AF821387

Database Management Systems

ITL Education Solutions Limited
Research and Development Wing
New Delhi

Copyright © 2012 Dorling Kindersley (India) Pvt. Ltd

This book is sold subject to the condition that it shall not, by way of trade or otherwise, be lent, resold, hired out, or otherwise circulated without the publisher's prior written consent in any form of binding or cover other than that in which it is published and without a similar condition including this condition being imposed on the subsequent purchaser and without limiting the rights under copyright reserved above, no part of this publication may be reproduced, stored in or introduced into a retrieval system, or transmitted in any form or by any means (electronic, mechanical, photocopying, recording or otherwise), without the prior written permission of both the copyright owner and the publisher of this book.

ISBN 978-81-317-6080-2

First Impression

Published by Dorling Kindersley (India) Pvt. Ltd, licensees of Pearson Education in South Asia.

Head Office: 7th Floor, Knowledge Boulevard, A-8(A), Sector 62, Noida 201 309, UP, India.
Registered Office: 11 Community Centre, Panchsheel Park, New Delhi 110 017, India.

Compositor: Tulyasys Technologies Pvt. Ltd

Printed in India by Sai Print O Pack Pvt. Ltd.

Contents

Preface

As organizations strive to excel in a modern competitive environment, managing information acquires greater relevance. Database systems now play a vital role in the effective management of information. Database being an essential ingredient of modern computing systems, the subject Database Management Systems is compulsory for students enrolled in various computer science courses in most universities. The book *Database Management Systems* aims to provide an in-depth knowledge of most important aspects of database systems in an easy-to-understand question-and-answer format.

The book comprises questions and their corresponding answers on fundamental concepts like database design, languages and implementation as well as advanced concepts like distributed databases and query processing and optimization. In addition, some miscellaneous questions on emerging technologies like object-based databases and XML are also included. The organized and accessible format allows students to quickly find questions on specific topics.

The book *Database Management Systems* is a part of series named *Express Learning Series*, which has a number of books designed as quick reference guides.

Unique Features

1. Designed as a student friendly self-learning guide. The book is written in a clear, concise and lucid manner.
2. Easy-to-understand question-and-answer format.
3. Includes previously asked as well as new questions organized in chapters.
4. All types of questions including MCQs, short and long questions are covered.
5. Solutions to numerical questions asked at examinations are provided.
6. All ideas and concepts are presented with clear examples.
7. Text is well structured and well supported with suitable diagrams.
8. Inter-chapter dependencies are kept to a minimum.

Chapter Organization

All the questions–answers are organized into 16 chapters. The outline of the chapters is as follows:

- *Chapter 1* provides an introduction of database and database management system, its advantages over the traditional file system, the DBMS environment, various data models and the steps involved in database design.
- *Chapter 2* deals with conceptual modeling using E-R and the enhanced E-R model. It represents all the concepts with the help of an example of the *Online Book* database.
- *Chapter 3* describes the basic concepts of the relational model, which is the most commonly used data model. It also covers integrity constraints and deals with constraint violations.

- *Chapter 4* discusses two formal query languages, namely, relational algebra and relational calculus. The concepts of relational algebra and calculus are explained in a simple way that helps in the easy understanding of these query languages.
- *Chapter 5* discusses the structured query language (SQL), which is used as the standard query language in most of the commercial databases.
- *Chapter 6* deals with normalization, which is the most important process in database design. It begins with various issues that are confronted while designing a database schema. It then discusses the formal methodology (normalization) that is used to resolve these issues and design an efficient database system.
- *Chapter 7* covers the concepts of physical database design including database storage and indexing. It describes the primary methods of organizing files on the disks and various indexing techniques that help in fast retrieval of data.
- *Chapter 8* introduces the basics of query processing and optimization. It provides an understanding of how queries are evaluated and how data are retrieved from the database.
- *Chapter 9* introduces the properties of transaction including atomicity, consistency, isolation and durability. It then discusses fundamentals of transaction processing and introduces the concept of serializability.
- *Chapter 10* covers a number of concurrency control techniques including locking, timestamping and optimistic concurrency control technique. It also covers deadlock handling.
- *Chapter 11* describes the database recovery system to ensure the normal execution of transactions regardless of any type of system failure. It discusses various recovery techniques such as system log, checkpoints, etc.
- *Chapter 12* focuses on database security and presents various security issues, the types of threats to the database and the role of DBA in implementing database security. In addition, it discusses how the user access to database is controlled.
- *Chapter 13* explores the concepts of database storage, query processing, transaction management, concurrency control and recovery in distributed database systems.
- *Chapter 14* introduces data warehousing, online transaction processing (OLAP) and data mining.
- *Chapter 15* discusses information retrieval techniques to extract information from unstructured textual data along with the retrieval techniques used in Web search engines.
- *Chapter 16* covers miscellaneous topics such as object-relational and object-oriented databases, XML and four leading database systems that include PostgreSQL, Oracle, Microsoft SQL Server and IBM DB2.

Acknowledgements

- Our publisher, Pearson Education, their editorial team and panel reviewers for their valuable contributions toward content enrichment.
- Our technical and editorial consultants for devoting their precious time to improve the quality of the book.
- Our entire research and development team who have put in their sincere efforts to bring out a high-quality book.

Feedback

For any suggestions and comments about this book, please send an e-mail to itlesl@rediffmail.com. Hope you enjoy reading this book as much as we have enjoyed writing it.

Rohit Khurana
Founder and CEO
ITL ESL

1

Database System

1. Define the term database.

Ans: A **database** can be defined as a collection of related data from which users can efficiently retrieve the desired information. A database can be anything from a simple collection of roll numbers, names, addresses and phone numbers of students to a complex collection of sound, images and even video or film clippings. Though databases are generally computerized, instances of non-computerized databases from everyday life can be cited in abundance. A dictionary, a phone book, a collection of recipes and a TV guide are examples of non-computerized databases. The examples of computerized databases include customer files, employee rosters, books catalog, equipment inventories and sales transactions.

2. What do you mean by a Database Management System?

Ans: A **Database Management System (DBMS)** is an integrated set of programs used to create and maintain a database. The main objective of a DBMS is to provide a convenient and effective method of defining, storing, retrieving and manipulating the data contained in the database.

3. What is a file-processing system? What are the disadvantages of a file-processing system that led to the development of the database system?

Ans: In the **file-processing system**, the data are stored in the form of files, and a number of application programs are written by programmers to add, modify, delete and retrieve data to and from appropriate files. New application programs are written as and when needed by the organization. For example, consider a bookstore that uses a file-processing system to keep track of all the available books. The system maintains a file named `BOOK` to store the information related to books. This information includes the book title, ISBN, price, year of publishing, copyright date, category, number of pages, name of the author and the name and address of the publisher.

In addition, the system has many application programs that allow users to manipulate the information stored in the `BOOK` file. For example, a system may contain programs to add information about a new book, modify any existing book information, print the details of books according to their categories, etc. If a need arises to keep additional information about the publishers of the books, which include the phone number and email id, the system creates a new file, say `PUBLISHER`, which includes the name, address, phone number and email id of the publishers. New application programs are written and added to the system to manipulate the information in the `PUBLISHER` file. In this way, as time goes by, more files and application programs are added to the system.

The file-processing system has a number of disadvantages that lead to the development of database systems. These disadvantages are given below:

- Same information may be duplicated in several files. For example, the name and the address of the publisher are stored in the `BOOK` file as well as in the `PUBLISHER` file. This duplication of data is known as **data redundancy**, which leads to wastage of storage space. The other problem with the file-processing system is that the data may not be updated consistently. Suppose a publisher requests for a change in his address. Since the address of the publisher is stored in the `BOOK` as well as the `PUBLISHER` file, both the files must be updated. If the address of the publisher is not modified in any of the two files, then the same publisher will have different addresses in two different files. This is known as **data inconsistency**.
- In any application, there are certain data integrity rules that need to be maintained. These rules could be in the form of certain conditions or constraints. In a file-processing system, all these rules need to be explicitly programmed in all application programs that use that particular data item. For example, the integrity rule that each book should have a book title has to be implemented in all the application programs separately that use the `BOOK` file. In addition, when new constraints are to be enforced, all the application programs should be changed accordingly.
- The file-processing system lacks the insulation between program and data. This is because the file structure is embedded in the application program itself; thus, it is difficult to change the structure of a file as it requires changing all the application programs accessing it. For example, an application program in C++ defines the file structure using the keyword `struct` or `class`. Suppose the data type of the field ISBN is changed from string to number, changes have to be made in all the application programs that are accessing the `BOOK` file.
- Handling new queries is difficult, since it requires change in the existing application programs or requires a new application program. For example, suppose a need arises to print the details of all the textbooks published by a particular publisher. One way to handle this request is to use the existing application program that prints the details of the books according to their categories, and then manually generate the list of textbooks published by a particular publisher. Obviously, it is unacceptable. Alternatively, the programmer is requested to write a new application program. Suppose such a new application program is written. Now suppose after some time, a request arises to filter the list of textbooks with a price greater than $50. Then again we have to write a new application program.
- Since many users are involved in creating files and writing application programs, the various files in the system may have different file structures. Moreover, the programmers may choose different programming languages to write application programs.
- Since application programs are added in an unplanned manner, due to which the details of each file are easily available to every user. Thus, the file-processing system lacks the security feature.

4. Explain DBMS catalog and metadata.

Ans: To provide a high degree of data independence, the definition or the description of the database structure (structure of each file, the type and storage format of each data item) and various constraints on the data are stored separately in a table. This table is known as the **DBMS catalog**. The information contained in the catalog is called the **metadata** (data about data).

5. What do you understand by the term data abstraction?

Ans: The property of DBMS that allows program-data independence is known as **data abstraction**. Data abstraction allows the database system to provide an abstract view of the data to its users without giving the physical storage and implementation details.

6. Discuss the advantages of a database system. Explain the various cost and risk factors involved in implementing a database system.

Ans: The main advantage of DBMS is **centralized data management** where the data are stored at a centralized location and are shared among multiple users. The centralized nature of the database system provides several advantages, which overcome the limitations of the conventional file-processing system. These advantages are as follows:

- **Controlled data redundancy:** During database design, various files are integrated, and each logical data item is stored at a central location. This eliminates replicating the data item in different files, and ensures consistency and saves the storage space.
- **Enforcing data integrity:** In the database approach, enforcing data integrity is much easier. Various integrity constraints are identified by the database designer during the database design.
- **Data sharing:** The data stored in the database can be shared among multiple users or application programs. Due to shared data, it is possible to satisfy the data requirements of the new applications without having to create any additional data or with minimal modification.
- **Ease of application development:** The application programmer develops the application programs according to the needs of the users. The other issues like concurrent access, security, data integrity, etc. are handled by the DBMS itself. This makes application development an easier task.
- **Data security:** The DBMS ensures that the only means of access to the database is through an authorized channel. To ensure security, a DBMS provides security tools such as user codes and passwords.
- **Multiple user interfaces:** DBMS provides different types of interfaces such as query languages, application program interfaces and graphical user interfaces (GUI) that include forms-style and menu-driven interfaces.
- **Backup and recovery:** The DBMS provides a backup and recovery subsystem, which is responsible for recovery from hardware and software failures.

In addition to centralized data management, DBMS also has some other advantages as follows:

- **Program-data independence:** The independence between the programs and the data is known as program-data independence. It allows changing the structure of the database without making any changes in the application programs that use the database.
- **Data abstraction:** The property of DBMS that allows program-data independence is known as data abstraction. Data abstraction allows the database system to provide an abstract view of the data to its users without giving the physical storage and implementation details.
- **Supports multiple views of the data:** A database can be accessed by many users and each of them may have a different perspective or view of the data. A database system provides a facility to define different views of the data for different users. A **view** is a subset of the database that contains virtual data derived from the database files but it does not exist in physical form.

The various cost and risk factors involved in implementing a database system are:

- **High cost:** Installing a new database system may require investment in hardware and software. The DBMS requires more main memory and disk storage. Moreover, DBMS is quite expensive.

Therefore, a company needs to consider the overhead cost of implementing a new database system.

- **Training new personnel:** When an organization plans to adopt a database system, it may need to recruit or hire a specialized data administration group, which can coordinate with different user-groups for designing views, establishing recovery procedures and fine tuning the data structures to meet the requirements of the organization. Hiring such professionals is expensive.
- **Explicit backup and recovery:** A shared corporate database must be accurate and available at all times. Therefore, a system using on-line updating requires explicit backup and recovery procedures.
- **System failure:** When a computer system containing the database fails, all users have to wait until the system is functional again. Moreover, if DBMS or the application program fails, a permanent damage may occur to the database.

7. What are the different types of database users who interact with the database system?

Ans: Database users are those who interact with the database in order to query and update the database and generate reports. Database users are classified into the following categories:

- **Naïve users:** The users who query and update the database by invoking some already written application programs. For example, the owner of the bookstore enters the details of various books in the database by invoking an appropriate application program.
- **Sophisticated users:** The users, such as a business analyst, scientist, etc., who are familiar with the facilities provided by a DBMS interact with the system without writing any application programs. Such users use database query language to retrieve information from the database to meet their complicated requirements.
- **Specialized users:** The users who write specialized database programs that are different from traditional data-processing applications such as banking and payroll management use simple data types. Specialized users write applications such as computer-aided design systems, knowledge-base and expert systems that store data having complex data types.

8. Explain the roles of a system analyst and an application programmer in a database system.

Ans: System analysts determine the requirements of the database users (especially naïve users) to create a solution for their business need and focus on non-technical and technical aspects. The non-technical aspects involve defining system requirements, facilitating interaction between business users and technical staff, etc. Technical aspects involve developing the specification for the user interface (application programs).

Application programmers are computer professionals who implement the specifications given by the system analysts and develop application programs. They can choose tools, such as rapid application development (RAD) to develop the application program with minimal effort. The database application programmer develops an application program to facilitate easy data access for the database users.

9. Who is a database administrator (DBA)? What are the various responsibilities of a DBA?

Ans: A database administrator (DBA) is a person who has central control over both data and application programs. Some of the responsibilities of DBA are as follows:

- **Schema definition and modification:** The overall structure of the database is known as the **database schema**. It is the responsibility of the DBA to create the database schema by executing a set of data definition statements in DDL.

- **New software installation:** It is the responsibility of the DBA to install new DBMS software, application software and other related software. After installation, the DBA must test the new software.
- **Security enforcement and administration:** DBA is responsible for establishing and monitoring the security of the database system. It involves adding and removing users, auditing and checking for security problems.
- **Data analysis:** DBA is responsible for analyzing the data stored in the database and studying its performance and efficiency in order to effectively use indexes, parallel query execution, etc.
- **Preliminary database design:** The DBA works along with the development team during the database-design stage due to which many potential problems that can arise later can be avoided.
- **Physical organization modification:** The DBA is responsible for carrying out the modifications in the physical organization of the database for better performance.
- **Routine maintenance checks:** The DBA is responsible for taking the database backup periodically in order to be able to recover from any hardware or software failure and restore the database to a consistent state.

10. Explain the three-level architecture of DBMS with the help of an example. Mention its advantages also.

Ans: The DBMS architecture describes how data in the database are viewed by the users. It is not concerned with how the data are handled and processed by the DBMS. In this architecture, the overall database description can be defined at three levels namely, *internal*, *conceptual* and *external levels* and, thus, named **three-level DBMS architecture** (Figure 1.1). The three levels are as follows:

- **Internal level:** It is the lowest level of data abstraction that deals with the physical representation of the database on the computer and, thus, is also known as the **physical level**. It describes *how* the data are physically stored and organized on the storage medium.

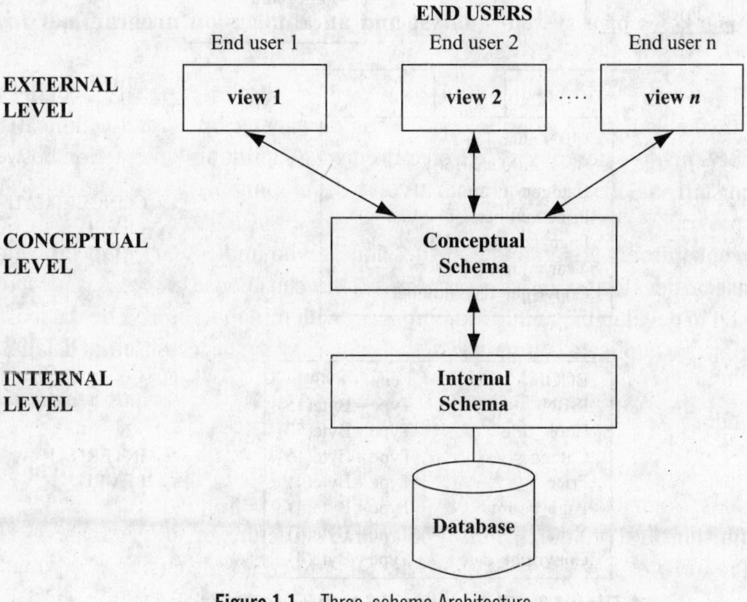

Figure 1.1 Three-schema Architecture

- **Conceptual level:** This level of abstraction deals with the logical structure of the entire database and, thus, is also known as the **logical level**. It describes *what* data are stored in the database, the relationships among the data and a complete view of the user's requirements without any concern for the physical implementation.
- **External level:** It is the highest level of abstraction that deals with the user's view of the database and, thus, is also known as the **view level**. It permits users to access data in a way that is customized according to their needs, so that the same data can be seen by different users in different ways, at the same time. In this way, it provides a powerful and flexible security mechanism by hiding the parts of the database from certain users as the user is not aware of the existence of any attributes that are missing from the view.

These three levels are used to describe the schema of the database at various levels. Thus, the three-level architecture is also known as **three-schema architecture**.

To illustrate three-schema architecture, we consider an *Online Book* database that maintains the details such as ISBN, title, price, year of publishing, number of pages, author and publisher of various textbooks, language books and novels. The user can also view the details of various authors and publishers. The author details include the name, address, URL and phone number. The publisher details include the publisher name, address, e-mail ID and phone number. The database also maintains the details of the ratings and feedbacks of other authors about a particular book. The ratings of a particular book are displayed along with the other details of the book. However, the detailed feedback about the book can be viewed on the URL of the authors who have reviewed the book.

Figure 1.2 shows the three levels of the BOOK file in the *Online Book* database. In this figure, two views (*view 1* and *view 2*) of the BOOK file have been defined at the external level. Different database

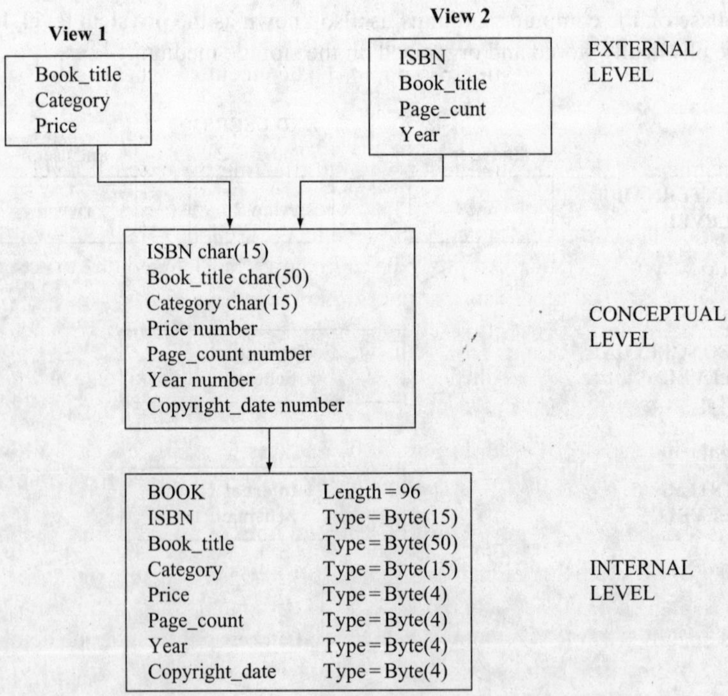

Figure 1.2 Three Levels of *Online Book* Database (BOOK file)

users can see these views. The details of the data types are hidden from the users. At the conceptual level, the BOOK records are described by a type definition. The application programmers and the DBA generally work at this level of abstraction. At the internal level, the BOOK records are described as a block of consecutive storage locations such as words or bytes. The database users and the application programmers are not aware of these details; however, the DBA may be aware of certain details of the physical organization of the data.

The main advantage of three-schema architecture is that it provides data independence. **Data independence** is the ability to change the schema at one level of the database system without having to change the schema at the other levels. The database users are provided with an abstract view of the data by hiding certain details of how data are physically stored. This enables the users to manipulate the data without worrying about where they are located or how they are actually stored.

11. Explain mapping in three-schema architecture.

Ans: In three-schema architecture, each user group refers only to its own external view. Whenever a user specifies a request to generate a new external view, the DBMS must transform the request specified at the external level into a request at the conceptual level, and then into a request at the physical level. If the user requests for data retrieval, the data extracted from the database must be presented according to the need of the user. This process of transforming the requests and results between various levels of DBMS architecture is known as **mapping.**

12. What is data independence and why is it important? What is the difference between logical and physical data independence?

Ans: **Data independence** is the ability to change the schema at one level of the database system without having to change the schema at the other levels. Data independence is of two types, namely, *logical data independence* and *physical data independence*.

- **Logical data independence:** It is the ability to change the conceptual schema without affecting the external schemas or application programs. The conceptual schema may be changed due to change in constraints or addition of new data items or removal of existing data items, etc. from the database. The separation of the external level from the conceptual level enables the users to make changes at the conceptual level without affecting the external level or the application programs.
- **Physical data independence:** It is the ability to change the internal schema without affecting the conceptual or external schema. An internal schema may be changed due to several reasons such as for creating additional access structure, changing the storage structure, etc. The separation of internal schema from the conceptual schema facilitates physical data independence.

Logical data independence is more difficult to achieve than the physical data independence because the application programs are always dependent on the logical structure of the database.

Importance: Data independence is an important characteristic of DBMS as it allows changing the structure of the database without making any changes in the application programs that use the database.

13. What is a database schema? Explain with the help of an example.

Ans: The overall structure of the database, which specifies the structure of each relation including its attributes, is known as **database schema**. The database schema is also known as intension of the database, and is specified while designing the database. It does not include the actual records of the relations. Figure 1.3 shows the database schema for *Online Book* database (described in Question 11).

BOOK

ISBN	Book_title	Category	Price	Copyright_date	Year	Page_count	P_ID

PUBLISHER

P_ID	Pname	Address	State	Phone	Email_ID

AUTHOR

A_ID	Aname	City	State	Zip	Phone	URL

AUTHOR_BOOK

A_ID	ISBN

REVIEW

R_ID	ISBN	Rating

Figure 1.3 Database Schema for *Online Book* Database

14. What is a database state? What are the various states of the database?

Ans: The data in the database at a particular point of time are known as **database instance** or **database state** or **snapshot**. The database state is also called an **extension** of the schema. The various states of the database are:

- **Empty state:** When a new database is defined, only its schema is specified. At this point, the database is said to be in an empty state as it contains no data.
- **Initial state:** When the database is loaded with data for the first time, it is said to be in an initial state.
- **Current state:** The data in the database are updated frequently. Thus, at any point of time, the database is said to be in the current state.

15. Define the term data model. Explain different types of data models.

Ans: A **database model** or simply a **data model** is an abstract model that describes how the data are represented and used. A data model consists of a set of data structures and conceptual tools, which is used to describe the structure of a database. Depending on the concept used to model the structure of the database, data models are categorized into three types, namely *High-level* or *conceptual data models*, *representational* or *implementation data models* and *low-level* or *physical data models*.

- **Conceptual data model:** A conceptual data model describes the information used by an organization in a way that is independent of any implementation-level issues and details. The main advantage of the conceptual data model is that it is independent of implementation details and, hence, can be understood even by the end users having non-technical background. The most popular conceptual data model is the entity–relationship model.
- **Representational data model:** The representational or implementation data models hide some data storage details from the users; however, they can be implemented directly on a computer system. The various representational data models are as follows:
  - *Hierarchical data model:* This data model organizes the data in a tree-like structure in which each **child node** (also known as **dependents**) can have only one **parent node**. The database

based on the hierarchical data model comprises a set of records connected to one another through links. The link is an association between two or more records. The top of the tree structure consists of a single node that does not have any parent and is called the **root node.** The root may have any number of dependents; each of these dependents may have any number of lower-level dependents. Each child node can have only one parent node, and a parent node can have any number of (many) child nodes. It, therefore, represents only one-to-one and one-to-many relationships. A collection of the same type of records is known as a **record type**. Figure 1.4 shows the hierarchical model of the *Online Book* database. The main advantage of the hierarchical data model is that the data access is quite predictable in the structure and, therefore, both the retrieval and updates can be highly optimized by the DBMS. However, the main drawback of this model is that the links are 'hard coded' into the data structure, that is, the link is permanently established and cannot be modified.

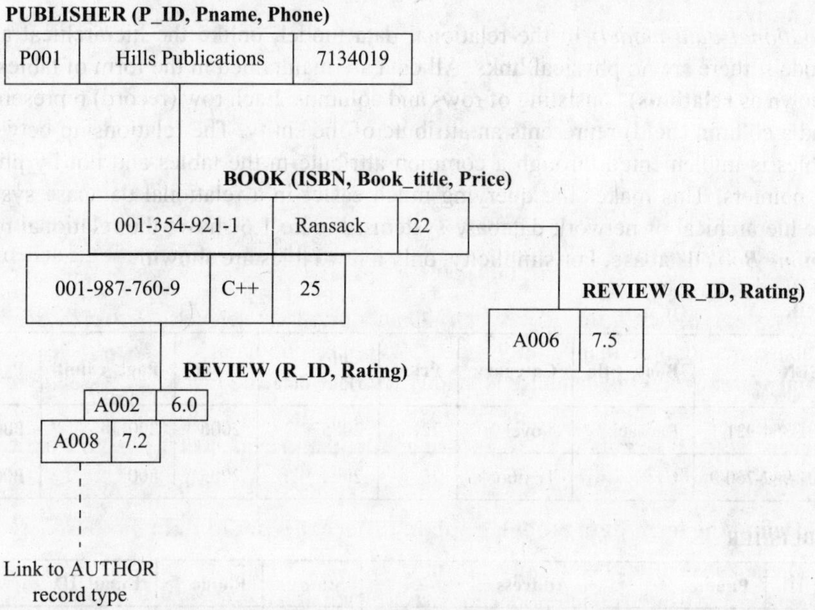

Figure 1.4 Hierarchical Data Model for *Online Book* Database

- *Network data model:* In a network model, the data are also represented by a collection of records, and relationships among data are represented by links. However, the link in a network data model represents an association between precisely two records. Like the hierarchical data model, each record of a particular record type also represents a node. However, unlike the hierarchical data model, all the nodes are linked to each other without any hierarchy. In the network data model, the data are organized in the form of graphs. The main advantage of the network data model is that a parent node can have many child nodes, and a child can also have many parent nodes. Thus, the network model permits the modeling of many-to-many relationships in data. The main limitation of the network data model is that it can be quite complicated to maintain all the links, and a single broken link can lead to problems in the database. Figure 1.5 shows the network model of the *Online Book* database.

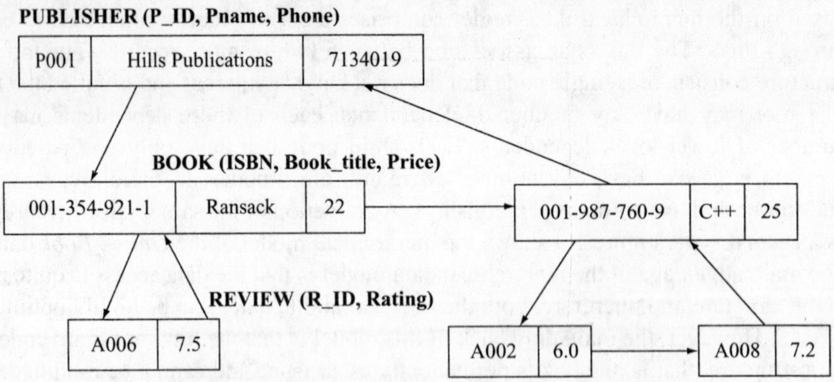

Figure 1.5 Network Data Model for the *Online Book* Database

- *Relational data model:* In the relational data model, unlike the hierarchical and network models, there are no physical links. All data are maintained in the form of tables (generally, known as **relations**) consisting of rows and columns. Each row (record) represents an entity, and a column (field) represents an attribute of the entity. The relationship between the two tables is implemented through a common attribute in the tables and not by physical links or pointers. This makes the querying much easier in a relational database system than in the hierarchical or network database systems. Figure 1.6 shows the relational model of the *Online Book* database. For simplicity, only a few tables are shown.

BOOK

ISBN	Book_title	Category	Price	Copy right_date	Year	Page_count	P_ID
001-354-921-1	Ransack	Novel	22	2005	2006	200	P001
001-987-760-9	C++	Textbook	25	2004	2005	800	P001

PUBLISHER

P_ID	Pname	Address	State	Phone	Email_ID
P001	Hills Publications	12, Park street, Atlanta	Georgia	7134019	H_pub@hills.com

REVIEW

R_ID	ISBN	Rating
A002	001-987-760-9	6.0
A006	001-354-921-1	7.5
A008	001-987-760-9	7.2

Figure 1.6 Relational Data Model for the *Online Book* Database

- *Object-based data model:* The object-oriented paradigm has been applied to database technology to create two new data models, known as the object-oriented data model and the object-relational data model. The **object-oriented data model** extends the concepts of object-oriented programming language with persistence, versioning, concurrency control, data recovery, security, and other database capabilities. On the other hand, the **object-relational data model** is an extension of the relational data model. It combines the features of both the relational data model and the object-oriented data model.

- **Physical data model:** The physical data model describes the data in terms of a collection of files, indices and other storage structures such as record formats, record ordering and access paths. This model specifies how the database will be executed in a particular DBMS software such as Oracle, Sybase, etc. by taking into account the facilities and constraints of a given database management system. It also describes how the data are stored on a disk and what access methods are available to it.

16. Define the term database languages.

Ans: To provide various facilities to different types of users, a DBMS normally provides one or more specialized programming languages called **Database** (or **DBMS**) **Languages**. The DBMS mainly provides two database languages, namely, *Data Definition Language* (*DDL*) and *Data Manipulation Language* (*DML*) to implement the databases.

17. Write a short note on data definition language and data manipulation language.

Ans: Data definition language: Data definition language (DDL) is used for defining the database schema. The DBMS comprises DDL compiler that identifies and stores the schema description in the DBMS catalog. A separate language, namely *storage definition language* (SDL) is used to define the internal schema and a third language, namely, *view definition language* (VDL) is used to define the external schema. DDL also accepts input in the form of instructions (statements) and generates the description of schema as output. The output is placed in the data dictionary. The DDL statements are also used to specify the integrity rules.

Data manipulation language: The DBMS provides data manipulation language (DML) that enables users to retrieve and manipulate the data. The statement that is used to retrieve the information is called a query. The part of the DML used to retrieve the information is called a query language. The DML are of two types, namely, *non-procedural DML* and *procedural DML*. The non-procedural or high-level or declarative DML requires a user to specify *what* data are required without specifying *how* to retrieve the required data. For example, SQL (Structured Query Language) is a non-procedural query language. The procedural or low-level DML requires the user to specify *what* data are required and *how* to access that data by providing a step-by-step procedure. For example, relational algebra is a procedural query language.

18. Explain the various functional components of a DBMS with the help of a suitable diagram.

Ans: A database system is partitioned into several software components that handle various tasks such as data definition and manipulation, security and data integrity, data recovery and concurrency control and performance optimization (Figure 1.7).

- **Data definition:** It is the responsibility of the database administrator to define the database and make changes to its definition (if required) using the DDL and other privileged commands. The **DDL compiler** component of DBMS processes these schema definitions and stores the schema descriptions in the DBMS catalog (data dictionary).
- **Data manipulation:** Once the data structure is defined, data need to be manipulated. The manipulation of data includes insertion, deletion and modification of records.
  - The queries that are defined as a part of the application programs are known as **planned queries**. The application programs are submitted to a **precompiler**, which extracts DML

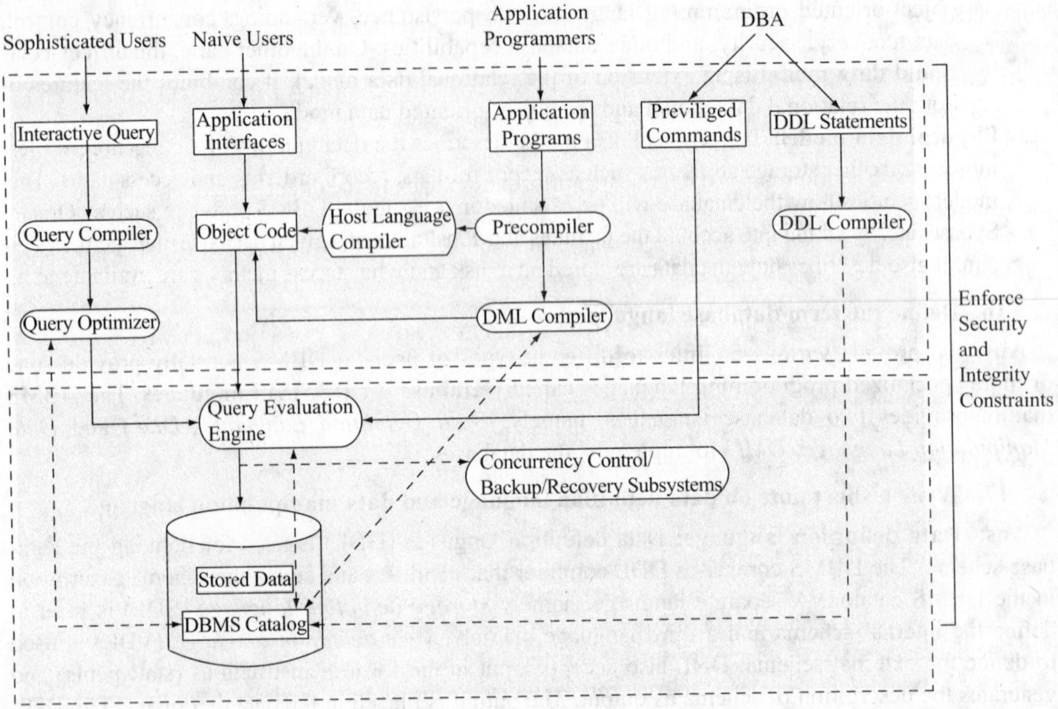

Figure 1.7 Component Modules of DBMS

commands from the application program and sends them to the **DML compiler** for compilation. The rest of the program is sent to the **host language compiler**. The object codes of both the DML commands and the rest of the program are linked and sent to the **query evaluation engine** for execution.

- The sudden queries that are executed as and when they arise are known as **unplanned queries (interactive queries)**. These queries are compiled by the **query compiler**, and then optimized by the **query optimizer**. The query optimizer consults the data dictionary for statistical and other physical information about the stored data. The optimized query is finally passed to the query evaluation engine for execution. The naïve users of the database can also query and update the database by using some already given application program interfaces. The object code of these queries is also passed to the query evaluation engine for processing.

- **Data security and integrity:** The DBMS contains functions that handle the security and integrity of data stored in the database. Since these functions can be easily invoked by the application, the application programmer need not code these functions in the programs.
- **Concurrency and data recovery:** The DBMS also contains some functions that deal with the concurrent access of records by multiple users and the recovery of data after a system failure.
- **Performance optimization:** The DBMS has a set of functions that optimize the performance of the queries by evaluating the different execution plans of a query and choosing the best among them.

19. What is the difference between a centralized and a client/server database system?

Ans: In **centralized database systems**, the database system, application programs and user-interface all are executed on a single system, and dummy terminals with no processing capabilities are connected to it. The processing power of a single system is utilized and dummy terminals are used only to display the information.

In **client/server architecture**, the processing power of the computer system at the user's end is utilized by processing the user-interface on that system. A **client** is a computer system that sends a request to the server connected to the network, and a **server** is a computer system that receives the request, processes it and returns the requested information back to the client. The client and the server are usually present at different sites. The end users (remote database users) work on a client computer system and a database system runs on the server. Client server architecture is best suited where large numbers of workstations, databases, Web servers, etc. are connected in a network.

20. What is the difference between two-tier architecture and three-tier architecture?

Ans: There are two approaches to implement client/server architecture. In the first approach, the user interface and application programs are placed on the client side and the database system on the server side. This architecture is called **two-tier architecture**. The application programs that reside at the client side invoke the DBMS at the server side. The application program interface standards like Open Database Connectivity (ODBC) and Java Database Connectivity (JDBC) are used for interaction between the client and the server. Figure 1.8 shows two-tier architecture.

The second approach is the **three-tier architecture**, which is used for Web-based applications. It adds an intermediate layer known as the **application server** (or **Web server**) between the client and the database server. The client communicates with the application server, which in turn communicates with the database server. The application server stores the business rules (procedures and constraints) used for accessing data from the database server. It checks the client's credentials before forwarding a request to the database server. When a client requests for information, the application server accepts the request, processes it and sends corresponding database commands to the database server. The database server sends the result back to the application server, which is converted into GUI format and presented to the client. Figure 1.9 shows the three-tier architecture.

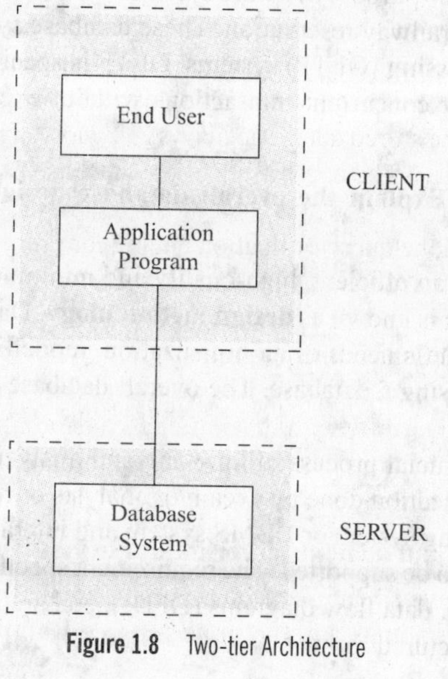

Figure 1.8 Two-tier Architecture

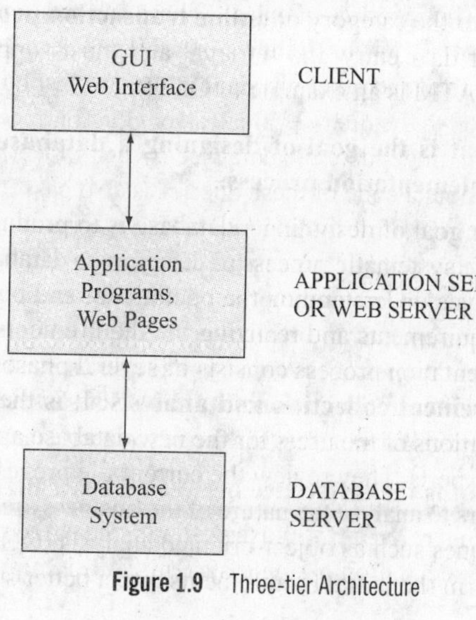

Figure 1.9 Three-tier Architecture

21. Explain the different criteria on the basis of which DBMS is classified into different categories.

Ans: The DBMSs can be classified into different categories on the basis of several criteria as follows:

- **Based on data models:** Depending on the data model they use, the DBMSs can be classified as hierarchical, network, relational, object oriented and object relational. The hierarchical and network data models are also known as **legacy data models**. Most of the popular and current commercial DBMSs are based on the relational data model. A new class of DBMSs called **object-relational DBMSs** has also been developed.
- **Based on the number of users:** Depending on the number of users the DBMS supports, it is divided into two categories, namely, *single-user system* and *multi-user system*. In a **single-user system**, the database resides on one computer and is only accessed by one user at a time. In the **multi-user system**, multiple users can access the database simultaneously. In multi-user DBMS the data are both integrated and shared.
- **Based on the number of sites:** Depending on the number of sites, it is divided into two types, namely, *centralized* or *distributed database systems*. In **centralized database systems**, both the database and DBMS software reside at a single computer site. The user interacts with the centralized system through a dummy terminal connected to it for information retrieval. In **distributed database systems**, the database and DBMS are distributed over several computers located at different sites. The computers communicate with each other through various communication media such as high-speed networks or telephone lines. Distributed databases can be classified as homogeneous and heterogeneous. In a **homogeneous** distributed database system, all sites have identical database management system software, whereas in **heterogeneous** distributed database system, different sites use different database management system software.
- **Based on the purpose:** Depending on the purpose the DBMS serves, it can be classified as **general purpose** or **specific purpose**. DBMS is a general-purpose software system. It can, however, be designed for specific purposes such as airline or railway reservation. These database systems fall under the category of **online transaction processing** (OLTP) systems. OLTP is specifically used for data entry and retrieval and must support concurrent transactions without excessive delays. ATM is an example of OLTP.

22. What is the goal of designing a database? Explain the overall database design and implementation process.

Ans: The goal of designing a database is to produce an efficient, high-quality and minimum cost database. The systematic process of designing a database is known as **design methodology**. Database design involves understanding the operational and business needs of an organization, modelling the specified requirements and realizing the requirements using a database. The overall database design and implementation process consists of several phases.

1. **Requirement collection and analysis:** It is the crucial process of knowing and analyzing the expectations of the users for the new database application done by a team of analysts or requirement experts. They review the current file processing system or DBMS system and interact with the users to analyse the nature of the business area to be supported. The requirement specification techniques such as object-oriented analysis (OOA), data flow diagrams (DFDs), etc. are used to transform the initial requirements into a better structured form.

2. **Conceptual database design:** In this phase, the database designer selects a suitable data model and translates the data requirements resulting from the previous phase into a conceptual database schema by applying the concepts of the chosen data model. The entity–relationship (E–R) diagram is generally used to represent the conceptual database design.
3. **Choice of a DBMS:** The choice of a DBMS depends on many factors such as cost, DBMS features and tools, underlying model, portability and DBMS hardware requirements. The technical factors that affect the choice of a DBMS are the type of DBMS, storage structures and access paths that DBMS supports, the interfaces available, the types of high-level query languages and the architecture it supports.
4. **Logical database design:** Once an appropriate DBMS is chosen, the next step is to map the high-level conceptual schema onto the implementation data model of the selected DBMS. In this phase, the database designer moves from an abstract data model to the implementation of the database.
5. **Physical database design:** In this phase, the physical features such as storage structures, file organization and access paths for the database files are specified to achieve good performance. The various options for file organization and access paths include various types of indexing, clustering of records, hashing techniques, etc.
6. **Database system implementation:** Once the logical and physical database designs are completed, the database system can be implemented. DDL statements of the selected DBMS are used and compiled to create the database schema and database files, and finally the database is loaded with the data.
7. **Testing and evaluation:** In this phase, the database is tested and fine-tuned for the performance, integrity, concurrent access and security constraints. This phase is carried out in parallel with application programming. If the testing fails, various actions are taken such as modification of physical design, modification of logical design or upgrading or changing DBMS software or hardware.

Multiple-choice Questions

1. Which of these is an advantage of database systems?
   (a) Data abstraction (b) Program-data independence
   (c) Centralized data management (d) All of these
2. The information about data in a database is called ________.
   (a) Tera data (b) Metadata (c) Hyper data (d) None of these
3. The users who query and update the database by invoking some already-written application programs are known as ________.
   (a) System analysts (b) Naïve users (c) Special users (d) Sophisticated users
4. The person who has the central control over data and application programs is ________.
   (a) DBA (b) System analysts (c) Database designer (d) None of these
5. Which of these individuals plays an important role in defining and maintaining a database for an organization?
   (a) Application programmer (b) System analyst
   (c) Database administrator (d) Both (a) and (b)
6. Which of the following levels deals with the physical representation of the database on the computer?
   (a) Internal level (b) Conceptual level (c) External level (d) None of these

7. Which of the following levels of abstraction deals with the user's view of the database?
   (a) External level (b) Conceptual level (c) Physical level (d) None of these
8. The process of transforming the requests and results between various levels of DBMS architecture is known as ________.
   (a) Mapping (b) Scheming (c) Viewing (d) None of these
9. The ability to change the conceptual schema without affecting the external schemas or application programs is known as ________.
   (a) Program-data independence (b) Logical data independence
   (c) Physical data independence (d) Data abstraction
10. Which of these is not a representational data model?
   (a) Entity–relationship model (b) Network data model
   (c) Hierarchical data model (d) Relational data model
11. Which of these is not a feature of the hierarchical model?
   (a) Organizes the data in a tree-like structure
   (b) Root node does not have any parent
   (c) Parent node can have any number of child nodes
   (d) Child node can have any number of parent nodes
12. The ________ model is an extension of the relational data model.
   (a) Object-oriented data model (b) Object-relational data model
   (c) Semistructured data model (d) None of these
13. The type of data structure that is used in a relational model is ________.
   (a) Table (b) Tree (c) Graph (d) None of these
14. Which of these DBMS languages is employed by end users and programmers to manipulate data in the database?
   (a) Data definition language (b) Data presentation language
   (c) Data manipulation language (d) Data translation language
15. The ________ is a special type of table that contains data descriptions and defines the name, data type and length of each field in the database.
   (a) Data dictionary (b) Data table (c) Data record (d) None of these
16. In a ________ distributed database system, all sites have identical database management system software.
   (a) Heterogeneous (b) Homogeneous (c) Centralized (d) Client/Server
17. What is the correct sequence of these phases of database design and implementation process?
   (i) Conceptual database design (ii) Requirement collection and analysis
   (iii) Physical database design (iv) Testing and evaluation
   (a) i, ii, iii and iv (b) ii, i, iii and iv (c) ii, iii, i and iv (d) i, ii, iv and iii

Answers

1. (d)	2. (b)	3. (b)	4. (a)	5. (c)	6. (a)	7. (a)
8. (a)	9. (b)	10. (a)	11. (d)	12. (b)	13. (a)	14. (c)
15. (a)	16. (b)	17. (b)				

2

Conceptual Modeling

1. Briefly describe conceptual data modeling.

Ans: The overall database design and implementation process starts with requirements gathering and specifications. Once the requirements of the user have been specified, the next step is to construct an abstract or conceptual model of a database based on the requirements of the user. This phase is known as **conceptual modeling** or **semantic modeling**. Conceptual modeling is an important phase in designing a successful database. It represents various pieces of data and their relationships at a very high level of abstraction. It mainly focuses on what data are required and how they should be organized rather than what operations are to be performed on the data. The model is independent of any hardware (physical storage) and software (DBMS) constraints and hence, can be modified easily according to the changing needs of the user. The conceptual model can be represented using two major approaches, namely, *Entity–Relationship Modeling* and *Object Modeling*.

2. What is an E–R model? What are its advantages?

Ans: The Entity–Relationship Model is the most popular conceptual model used for designing a database. It was originally proposed by Dr Peter Chen in 1976 as a way to unify the network and relational database views. The E–R model views the real world as a set of basic objects (known as **entities**), their characteristics (known as **attributes**) and associations among these objects (known as **relationships**). The *entities*, *attributes* and *relationships* are the basic constructs of an E–R model. The E–R model has several advantages as listed below:

- It is simple and easy to understand and, thus, can be used as an effective communication tool between the database designer and the end user.
- It captures the real-world data requirements in a simple, meaningful and logical way.
- It can be easily mapped to the relational model. The basic constructs, that is, the entities and attributes of the E–R model can be easily transformed into relations (or tables) and columns (or fields) in a relational model.
- It can be used as a design plan and can be implemented in any database management software.

3. Define the term entity. What is the difference between tangible and non-tangible entity?

Ans: An **entity** is a distinguishable object that has an independent existence in the real world. It includes all those 'things' of an organization about which the data are collected. For example, each book, publisher and author in an *Online Book* database is an entity. An entity can exist either physically or conceptually.

- **Tangible entity:** If an entity has a physical existence, it is termed as **tangible** or **concrete entity**. For example, a book, an employee, a place or a part.
- **Non-tangible:** If an entity has a conceptual existence, it is termed as **non-tangible** or **abstract entity**. For example, an event, a job title or a customer account.

4. What is the difference between an attribute and a domain?

Ans: The **attributes** are the properties of an entity that characterize and describe it. Figure 2.1 shows the `BOOK` entity b_1 described by the attributes `Book_title`, `Price` (in dollars), `ISBN`, `Year`, `Page_count` and `Category`. Each attribute can accept a value from a set of permitted values, which is called the **domain** or the **value set** of the attribute. For example, the domain of the attribute `Page_count` is a set of positive integers. On the other hand, the category of a book can be a textbook, a language book or a novel. Thus, the domain of the attribute `Category` is {Textbook, Language book, Novel}. Only one of these three permitted values can be assigned to the category attribute.

5. Define the terms entity type and entity set.

Ans: A set or a collection of entities that share the same attributes but different values is known as an **entity type**. For example, the set of all publishers who publish books can be defined as the entity type `PUBLISHER`. A specific occurrence of an entity type is called its **instance**. For example, the publisher *Hills Publications* is the instance of the entity type `PUBLISHER`. An entity set is a collection of all instances of a particular entity type in the database at any point of time. Each entity is referred to by its name and attribute values. An entity type describes the **schema (intension)** for the entity set that shares the same structure. The entity set, on the other hand, is called the **extension** of the entity type.

6. Explain the various types of attributes. What are the various situations in which an attribute can use a *null* value?

Ans: The attributes of an entity are classified into the following categories:

- **Identifying and descriptive attributes:** The attribute that is used to uniquely identify an instance of an entity is known as an **identifying attribute** or simply an **identifier**. For example, the attribute

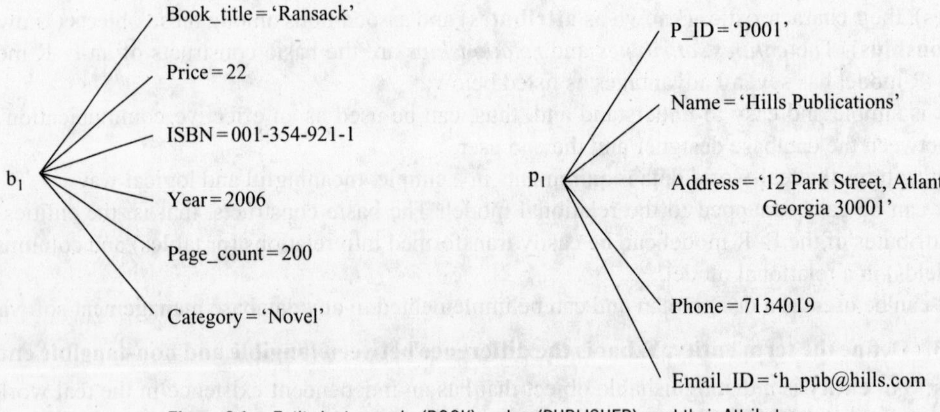

Figure 2.1 Entity Instances b_1 (BOOK) and p_1 (PUBLISHER), and their Attributes

P_ID of the entity type PUBLISHER is an identifying attribute, as two publishers cannot have the same publisher ID. A **descriptive attribute** or simply a **descriptor**, on the other hand, describes a non-unique characteristic of an entity instance. For example, the attributes Price and Page_count are the descriptive attributes as two books can have the same price and number of pages.

- **Simple and composite attributes:** The attributes that are indivisible are known as **simple** (or **atomic**) **attributes**. For example, the attributes Book_title, Price, Year, Page_count and Category of the entity type BOOK are simple attributes as they cannot be further divided into smaller subparts. On the other hand, **composite attributes** can be divided into smaller subparts. For example, the attribute Address can be further divided into House_number, Street, City, State and Zip_code (Figure 2.2).
- **Stored and derived attributes:** In some cases, two or more attribute values are related in such a way that the value of one attribute can be determined from the value of other attributes or related entities. Consider an entity type PERSON and its attributes Date_of_birth and Age. The value of the attribute Age can be determined from the current date and the value of Date_of_birth. Thus, the attribute Age is known as a **derived attribute** and the attribute Date_of_birth is known as a **stored attribute**.
- **Single-valued and multi-valued attributes:** The attributes that can have only one value for a given entity are called the **single-valued attributes**. For example, the attribute Book_title is a single-valued attribute as one book can have only one title. The attributes that can have multiple values for a given entity are called **multi-valued attributes**. For example, the attributes Email_ID and Phone of the entity type PUBLISHER are multi-valued attributes, as a publisher can have zero, one or more e-mail IDs and phone numbers.
- **Complex attributes:** The attributes that are formed by arbitrarily nesting the composite and multi-valued attributes are called **complex attributes**. This is represented by grouping the components of a composite attribute between parentheses '()' and by displaying the multi-valued attributes between braces '{}', and attributes separated by commas. For example, a publisher can have offices at different places, each with different addresses and each office having multiple phones (Figure 2.3).

There are various situations in which an attribute can use a NULL value. One such situation is when a particular entity does not have an appropriate value for an attribute. In such a situation, the attribute takes a special value called the **NULL** value. A null value of an attribute may indicate "not applicable". For example, consider an entity type PERSON with three attributes First_name, Middle_name and Last_name. Since not every person has a middle name, the person without any middle name wiil have a NULL value for the attribute Middle_name. Another situation when

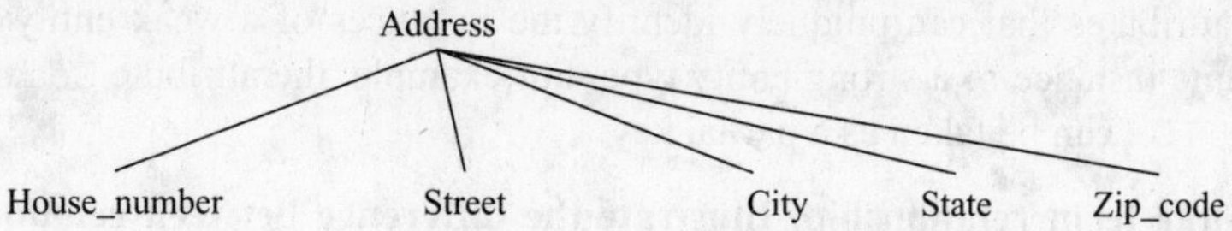

Figure 2.2 Composite Attributes

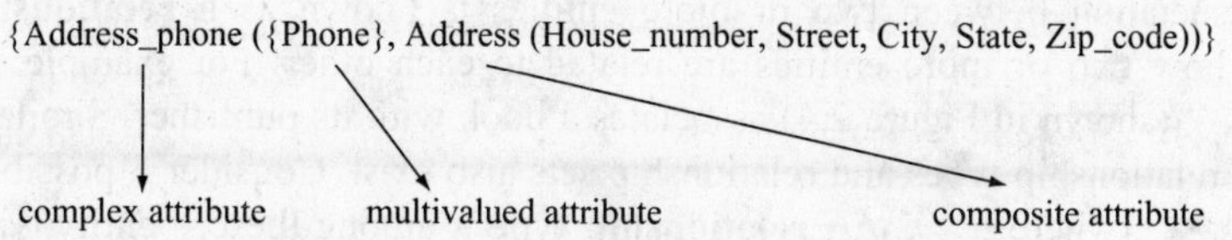

Figure 2.3 Complex Attribute—Address_phone

the NULL value is used is when the value of a particular attribute is unknown. An unknown category can further be classified as *missing* and *not known*. For example, if the attribute Book_title has the value NULL, it indicates that the title of the book is missing, as every book must have a title. However, if the attribute Phone has a NULL value, it indicates that it is not known whether the value for Phone exists or not.

7. Differentiate between a superkey, a candidate key and a primary key.

Ans: A set of one or more attributes, when taken together, helps in uniquely identifying each entity is called a **superkey**. For example, the attribute P_ID of the entity type PUBLISHER can be used to uniquely identify each entity instance. Thus, P_ID is a superkey. The combination of the attributes P_ID and Name is also a superkey. One can also use the set of all attributes (P_ID, Name, Address, Phone, Email_ID) to uniquely identify each entity instance of the type PUBLISHER. Thus, the combination of all attributes is also a superkey.

However, P_ID itself can uniquely identify each entity instance, thus, other attributes are not required. Such a minimal superkey that does not contain any superfluous (extra) attribute in it is called a **candidate key**. A candidate key contains a minimized set of attributes that can be used to uniquely identify a single entity instance. For example, the attributes P_ID and Name are the candidate keys. However, the combination of P_ID and Name is not a candidate key. The candidate key, which is chosen by the database designer to uniquely identify entities, is known as the **primary key**. For example, the attribute P_ID can be chosen as the primary key. If a primary key is formed by the combination of two or more attributes, it is known as a **composite key**. A composite key must be minimal, that is, all the attributes that form the composite key must be included in the key attribute to uniquely identify the entities.

8. Explain the difference between strong and weak entity type.

Ans: An entity type that does not have any key attribute of its own is called a **weak entity type**. On the other hand, an entity type that has a key attribute is called a **strong entity type**. The weak entity is also called a **dependent entity** as it depends on another entity for its identification. The strong entity is called an **independent entity**, as it does not rely on another entity for its identification. The weak entity has no meaning and relevance in an E–R diagram if shown without the entity on which it depends. For example, consider an entity type EDITION with attributes Edition_no and Type (Indian or International). It depends on another entity type BOOK for its existence, as an edition cannot exist without a book. Thus, EDITION is a weak entity type and BOOK is a strong entity type.

A weak entity does not have its own identifying attribute that can uniquely identify each instance. It has a partial identifying attribute, which is known as the **partial key** (or **discriminator**). A partial key is a set of attributes that can uniquely identify the instances of a weak entity type, which are related to the same instance of a strong entity type. For example, the attribute Edition_no of the entity type EDITION can be taken as a partial key.

9. Define the term relationship. Illustrate the difference between relationship type and relationship instance.

Ans: An association between two or more entities is known as a **relationship**. A relationship describes how two or more entities are related to each other. For example, the relationship PUBLISHED_BY (shown in Figure 2.4) associates a book with its publisher. Similar to entity types and entity sets, relationship types and relationship sets also exist. Consider n possible distinct entity types E_1, E_2,..., E_n (where n>=2). A **relationship type** R among these n entity types defines a set of associations (known as **relationship set**) among instances from these entity types. A **relationship**

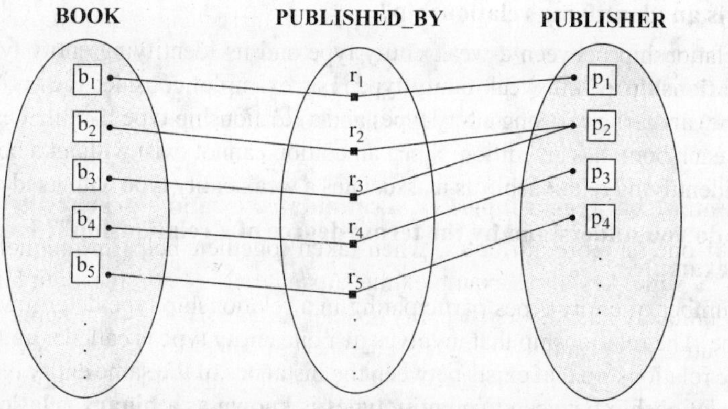

Figure 2.4 Relationship PUBLISHED_BY between two Entity Types BOOK and PUBLISHER

instance represents an association between individual entity instances. For example, an association between the entity types BOOK and PUBLISHER represents a relationship type; however, an association between the instances C++ and P001 represents a relationship instance.

Mathematically, a relationship type R can be defined as a subset of the Cartesian product $E_1 X E_2 X \ldots X E_n$. Similarly, the relationship set R can be defined as a set of relationship instances r_i, where each r_i associates n individual entity instances $e_1, e_2, \ldots, e_n$ of each entity type $E_1, E_2, \ldots, E_n$, respectively. Each of the individual entity types $E_1, E_2, \ldots, E_n$ is said to **participate** in the relationship type R and each of the individual entity instances $e_1, e_2, \ldots, e_n$ is said to participate in the relationship instance r_i. Figure 2.4 shows a relationship type PUBLISHED_BY between two entity types BOOK and PUBLISHER, which associates each book with its publisher. Here, $r_1, r_2, r_3, \ldots, r_n$ denote relationship instances.

10. Can a relationship type have attributes? Explain with the help of an example.

Ans: A relationship type may also have descriptive attributes. Consider two entity types AUTHOR and BOOK of the *Online Book* database, which are associated with the relationship type REVIEWS. Each author reviews some books and gives a rating to that book. An attribute Rating could be associated with the relationship to specify the rating of the book given by the author (see Figure 2.5).

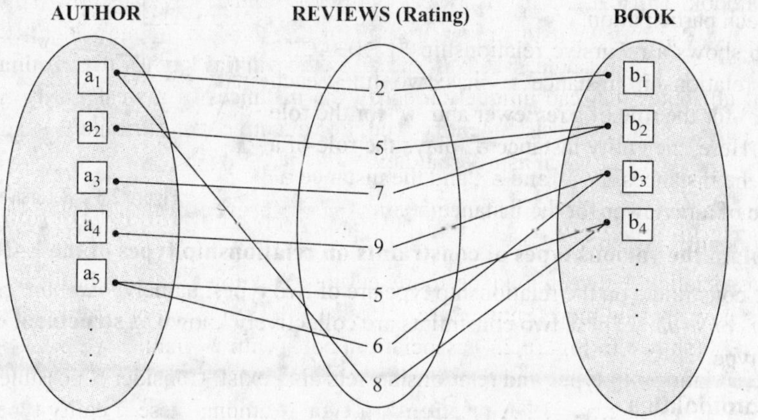

Figure 2.5 Relationship Type REVIEWS with attribute 'Rating'

11. What is an identifying relationship?

Ans: The relationship between a weak entity type and its identifying entity type is known as the **identifying relationship** of the weak entity type. For example, consider the entity types `EDITION` (weak entity type) and `BOOK` (strong entity type) and a relationship type `HAS` that exists between them. It specifies that each book has an edition. Since an edition cannot exist without a book, the relationship type `HAS` is an identifying relationship as it associates a weak entity type with its identifying entity type.

12. What do you understand by the term "degree of a relationship"? Explain with the help of an example.

Ans: The number of entity types participating in a relationship type determines the degree of the relationship type. The relationship that involves just one entity type is called a **unary relationship**. In other words, the relationship that exists between the instances of the same entity type is the unary relationship. The relationship between two entity types is known as a **binary relationship** and the relationship between three entity types is known as the **ternary relationship**. In general, the relationship between *n* entity types is known as an *n*-ary relationship. Thus, a unary relationship has a degree 1, a binary relationship has a degree 2, a ternary relationship has a degree 3 and an *n*-ary relationship has a degree *n*. For example, the relationship type `PUBLISHED_BY` (shown in Figure 2.4) between the entity types `BOOK` and `PUBLISHER` is a binary relationship.

13. What is a role name? In what situations is it necessary to use role names in the description of relationship types?

Ans: Each entity type that participates in a relationship type plays a specific function or a role in the relationship. The role of each participating entity type is represented by the **role name**. If the participating entity types are distinct, their role names are implicit and are not usually specified. For example, in the `PUBLISHED_BY` relationship, the entity type `BOOK` plays the role of a *book* and the entity type `PUBLISHER` plays the role of a *publisher*. Thus, the role names in this relationship are implicit. Now, consider another entity `AUTHOR` from the *Online Book* database, where the entity type `AUTHOR` plays two different roles (author and reviewer). Such a relationship is called a **recursive relationship**. In such situations, where role names are not implicit, it is necessary to explicitly specify role names to distinguish the meaning of each participation.

Figure 2.6 shows a recursive relationship `FEEDBACKS` where each relationship instance r_i has two lines each marked by '`r`' for the role of a reviewer and '`w`' for the role of an author. Here, the entity instance a_1 plays the role of a reviewer for the instances a_2, a_3 and a_4, and the instance a_2 plays the role of a reviewer for the instance a_5.

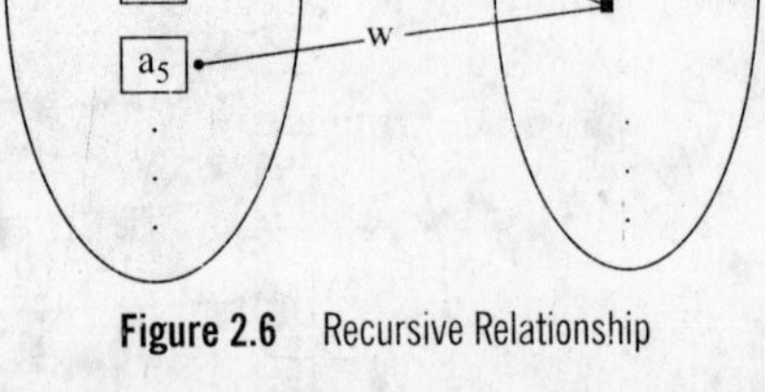

Figure 2.6 Recursive Relationship

14. Explain the various types of constraints on relationship types of the E–R model.

Ans: The constraints on the relationship type are of two types, namely, *mapping cardinalities* and *participation constraint*. These two constraints are collectively known as **structural constraints** of a relationship type.

Mapping cardinalities

The maximum number of instances of one entity type to which an instance of another entity type can relate to is expressed by the **mapping cardinalities** or **cardinality ratio** (Figure 2.7). The

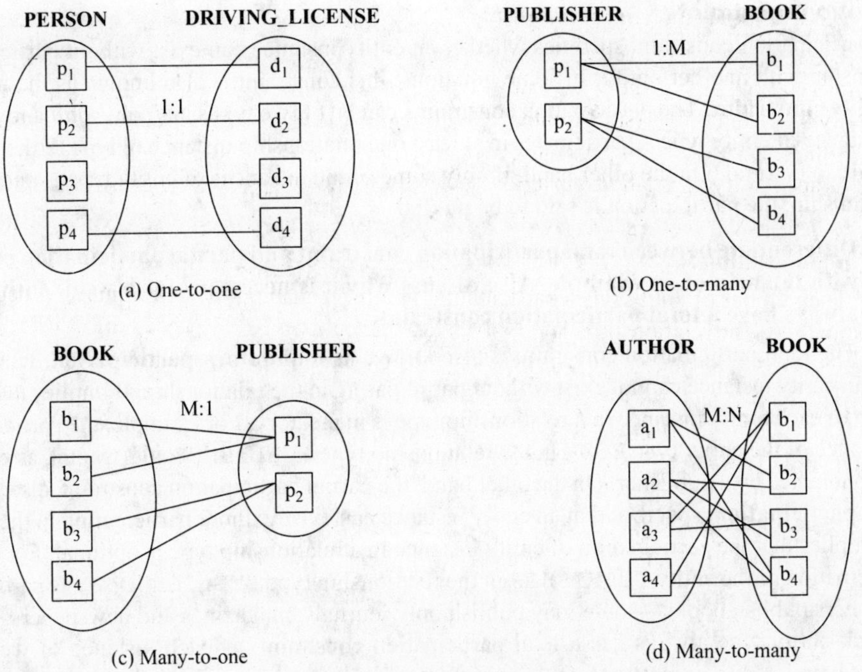

Figure 2.7 Mapping Cardinalities

mapping cardinalities can be used to describe the relationship between two or more entities. For a binary relationship between two entity types E_1 and E_2, the mapping cardinalities can be of four types:

- **One-to one:** In one-to-one mapping, each instance of entity type E_1 is associated with at most one instance of entity type E_2 and vice-versa. It is represented by 1:1 relationship. For example, consider two entities `PERSON` and `DRIVING_LICENSE`. Each person can only have one driving license, and one driving license with a particular number can only be issued to a single person. That is, no two persons can have the same driving license. Thus, these two entities have 1:1 relationship.
- **One-to-many:** In one-to-many mapping, each instance of entity type E_1 can be associated with zero or more instances of type E_2. However, an instance of type E_2 can only be associated to at most one instance of E_1. It is represented by 1:M relationship. For example, one publisher can publish many books; however, one book (with a particular ISBN) can only be published by one publisher. Thus, the entities `PUBLISHER` and `BOOK` have 1:M relationship.
- **Many-to-one:** In many-to-one mapping, each instance of entity type E_1 can be associated with at most one instance of type E_2. However, an instance of type E_2 can be associated with zero or more instances of type E_1. It is represented by M:1 relationship. For example, different books can be published by one publisher; however, one book can only be published by one publisher. Thus, the entities `BOOK` and `PUBLISHER` have M:1 relationship.
- **Many-to-many:** In many-to-many mapping, each instance of entity type E_1 can be associated with zero or more instances of type E_2 and an instance of type E_2 can also be associated with zero or more instances of type E_1. It is represented by M:N relationship. For example, one author can write many books and one book can be written by more than one author. Thus, the entities `AUTHOR` and `BOOK` have M:N relationship.

Participation constraint

The participation constraint specifies whether an entity instance can exist without participating in a relationship with another entity. In some notations, this constraint is also known as the **minimum cardinality constraint**. The participation constraints can be of two types, namely, *total* and *partial*. If every instance of entity type E participates in at least one relationship instance of type R, the participation is said to be **total**. On the other hand, if only some of the instances of entity type E participate in the relationship, the participation is said to be **partial**.

15. Differentiate between total participation constraint and partial participation constraint with the help of an example. Also discuss why it is necessary for a weak entity type to always have a total participation constraint.

Ans: The total participation constraint is also known as **mandatory participation**, which specifies that an entity instance cannot exist without participating in the relationship. It implies that the participation of each entity instance in a relationship type is mandatory. For example, the participation of each instance of the entity type BOOK in the relationship type PUBLISHED_BY is total, as each book must be published by a publisher. On the other hand, the partial participation constraint, also known as **optional participation**, specifies that an entity instance can exist without participating in the relationship. It implies that the participation of entity instance in a relationship type is optional. For example, the participation of the entity PUBLISHER in the relationship type PUBLISHED_BY is partial, as not all publishers publish books—some may publish only journals, magazines and newspapers.

A weak entity type always has a total participation constraint, as each instance of weak entity type must be related to at least one of the instances of its parent entity type. For example, the entity type EDITION in the *Online Book* database has a total participation constraint as an edition must be related to at least one of instances of the entity type BOOK.

16. Discuss the E–R diagram notations.

Ans: There are various symbols that are used in the E–R diagrams to represent various types of information. The symbols include rectangles, ellipses, diamonds, lines, double lines, double ellipses, dashed ellipses and double rectangles. The symbols and their purpose are shown in Figure 2.8.

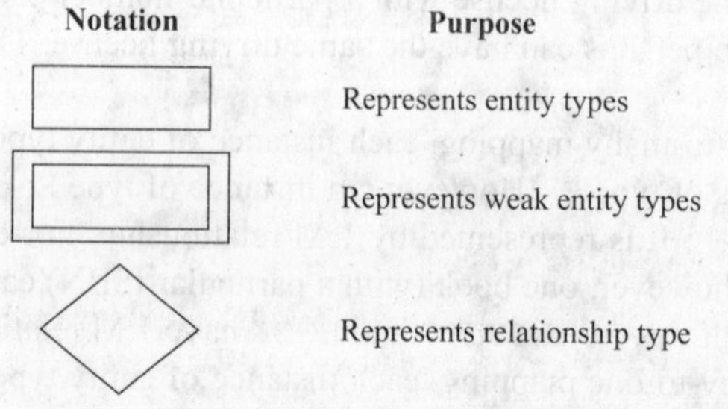

Figure 2.8 E–R Diagram Notations

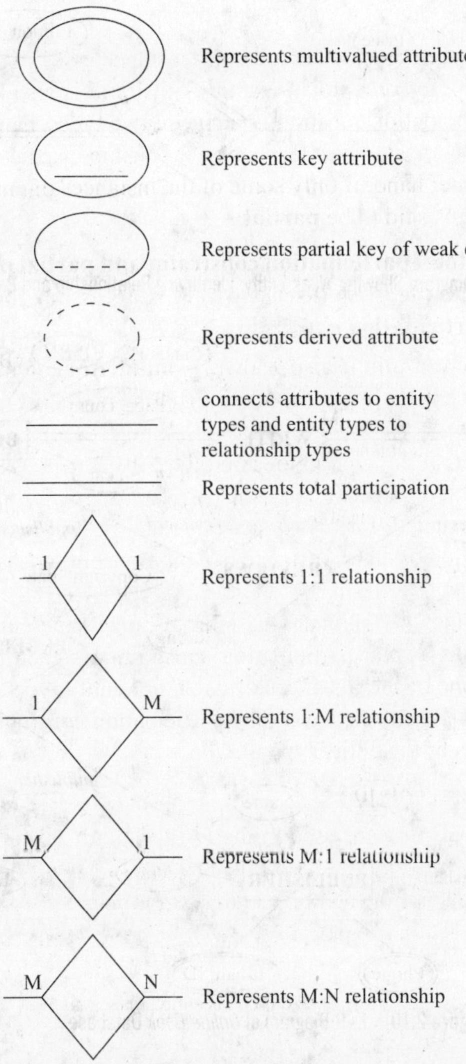

Figure 2.8 (Contd...)

17. How are weak entity types represented in an E–R diagram? Explain with help of an example.

Ans: To illustrate how weak entity types are represented in an E–R diagram, consider the *Online Book* database in which the entity type `EDITION` is a weak entity type with `Edition_no` as its partial key. It depends on the strong entity type `BOOK`. It has a total participation in the identifying relationship type `HAS`, which specifies that an edition cannot exist without a book (Figure 2.9).

18. Give the complete E–R diagram for the *Online Book* database.

Ans: The complete E–R diagram for the *Online Book* database is shown in Figure 2.10.

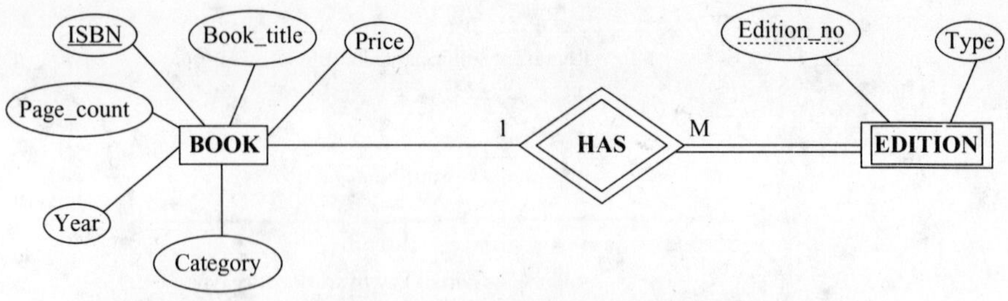

Figure 2.9 E–R Diagram Showing Weak Entity, Identifying Relationship and Partial Key

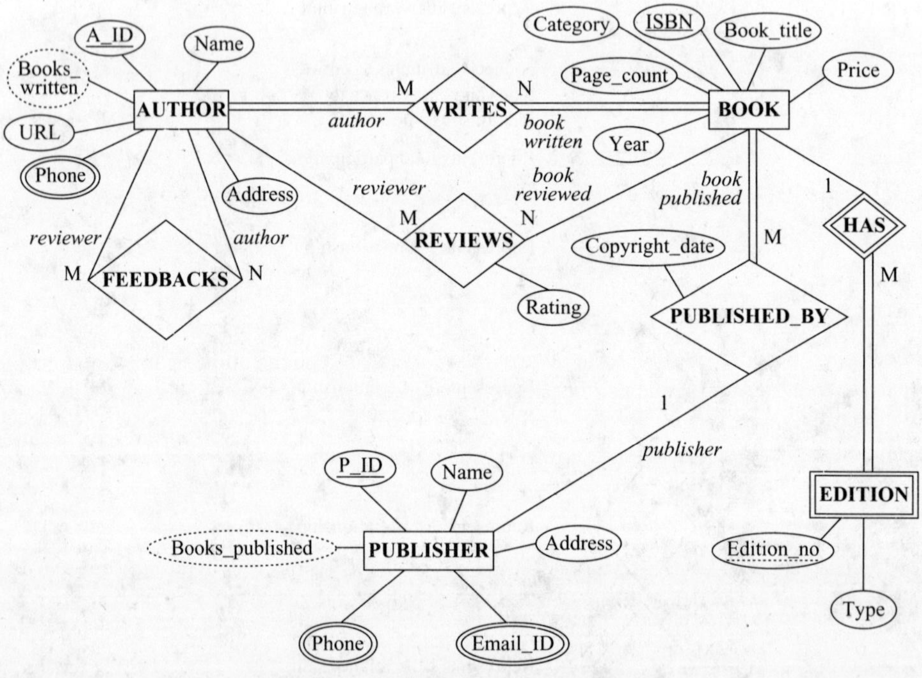

Figure 2.10 E–R Diagram of *Online Book* Database

19. Discuss with the help of an example how we can represent ternary relationships using the E–R diagram.

Ans: An E–R diagram can also be used to represent higher degree relationships (relationships of degree greater than two). The most common higher degree relationship is the ternary relationship, which describes the relationship between three entity types. For example, consider the entity types `AUTHOR`, `BOOK` and `SUBJECT`. The entity type `SUBJECT` has the attributes `S_ID` and `Subject_name`. The subject name could be Database Systems, C++, C, Computer Architecture, etc. Each author writes a book on a particular subject. This relationship is ternary as it associates three entity types. Figure 2.11 shows the relationship type `WRITES` among three entity types `AUTHOR`, `BOOK` and `SUBJECT`. The mapping cardinality of the relationship type `WRITES` is M:1:1, which implies that a group of particular authors (many authors) can write at most one book on a particular subject.

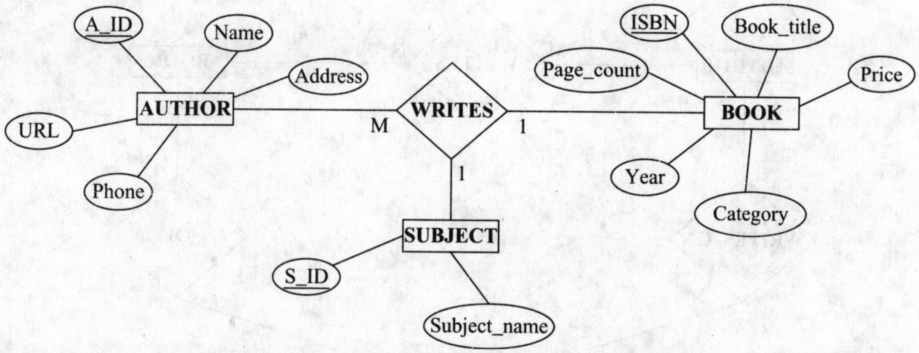

Figure 2.11 E–R Diagram Showing a Ternary Relationship

20. Discuss the design issues that are to be considered while designing an E–R diagram.

Ans: While designing an E–R diagram, a number of design choices are to be considered. They are as follows:

Entity types versus attributes

When the attributes of a particular entity type are identified, it becomes difficult to determine whether a property of the entity should be represented as an entity type or as an attribute. For example, consider the entity type `AUTHOR` with attributes `A_ID`, `Name`, `Address`, `Phone` and `URL`. Treating phone as an attribute implies that each author can have at the most one telephone number. In case multiple phone numbers have to be stored for each author, the attribute `Phone` can be taken as a multivalued attribute. However, treating telephone number as a separate entity type better models a situation where the user may want to store some extra information such as location (*home*, *office* or *mobile*) of the telephone. Thus, `Phone` can be taken a separate entity type with attributes `Phone_number` and `location`, which implies that an author can have multiple phones numbers at different locations (Figure 2.12).

Binary versus ternary relationship

Generally, a database contains binary relationships, as it is easy to represent and understand the binary relationships. However, in some cases, ternary relationships need to be created to represent certain situations. For example, consider the ternary relationship `WRITES` in the Figure 2.11. Its equivalent E–R diagram comprising three distinct binary relationships, `WRITES_ON`, `WRITES` and `OF` with cardinality ratios M:N, M:N and M:1, respectively, is shown in Figure 2.13. The information conveyed by these three binary relationships is not the same as that of the ternary relationship shown in Figure 2.11. Thus, it is the responsibility of the database designer to make an appropriate decision depending on the situation being represented.

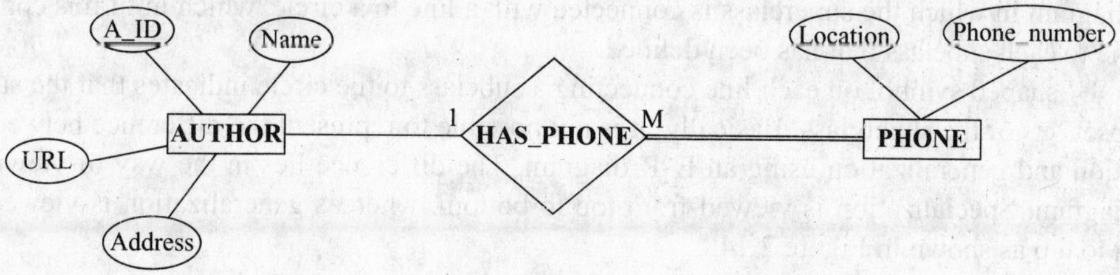

Figure 2.12 E–R Diagram Showing `Phone` as an Entity Type

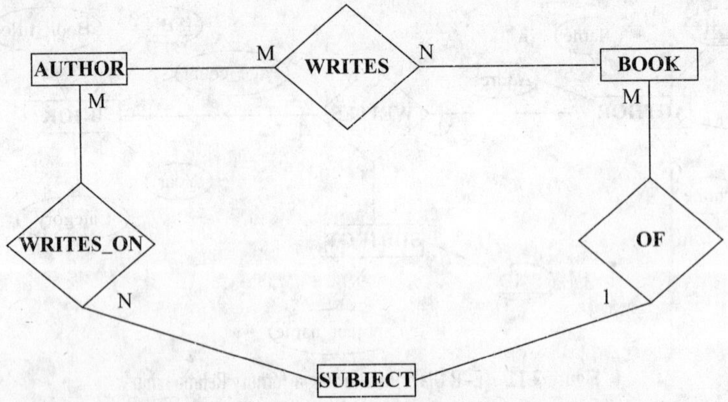

Figure 2.13 E–R Diagram Showing Three Binary Relationships

21. Discuss the difference between specialization and generalization with the help of an example. Is it possible to represent their differences with the help of an E–R diagram? Explain.

Ans: An entity type may include subgroups of its entities in such a way that entities of one subgroup are distinct in some way from the entities of other subgroups. For example, the entity type BOOK can be classified into three types, namely, TEXTBOOK, LANGUAGE_BOOK and NOVEL. These entity types are described by a set of attributes that includes all the attributes of the entity type BOOK and some additional sets of attributes. These additional attributes are also known as **local** or **specific** attributes. For example, the entity type TEXTBOOK may have the additional attribute Subject (for example, Computer, Maths, Science, etc.). This process of defining the subgroups of a given entity type is called **specialization**.

The entity type containing the common attributes is known as the **superclass** and the entity type, which is a subset of the superclass, is known as its **subclass**. The design process in which multiple lower-level entity types are combined on the basis of common features to form higher-level entity types is known as **generalization**. For example, the database designer may first identify the entity types TEXTBOOK, LANGUAGE_BOOK and NOVEL and then combine the common attributes of these entity types to form a higher-level entity type BOOK. Specialization starts with a single higher-level entity type and ends with a set of lower-level entity types having some additional attributes that distinguish them from each other. Generalization, on the other hand, starts with the identification of a number of lower-level entity types and ends with the grouping of the common attributes to form a single higher-level entity type.

Specialization and generalization can be represented graphically with the help of an EER (enhanced E–R) diagram in which the superclass is connected with a line to a circle, which in turn is connected by a line to each subclass that has been defined.

The 'U' shaped symbol on each line connecting a subclass to the circle indicates that the subclass is a subset '⊂' of the superclass. Basically, it is not possible to represent the difference between specialization and generalization using an E–R diagram. The difference lies in the way of viewing the E–R diagram. Specialization is viewed from top to bottom, whereas generalization is viewed from bottom to top as shown in Figure 2.14.

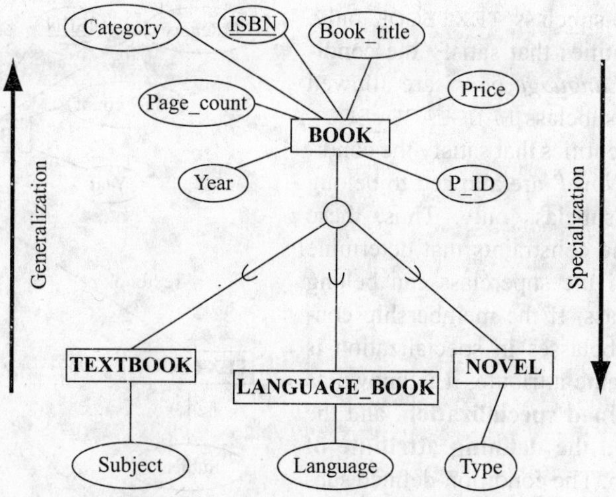

Figure 2.14 Specialization and Generalization

22. Define attribute inheritance.

Ans: The higher-level entity type (or superclass) has the attributes that are common to all of its lower-level entity types (or subclasses). These common attributes of the superclass are inherited by all its subclasses. This property is known as **attribute inheritance**.

23. Differentiate between specialization hierarchy and specialization lattice.

Ans: If a subclass is a subset of only one superclass, that is, it has only one parent, it is known as **single inheritance**, and the resulting structure is known as a **specialization** (or **generalization**) **hierarchy**. For example, Figure 2.14 shows a single inheritance as three subclasses are derived from only one superclass. On the other hand, if a subclass is derived from more than one superclass, it is known as **multiple inheritance**, and the resulting structure is known as a **specialization** (or **generalization**) **lattice**. In this case, the subclass is known as a **shared subclass**. For example, consider two entity types `EMPLOYEE` and `STUDENT`. A student who is working as a part-time employee in an organization as well as pursuing a course from a university can be derived from these two entity types. Figure 2.15 shows a specialization lattice with a shared subclass `PARTTIME_EMPLOYEE`.

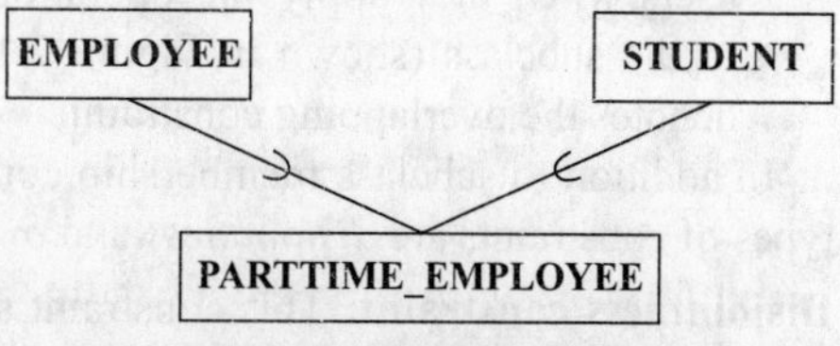

Figure 2.15 Specialization Lattice with Shared Subclass `PARTTIME_EMPLOYEE`

24. Discuss the various constraints that can be placed on specialization and generalization.

Ans: The constraints that can be placed on generalization and specialization are as follows:

- **Condition defined:** In condition defined, the membership of entities is determined by placing a condition on the value of some attribute of the superclass. The subclasses formed on the basis of the specified condition are called **condition-defined** (or **predicate-defined**) **subclasses**. For example, all the instances of type `BOOK` can be evaluated based on the value of the attribute `Category`. The entities that satisfy the condition *Category='Textbook'* are allowed to belong to the subclass TEXTBOOK only. Similarly, the entities that satisfy the condition *Category*='*Language book*' are allowed to belong to the subclass LANGUAGE_BOOK only. Lastly, the entities that satisfy the condition *Category*='*Novel*' are allowed to belong to the NOVEL subclass only. Thus, these conditions are the constraints that determine which entities of the superclass can belong to a given subclass. If the membership condition for all subclasses in specialization is defined on the same attribute, it is known as an **attribute-defined specialization**, and the attribute is called the **defining attribute** of the specialization. The condition-defined subclass is shown by writing the condition next to the line connecting the subclass to the specialization circle (shown in Figure 2.16). The symbol **d** denotes the disjointness constraint.

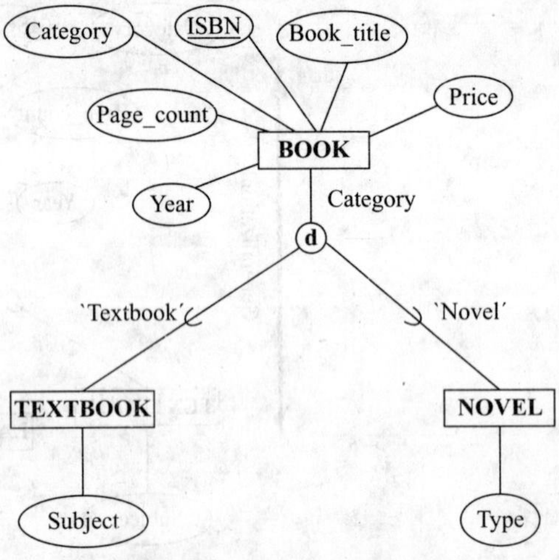

Figure 2.16 EER Diagram for an Attribute-defined Specialization with Disjoint Constraint

- **User defined:** If the membership of the superclass entities in a given subclass is determined by the database users and not by any membership condition, it is called **user-defined specialization**, and the subclasses that are formed are known as **user-defined subclasses**. For example, consider an entity CELEBRITY. A celebrity could be a film star, a politician, a newsreader or a player. Thus, the assignment of the entities of type CELEBRITY to a given subclass is specified explicitly by the database users when they apply the operation to add an entity to the subclass (shown in Figure 2.17). The symbol **o** denotes the overlapping constraint.

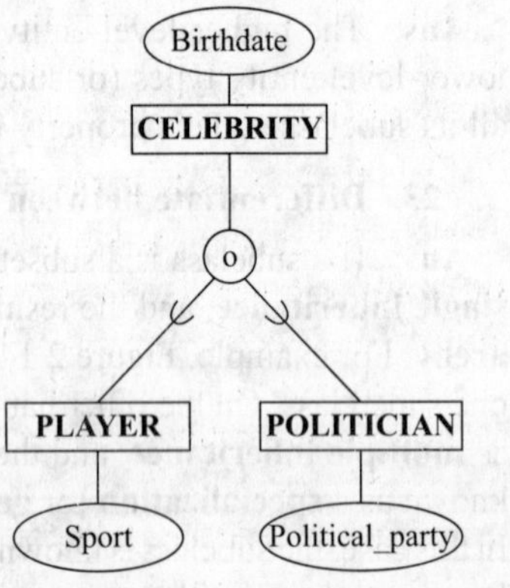

Figure 2.17 EER Diagram for a User-defined Specialization with Overlapping Constraint

In addition to subclass membership constraints, two other types of constraints are *disjointness* and *overlapping*.

Disjointness constraint: This constraint specifies that the same higher-level entity instance cannot belong to more than one lower-level entity type. That is, the subclasses of any superclass must be disjoint. For example, an entity of type BOOK can belong to either TEXTBOOK or NOVEL but not both. An attribute-defined specialization in which the defining attribute is single-valued implies a disjointness constraint. The disjoint constraint is represented by a symbol **d** written in a circle in an EER diagram as shown in Figure 2.18.

Overlapping constraint: This constraint specifies that the same higher-level entity instance can belong to more than one lower-level entity types. That is, the subclasses of any superclass need not be disjointed and entities may overlap. In terms of the EER diagram, the overlapping constraint is represented by a symbol **o** written in a circle joining the superclass with its subclasses. For example, the entity types PLAYER and POLITICIAN show an overlapping constraint, as the celebrity can be a player as well as a politician (see Figure 2.19).

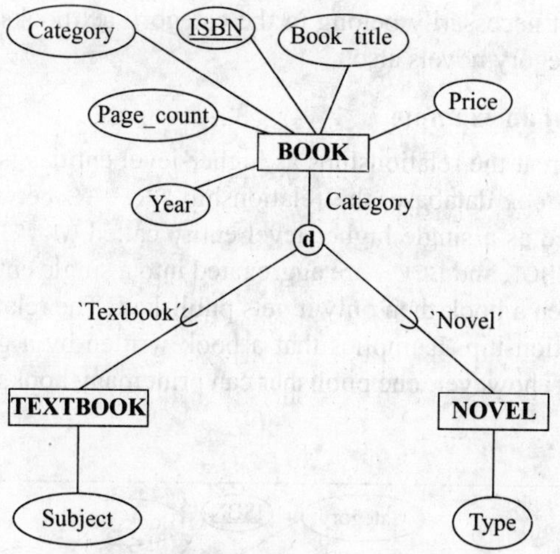

Figure 2.18 EER Diagram for an Attribute-defined Specialization with Disjoint Constraint

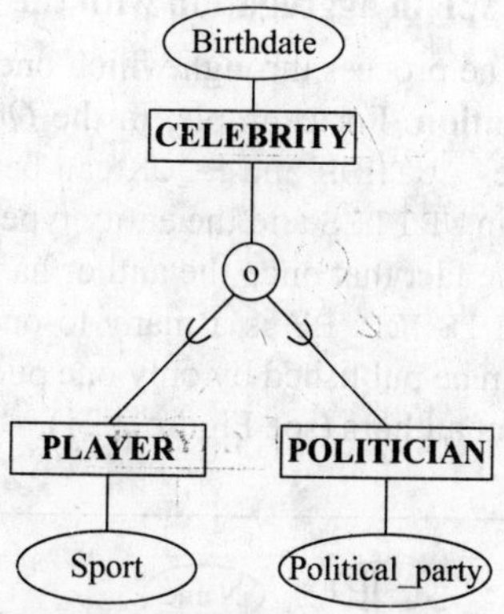

Figure 2.19 EER Diagram for a User-defined Specialization with Overlapping Constraint

Completeness constraint: The last constraint that can be applied to generalization or specialization is the completeness constraint. It determines whether an entity in the higher-level entity set must belong to at least one of the lower-level entity sets or not. The completeness constraint can be total or partial.

- **Total specialization:** It specifies that each higher-level entity must belong to at least one of the lower-level entity types in the specialization. Figure 2.20(a) shows the total specialization of the entity type BOOK. Here, each book entity must belong to either textbook or language book or novel category. The total specialization is represented by double lines connecting the superclass with the circle.
- **Partial specialization:** It allows some of the instances of the higher-level entity type not to belong to any of the lower-level entity types. Figure 2.20(b) shows the partial specialization of

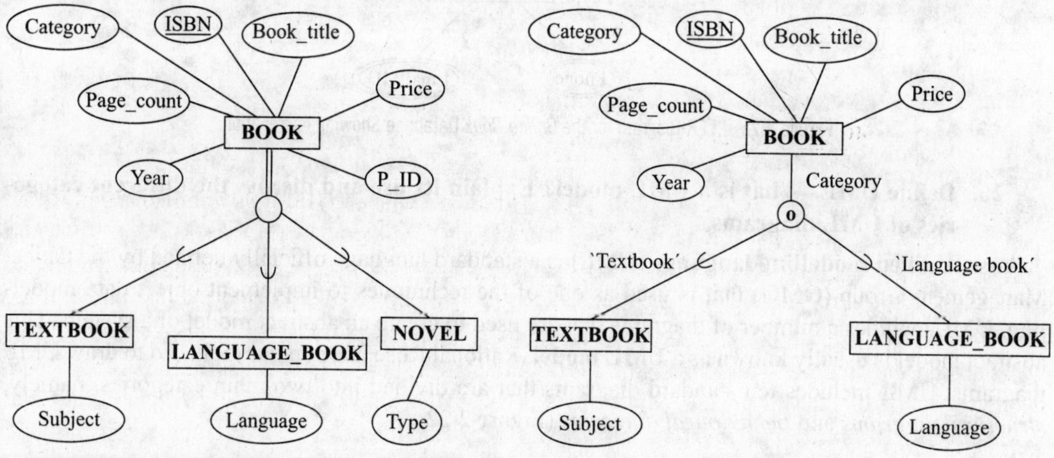

Figure 2.20 EER Diagrams Showing Completeness Constraints: (a) EER Diagram Showing Total Participation and (b) EER Diagram Showing Partial Participation

the entity type BOOK, as all books do not necessarily belong to the category textbooks or language books; some may belong to the category novels also.

25. Explain aggregation with the help of an example.

Ans: The process through which one can treat the relationships as higher-level entities is known as **aggregation**. For example, in the *Online Book* database, the relationship WRITES between the entity types AUTHOR and BOOK can be treated as a single higher-level entity called WRITES. The relationship WRITES and the entity types AUTHOR and BOOK are aggregated into a single entity type to show the fact that once the author has written a book then only it gets published. The relationship type PUBLISHED_BY is a many-to-one relationship. It implies that a book written by a group of authors can be published by only one publisher; however, one publisher can print many books written by different authors (see Figure 2.21).

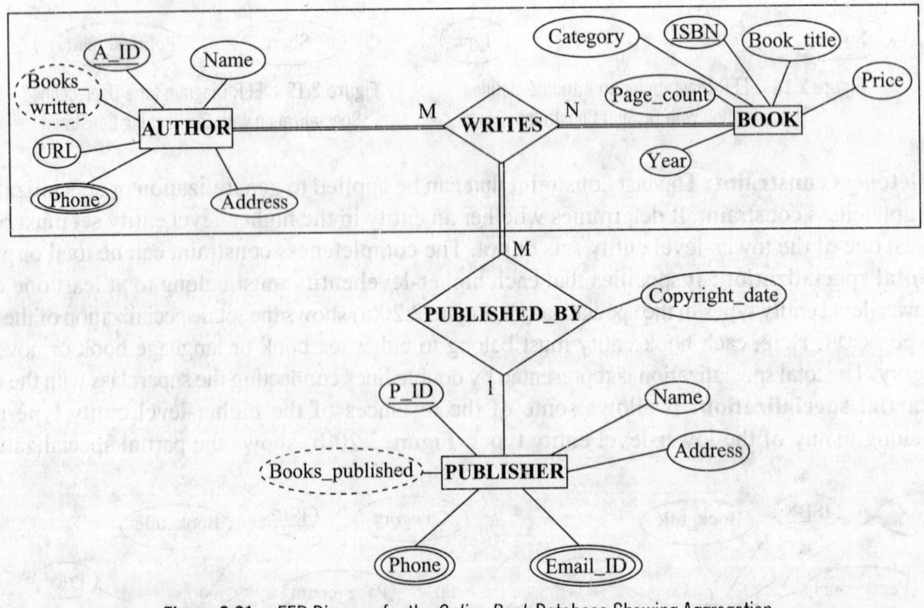

Figure 2.21 EER Diagram for the *Online Book* Database Showing Aggregation

26. Define UML. What is a UML model? Explain its use and discuss the different categories of UML diagrams.

Ans: Unified modelling language (UML) is a standard language officially defined by the Object Management Group (OMG) that is used as one of the techniques to implement object data modelling. UML includes a number of diagrams that are used to create an abstract model of a system. This abstract model is usually known as a **UML model**. Rational Rose is a popular tool used to draw UML diagrams. UML includes ten standard diagrams that are divided into two main categories, namely, *structural diagrams* and *behavioural diagrams* (Figure 2.22).

Structural diagrams

The **structural diagrams** describe the static or structural relationships among various components of the system. The structural diagrams are of five types:

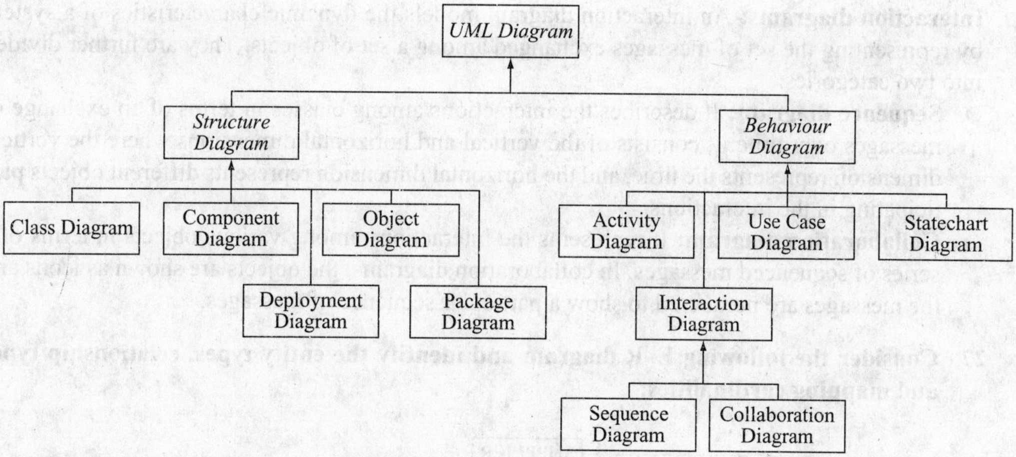

Figure 2.22 Hierarchy of UML Diagrams

- **Class diagram:** A class diagram describes the static structure of the entire system by showing the classes of the system, their attributes and the relationships between them. Like E–R diagrams, a UML class diagram is also used to represent the conceptual database schema. The entity types in an E–R diagram become the classes in the UML class diagram.
- **Package diagram:** A package diagram can be treated as a subset of a class diagram. It organizes the elements of a system into related groups such that the dependencies between the various packages are minimized.
- **Object diagram:** An object diagram describes a set of objects and their relationships. It is used to represent the static view of a system at a particular point of time and is typically used to test the class diagrams for accuracy.
- **Component diagram:** A component diagram displays the dependencies among various components of the system. The components include source code, run-time (binary) code and executable code.
- **Deployment diagram:** A deployment diagram displays the physical resources in the system such as nodes, components and connections. The **nodes** are the run-time processing elements.

Behavioural diagrams

The **behavioural diagrams** describe the dynamic or behavioural relationships among various components of the system. The behavioural diagrams are of four types:

- **Use case diagram:** A use case diagram displays the relationship among actors and use cases. An **actor** represents a user or another system that interacts with the system, and a **use case** is an external view of the system that represents some action.
- **Statechart diagram:** A statechart diagram describes the dynamic behaviour of the system by displaying the sequences of states that an object goes through during its life in response to some external events. It shows the start/initial state of an object before the occurrence of an external event and its stop/final state in response to that external event.
- **Activity diagram:** An activity diagram describes the dynamic behaviour of the system by modelling the flow of control from one activity to another. An **activity** is an operation performed on any class in the system that results in a change in the system state.

- **Interaction diagrams:** An interaction diagram models the dynamic characteristics of a system by representing the set of messages exchanged among a set of objects. They are further divided into two categories:
  - **Sequence diagram:** It describes the interactions among classes in terms of an exchange of messages over time. It consists of the vertical and horizontal dimensions where the vertical dimension represents the time, and the horizontal dimension represents different objects participating in the interactions.
  - **Collaboration diagram:** It represents the interactions among various objects in terms of a series of sequenced messages. In collaboration diagrams, the objects are shown as icons and the messages are numbered to show a particular sequence of messages.

27. Consider the following E–R diagram and identify the entity types, relationship types and mapping cardinalities:

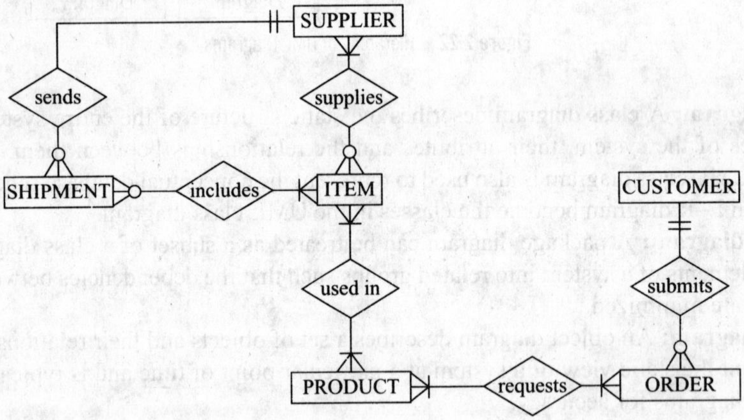

Ans: **Entity types** are Supplier, Item, Shipment, Product, Order and Customer.

Relationship types are Sends, Includes, Supplies, Used in, Requests and Submits.

Mapping cardinalities are Supplier–Item: M:N, Shipment–Supplier: M:1, Item–Product: M:N, Product–Order: M:N, Shipment–Item: M:N and Order–Customer: M: 1.

28. Design an E–R diagram for an IT training group database that will meet the information needs for its training program. Clearly indicate the entities, relationships and the key constraints. The description of the environment is as follows: The company has 12 instructors and can handle up to 100 trainees for each training session. The company offers 5 advanced technology courses, each of which is taught by a team of 2 or more instructors. Each instructor is assigned to a maximum of two teaching teams or may be assigned to do research. Each trainee undertakes one advanced technology course per training session.

Ans:

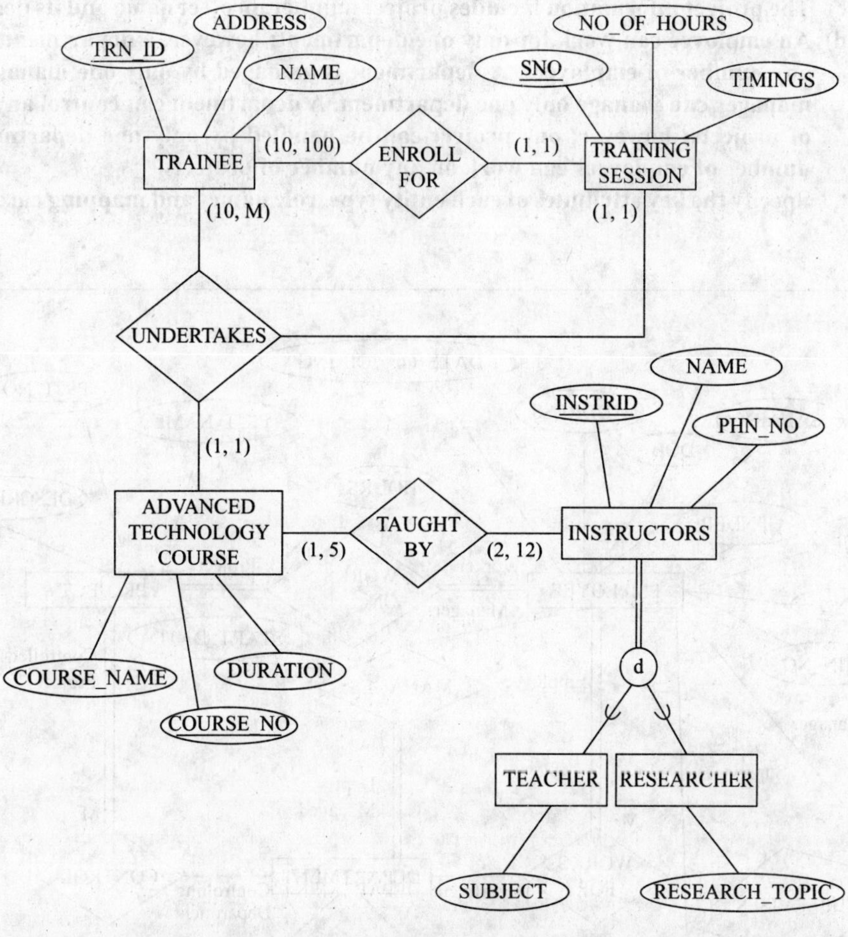

29. Design an E–R diagram for a COMPANY database as per the requirements given below. Make appropriate assumptions to complete the specification.

(a) The company stores the information about the currently working employees. The information includes employee number, name, gender, salary, and date of birth, date of joining, address and phone number. Each employee works for a department on a particular project for a particular number of hours.

(b) The information about departments includes department number and department name. Each department controls some projects currently running in the company. Also each department is managed by a particular employee who becomes the

manager for that department. This employee also supervises all the other employees in that department.

(c) The project information includes project number, project name and its description.

(d) An employee can work for only one department; however, a department can have any number of employees. A department is managed by only one manager and a manager can manage only one department. A department can control any number of projects; however, one project can be handled by only one department. Any number of employees can work on any number of projects.

Specify the key attributes of each entity type, role names and mapping cardinalities.

Ans:

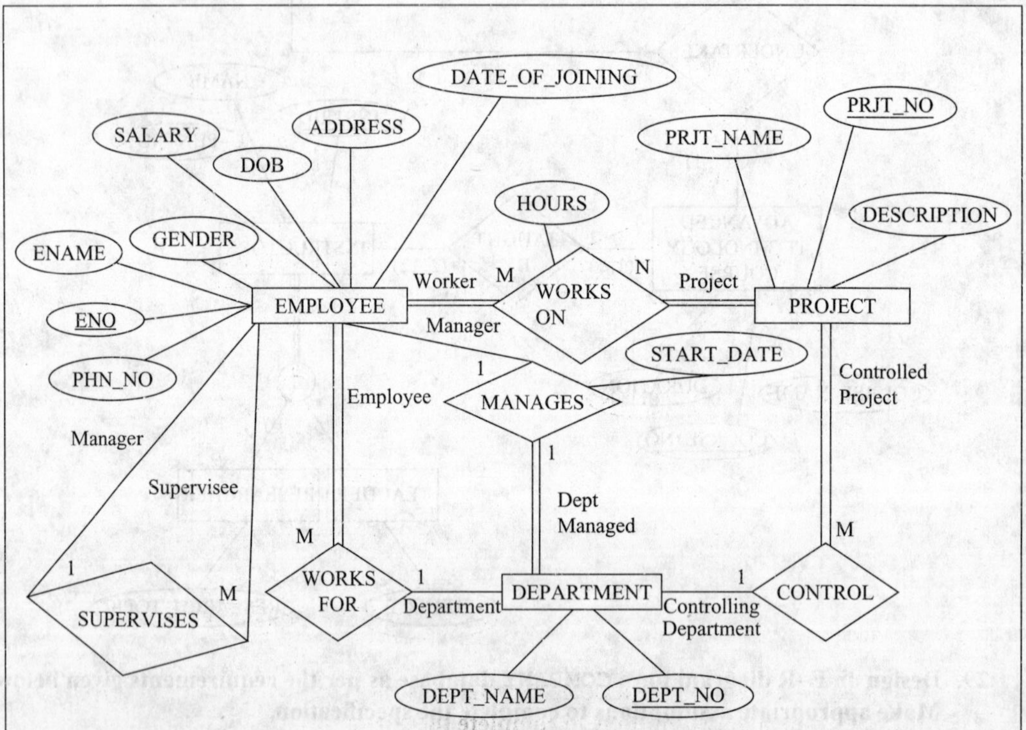

30. Consider a BANK database having customer, loan, account, employee and branch as entity types. Each branch of bank allows customers to open accounts and borrow loans. A customer can open more than one account, and one account may also belong to one or more customers. Similarly, a customer can take out more than one loan and a loan may be held by more than one customer. The bank has a number of employees working in different branches of the bank. Add appropriate attributes for each entity type. Represent the key attribute, weak entity types (if any) and cardinality ratios. Make appropriate assumptions to complete the specification. Design an E–R diagram for the BANK database.

Ans:

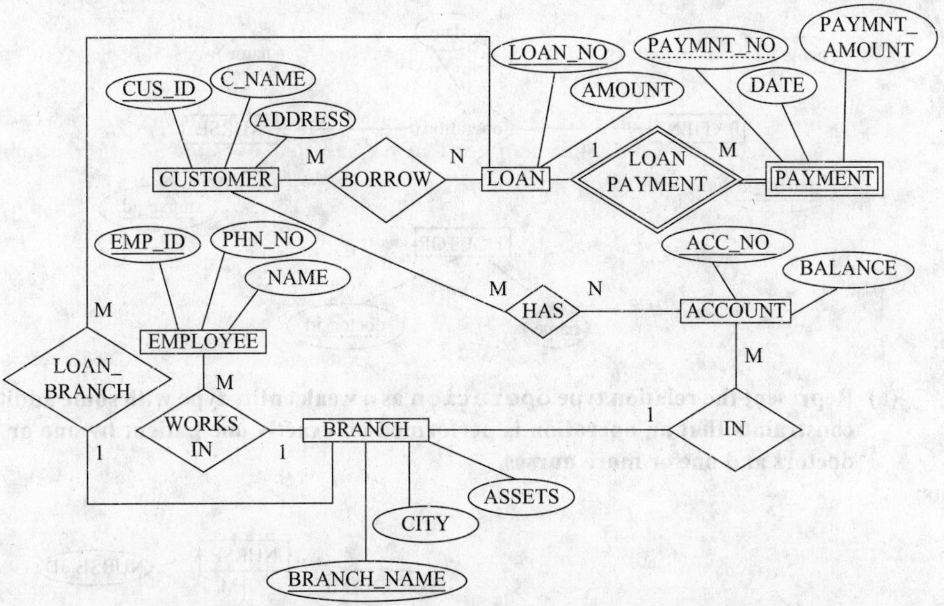

31. Construct an EER diagram for the company database described in Question 35 by showing the specialization of employee entity type. The subclasses include *clerk*, *technician*, *engineer*, *fulltime employee* and *part-time employee*. Show all the possible constraints. Make appropriate assumptions, wherever necessary.

Ans:

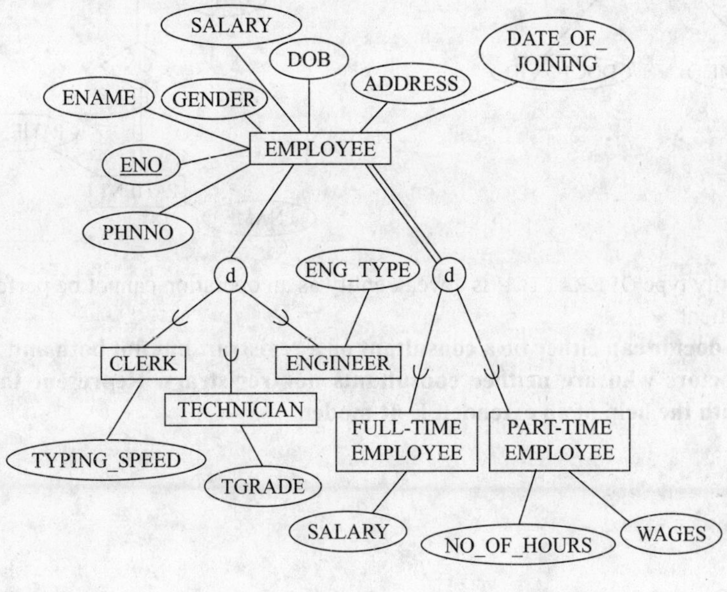

32. The following E–R diagram describes surgeries or operations in a HOSPITAL database:

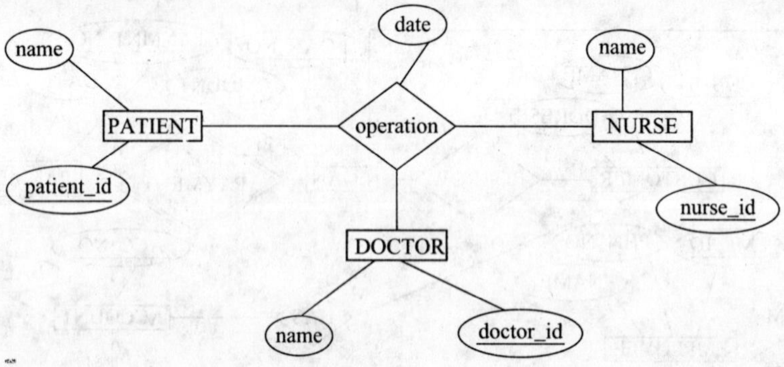

(a) Represent the relation type operation as a weak entity type with some additional constraints that an operation is performed on exactly one patient by one or more doctors and one or more nurses.

Ans:

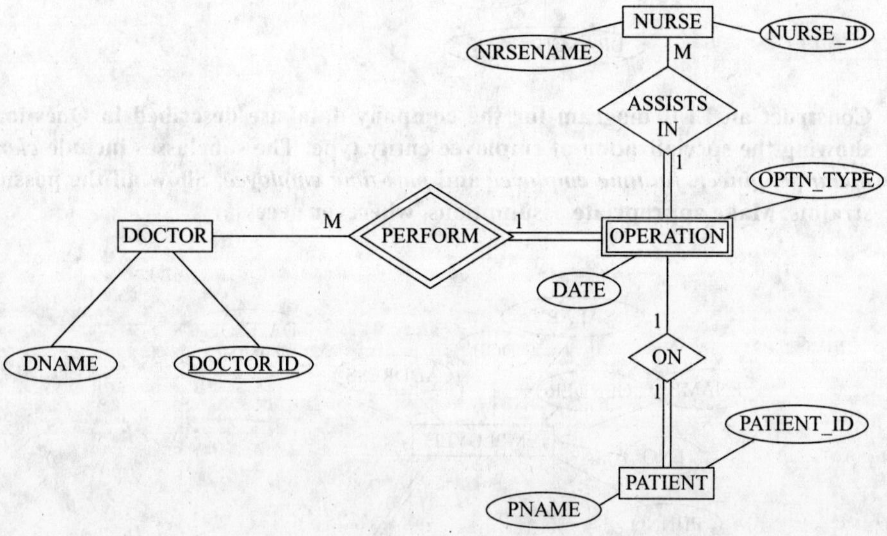

Here, the entity type OPERATION is a weak entity as an operation cannot be performed without a doctor and a patient.

(b) A doctor can either be a consultant or a registrar, but not both and there are some doctors who are neither consultants nor registrars. Represent this information with the help of an extended E–R model.

Ans:

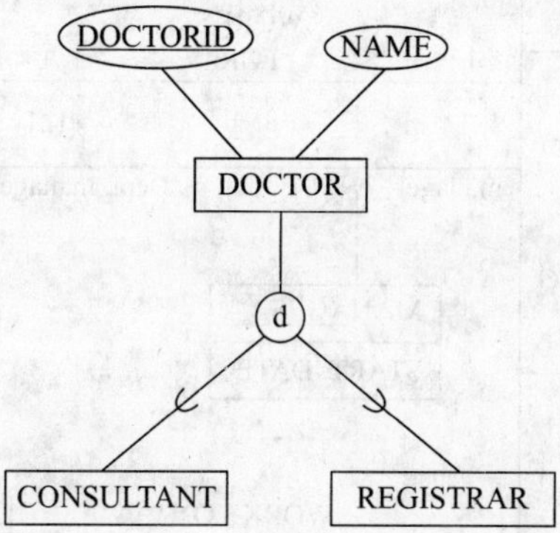

33. Draw the UML diagrams equivalent to the E–R diagrams constructed for Questions 27 and 29.

Ans: UML diagram for Question 27:

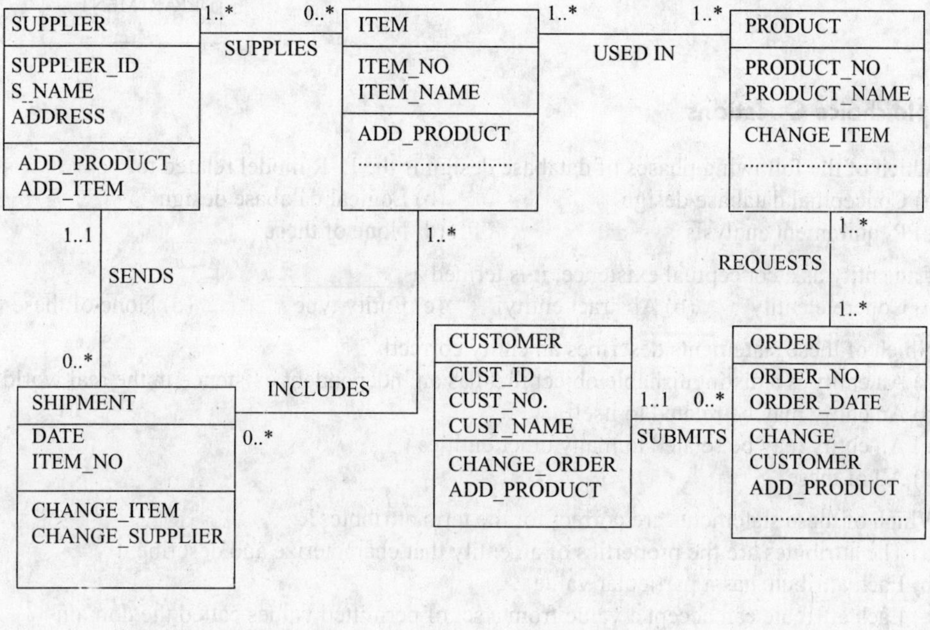

UML diagram for Question (29):

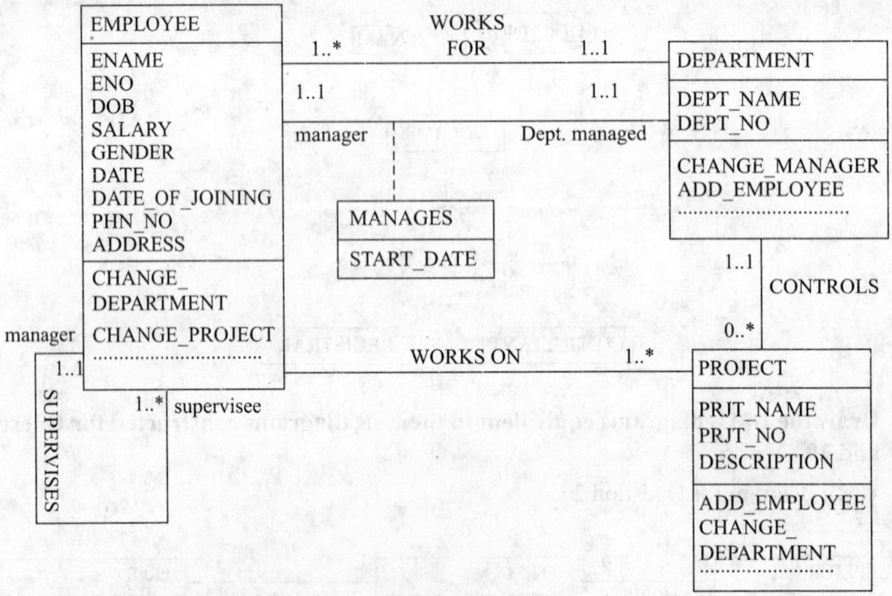

Multiple-choice Questions

1. Which of the following phases of database design is the E–R model related to?
   (a) Conceptual database design (b) Logical database design
   (c) Requirement analysis (d) None of these
2. If an entity as a conceptual existence, it is termed as __________.
   (a) Concrete entity (b) Abstract entity (c) Entity type (d) None of these
3. Which of these statements describes an entity correctly?
   (a) An entity is a distinguishable object that has an independent existence in the real world
   (b) An entity may be related to itself
   (c) An entity may be related to many other entities
   (d) All of these
4. Which of these statements are correct for the term attributes?
   (a) The attributes are the properties of an entity that characterize and describe it
   (b) Each attribute has a particular value
   (c) Each attribute can accept a value from a set of permitted values called the domain
   (d) All of these
5. The entity set that participates in a relationship__________.
   (a) May or may not be distinct (b) Is distinct
   (c) Need not be distinct (d) None of these
6. Which of the following attributes is used to uniquely identify an instance of an entity?
   (a) Unique attribute (b) Simple attribute
   (c) Identifying attribute (d) Multi-valued attribute

7. Which of these attributes can be considered as the identifying attribute for an entity student?
(a) Address (b) Roll number (c) Marks (d) Any of these
8. The relationship that exists between a weak entity type and its identifying entity type is known as __________.
(a) Identifying relationship (b) Weak relationship
(c) Strong relationship (d) Relationship type
9. The relationship between two entity types is known as __________.
(a) Two-way relationship (b) Double relationship
(c) Binary relationship (d) Multiple relationship
10. A person has a PAN card. Which of the following relationships is correct for this condition?
(a) One-to-one (b) One-to-many (c) Many-to-many (d) Many-to-one
11. The strong entity type and weak entity type participates in __________.
(a) One-to-one relationship (b) One-to-many relationship
(c) Many-to-one relationship (d) Many-to-many relationship
12. In an E–R diagram, __________ is used for representing an entity.
(a) Square (b) Rectangle
(c) Diamond-shaped box (d) Ellipse
13. The process of defining the subgroups of a given entity type is known as __________.
(a) Generalization (b) Aggregation (c) Participation (d) Specialization
14. When common attributes of entity types are combined to form higher-level entity type, it is called __________.
(a) Inheritance (b) Specialization (c) Aggregation (d) Generalization
15. Rational Rose is a popular tool used to draw __________ diagrams.
(a) E–R (b) EER (c) UML (d) None of these
16. UML class diagram is used to represent the __________ database schema.
(a) Conceptual (b) Relational (c) Both (a) and (b) (d) None of these

Answers

1. (a)	2. (b)	3. (d)	4. (d)	5. (c)	6. (c)	7. (b)
8. (a)	9. (c)	10. (a)	11. (b)	12. (b)	13. (d)	14. (d)
15. (c)	16. (a)					

3

Relational Model

1. What do you understand by the term relation?

Ans: A **relation** is used to represent information about any entity and its relationship with other entities in the form of attributes (or columns) and tuples (or rows). It comprises a relation schema and a relation instance.

2. What is a relational database?

Ans: A **relational database** is a collection of relations (or two-dimensional tables) having distinct names. It is a persistent storage mechanism that conforms to the relational model.

3. Illustrate the difference between relation schema and relation instance.

Ans: A **relation schema** (also termed as relation intension) depicts the attributes of the table. It consists of a relation name R and a set of attributes (or fields) $A_1, A_2, \ldots, A_n$. It is represented by R $(A_1, A_2, \ldots, A_n)$ and is used to describe a relation R. To understand the concept of relation schema, consider the book, publisher and author information stored in an *Online Book* database with the schema of the relations given as:

```
BOOK (ISBN, Book_title, Category, Price, Copyright_date, Year,
Page_count, P_ID)
AUTHOR (A_ID, Aname, City, State, Zip, Phone, URL)
PUBLISHER (P_ID, Pname, Address, State, Phone, Email_id)
```

In these statements, ISBN, Book_title, Category, Price, Copyright_date, Year, Page_count and P_ID are the attributes of relation BOOK. A_ID, Aname, City, State, Zip, Phone and URL are the attributes of relation AUTHOR. P_ID, Pname, Address, State, Phone and Email_id are the attributes of relation PUBLISHER.

A **relation instance** (also termed as relation extension) is a two-dimensional table with a time-varying set of tuples. A relation instance (or relation) r of the relation schema R $(A_1, A_2, \ldots, A_n)$ is a set of *n*-tuples t. It is also denoted by r(R). A relation instance is an ordered set of attributes values v that belongs to the domain D and it can be denoted as $r = \{t_1, t_2, \ldots, t_m\}$ where, $t = \{v_1, \ldots, v_n\}$. It can be considered as a *table*, which is a collection of tuples having same number of attributes.

Attributes (or Fields or Columns)

Tuples (Records or rows)

ISBN	Book_title	Category	Price	Copyright_ date	Year	Page_count	P_ID
001-354-921-1	Ransack	Novel	22	2005	2006	200	P001
001-987-650-5	Differential Calculus	Textbook	30	2003	2003	450	P001
002-678-880-2	Call Away	Novel	22	2001	2002	200	P002

Figure 3.1 Instance `B1` of the `BOOK` Relation

Figure 3.1 shows an instance `B1` of `BOOK` relation which contains three tuples and eight attributes. If the tuple `t` denotes the first tuple of the relation, the notation `t[ISBN]` refers to the value of `t` on the `ISBN` attribute. Hence, `t[ISBN]="001-354-921-1",t[Book_title]="Ransack"` and so on.

4. Define the term degree.

Ans: The number of attributes in a relation is known as **degree** or **arity**.

5. What do you mean by the term cardinality?

Ans: The number of tuples in a relation is known as **cardinality**.

6. What are unary, binary, and ternary relations?

Ans: A relation of degree one is known as **unary relation.** A relation of degree two is known as **binary relation.** A relation of degree three is known as **ternary relation**.

7. Explain the characteristics of relations?

Ans: A relation has certain characteristics, which are given here.

- **Ordering of tuples in a relation:** Since a relation is a set of tuples and a set has no particular order among its elements, hence, tuples in a relation do not have any specified order. However, tuples in a relation can be logically ordered by the values of various attributes. In that case, information in a relation remains same, only the order of tuple varies. Hence, tuple ordering in a relation is irrelevant.
- **Ordering of values within a tuple:** An *n*-tuple is an ordered set of attribute values that belongs to the domain `D`, so, the order in which the values appear in the tuples is significant. However, if a tuple is defined as a set of (`<attribute>` : *<value>*) pairs, the order in which attributes appear in a tuple is irrelevant. This is due to the reason that there is no preference for one attribute value over another.
- **Values and nulls in the tuples:** Relational model is based on the assumption that each tuple in a relation contains a single value for each of its attribute. Hence, a relation does not allow composite and multivalued attributes. Moreover, it allows denoting the value of the attribute as *null*, if the value does not exist for that attribute or the value is unknown.
- **No two tuples are identical in a relation:** Since a relation is a set of tuples and a set does not have identical elements. Therefore, each tuple in a relation must be uniquely identified by its contents. In other words, two tuples with the same value for all the attributes (that is, duplicate tuples) cannot exist in a relation.

- **Interpretation of a relation:** A relation can be used to interpret facts about entities as a type of assertion. A relation can also be used to interpret facts about relationships.

8. Differentiate between relational database schema and relational database instance with the help of an example.

Ans: A set of relation schemas {R_1, R_2, ..., R_m} together with a set of integrity constraints in the database constitutes **relational database schema**. A relational database schema, say S, is represented as S = {R_1, R_2, ..., R_m}.

For example, the relational database schema for *Online Book* database is a set of relation schemas, namely, BOOK, PUBLISHER, AUTHOR, AUTHOR_BOOK and REVIEW, which is shown in Figure 3.2.

BOOK

ISBN	Book_title	Category	Price	Copyright_date	Year	Page_count	P_ID

PUBLISHER

P_ID	Pname	Address	State	Phone	Email_id

AUTHOR

A_ID	Aname	City	State	Zip	Phone	Url

AUTHOR_BOOK

A_ID	ISBN

REVIEW

R_ID	ISBN	Rating

Figure 3.2 Relational Database Schema

Hence, the relational database schema for *Online Book* database can be represented as:

```
Online Book= {BOOK, PUBLISHER, AUTHOR, AUTHOR_BOOK, REVIEW}
```

A **relational database instance** s of relational database schema S = {R_1, R_2, ..., R_m} is a set of relation instances {r_1, r_2, ..., r_m} such that each relation instance r_i is a state of corresponding relation schema R_i. Each relation instance must satisfy the integrity constraints specified in the relation schema.

For example, a relational database instance corresponding to the *Online Book* database is shown in Figure 3.3.

BOOK

ISBN	Book_title	Category	Price	Copy right_date	Year	Page_count	P_ID
001-354-921-1	Ransack	Novel	22	2005	2006	200	P001
002-678-880-2	Call Away	Novel	22	2001	2002	200	P002

Figure 3.3 Relational Database Instance (Contd...)

AUTHOR

A_ID	Aname	State	City	Zip	Phone	URL
A001	Thomas William	New York	New York	14998	923673	www.thomas.com
A002	James Erin	Georgia	Atlanta	31896	376045	www.ejames.com

PUBLISHER

P_ID	Pname	Address	State	Phone	Email_id
P001	Hills Publications	12, Park street, Atlanta	Georgia	7134019	h_pub@hills.com
P003	Bright Publications	123, Main street, Honolulu	Hawai	767898	bright@bp.com

AUTHOR_BOOK

A_ID	ISBN
A001	001-987-760-9
A002	002-678-980-4

REVIEW

R_ID	ISBN	Rating
A001	002-678-980-4	2
A002	001-987-760-9	6

Figure 3.3 Relational Database Instance

9. **All candidate keys are superkeys, whereas all superkeys are not candidate keys. Justify this statement with a suitable example.**

Ans: A superkey `SK` is a subset of attributes of a relation schema `R`, such that for any two distinct tuples t_1 and t_2 in relation state `r` of `R`, we have $t_1[SK] \neq t_2[SK]$. For example, consider a relation schema `BOOK` with three attributes `ISBN`, `Book_title`, and `Category`. The value of `ISBN` is unique for each tuple; hence, {`ISBN`} is a superkey. In addition, the combination of all the attributes, that is, `{ISBN, Book_title, Category}` is a default superkey for this relation schema.

Generally, all the attributes of a superkey are not required to identify each tuple uniquely in a relation. Instead, only a subset of attributes of the superkey is sufficient to uniquely identify each tuple. Further, if any attribute is removed from this subset, the remaining set of attributes can no longer serve as a superkey. Such a minimal set of attributes, say `K`, is a **candidate key** (also known as **irreducible superkey**). For example, the superkey `{ISBN, Book_title, Category}` is not a candidate key, since its subset `{ISBN}` is a minimal set of attributes that uniquely identify each tuple of `BOOK` relation. So, `ISBN` is a candidate key as well as superkey. Hence, it is concluded that all candidate keys are superkeys, whereas all superkeys are not candidate keys.

10. **Illustrate the difference between primary key and foreign key.**

Ans: A candidate key that is chosen to uniquely identify a tuple in a relation is known as **primary key (`PK`).** Other candidate keys that are not chosen as primary key are known as **alternate keys**. The attribute whose value is never or rarely changed should be chosen as primary key. For example, in `PUBLISHER` relation (shown in Figure.3.3), the attribute `Address` should not be chosen as a primary key since it can be changed often. However, the attribute `P_ID` can be chosen as a primary key since each publisher has a unique publisher id and generally, it does not change.

Attribute of one relation can be accessed in another relation by enforcing a link between the attributes of two relations. This can be done by defining the attribute of one relation as the **foreign key** that refers to the primary key of another relation. For example, consider two relations, namely, PUBLISHER and BOOK. Here, all the books must be associated with a publisher that is already in the PUBLISHER relation. In this case, a foreign key will be defined on the BOOK relation, which will be related to the primary key of the PUBLISHER relation. Thus, all books in the BOOK relation would be related to a publisher in the PUBLISHER relation. A relation that references another relation is known as **referencing relation** whereas a relation that is being referenced is known as **referenced relation**. Figure 3.4 shows that the attribute P_ID is a primary key in PUBLISHER relation whereas it is a foreign key in BOOK relation.

BOOK

ISBN	Book_title	Category	Price	Copy right_ date	Year	Page_ count	P_ID
001-354-921-1	Ransack	Novel	22	2005	2006	200	P001
001-987-650-5	Differential Calculus	Textbook	30	2003	2003	450	P001

FOREIGN KEY

PRIMARY KEY

PUBLISHER

P_ID	Pname	Address	State	Phone	Email_id
P001	Hills Publications	12, Park street, Atlanta	Georgia	7134019	h_pub@hills.com
P002	Sunshine Publishers Ltd.	45, Second street, Newark	New Jersey	6548909	null

Figure 3.4 Foreign Key

11. What do you mean by a self-referencing foreign key? Explain with the help of an example.

Ans: A foreign key that refers to its own relation is called self-referencing foreign key. It is also known as recursive foreign key. To understand the concept of self-referencing foreign key, consider the EMPLOYEE relation shown in Figure 3.5. In this relation, EMP_NO is the primary key and the attribute MANAGER refers to EMP_NO and thus, is the self-referencing foreign key.

EMP_NO	EMP_NAME	DEPT_NO	SALARY	MANAGER
E01	NANCY	D101	24 000	E01
E04	PETER	D105	30 000	E10
E07	ALWIN	D107	25 000	E10
E10	STELLA	D109	24 000	NULL

Figure 3.5 EMPLOYEE Relation with Self-referencing Foreign Key

12. Can a relation have more than one foreign key? Explain with the help of an example.

Ans: Yes, a relation can have more than one foreign keys and each foreign key can refer to a different relation. For example, consider `REVIEW` relation that includes the details of ratings given by the reviewer to a particular book. Here, books and reviewers (or authors) must be associated with book and author that are already in the `BOOK` and `AUTHOR` relations respectively. In this case, two foreign keys `R_ID` and `ISBN` will be defined on the `REVIEW` relation that will be related to the primary keys of the `AUTHOR` and `BOOK` relation respectively (see Figure 3.6).

AUTHOR

A_ID	Aname	State	City	Zip	Phone	URL
A001	Thomas William	New York	New York	14998	923673	www.thomas.com
A002	James Erin	Georgia	Atlanta	31896	376045	www.ejames.com

(Referenced Relation)

REVIEW

R_ID	ISBN	Rating
A001	002-678-980-4	2
A002	001-987-760-9	6

(Referenced Relation)

BOOK

ISBN	Book_title	Category	Price	Copy right_date	Year	Page_count	P_ID
001-354-921-1	Ransack	Novel	22	2005	2006	200	P001
002-678-880-2	Call Away	Novel	22	2001	2002	200	P002

(Referenced Relation)

Figure 3.6 More Than One Foreign Key in One Referencing Relation

13. Define the term data integrity and explain its types.

Ans: **Data integrity** ensures that the data in the database is consistent, accurate, correct and valid. It ascertains that the data adhere to the set of rules defined by the database administrator and hence, prevents the entry of the invalid information into database. Data integrity is of four types, namely, *domain integrity*, *entity integrity*, *referential integrity* and *semantic integrity*.

Domain integrity

Domain integrity can be specified for each attribute by defining its specific range or domain. It requires that the attribute value must fall under a particular range in order to be valid. It ensures correct values for an attribute by defining the restrictions on the data type, format or range of possible values. For example, the domain of the attribute `Price` of the `BOOK` relation for the `Category`: *Textbook* may be between *$20* and *$200*. Similarly, the domain of the attribute `Category` may be *Textbook, Novel* or *Language Book*.

Entity integrity

Entity integrity assigns restriction on the tuples of a relation and ascertains the accuracy and consistency of the database. It ensures that each tuple in a relation is uniquely identified in order to retrieve each tuple separately. Entity integrity is a rule, which ensures that the set of attribute(s) that participates in the primary key cannot have duplicate value or *null* value. This is because each tuple in a relation is uniquely identified by a primary key attribute and if the value of the primary key attribute is duplicate or *null*, it becomes difficult to identify such tuple uniquely. For example, if the attribute `ISBN` is declared as a primary key of a `BOOK` relation, entity integrity ensures that any two tuples of `BOOK` relation must have unique value for the attribute ISBN and must not be *null*. Entity integrity rule requires that various operations like `INSERT`, `DELETE` and `UPDATE` on a relation maintains uniqueness and existence of a primary key.

Referential integrity

Referential integrity condition ensures that the domain for a given set of attributes, say `S1`, in a relation `r1` should be the values that appear in certain set of attributes, say `S2`, in another relation `r2`. Here, the set `S1` is foreign key for the referencing relation `r1` and `S2` is primary key for referenced relation `r2`. In other words, the value of foreign key in the referencing relation must exist in the primary key attribute of the referenced relation, or that the value of foreign key is *null*.

Referential integrity also ensures that the data type of the foreign key in referencing relation must match the data type of the primary key of referenced relation. For example, the data type of both foreign key attribute `P_ID` in a `BOOK` relation and primary key attribute `P_ID` in a `PUBLISHER` relation is same, that is, string.

Semantic integrity

To represent real world accurately and consistently, the business rules and logical rules (that are derived from our knowledge of the semantics of the real world) must be enforced on database. These rules are known as semantic integrity. Semantic integrity ensures that the data in the database is logically consistent and complete with respect to the real world. Examples of semantic integrity are:

- Number of pages of a book cannot be zero.
- One book can be published by one publisher only.
- Copyright date of a book cannot be later than its published date.
- An author cannot review his own book.

14. Explain integrity constraints. Describe their importance.

Ans: Integrity constraints are the rules defined on a relational database schema and satisfied by all the instances of database in order to model the real-world concepts correctly. They ensure the consistency of database while the modifications are made by the users. For example, the integrity constraint ensures that the value of `ISBN` in `BOOK` relation cannot be duplicated or *null*.

15. Differentiate between primary key constraint and unique constraint. Why is unique constraint preferred over primary key constraint?

Ans: The **primary key** constraint ensures that the attributes, which are declared as primary keys must be unique and not *null*. The primary key constraint enforces entity integrity for the relation and constrains the relation in the following ways:

- The primary key attribute must have unique set of values for all the tuples in a relation.
- The primary key attribute cannot have *null* value.
- A relation can have only one primary key attribute.

The **unique** constraint ensures that a particular set of attributes contains unique values and hence, two tuples cannot have duplicate values in specified attributes. Like primary key, it also enforces entity integrity.

Unique constraint is preferable over primary key constraint to enforce uniqueness of a non-primary key attribute. This is because

- Multiple unique constraints can be applied on a relation whereas only one primary key constraint can be defined on a relation.
- Unlike primary key constraint, unique constraint allows the attribute value to be *null*.

16. Explain not null constraint. How does a not null constraint enforce domain integrity?

Ans: Every attribute has a nullability characteristic that shows whether a particular attribute accepts a *null* value or not. By default, every attribute accepts *null* values but this default nullability characteristic can be overridden by using the **not null** constraint. The not null constraint ensures that the attribute must not accept *null* values. For example, consider a tuple in the `BOOK` relation where the attribute `ISBN` contains a *null* value. Such a tuple provides book information for an unknown `ISBN` and, hence, it does not provide appropriate information. In such case, *null* value must not be allowed and this can be done by constraining the attribute `ISBN` using not null constraint. Here, the not null constraint prevents the *null* value to be inserted into the attribute `ISBN`. Any attempt to change the attribute value of `ISBN` to *null* value results in an error. The *null* values are not allowed in the primary key attribute of a relation. Since `ISBN` is a primary key attribute of `BOOK` relation, it cannot accept *null* values. Hence, it is not necessary to explicitly specify not null constraint for the attribute `ISBN`.

The not null constraint enforces *domain integrity* by ensuring that the attribute of a particular domain is not permitted to take *null* values. For example, a domain, say `dom2`, can be restricted to take non-*null* values. If the domain `dom2` is assigned to the attribute `Category` of a `BOOK` relation, it ensures that the attribute `Category` must have some values. As a result, if *null* value is inserted into the constrained attribute, it will not be accepted as it violates the not null constraint.

17. Explain foreign key constraint and its importance.

Ans: A **foreign key** constraint allows certain attributes in one relation to refer to attributes in another relation. The relation on which foreign key constraint is defined contains the partial information. Its detailed information can be searched from another relation with a matching entry. A foreign key constraint not only controls the data that can be stored in the referencing relation but also controls the changes made to the referenced relation. For example, if the tuple for a publisher is deleted from the `PUBLISHER` relation, and the publisher's ID is used in the `BOOK` relation, the deleted publisher's ID becomes orphaned in the `BOOK` relation. This situation can be prevented by a foreign key constraint.

Foreign key constraint enforces *referential integrity* by ensuring that an attribute in a relation `S` whose value in each tuple either matches with the values of the primary key in another relation `R` or is *null*. For example, the foreign key attribute `R_ID` in the `REVIEW` relation must have either the same values as that of the primary key `A_ID` of the `AUTHOR` relation or must be *null*.

18. Discuss the various update operations that can be performed on a relation.

Ans: The update operations that can be operated on a relation are *insert*, *delete* and *update* (or *modify*).

Insert operation

The **insert** operation creates a new tuple or a set of tuples into a relation and provides attribute values to the inserted tuples. These inserted values must satisfy all the integrity constraints to maintain the consistency of the database. For example, the statement Insert<‘*003-456-654-3*’, ‘*Discrete Mathematics*’, ‘*Textbook*’, *60*, *2007*, *2007*, *650*, ‘*P002*’> satisfies all the integrity constraints and hence, these values can be inserted into the BOOK relation. However, if the attribute values violate one or more integrity constraints, the attribute values are rejected and the insert operation cannot be performed. Consider some cases as given here.

- If the attribute value is inserted into a tuple of BOOK relation, it must belong to the associated domain of possible values otherwise the domain integrity will be violated.
- If the attribute value is inserted into a primary key attribute of BOOK relation, it must be unique and non-*null* otherwise the entity integrity will be violated.
- If the attribute value is inserted into a foreign key attribute of BOOK relation, it must exist in the PUBLISHER relation otherwise the referential integrity will be violated.
- If the attribute value is inserted into a foreign key attribute of BOOK relation, it must be logically correct otherwise the semantic integrity will be violated.

Delete operation

A tuple or a set of tuples can be deleted from a relation using the **delete** operations. If deletion violates the referential integrity then it is either rejected or cascaded. For example, if an attempt is made to delete the tuple with P_ID = ‘*P001*’ in PUBLISHER (shown in Figure.3.3) relation, the delete operation is rejected as it violates the referential integrity. On the other hand, if the tuple of PUBLISHER relation with P_ID = ‘*P003*’ is deleted; the attribute values of this tuple will be deleted since this tuple is not referenced by any tuple of BOOK relation and does not violate the referential integrity.

Deletion can be cascaded by deleting the tuples in the referencing relation that references the tuple to be deleted in the referenced relation. For example, in order to delete P_ID = ‘*P001*’ from PUBLISHER relation, the tuples with P_ID = ‘*P001*’ of BOOK relation must be first deleted. In addition to rejecting and cascading the deletion, the tuples that reference the tuple to be deleted can be modified either to *null* value or to the value of another existing tuple. However, assigning *null* value to the tuple must not violate the entity integrity. If it violates then the *null* value should not be assigned to the tuple.

Update operation

The attribute values in a tuple or a set of tuples can be modified using the **update** operation. Update operation changes the existing value of the attribute in a tuple to the new and valid value. It ensures that the new value satisfies all the integrity constraints. For example, if the value of the attribute Price with ISBN = “001-987-760-9” is updated from *$25* to *$50*, the changes are reflected in a relation since it satisfies all the integrity constraints.

Changing the value of attributes does not create any problem as long as the valid values are entered in a relation. However, changing the value of primary key attribute or foreign key attribute can be a critical issue. Since the primary key attribute identifies each tuple, changing this attribute value must satisfy all the integrity constraints. For example, if the value of the attribute P_ID in the PUBLISHER relation is updated from *P001* to *P002*, the changes are reflected in a relation only if it satisfies all the integrity constraints.

Similarly, the foreign key attribute must be modified in such a manner which ensures that the new value either refers to the existing value in the referenced relation or is *null*. For example, if the

P_ID of the BOOK relation with ISBN = "001-987-760-9" is updated to *null* or any other value that exists in the attribute P_ID of PUBLISHER relation, the value of the foreign key attribute is modified. However, if the new value of P_ID of the BOOK relation does not exist in the P_ID of the PUBLISHER relation, it violates the referential integrity and hence, the values are rejected.

19. How entity types and attributes are mapped to relation schemas? Explain with the help of an example.

Ans: An entity type is mapped to a relation by representing different attributes $A_1, A_2, ..., A_n$ of an entity type E as attributes $A_1, A_2, ..., A_n$ of a relation R. Each entity instance of the entity type E represents a tuple in the relation R and the primary key of the entity type E becomes the primary key of the relation R. For example, consider the E-R diagram of the entity type BOOK of *Online Book* database (Refer question 22 of *Chapter 2*) shown in Figure 3.7.

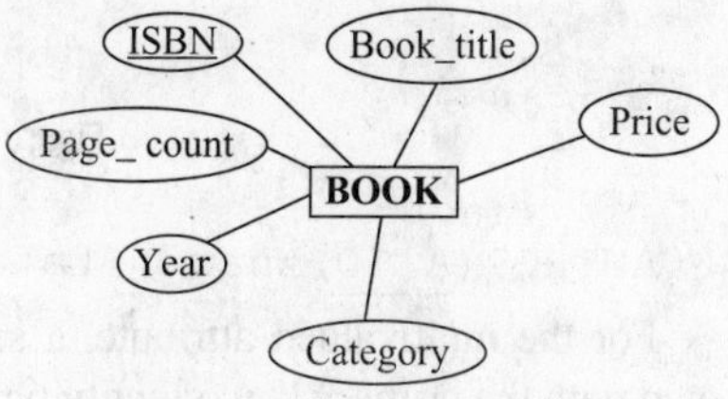

Figure 3.7 The BOOK Entity Type

The entity type BOOK can be represented by a relation schema BOOK with six attributes

BOOK (<u>ISBN</u>, Book_title, Category, Price, Year, Page_count)

Representation of weak entity types

Representation of weak entity type with attributes $a_1, a_2, ..., a_m$ depends on the strong entity type with the attributes $A_1, A_2, ..., A_n$. Weak entity type can be represented by the relation schema R with one attribute for each member of the set as

$$\{a_1, a_2, ..., a_m\} \cup \{A_1, A_2, ..., A_n\}$$

The primary key of the weak entity type consists of the primary key of the strong entity type as a foreign key and its own partial key. For example, consider the E-R diagram of entity type BOOK having weak entity type EDITION shown in Figure 3.8.

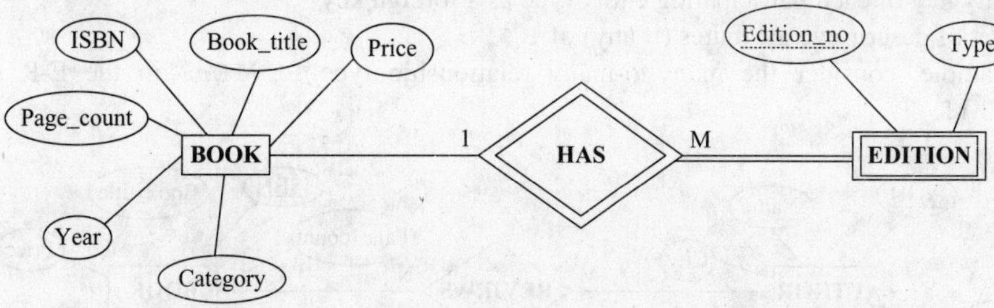

Figure 3.8 The Entity Type BOOK with Weak Entity Type EDITION

The primary key of the entity type BOOK, on which weak entity type EDITION depends, is ISBN. Thus, the relation schema of the weak entity type EDITION can be represented as

EDITION = (<u>ISBN, Edition_no</u>, Type)

Representation of composite and multivalued attributes

If an entity type has composite attributes, no separate attribute is created for the composite attribute itself. Instead, separate attributes for each of its component attributes are created. For example, consider the E-R diagram of the entity type AUTHOR with the composite attribute Address shown in Figure 3.9.

The schema of the AUTHOR relation can be shown as

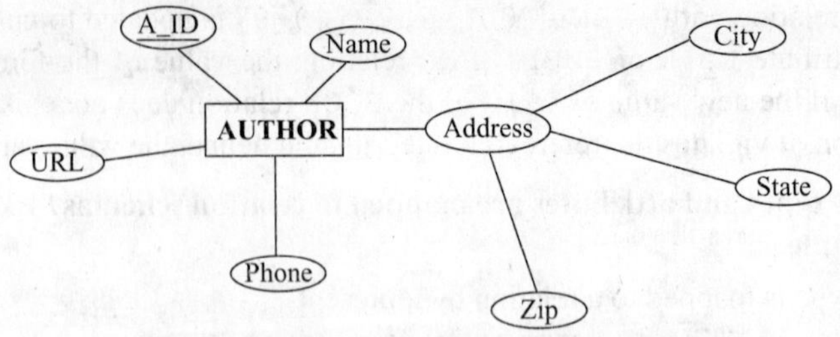

Figure 3.9 E-R Diagram of Entity Type AUTHOR

AUTHOR(A_ID,Aname,State,City,Zip, Phone,URL)

For the multivalued attribute, a separate relation is created with the primary key of entity type and with an attribute corresponding to the multivalued attribute of the entity type. For example, the attribute Phone of entity type AUTHOR is a multivalued attribute. Consider the E-R diagram of multivalued attribute Phone of entity type AUTHOR in Figure 3.10.

Multivalued attribute Phone of entity type AUTHOR can be represented by relation schema as

AUTHOR_PHONE (A_ID, Phone)

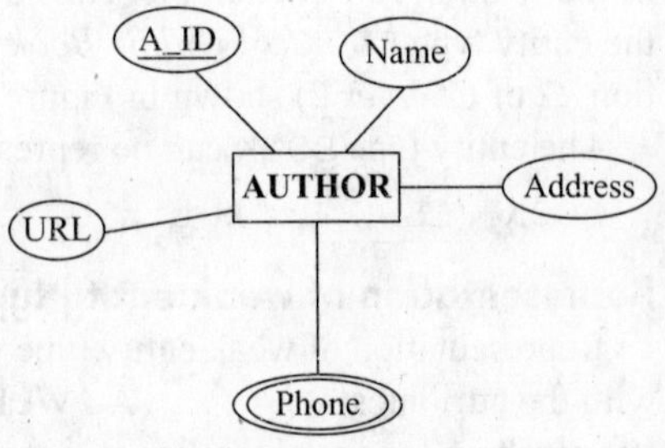

Figure 3.10 The Entity Type AUTHOR with Multivalued Attributes

20. Explain with the help of an example the mapping of relationship types into relation schemas.

Ans: In case of **many-to-many** relationship type, the relationship type R is mapped to a relation, which includes

- ❑ Primary key of each participating entity type as a foreign key
- ❑ The set of descriptive attributes (if any) of R

For example, consider the many-to-many relationship type REVIEWS in the E-R diagram of Figure 3.11.

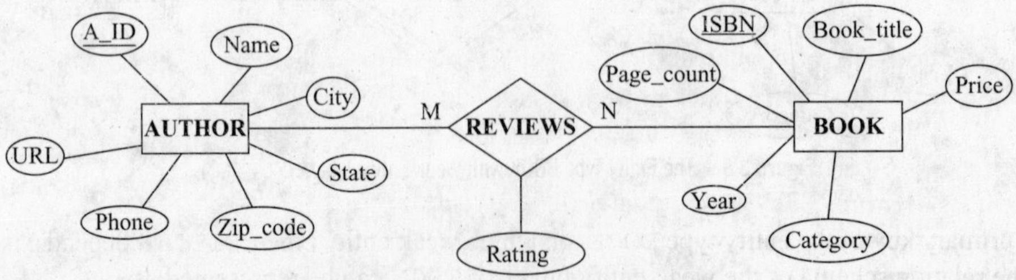

Figure 3.11 A Relationship Type REVIEWS

The relationship type REVIEWS has two entity types, namely, AUTHOR with the primary key A_ID and BOOK with the primary key ISBN. Since the relationship type has one descriptive attribute, namely, Rating, the REVIEW schema of the relationship type REVIEWS has three attributes which can be shown as

REVIEW (R_ID, ISBN, Rating)

Since the relationship type is many-to-many, the primary key for the REVIEW relation is the union of the primary key of entity type AUTHOR, that is, R_ID and primary key of entity type BOOK, that is, ISBN.

In case of **one-to-many** and **many-to-one** relationship types, there is no need to map relationship type R to a different schema. Rather the schema of R can be merged with the schema of the participating entity type on the many-side of relationship type R. For example, consider a many-to-one relationship type PUBLISHED_BY shown in Figure 3.12.

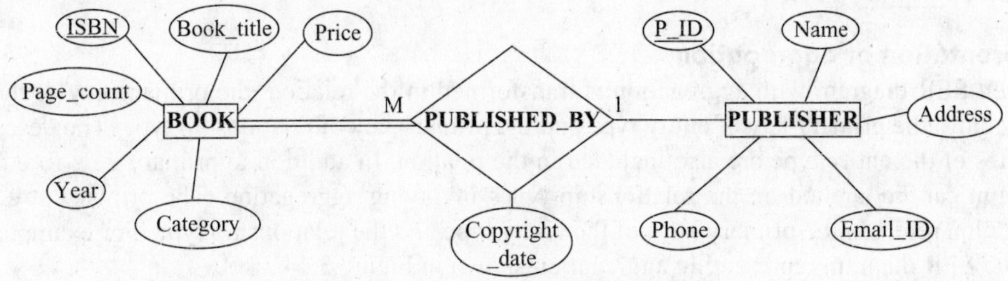

Figure 3.12 E-R Diagram of Relationship Type PUBLISHED_BY

The relation schema for this relationship type can be shown as

```
BOOK(ISBN,Book_title,Category,Price,Copyright_date,Year,
Page_count,P_ID)
PUBLISHER(P_ID,Pname,Address,State,Phone,Email_id)
```

The primary key of entity type, into whose schema the relationship type schema is combined, becomes the primary key of combined schema. So, the primary key of the combined schema is the primary key of BOOK, that is, ISBN.

In case of **one-to-one** relationship type also, it is not required to map the relationship type to a separate schema; rather the schema of the relationship type can be merged with the relation schema of either of the participating entity types.

21. Explain with the help of an example the mapping of extended E-R features into relation schemas.

Ans:

Representation of generalization

A separate relation is created for the higher-level entity type as well as for all the lower-level entity types. The relation for higher-level entity type includes its primary key attributes and all other attributes. Each relation for lower-level entity type includes the primary key of higher-level entity type and its own attributes. The primary key attribute of lower-level entity type refers to the primary key attribute of the higher-level entity type and hence, creates the foreign key constraint. For example, consider the EER diagram of entity type BOOK representing generalization in Figure 3.13.

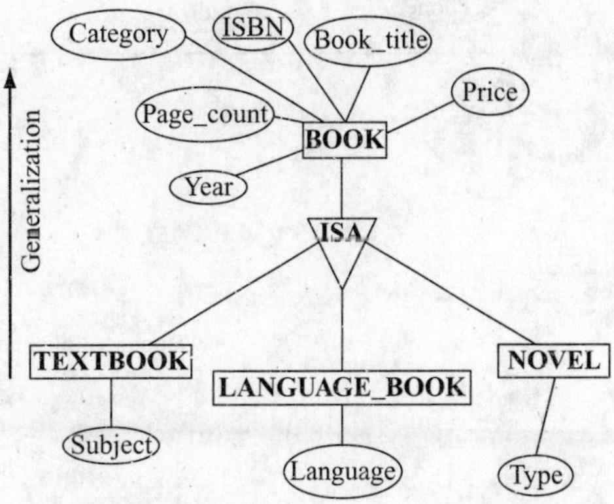

Figure 3.13 EER Diagram Representing Generalization

In this figure, the higher-level entity type is BOOK and the lower-level entity types are TEXTBOOK, LANGUAGE_BOOK and NOVEL. The relation schemas for the higher-level entity type and lower-level entity types can be given as

```
BOOK(ISBN, Book_title,Category,Price,Year,Page_count)
TEXTBOOK(ISBN,Subject)
LANGUAGE_BOOK(ISBN,Language)
NOVEL(ISBN,Type)
```

Representation of aggregation

When EER diagram with aggregation is transformed in the relation, the primary key of the relation includes the primary key of entity type and the primary key of relationship type. The descriptive attributes of the entity type are also included in the relation. In addition to primary key, foreign key constraint can be applied on the relationship types involving aggregation. The primary key of the aggregation refers to the primary keys of the entity type and the relationship type. For example, consider the EER diagram representing aggregation shown in Figure 3.14.

Since the primary key for the relationship type is the union of the primary keys of the entity types involved, the primary key for the relationship type WRITES is the union of the primary keys of the entity type BOOK and AUTHOR. Hence, the schema for the relationship type WRITES can be written as

{ISBN,A_ID}

The primary key of the relation, say COPYRIGHT, includes the primary key of the entity type Publisher and the primary key of the relationship type WRITES. The descriptive attribute COPYRIGHT_DATE of the relation COPYRIGHT is also included. Now, the schema for the relation COPYRIGHT can be represented as

{ISBN, A_ID, P_ID, Copyright_date}

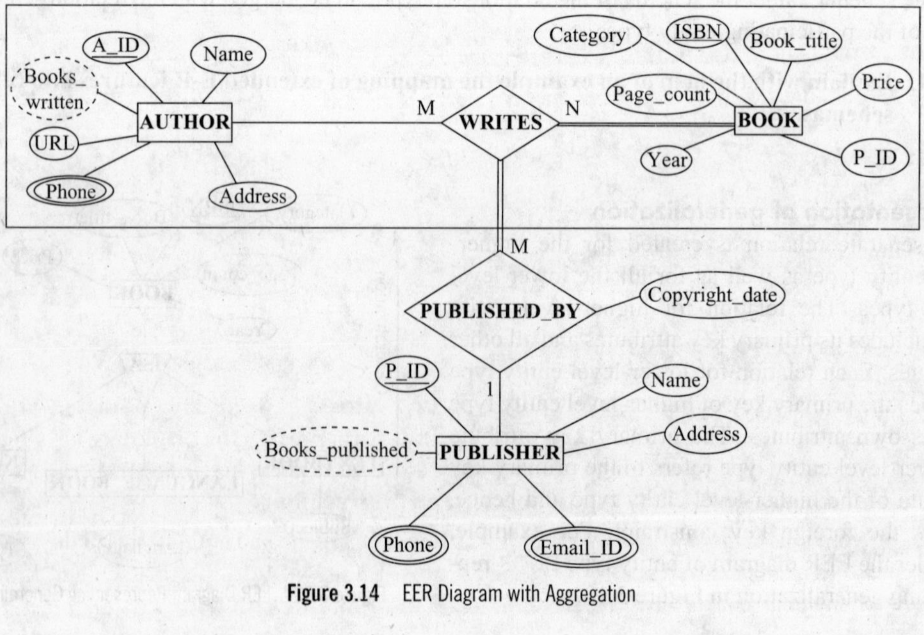

Figure 3.14 EER Diagram with Aggregation

22. Construct appropriate relation schemas for the E-R diagrams given in Practical Questions 27 and 32 in *Chapter 2*. Make appropriate assumptions, if necessary.

Ans: (i) The relation schemas for the E-R diagram shown in Question 27 of Chapter 2 are:

```
CUSTOMER(CUST_ID, CUST_NAME, CUST_ADDRESS, CUST_CITY)
ORDER(ORDER_ID, ORDER_DESC, ORDER_DATE, CUST_ID)
SUPPLIER(SUP_ID, SUP_NAME, SUP_ADDRESS)
PRODUCT(PROD_NO, PROD_NAME, PROD_DESC)
SHIPMENT(SHIP_NO, SHIP_DATE, SUP_ID)
ITEM(ITEM_NO, ITEM_NAME, ITEM_DESC)
SUPPLIES(SUP_ID, ITEM_NO)
INCLUDES(SHIP_NO, ITEM_NO)
USEDIN(ITEM_NO, PROD_NO)
REQUESTS(OREDR_ID, PROD_NO)
```

(ii) The relation schemas for the E-R diagram shown in Question 32 of Chapter 2 are:

```
DOCTOR(DOCTOR_ID, NAME)
PATIENT(PATIENT_ID, NAME)
NURSE(NURSE_ID, NAME)
OPERATION(DOCTOR_ID, PATIENT_ID, NURSE_ID, DATE, OPRN_DESC)
```

23. Construct appropriate relation schemas for the COMPANY, BANK databases given in Practical questions 29 and 30, respectively, in *Chapter 2*. Make appropriate assumptions, wherever necessary.

Ans: (i) The relation schemas for COMPANY database are:

```
EMPLOYEE(ENO, ENAME, ADDRESS, PHN_NO, GENDER, DOB, SALARY, DATE_
OF_JOINING, DEPT_NO, SUPERVISOR_NO)
DEPARTMENT(DEPT_NO, DEPT_NAME, DEPT_MNGR, MNGR_START_DATE)
PROJECT(PRJT_NO, PRJT_NAME, PRJT_DESC, DEPT_NO)
WORKS_ON(ENO, PRJT_NO, HOURS)
```

(ii) The relation schemas for BANK database are:

```
CUSTOMER(CUS_ID, CUS_NAME, ADDRESS)
BRANCH(BRANCH_NAME, CITY, ASSETS)
LOAN(LOAN_NO, AMOUNT, BRANCH_NAME)
ACCOUNT(ACC_NO, BALANCE, BRANCH_NAME)
EMPLOYEE(EMP_ID, PHN_NO, NAME, BRANCH_NAME)
PAYMENT(LOAN_NO, PAYMNT_NO, PAYMNT_AMOUNT, DATE)
BORROWER(LOAN_NO, CUS_ID)
DEPOSITOR(ACC_NO, CUS_ID)
```

24. Consider the relation STUDENT (`Enroll#`, `SemRoll#`, `Stud_name`, `Gender`, `Course`, `Semester`, `Address`, `Phone_no`). Specify the candidate keys for this schema and the constraints under which each candidate key would be valid. What other constraints (if any) can be specified on this relation?

Ans: One obvious candidate key is `Enroll#` as it will be unique and not null for all the students. Another possible candidate key can be `SemRoll#` only if no two students (from same or different semesters) of any course are allowed to have the same value for `SemRoll#`.

Other constraints that can be specified on this relation are as follows:

- The attributes `Stud_name`, `Gender`, `Course`, and `Semester` must not be null.
- The value of `Semester` must be between *1* and *8*.

25. Consider the following relation schema for a `UNIVERSITY` database:

`PROFESSOR (PID, P_Name, Dept_ID)`
`COURSE (Code, Dept_ID, C_Name, Syllabus)`
`PROF_COURSE (PID, Code, Semester)`

Identify the primary keys and foreign keys for this schema. Now populate these relations with some tuples, and then give an example of insertion in the PROF_COURSE relation that violates the referential integrity constraints and of another that does not. Identify what you think should be the various candidate keys for this schema. Make any assumption, wherever necessary.

Ans: The primary key for `PROFESSOR` relation is `PID`, for `COURSE` relation is `Code`, and for `PROF_COURSE` relation is (`PID`, `CODE`).

Foreign keys for `PROF_COURSE` relation is `PID` and `Code`.
Insert<'*P001*', '*Sachin Rana*', '*D01*'> into `PROFESSOR` relation.
Insert<'*P002*', '*Vinay Kumar*', '*D02*'> into `PROFESSOR` relation.
Insert<'*P003*', '*Sumit Balakrishnan*', '*D03*'> into `PROFESSOR` relation.
Insert<'*P004*', '*Poonam Sharma*', '*D04*'> into `PROFESSOR` relation.

PROFESSOR

PID	P_Name	Dept_ID
P001	Sachin Rana	D01
P002	Vinay Kumar	D02
P003	Sumit Balakrishnan	D03
P004	Poonam Sharma	D04

Insert<'*01*', '*D01*', '*CS101*', 'C++'> into `COURSE` relation.
Insert<'*02*', '*D02*', '*CS102*', '*Networking*'> into `COURSE` relation.
Insert<'*03*', '*D03*', '*CS103*', '*Java*'> into `COURSE` relation.
Insert<'04', '*D04*', '*CS104*', '*OS*'> into `COURSE` relation.

COURSE

Code	Dept_ID	C_Name	Syllabus
01	D01	CS101	C++
02	D02	CS102	Networking
03	D03	CS103	Java
04	D04	CS104	OS

Insert<'*P001*', '*01*', '*S01*'> into `PROF_COURSE` relation.
Insert<'*P002*', '02', '*S02*'> into `PROF_COURSE` relation.
Insert<'*P003*', '03', '*S03*'> into `PROF_COURSE` relation.

PROF_COURSE

PID	Code	Semester
P001	01	S01
P002	02	S02
P003	03	S03

The statement Insert<'*P005*', '*07*', '*S05*'> into `PROF_COURSE` relation violates the referential integrity as the `PID` '*P005*' and `Code` *07* does not exist in `PROFESSOR` and `COURSE` relation, respectively.

However, the statement Insert<'*P004*', '*04*', '*S04*'> into `PROF_COURSE` relation does not violate referential integrity.

26. Consider the following relation schema for the SALES database:

CUSTOMER (<u>CustNo</u>, Cust_Name, Address)
ORDER (<u>OrderNo</u>, Order_date, Cust_no, Qty, Amount)
PRODUCT (<u>ProdNo</u>, Price, Order_no)

Specify the foreign key constraints for the SALES database. Also insert some tuples in the relations and show some examples of deletion of tuples that violate referential integrity constraints. Make any assumption, wherever necessary.

Ans: The foreign key constraints for SALES database can be given as follows:

- The `Cust_no` attribute of `ORDER` relation can have values that either exist in `CustNo` attribute of `CUSTOMER` relation or null values.
- The `Order_no` attribute of `PRODUCT` relation can have values that either exist in `OrderNo` attribute of `ORDER` relation or null values.
- Delete the tuple with `CustNo` '*C03*' from `CUSTOMER` relation. This statement violates referential integrity as the `CustNo` of `CUSTOMER` relation is referenced by `Cust_no` of `ORDER` relation.

CUSTOMER

CustNo	Cust_Name	Address
C01	Jim	House No.10, Park street, Georgia
C02	Carol	Bld.25, Main street, Hawaii
C03	Susan	House 45, First Street, Las Vegas

PRODUCT

ProdNo	Price	Order_no
P1	220	101
P2	300	102
P3	100	103

ORDER

OrderNo	Order_date	Cust_no	Qty	Amount
101	09/06/2010	C01	10	210
102	10/25/2010	C02	50	180
103	12/10/2010	C03	20	300

- Delete the tuple with `OrderNo` '*102*' from `ORDER` relation. This statement violates the referential integrity as the `OrderNo` of `ORDER` relation is referenced by `Order_no` of `PRODUCT` relation.

27. Consider the following update operations performed on the database instance shown in the Figure. Discuss the integrity constraints violated by each operation. Consider the following restriction on the domain of the attribute `Price` of `BOOK` relation.

If `Category` is *Textbook*, `Price` must be between *$20* and *$200*
If `Category` is *Language Book*, `Price` must be between *$20* and *$150*
If `Category` is *Novel*, `Price` must be between *$20* and *$100*

BOOK

ISBN	Book_title	Category	Price	Copyright_date	Year	Page_count	P_ID
001-354-921-1	Ransack	Novel	22	2005	2006	200	P001
001-987-650-5	Differential Calculus	Textbook	30	2003	2003	450	P001
001-987-760-9	C++	Textbook	40	2004	2005	800	P001
002-678-880-2	Call Away	Novel	22	2001	2002	200	P002
002-678-980-4	DBMS	Textbook	40	2004	2006	800	P002
003-456-433-6	Introduction to German language	Language Book	22	2003	2004	200	P004
003-456-533-8	Learning French language	Language Book	32	2005	2006	500	P004
004-765-359-3	Coordinate Geometry	Textbook	35	2006	2006	650	P003
004-765-409-5	UNIX	Textbook	26	2006	2007	550	P003

PUBLISHER

P_ID	Pname	Address	State	Phone	Email_id
P001	Hills Publications	12, Park street, Atlanta	Georgia	7134019	h_pub@hills.com
P002	Sunshine Publishers Ltd.	45, Second street, Newark	New Jersey	6548909	Null
P003	Bright Publications	123, Main street, Honolulu	Hawai	7678985	bright@bp.com
P004	Paramount Publishing House	789, Oak street, New York	New York	9254834	param_house@param.com
P005	Wesley Publications	456, First street, Las Vegas	Nevada	5683452	Null

AUTHOR						
A_ID	Aname	State	City	Zip	Phone	URL
A001	Thomas William	New York	New York	14998	923673	www.thomas.com
A002	James Erin	Georgia	Atlanta	31896	376045	www.ejames.com
A003	Charles Smith	California	Los Angeles	95031	419562	www.csmith.com
A004	Lewis Ian	Washington	Seattle	98012	578932	www.au_lewis.com
A005	Allen Ford	Alaska	Juneau	99502	581231	www.allenford.com
A006	Jones Martin	New York	Albany	14521	218161	www.martin.com
A007	John Stephen	Texas	Austin	75112	316292	www.john_stepen.com
A008	Annie George	Michigan	Detroit	48011	321313	www.annie.com
A009	Suzanne Hedley	Washington	Seattle	98001	785236	www.suzz.com
A010	Richard Flaming	Virginia	Virginia Beach	22111	456163	www.richard.com

AUTHOR_BOOK	
A_ID	ISBN
A001	001-987-760-9
A002	002-678-980-4
A003	001-987-760-9
A004	003-456-433-6
A005	001-354-921-1
A006	002-678-880-2
A007	001-987-650-5
A008	002-678-980-4
A008	004-765-409-5
A009	004-765-359-3
A010	003-456-533-8

REVIEW		
R_ID	ISBN	Rating
A001	002-678-980-4	2
A002	001-987-760-9	6
A003	002-678-980-4	5
A003	004-765-409-5	4
A004	003-456-533-8	9
A005	002-678-980-4	7
A006	001-354-921-1	7
A006	002-678-880-2	4
A007	004-765-359-3	3
A008	001-987-760-9	7
A009	001-987-650-5	8
A010	003-456-433-6	5

a. Insert<*'002-678-999-6', 'Operating System', 'Textbook', 500, 2006, 2007, 700, 'P001'*> into BOOK relation.

Ans: The price of the book in this statement (that is, 500) does not adhere to domain integrity rule, according to which price of a textbook should be between \$20 and \$200. So, this statement violates the domain integrity.

b. Insert<*'P003', 'Express Publications', '100, Second street, Atlanta', 'Georgia', 7134000, 'Express@publications.com'*> into `PUBLISHER` relation.

Ans: The `P_ID` *'P003'* already exists in the `PUBLISHER` relation. So, this statement violates the primary key constraint.

c. Insert<*NULL, 'Richard Martin', 'Washington', 'Seattle', 98012570732, 'www.rmartin.com'*> into `AUTHOR` relation.

Ans: The attribute `A_ID` is the primary key of `AUTHOR` relation and thus, cannot have null value. So, this statement violates the primary key constraint.

d. Insert<*'004-765-200-1', 'VC++', 'Textbook', 40, 2007, 2008, 550, 'P010'*> into BOOK relation.

Ans: The `P_ID` *'P010'* does not exist in the `P_ID` of the `PUBLISHER` relation. So, this statement violates the foreign key constraint.

e. Insert<*'002-876-680-2', 'Sunlight', 'Novel', 25, 2003, 2001, 250, 'P002'*> into BOOK relation.

Ans: The copyright date of a book cannot be later than its published date. So, this statement violates the semantic integrity.

f. Insert<*'A001', '001-987-760-9', 8*> into `REVIEW` relation.

Ans: This statement does not violate any integrity constraint.

g. Delete the tuple with `P_ID` = `'P004'` from `PUBLISHER` relation.

Ans: The `P_ID` *'P004'* exists in a tuple of `BOOK` relation. So, this statement violates the foreign key constraint.

h. Delete the tuple with A_ID = `'A003'` from AUTHOR relation.

Ans: The `A_ID` *'A003'* is being used in `AUTHOR_BOOK` and `REVIEW` relation. So, this statement violates the foreign key constraint.

i. Delete the tuple with `ISBN` = `'004-765-409-5'` from BOOK relation.

Ans: The `ISBN` *'004-765-409-5'* is being used in `AUTHOR_BOOK` and `REVIEW` relation. So, this statement violates foreign key constraint.

j. Modify the `Rating` attribute of the `REVIEW` relation with `R_ID` = `'A001'` and `ISBN` = `'002-678-980-4'` to *'6'*.

Ans: This statement does not violate any integrity constraint.

k. Modify the `P_ID` attribute of the `PUBLISHER` relation to *'P002'*.

Ans: The `P_ID` is the primary key of `PUBLISHER` relation and thus, cannot have same values for all the tuples. So, this statement violates the primary key constraint.

Multiple-choice Questions

1. The relational model is based on the branches of __________.
   (a) Engineering (b) Mathematics (c) Science (d) None of these
2. The relational model includes:
   (a) Manipulative components (b) Integrity constraints
   (c) Structural components (d) All of these

3. Which of the following data structures is used in relational model?
   (a) Table (b) Tree (c) Node (d) None of these
4. Which of the following does not belong to relation schema?
   (a) Tuples (b) Set of attributes (c) Relation name (d) Both (b) and (c)
5. Which of the following factors indicates that a table is not well-structured?
   (a) The primary key consists of more than one attribute.
   (b) Referential integrity is violated when attempting to enter data.
   (c) It contains multiple foreign keys.
   (d) All of these.
6. Candidate key is also known as __________.
   (a) Superkey (b) Irreducible superkey
   (c) Foreign key (d) Primary key
7. Which of the following keys describes a field, or a combination of fields, that has a unique value?
   (a) Secondary key (b) Foreign key (c) Primary key (d) Alternate key
8. When more than one attribute forms the primary key, the key is known as __________.
   (a) Foreign key (b) Alternate key (c) Candidate key (d) Composite key
9. A foreign key must
   (a) Be numeric.
   (b) Match the field value of a primary key in a related table.
   (c) Be defined in all tables in the database.
   (d) Be unique.
10. Integrity constraints can be divided into __________ parts.
    (a) One (b) Two (c) Three (d) Four
11. Which of the following integrity is applied on the tuple?
    (a) Semantic integrity (b) Referential integrity
    (c) Entity integrity (d) Domain integrity
12. What does referential integrity prevent?
    (a) Recursive joins
    (b) Loss of data from employee sabotage
    (c) Loss of data from any one corrupted table
    (d) Data redundancy
13. The constraint that can be applied only at column level is __________.
    (a) Primary key constraint (b) Foreign key constraint
    (c) Unique constraint (d) Not Null constraint
14. Which of the following is not true with primary key constraint?
    (a) Primary key attribute cannot have null value.
    (b) Primary key constraint enforces entity integrity.
    (c) Unique key constraint is preferable over primary key constraint.
    (d) Multiple primary key constraints can be defined on a relation.
15. While mapping relationship types to a relation, which of the following relationship types allows us to choose the primary key of either participating entity type as the primary key of the relation?
    (a) Many-to-many (b) One-to-many (c) One-to-one (d) All of these

Answers

1. (b)	2. (d)	3. (a)	4. (a)	5. (d)	6. (b)	7. (c)
8. (d)	9. (b)	10. (c)	11. (c)	12. (d)	13. (d)	14. (d)
15. (c)						

4

Relational Algebra and Calculus

1. What are the similarities and differences between relational algebra and relational calculus?

Ans: Both relational algebra and relational calculus are formal languages associated with relational model that are used to specify the basic retrieval requests.

Relational algebra consists of a basic set of operations, which can be used for carrying out basic retrieval operations. Relational calculus, on the other hand, provides declarative notations based on mathematical logic for specifying relational queries. Relational algebra uses a procedural approach by providing a step-by-step procedure for carrying out a query, whereas relational calculus uses the non-procedural approach as it describes the information to be retrieved without specifying the method for obtaining that information.

2. What do you understand by unary and binary operations in relational algebra?

Ans: The operations operating on a single relation are known as **unary operations**. The various unary operations in relational algebra are *select*, *project* and *rename*. The operations operating on two relations are known as **binary operations**. The various binary operations in relational algebra are *set operations*, *join operations* and *division operation*.

3. What are the various unary operations in relational algebra? Explain with examples.

Ans: Various unary operations in relational algebra are *select*, *project* and *rename*.

Select operation: The select operation retrieves all those tuples from a relation, which satisfy a specific condition. It can also be considered as a filter that displays only those tuples, which satisfy a given condition. The Greek letter sigma (σ) is used as a select operator. In general, the select operation is specified as

$$\sigma_{\text{<selection\_condition>}}(\text{R})$$

where `selection_condition` is the condition on the basis of which the subset of tuples is selected and R is the name of the relation. For example, to retrieve those tuples from the BOOK relation whose Category is *Novel*, the select operation can be specified as

$$\sigma_{\texttt{Category="Novel"}}(\texttt{BOOK})$$

The sequence of select operations can be applied in any order, as it is commutative in nature, that is,

$$\sigma_{\texttt{<condition\_1>}}(\sigma_{\texttt{<condition\_2>}}\texttt{R}) = \sigma_{\texttt{<condition\_2>}}(\sigma_{\texttt{<condition\_1>}}\texttt{R})$$

Project operation: The project operation is used to select the required attributes from a relation while discarding the other attributes. The Greek letter pi (π) is used as the project operator. In general, the project operation is specified as

$$\pi_{\texttt{<attribute\_list>}}(\texttt{R})$$

where `attribute_list` is the list of required attributes separated by comma and R is the name of the relation. For example, to retrieve only ISBN, Book_title and Price attributes from the BOOK relation, the project operation can be specified as

$$\pi_{\texttt{ISBN, Book\_title, Price}}(\texttt{BOOK})$$

Unlike the select operation, the commutative property does not hold on project operation, that is,

$$\pi_{\texttt{<list\_1>}}(\pi_{\texttt{<list\_2>}}(\texttt{R})) \neq \pi_{\texttt{<list\_2>}}(\pi_{\texttt{<list\_1>}}(\texttt{R}))$$

Note that the select and project operations can also be combined together to create more complex queries.

Rename operation: Rename operation is used to provide a name to the relation obtained after applying any relational algebra operation. The Greek letter rho (ρ) is used as a rename operator. The relation obtained from any operation can be renamed by using the rename operator as given here.

$$\rho(\texttt{R, E})$$

where ρ is the rename operator, E is the expression representing relational algebra operations and R is the name given to relation obtained by applying relational algebra operations specified in expression E.

For example, consider the following expression:

$$\rho(R_1, \sigma_{\texttt{Category="Novel"}}(\texttt{BOOK}))$$

where R_1 is the name given to the relation obtained from the specified relational algebra expression.

The rename operation can also be used to rename attributes in a new relation. For example, consider the following expression

$$\rho(R_2(P_1, P_2, P_3), \pi_{\texttt{P\_ID, State, Phone}}(\texttt{PUBLISHER}))$$

In this example, P_1, P_2, P_3 are new attribute names in the relation R_2 for the attributes P_ID, State and Phone of the relation PUBLISHER, respectively.

4. When are two relations said to be union compatible? Give an example.

Ans: Two relations are said to be union compatible if they satisfy the following conditions:

1. The degree of both the operand relations must be the same.
2. The domain of the nth attribute of relation R_1 must be the same as that of the nth attribute of relation R_2.

For example, the two relations PUBLISHER_1 and PUBLISHER_2 given in Figure 4.1 are union compatible.

PUBLISHER_1

P_ID	Pname
P001	Hills Publications
P002	Sunshine Publishers Ltd.
P003	Bright Publications
P004	Paramount Publishing House
P005	Wesley Publications

PUBLISHER_2

P_ID	Pname
P001	Hills Publications
P002	Sunshine Publishers Ltd.
P006	ESL Publications
P007	Arizon Publishers Ltd.

Figure 4.1 Union Compatible Relations

5. What are the various set operations in relational algebra? Explain with examples.

Ans: Various set operations in relational algebra are union, intersection, difference and cartesian product.

Union operation: The **union operation,** denoted by È, returns a third relation that contains tuples from both or either of the operand relations. The union of relations R_1 and R_2 is denoted by $R_1 \cup R_2$. The duplicate tuples are automatically removed from the resultant relation.

For example, consider the two union-compatible relations PUBLISHER_1 and PUBLISHER_2. The union of these two relations consists of tuples from both relations without any duplicate tuples as shown in Figure 4.2.

Note that the union operation is commutative and associative in nature.

PUBLISHER_1

P_ID	Pname
P001	Hills Publications
P002	Sunshine Publishers Ltd.
P003	Bright Publications
P004	Paramount Publishing House
P005	Wesley Publications

PUBLISHER_2

P_ID	Pname
P001	Hills Publications
P002	Sunshine Publishers Ltd.
P006	ESL Publications
P007	Arizon Publishers Ltd.

PUBLISHER_1 ∪ PUBLISHER_2

P_ID	Pname
P001	Hills Publications
P002	Sunshine Publishers Ltd.
P003	Bright Publications
P004	Paramount Publishing House
P005	Wesley Publications
P006	ESL Publications
P007	Arizon Publishers Ltd.

Figure 4.2 Union Operation

Intersection operation: The **intersection operation**, denoted by ∩, returns a third relation that contains tuples common to both the operand relations. The intersection of relations R_1 and R_2 is denoted by $R_1 \cap R_2$.

For example, consider the two union-compatible relations PUBLISHER_1 and PUBLISHER_2. The intersection of these two relations consists of tuples common to both the relations as shown in Figure 4.3.

PUBLISHER_1 ∩ PUBLISHER_2

P_ID	Pname
P001	Hills Publications
P002	Sunshine Publishers Ltd.

Figure 4.3 Intersection Operation

Like union, intersection operation is also commutative and associative in nature.

Difference operation: The **difference operation**, denoted by – (minus), returns a third relation that contains all tuples present in one relation, which are not present in the second relation. The difference of the relations R_1 and R_2 is denoted by $R_1 - R_2$. The expression $R_1 - R_2$ results in a relation containing all tuples from relation R_1, which are not present in relation R_2. Similarly, the expression $R_2 - R_1$ results in a relation containing all tuples from relation R_2, which are not present in relation R_1.

For example, consider the two union-compatible relations PUBLISHER_1 and PUBLISHER_2. The difference of these two relations is shown in Figure 4.4.

PUBLISHER_1–PUBLISHER_2

P_ID	Pname
P003	Bright Publications
P004	Paramount Publishing House
P005	Wesley Publications

PUBLISHER_2–PUBLISHER_1

P_ID	Pname
P006	ESL Publications
P007	Arizon Publishers Ltd.

Figure 4.4 Difference Operation

The difference operation is not commutative in nature.

Cartesian product operation: The **cartesian product** (also known as **cross product** or **cross join**), denoted by the symbol, X, returns a third relation that contains all possible combinations of the tuples from the two operand relations. The cartesian product of the relations R_1 and R_2 is denoted by $R_1 X R_2$. Each tuple of the first relation is concatenated with all the tuples of the second relation to form the tuples of a new relation. The cartesian product creates tuples with the combined attributes of two relations. Therefore, the degree of a new relation is the sum of the degree of both the operand relations. In addition, the cardinality of the resultant relation is the product of the cardinality of both the operand relations. For example, consider the relations AUTHOR_1 and BOOK_1. Their cartesian product is shown in Figure 4.5.

AUTHOR_1

A_ID	Aname	City
A001	Thomas William	New York
A002	James Erin	Atlanta

BOOK_1

ISBN	Book_title	Price
001-987-760-9	C++	40
001-354-921-1	Ransack	22

AUTHOR_1 X BOOK_1

A_ID	Aname	City	ISBN	Book_title	Price
A001	Thomas William	New York	001-987-760-9	C++	40
A001	Thomas William	New York	001-354-921-1	Ransack	22
A002	James Erin	Atlanta	001-987-760-9	C++	40
A002	James Erin	Atlanta	001-354-921-1	Ransack	22

Figure 4.5 Cartesian Product

6. What is the role of join operations in relational algebra? Differentiate between equijoin and natural join?

Ans: The **join** operation is one of the most useful and commonly used operations to extract information from two or more relations. The **join operation**, denoted by ⋈, is used to join two relations to form a new relation on the basis of a common attribute present in the two operand relations. It results in a new wider relation in which each tuple is formed by concatenating the two tuples, one from each of the operand relations, such that two tuples have the same value for that common attribute.

The join operation is specified as

$$R_1 \bowtie_{cond} R_2 = \sigma_{cond} (R_1 \mathbf{X} R_2)$$

Equijoin: Equijoin operation is one in which the join condition consists only of the equality condition. The resultant relation of an equijoin operation always has one or more pairs of attributes that have identical values in every tuple.

For example, consider the relations BOOK and PUBLISHER. The two relations can be joined for the tuples where BOOK.P_ID is the same as PUBLISHER.P_ID. This is specified as

$$BOOK \bowtie_{BOOK.P\_ID = PUBLISHER.P\_ID} PUBLISHER$$

BOOK

ISBN	Book_title	Category	Price	Copyright_ date	Year	Page_count	P_ID
001-354-921-1	Ransack	Novel	22	2005	2006	200	P001
001-987-650-5	Differential Calculus	Textbook	30	2003	2003	450	P001
002-678-880-2	Call Away	Novel	22	2001	2002	200	P002
004-765-359-3	Coordinate Geometry	Textbook	35	2006	2006	650	P003

PUBLISHER

P_ID	Pname	Address	State	Phone	Email_id
P001	Hills Publications	12, Park street, Atlanta	Georgia	7134019	h_pub@hills.com
P002	Sunshine Publishers Ltd.	45, Second street, Newark	New Jersey	6548909	null
P003	Bright Publications	123, Main street, Honolulu	Hawaii	7678985	bright@bp.com
P005	Wesley Publications	456, First street, Las Vegas	Nevada	5683452	null

ISBN	Book_title	…	BOOK.P_ID	PUBLISHER.P_ID	Pname	…	Email_id
001-354-921-1	Ransack	…	P001	P001	Hills Publications	…	h_pub@hills.com
001-987-650-5	Differential Calculus	…	P001	P001	Hills Publications	…	h_pub@hills.com
002-678-880-2	Call Away	…	P002	P002	Sunshine Publishers Ltd.	…	null
004-765-359-3	Coordinate Geometry	…	P003	P003	Bright Publications	…	bright@bp.com

Figure 4.6 Equijoin Operation

Natural join operation: If one of the two identical attributes is removed from the result of equijoin, it is known as a **natural join**. The natural join of two relations R_1 and R_2 is obtained by applying a project operation to the equijoin of these two relations in a sequence given here.

1. Find the equijoin of two relations R_1 and R_2.
2. For each attribute A that is common to both relations R_1 and R_2, project operation is applied to remove the column $R_1.A$ or $R_2.A$. Therefore, if there are *m* attributes common in both the relations, then *m* duplicate columns are removed from the resultant relation of equijoin.

The expression to obtain the natural join of relations BOOK and PUBLISHER can be specified as

$$\pi_{\texttt{ISBN, Book\_title, Category, BOOK.P\_ID, Pname, Address, Email\_id}}(\texttt{BOOK} \bowtie_{\texttt{BOOK.P\_ID = PUBLISHER.P\_ID}} \texttt{PUBLISHER})$$

ISBN	Book_title	Category	BOOK.P_ID	Pname	Address	Email_id
001-354-921-1	Ransack	Novel	P001	Hills Publications	12, Park street, Atlanta	h_pub@hills.com
001-987-650-5	Differential Calculus	Textbook	P001	Hills Publications	12, Park street, Atlanta	h_pub@hills.com
002-678-880-2	Call Away	Novel	P002	Sunshine Publishers Ltd.	45, Second street, Newark	null
004-765-359-3	Coordinate Geometry	Textbook	P003	Bright Publications	123, Main street, Honolulu	bright@bp.com

Figure 4.7 Natural Join Operation

7. What is the outer join? Explain how does it differ from the inner join?

Ans: The outer join selects all the tuples satisfying the join condition along with the tuples for which no tuples from the other relation satisfy the join condition. Thus, an outer join is a type of equijoin that can be used to display all the tuples from one relation, even if there are no corresponding tuples in the second relation, thus preventing information loss. An inner join on the other hand selects only those tuples from both the joining relations that satisfy the joining condition. There are three types of outer join operations, namely *left outer join*, *right outer join* and *full outer join*.

- **Left outer join:** The **left outer join** includes all the tuples from both the relations satisfying the join condition along with all the tuples in the left relation that do not have a corresponding tuple in the right relation. The tuples from the left relation not satisfying the join condition are concatenated with the tuples having null values for all the attributes from the right relation. The left outer join of relations R_1 and R_2 is specified as $R_1 ⟕_{cond} R_2$.
- **Right outer join:** The **right outer join** includes all the tuples from both the relations satisfying the join condition along with all the tuples in the right relation that do not have a corresponding tuple in the left relation. The tuples from the right relation not satisfying the join condition are concatenated with the tuples having null values for all the attributes from the left relation. The right outer join of relations R_1 and R_2 is specified as $R_1 ⟖_{cond} R_2$.
- **Full outer join:** The **full outer join** combines the results of both the left and the right outer joins. The resultant relation contains all records from both the relations, with null values for the missing corresponding tuples on either side. The full outer join of relations R_1 and R_2 is specified as $R_1 ⟗_{cond} R_2$.

Consider two relations, `Student` (Stud_name, S_id, City) and `Advisor` (Stud_name, Professor, Department).

Student

Stud_name	S_id	City
Jasvinder	01	Chandigarh
Bhavna	02	New Delhi
Ritu	03	Noida
Braham	04	Gwalior

Advisor

Stud_name	Professor	Department
Jasvinder	Saurabh	Commerce
Bhavna	Preeti	Computer
Ritu	Rohit	Science
Ashish	Harris	Maths

(a) Two given relations

Left outer join: `Student` $⟕_{\texttt{Student.Stud\_name=Advisor.Stud\_name}}$ `Advisor`

Stud_name	S_id	City	Professor	Department
Jasvinder	01	Chandigarh	Saurabh	Commerce
Bhavna	02	New Delhi	Preeti	Computer
Ritu	03	Noida	Rohit	Science
Braham	04	Gwalior	Null	Null

(b) Left outer join

Right outer join: `Student` $⟖_{\texttt{Student.Stud\_name=Advisor.Stud\_name}}$ `Advisor`

Stud_name	S_id	City	Professor	Department
Jasvinder	01	Chandigarh	Saurabh	Commerce
Bhavna	02	New Delhi	Preeti	Computer
Ritu	03	Noida	Rohit	Science
Ashish	Null	Null	Harris	Maths

(c) Right outer join

Full outer join: $\text{Student} ⟗_{\text{Student.Stud\_name=Advisor.Stud\_name}} \text{Advisor}$

Stud_name	S_id	City	Professor	Department
Jasvinder	01	Chandigarh	Saurabh	Commerce
Bhavna	02	New Delhi	Preeti	Computer
Ritu	03	Noida	Rohit	Science
Braham	04	Gwalior	Null	Null
Ashish	Null	Null	Harris	Maths

(d) Right outer join

Figure 4.8 Outer Join Operation

8. Explain the division operation by giving an example.

Ans: The division operation, denoted by ÷, is useful for queries of the form '*for all objects having all the specified properties*'. Consider a relation R_1 having exactly two attributes `A` and `B`, and a relation R_2 having just one attribute `B` with the same domain as in R_1. The division operation $R_1 \div R_2$ is defined as the set of all values of attribute `A`, such that for every value of attribute `B` in R_2, there is a tuple (`A`, `B`) in R_1. In general, for the relations R_1 and R_2, $R_1 \div R_2$ results in the relation R_3 such that $R_3 X R_2 \sqsubseteq R_1$.

For example, consider the relations R_1 and R_2 with the sample data as shown in Figure 4.9.

9. Discuss how aggregate functions and grouping is performed in relational algebra.

Ans: Aggregate functions take a collection of values as input, process them and return a single value as the result. For example, the aggregate function `SUM` returns a sum of the collection of numeric values taken as input. Similarly, aggregate functions, namely `AVG`, `MAX` and `MIN` are used to find the average, maximum and minimum of the collection of numeric values, respectively. The `COUNT` function is used for counting tuples or values in a relation.

R_1

A	B
a_1	b_1
a_1	b_2
a_1	b_3
a_1	b_4
a_2	b_1
a_2	b_2
a_3	b_2
a_4	b_2
a_4	b_4

(a) $R_1 \div R_2$

R_2

B
b_2

$R_1 \div R_2$

A
a_1
a_2
a_3
a_4

(b) $R_1 \div R_3$

R_3

B
b_2
b_4

$R_1 \div R_3$

A
a_1
a_4

(c) $R_1 \div R_4$

R_4

B
b_1
b_2
b_4

$R_1 \div R_4$

A
a_1

Figure 4.9 Division Operation

In addition, a situation may arise where tuples in a relation are required to be grouped, based on the values of an attribute. The aggregate functions can be applied on each group individually, thus, returning a result value for each group separately. For example, for calculating the average price for each category of the book, `AVG` function is applied on each category of the book separately. The grouping of tuples of a relation can be based on one or more attributes. For example, tuples in the relation `BOOK` can be grouped on two attributes, that is, first on the basis of the category and then on the basis of the publisher ID.

The aggregate function operation can be specified using the symbol ℑ (called "script F") as shown here:

$$_{\texttt{<attribute\_list>}}\Im_{\texttt{<function(attribute)\_list>}}(\texttt{R})$$

where <attribute_list> is the list of attributes on the basis of which tuples of a relation are to be grouped and <function(attribute)_list> is the list of functions to be applied on different attributes.

For example, consider a relation `BOOK`, where average, maximum and minimum price is to be calculated for each category of book separately. The expression to represent this query can be specified as

$$_{\texttt{Category}}\Im_{\texttt{AVG(Price), MAX(Price), MIN(Price)}}(\texttt{BOOK})$$

The list of attributes on the basis of which tuples are grouped can be omitted from an expression. If a grouping attribute is not specified in the expression, then the function is applied individually on all the tuples in the relation.

10. Write queries in relational algebra for the following based on the *Online Book* database.

- **(a) Retrieve the city, phone and url of the author whose name is *Lewis Ian.***
- **(b) Retrieve the name, address and phone of all the publishers located in *New York* state.**
- **(c) Retrieve the title and price of all the textbooks with a page count greater than *600.***
- **(d) Retrieve the ISBN, title and price of the books belonging to either novel or language book category.**
- **(e) Retrieve the ID, name, address and phone of publishers publishing novels.**
- **(f) Retrieve the title and price of all the books published by *Hills Publications.***
- **(g) Retrieve the book title, reviewers ID and rating of all the text books.**
- **(h) Retrieve the title, category and price of all the books written by *Charles Smith.***
- **(i) Retrieve the ID, name, url of the author and category of the book *C++.***
- **(j) Retrieve the book title, price, author name and url for the publishers *Bright Publications.***
- **(k) Retrieve the name and address of publishers who have not published any books.**
- **(l) Retrieve the name of all the publishers and the ISBN and the title of books published by them (if any).**
- **(m) Retrieve the ID and the number of books written by each author.**
- **(n) Retrieve the ISBN and the average rating given to each book.**
- **(o) Retrieve the name of the publishers who have published all categories of books.**

Ans:

(a) $\pi_{\texttt{City,Phone,URL}}(\sigma_{\texttt{Aname="Lewis Ian"}}(\texttt{AUTHOR}))$

(b) $\pi_{\texttt{Pname, Address, Phone}}(\sigma_{\texttt{State="New York"}}(\texttt{PUBLISHER}))$

(c) $\pi_{\texttt{Book\_title, Price}}(\sigma_{\texttt{Category="Textbook"} \wedge \texttt{Page\_count>600}}(\texttt{BOOK}))$

(d) $\pi_{\texttt{ISBN, Book\_title, Price}}(\sigma_{\texttt{Category="Novel"} \vee \texttt{Category="Language Book"}}(\texttt{BOOK}))$

(e) $\pi_{BOOK.P\_ID, Pname, Address, Phone}(\sigma_{Category=\text{"Novel"}}(BOOK \bowtie_{BOOK.P\_ID=PUBLISHER.P\_ID} PUBLISHER))$

(f) $\pi_{Book\_title, Price}(\sigma_{Pname=\text{"Hills Publications"}}(BOOK \bowtie_{BOOK.P\_ID=PUBLISHER.P\_ID} PUBLISHER))$

(g) $\pi_{Book\_title, R\_ID, Rating}(\sigma_{Category=\text{"Textbook"}}(BOOK \bowtie_{BOOK.ISBN=REVIEW.ISBN} REVIEW))$

(h) $\pi_{Book\_title, Category, Price}(\sigma_{Aname=\text{"Charles Smith"}}((BOOK \bowtie_{BOOK.ISBN=AUTHOR\_BOOK.ISBN} AUTHOR\_BOOK) \bowtie_{AUTHOR\_BOOK.A\_ID=AUTHOR.A\_ID} AUTHOR))$

(i) $\pi_{AUTHOR.A\_ID, Aname, URL, Category}(\sigma_{Book\_title=\text{"C++"}}((AUTHOR \bowtie_{AUTHOR.A\_ID=AUTHOR\_BOOK.A\_ID} AUTHOR\_BOOK) \bowtie_{AUTHOR\_BOOK.ISBN=BOOK.ISBN} BOOK))$

(j) $\pi_{Book\_title, Price, Aname, URL}(\sigma_{Pname=\text{"Bright Publications"}}(((BOOK \bowtie_{BOOK.ISBN=AUTHOR\_BOOK.ISBN} AUTHOR\_BOOK) \bowtie_{AUTHOR\_BOOK.A\_ID=AUTHOR.A\_ID} AUTHOR) \bowtie_{BOOK.P\_ID=PUBLISHER.P\_ID} PUBLISHER))$

(k) $\rho(R_1, \pi_{P\_ID}(PUBLISHER))$
$\rho(R_2, \pi_{P\_ID}(BOOK))$
$\rho(R_3, R_1 - R_2)$
$\rho(R_4, \pi_{Pname, Address}(R_3 \bowtie_{R3.P\_ID=PUBLISHER.P\_ID} PUBLISHER))$

(l) $\pi_{Pname, ISBN, Book\_title}(BOOK \bowtie_{BOOK.P\_ID=PUBLISHER.P\_ID} PUBLISHER)$

(m) $_{A\_ID}\Im_{COUNT(ISBN)}(AUTHOR\_BOOK)$

(n) $_{ISBN}\Im_{AVG(Rating)}(REVIEW)$

(o) $\rho(R_1, \pi_{Pname, Category}(BOOK \bowtie_{BOOK.P\_ID=PUBLISHER.P\_ID} PUBLISHER))$
$\rho(R_2, \pi_{Category}(BOOK))$
$\rho(R_3, R_1 \div R_2)$

11. What is relational calculus? What are its two forms? Differentiate between them.

Ans: Relational calculus is a non-procedural or declarative query language as it specifies what is to be retrieved rather than how to retrieve it. In relational calculus, queries are expressed in the form of variables and formulas consisting of these variables. The formula specifies the properties of the resultant relation without giving a specific procedure for evaluating it.

There are two forms of relational calculus, namely *tuple relational calculus* (*TRC*) and *domain relational calculus* (*DRC*).

The tuple relational calculus is based on tuple variables, which takes tuples of a specific relation as its values. The domain relational calculus on the other hand, is based on domain variables, which range over the values from the domain of an attribute, rather than values for an entire tuple.

12. What are the components of a tuple relational calculus expression? Explain with examples.

Ans: The tuple calculus expression consists basically of three components, which are

- The relation R for which the tuple variable T is defined.
- A condition P(T) on the basis of which a set of tuples is to be retrieved.
- An attribute list specifying the required attributes to be retrieved for the tuples satisfying the given condition.

A tuple relational calculus query is of the form:

$$\{T \mid P(T)\}$$

The resultant relation of this query is the set of all tuples T for which the condition P(T) evaluates to true. For example, the query to retrieve all books having a price greater than \$30 can be specified in the form of the tuple calculus expression as

$$\{T \mid BOOK(T) \wedge T.Price>30\}$$

The condition BOOK(T) specifies that the tuple variable T is defined for the relation BOOK. The query retrieves the set of all the tuples T satisfying the condition T.Price>30.

13. Discuss expressions and formulas in tuple relational calculus.

Ans: A general expression of the tuple relational calculus consists of a tuple variable T and a formula P(T). A formula can consist of more than one tuple variable. A formula is made up of atoms, and atoms can be of any of the forms given here.

1. R(T), where T is a tuple variable and R is a relation.
2. $T_1.A_1$ opr $T_2.A_2$, where opr is a comparison operator (=, ≠, <, ≤, >, ≥), T_1 and T_2 are tuple variables. A_1 is an attribute of the relation on which T_1 ranges and A_2 is an attribute of the relation on which T_2 ranges.
3. T.A opr c or c opr T.A, where opr is any comparison operator, T is a tuple variable, A is an attribute of the relation on which T ranges and c is a constant in the domain of attribute A.

Each of the atoms evaluates to either *true* or *false* for a specific combination of tuples known as the **truth-value** of an atom. A formula is built from one or more atoms concatenated with the help of the logical operators (¬, ∧, ∨) by using the following rules:

1. An atom is a formula.
2. If F is a formula, then so is ¬ F.
3. If F_1 and F_2 are formulae, then so are $F_1 \wedge F_2$, $F_1 \vee F_2$ and $F_1 \Rightarrow F_2$ where $F_1 \Rightarrow F_2$ is also equivalent to $(\neg (F_1) \vee F_2)$.
4. If F is a formula, then so is ∃T(F), where T is a tuple variable.
5. If F is a formula, then so is ∀T(F), where T is a tuple variable.

Note that in the last two clauses, special symbols called **quantifiers**, namely **existential quantifier** (∃) and **universal quantifier** (∀), are used to quantify the tuple variable T. The expression ∀T means "for every occurrence of T" and the expression ∃T means "for some occurrence of T".

14. What are the rules on the basis of which a tuple variable is said to be free or bound?

Ans: A tuple variable T is said to be **bound** if it is quantified, that is, it appears in (∃T) or (∀T) clause; otherwise, it is **free**. A tuple variable T can be said to be free or bound in a formula on the basis of the following rules:

- A tuple variable T is free in a formula F, which is an atom.
- A tuple variable T is free or bound in a formula of the forms $(F_1 \wedge F_2)$, $(F_1 \vee F_2)$ and ¬F depending on whether it is free or bound in F_1 or F_2 (if it occurs in either of the formulas). Note that in a formula of the form $F=(F_1 \vee F_2)$, a tuple variable may be free in F_1 and bound in F_2, or vice versa. In such cases, one occurrence of the tuple variable is bound and the other is free in F.
- All free occurrences of a tuple variable T in F are bound in a formula F′ of the form F′ = (∃T)(F) or F′ = (∀T)(F). The tuple variable is bound to the quantifier specified in F′.

15. How is a truth value of a formula in the tuple calculus expression derived?

Ans: A query can be evaluated on the basis of a given instance of the database. The truth value of a formula can be derived as follows:

(a) An atom (formula) is *true* if tuple variable T is assigned a tuple from a relation R; otherwise, it is *false*.
(b) ¬F is *true* if F is *false*, and it is *false* if F is *true*.
(c) $F_1 \wedge F_2$ is *true* if both F_1 and F_2 are *true*; otherwise, it is *false*.
(d) $F_1 \vee F_2$ is *false* if both F_1 and F_2 are *false*; otherwise, it is *true*.
(e) In $F_1 \Rightarrow F_2$, F_2 is *true* whenever F_1 is *true*; otherwise, it is *false*.
(f) (∃T) (F) is *true* if F is *true* for some (at least one) tuple assigned to free occurrences of T in F; otherwise, it is *false*.
(g) (∀T) (F) is *true* if F is *true* for every tuple (universal) assigned to free occurrences of T in F; otherwise, it is *false*.

16. What are the types of quantifiers? Explain the conversion of one quantifier into another by giving an example.

Ans: Quantifiers are special symbols that are used to quantify a tuple variable T. They are of two types: *existential quantifier* (∃) and *universal quantifier* (∀). The expression ∀T means "for every occurrence of T" and the expression ∃T means "for some occurrence of T". A tuple variable T is said to be **bound** if it is quantified, that is, it appears in (∃T) or (∀T) clause; otherwise, it is **free**.

An existential quantifier is transformed into a universal quantifier and vice versa by performing the following steps:

1. Replace one type of quantifier into the other and precede the quantifier by a NOT (¬) operator.
2. Replace the AND(∧) with the OR(∨) operator and vice versa.
3. Formula is preceded by the NOT (¬) operator; as a result, the negated formula becomes affirmed and vice versa.

Some examples of this transformation are:

$$(\exists T)\ (F) \equiv \neg (\forall T)\ (\neg F)$$

$$(\forall T)\ (F) \equiv \neg (\exists T)\ (\neg F)$$

$$(\exists T)\ (F_1 \wedge F_2) \equiv \neg (\forall T)\ (\neg F_1 \vee \neg F_2)$$

The symbol ≡ represents "equivalent to".

17. When is an expression in tuple relational calculus said to be unsafe? How can safe expressions be defined? Explain with an example.

Ans: An expression of tuple relational calculus containing a universal quantifier, existential quantifier or negation condition may lead to a relation of an infinite number of tuples. For example, consider the following expression:

$$\{T \mid \neg BOOK(T)\}$$

This expression appears to be syntactically correct but it refers to all the tuples in the universe not belonging to the BOOK relation, which are infinite in number. These types of expressions are known as **unsafe expressions**.

A **safe expression** is an expression, which results in a relation with a finite number of tuples. Safe expressions can be defined more precisely by introducing the concept of the domain of a tuple relational calculus expression, E. The domain of expression E, denoted by Dom(E), is the set of all values that appear as a constant in E or appear in one or more relations whose names appear in E. Therefore, the domain of the above expression includes all the values appearing in the relation BOOK. Hence, an expression E is said to be safe if all the values appearing in the resultant relation are from the domain of E, Dom(E). For example, consider the following expression:

{T.City, T.Phone, T.URL | AUTHOR(T) ∧ T.Aname="Lewis Ian"}

This expression is safe since all the values appearing in the resultant relation are from the domain, Dom(AUTHOR).

18. Express queries (a) to (k) of Question 10 in tuple relational calculus.

Ans:

(a) {T.City, T.Phone, T.URL | AUTHOR(T) ∧ T.Aname="Lewis Ian"}

(b) {T.Pname, T.Address, T.Phone | PUBLISHER(T) ∧ T.State="New York"}

(c) {T.Book_title, T.Price | BOOK(T) ∧ T.Category="Textbook" ∧ T.Page_count>600}

(d) {T.ISBN, T.Book_title, T.Price | BOOK(T) ∧ (T.Category="Novel" ∨ T.Category="Language Book") }

(e) {T.P_ID, T.Pname, T.Address, T.Phone | PUBLISHER(T) ∧ (∃S)(BOOK(S) ∧ S.P_ID=T.P_ID ∧ S.Category="Novel") }

(f) {T.Book_title, T.Price | BOOK(T) ∧ (∃S)(PUBLISHERS(S) ∧ S.P_ID=T.P_ID ∧ S.Pname = "Hills Publications") }

(g) {T.Book_title, S.R_ID, S.Rating | BOOK(T) ∧ REVIEW(S) ∧ T.Category="Textbook" ∧ T.ISBN = S.ISBN }

(h) {T.Book_title, T.Category, T.Price | BOOK(T) ∧ ((∃S)(∃P)(AUTHOR(S) ∧ AUTHOR_BOOK(P) ∧ S.Aname="Charles Smith" ∧ T.ISBN=P.ISBN ∧ P.A_ID=S.A_ID)) }

(i) {T.A_ID, T.Aname, T.URL, S.Category | AUTHOR(T) ∧ BOOK(S) ∧ S.Book_title="C++" ∧ ((∃P)(AUTHOR_BOOK(P) ∧ T.A_ID=P.A_ID ∧ P.ISBN=S.ISBN)) }

(j) {T.Book_title, T.Price, S.Aname, S.URL | BOOK(T) ∧ AUTHOR(S) ∧ ((∃P)(∃R)(PUBLISHER(P) ∧ AUTHOR_BOOK(R) ∧ T.ISBN=R.ISBN ∧ R.A_ID=S.A_ID ∧ T.P_ID=P.P_ID ∧ P.Pname="Bright Publications")) }

(k) {T.Pname, T.Address | PUBLISHER(T) ∧ (¬(∃S)(BOOK(S) ∧ T.P_ID=S.P_ID)) }

19. Explain the general form of domain relational calculus.

Ans: The domain relational calculus is based on domain variables, which range over the values from the domain of an attribute, rather than values for an entire tuple. A simple domain relational calculus query is of the form

{T | P(T)}

where T represents a set of domain variables (x_1, x_2, ..., x_n) that ranges over domains of attributes (A_1, A_2, ..., A_n), and P represents the formula on T.

20. Discuss the concept of formulas and atoms in domain relational calculus.

Ans: Formulae in domain relational calculus are built up from atoms, and an atom can be of any of the forms given here.

1. R(x_1, x_2, ..., x_n), where R is a relation with *n* attributes and x_1, x_2, ..., x_n are domain variables or domain constants for the corresponding *n* attributes.
2. x_1 opr x_2, where opr is a comparison operator (=, ≠, <, ≤, >, ≥) and x_1 and x_2 are domain variables.

3. `x opr c` or `c opr x`, where `opr` is a comparison operator, `x` is a domain variable and `c` is a constant in the domain of the attribute for which `x` is a domain variable.

Formulas are built from atoms by using the following rules:

1. An atom is a formula.
2. If F is a formula, then so is $\neg F$.
3. If F_1 and F_2 are formulae, then so are $F_1 \wedge F_2$, $F_1 \vee F_2$ and $F_1 \Rightarrow F_2$.
4. If F is a formula, then so is $\exists x(F)$, where x is a domain variable.
5. If F is a formula, then so is $\forall x(F)$, where x is a domain variable.

21. What do you understand by the expressive power of relational algebra? How are relational algebra and relational calculus logically equivalent? When is a query language said to be relationally complete?

Ans: The expressive power of relational algebra is frequently used as a metric to measure the power of any relational database query language.

Relational algebra and relational calculus are logically equivalent because for every safe relational calculus expression there exists equivalent relational algebra expression and vice versa. In other words, there is one-to-one mapping between the two and the difference lies only in the way the query is expressed.

A query language is said to be relationally complete if it is at least as powerful as relational algebra, that is, if it can express any query expressed in relational algebra.

22. Express queries (a) to (k) of Question 10 in domain relational calculus.

Ans:

(a) $\{a_4, a_6, a_7 \mid (\exists a_2)\ (\text{AUTHOR}(a_1,a_2,a_3,a_4,a_5,a_6,a_7) \wedge a_2=\text{"Lewis Ian"})\}$

(b) $\{p_2, p_3, p_5 \mid (\exists p_4)\ (\text{PUBLISHER}(p_1,p_2,p_3,p_4,p_5,p_6) \wedge p_4=\text{"New York"})\}$

(c) $\{b_2, b_4 \mid (\exists b_3)\ (\exists b_7)\ (\text{BOOK}(b_1,b_2,b_3,b_4,b_5,b_6,b_7,b_8) \wedge b_3=\text{"Textbook"} \wedge b_7>600)\}$

(d) $\{b_1, b_2, b_4 \mid (\exists b_3)\ (\text{BOOK}(b_1,b_2,b_3,b_4,b_5,b_6,b_7,b_8) \wedge (b_3=\text{"Novel"} \vee b_3=\text{"Language Book"}))\}$

(e) $\{p_1, p_2, p_3, p_5 \mid (\exists b_3)\ (\exists b_8)\ (\text{BOOK}(b_1,b_2,b_3,b_4,b_5,b_6,b_7,b_8) \wedge \text{PUBLISHER}(p_1,p_2,p_3,p_4,p_5,p_6) \wedge b_8=p_1 \wedge b_3=\text{"Novel"})\}$

(f) $\{b_2, b_4 \mid (\exists p_2)\ (\exists p_1)\ (\exists b_8)\ (\text{BOOK}(b_1,b_2,b_3,b_4,b_5,b_6,b_7,b_8) \wedge \text{PUBLISHER}(p_1,p_2,p_3,p_4,p_5,p_6) \wedge p_1=b_8 \wedge p_2=\text{"Hills Publications"})\}$

(g) $\{b_2, r_1, r_3 \mid (\exists b_3)\ (\exists b_1)\ (\exists r_2)\ (\text{BOOK}(b_1,b_2,b_3,b_4,b_5,b_6,b_7,b_8) \wedge \text{REVIEW}(r_1,r_2,r_3) \wedge b_1=r_2 \wedge b_3=\text{"Textbook"})\}$

(h) $\{b_2, b_3, b_4 \mid (\exists b_1)\ (\exists c_2)\ (\exists c_1)\ (\exists a_1)\ (\exists a_2)\ (\text{BOOK}(b_1,b_2,b_3,b_4,b_5,b_6,b_7,b_8) \wedge \text{AUTHOR}(a_1,a_2,a_3,a_4,a_5,a_6,a_7) \wedge \text{AUTHOR\_BOOK}(c_1,c_2) \wedge b_1=c_2 \wedge c_1=a_1 \wedge a_2=\text{"Charles Smith"})\}$

(i) $\{a_1, a_2, a_7, b_3 \mid (\exists c_1)\ (\exists b_1)\ (\exists c_2)\ (\exists b_2)\ (\text{BOOK}(b_1,b_2,b_3,b_4,b_5,b_6,b_7,b_8) \wedge \text{AUTHOR}(a_1,a_2,a_3,a_4,a_5,a_6,a_7) \wedge \text{AUTHOR\_BOOK}(c_1,c_2) \wedge a_1=c_1 \wedge c_2=b_1 \wedge b_2=\text{"C++"})\}$

(j) $\{b_2, b_4, a_2, a_7 \mid (\exists a_1)\ (\exists c_1)\ (\exists c_2)\ (\exists b_1)\ (\exists b_8)\ (\exists p_1)\ (\exists p_2)\ (\text{BOOK}(b_1,b_2,b_3,b_4,b_5,b_6,b_7,b_8) \wedge \text{AUTHOR}(a_1,a_2,a_3,a_4,a_5,a_6,a_7) \wedge \text{AUTHOR\_BOOK}(c_1,c_2) \wedge \text{PUBLISHER}(p_1,p_2,p_3,p_4,p_5,p_6) \wedge a_1=c_1 \wedge c_2=b_1 \wedge b_8=p_1 \wedge p_2=\text{"Bright Publications"})\}$

(k) $\{p_2, p_3 \mid (\exists p_1)\ (\text{PUBLISHER}(p_1,p_2,p_3,p_4,p_5,p_6) \wedge (\neg(\exists b_8)\ (\text{BOOK}(b_1,b_2,b_3,b_4,b_5,b_6,b_7,b_8) \wedge p_1=b_8)))\}$

23. Consider the following relation schema for the SALES database:

CUSTOMER(<u>CustNo</u>, CName, City)
ORDER(<u>OrderNo</u>, OrderDate, <u>CustNo</u>, Amount)
ORDER_ITEM(<u>OrderNo</u>, <u>ItemNo</u>, Qty)
ITEM(<u>ItemNo</u>, UnitPrice)

On the basis of this relational schema, write the following queries in relational algebra, tuple calculus and domain calculus:

(a) Retrieve the number and date of orders placed by customers residing at *Atlanta* city.
(b) Retrieve the number and unit price of items for which an order of quantity greater than *50* is placed.
(c) Retrieve the order number, date and item number for the order of items having a unit price greater than *20*.
(d) Retrieve details of customers who have placed an order for the item number *I010*.
(e) Retrieve the number and unit price of items for which an order is placed by the customer number *C001*.

Ans:

Queries in relational algebra

(a) $\pi_{OrderNo,OrderDate}(\sigma_{city=\text{"Atlanta"}}(CUSTOMER \bowtie_{CUSTOMER.CustNo=ORDER.CustNo} ORDER))$

(b) $\pi_{Item.ItemNo,UnitPrice}(\sigma_{Qty>50}(ORDER\_ITEM \bowtie_{ORDER\_ITEM.ItemNo=ITEM.ItemNo} ITEM))$

(c) $\pi_{Order.OrderNo,OrderDate,Item.ItemNo}(\sigma_{UnitPrice>20}((ORDER \bowtie_{ORDER.OrderNo=ORDER\_ITEM.OrderNo} ORDER\_ITEM) \bowtie_{ORDER\_ITEM.ItemNo=ITEM.ItemNo} ITEM))$

(d) $\pi_{Customer.CustNo,CName,City}(\sigma_{ItemNo=\text{"I010"}}((CUSTOMER \bowtie_{CUSTOMER.CustNo=ORDER.CustNo} ORDER) \bowtie_{ORDER.OrderNo=ORDER\_ITEM.OrderNo} ORDER\_ITEM))$

(e) $\pi_{Item.ItemNo,UnitPrice}(\sigma_{CustNo=\text{"C001"}}((ORDER \bowtie_{ORDER.OrderNo=ORDER\_ITEM.OrderNo} ORDER\_ITEM) \bowtie_{ORDER\_ITEM.ItemNo=ITEM.ItemNo} ITEM))$

Queries in tuple calculus

(a) {T.OrderNo, T.OrderDate | ORDER(T) ∧ (∃S) (CUSTOMER(S) ∧ S.CustNo= T.CustNo ∧ S.City="Atlanta")}

(b) {I.ItemNo, I.UnitPrice | ITEM(I) ∧ (∃R)(ORDER_ITEM(R) ∧ I.ItemNo= R.ItemNo ∧ R.Qty>50)}

(c) {T.OrderNo, T.OrderDate, R.ItemNo | ORDER(T) ∧ ((∃S) (∃R) (ITEM(S) ∧ ORDER_ITEM(R) ∧ T.OrderNo=R.OrderNo ∧ R.ItemNo=S.ItemNo ∧ S.UnitPrice>20))}

(d) {T.CustNo, T.CName, T.City | CUSTOMER(T) ∧ ((∃R) (∃S) (ORDER(R) ∧ ORDER_ITEM(S) ∧ T.CustNo=R.CustNo ∧ R.OrderNo=S.OrderNo ∧ S.ItemNo="I010"))}

(e) {T.ItemNo, T.UnitPrice | ITEM(T) ∧ ((∃R) (∃S) (ORDER(R) ∧ ORDER_ITEM(S) ∧ R.OrderNo=S.OrderNo ∧ S.ItemNo=T.ItemNo ∧ R.CustNo="C001"))}

Queries in domain relational calculus

(a) $\{o_1, o_2 \mid (\exists c_1)(\exists o_3)(\exists c_3)(CUSTOMER(c_1, c_2, c_3) \wedge ORDER(o_1, o_2, o_3, o_4) \wedge c_1=o_3 \wedge c_3=\text{"Atlanta"}\}$

(b) $\{i_1, i_2 \mid (\exists r_2)(\exists r_3)\ (ORDER\_ITEM(r_1, r_2, r_3) \wedge ITEM(i_1, i_2) \wedge r_2=i_1 \wedge r_3>50)\}$

(c) $\{o_1, o_2, i_1 \mid (\exists r_1)(\exists r_2)(\exists i_2)\ (ORDER(o_1, o_2, o_3, o_4) \wedge ORDER\_ITEM(r_1, r_2, r_3) \wedge ITEM(i_1, i_2) \wedge o_1=r_1 \wedge r_2=i_1 \wedge i_2>20)\}$

(d) $\{c_1, c_2, c_3 | (\exists o_1)(\exists o_3)(\exists r_2)(\exists r_1)$ (CUSTOMER(c_1, c_2, c_3) $\wedge$ ORDER(o_1, o_2, o_3, o_4) $\wedge$ ORDER_ITEM$(r_1, r_2, r_3) \wedge c_1=o_3 \wedge o_1=r_1 \wedge r_2=$"I010")$\}$

(e) $\{i_1, i_2 | (\exists o_1)(\exists o_3)(\exists r_1)(\exists r_2)$ (ORDER(o_1, o_2, o_3, o_4) $\wedge$ ORDER_ITEM$(r_1, r_2, r_3) \wedge$ ITEM$(i_1, i_2) \wedge o_1=r_1 \wedge r_2=i_1 \wedge o_3=$"C001")$\}$

24. Consider the relational database:
EMPLOYEE(Empname, Street, City)
WORKS(Empname, Companyname, Salary)
COMPANY(Companyname, City)
MANAGES(Empname, Managername)
On the basis of this relational schema, write the following queries in relational algebra, tuple calculus (for (a) to (c)) and domain calculus (for (a) to (c)):
(a) Find the names of all employees who work for *First Bank Corporation*.
(b) Find the names, street addresses and cities of residence of all employees who work for *First Bank Corporation* and earn more than *200,000* per annum.
(c) Find the names of all employees in this database who live in the same city as the company for which they work.
(d) Find the number of employees working in each company.
(e) Find the average, maximum and minimum salary for each company.

Ans:

Expression in relational algebra

(a) $\pi_{\text{Empname}}(\sigma_{\text{Companyname="First Bank Corporation"}}(\text{WORKS}))$

(b) $\pi_{\text{EMPLOYEE.Empname, Street, City}}(\sigma_{\text{Companyname="First Bank Corporation"} \wedge \text{Salary}>200000}(\text{EMPLOYEE} \bowtie_{\text{EMPLOYEE.Empname=WORKS.Empname}} \text{WORKS}))$

(c) $\pi_{\text{EMPLOYEE.Empname}}(\sigma_{\text{EMPLOYEE.City=COMPANY.City}}((\text{WORKS} \bowtie_{\text{WORKS.Companyname=COMPANY.Companyname.}} \text{COMPANY}) \bowtie_{\text{WORKS.Empname=EMPLOYEE.Empname}} \text{EMPLOYEE}))$

(d) $_{\text{Companyname}}\Im_{\text{Count(Empname)}}(\text{WORKS})$

(e) $_{\text{Companyname}}\Im_{\text{AVG(Salary), MAX(Salary), MIN(Salary)}}(\text{WORKS})$

Expression in tuple calculus

(a) {T.Empname | WORKS(T) $\wedge$ T.Companyname ="First Bank Corporation"}

(b) {T.Empname, T.Street, T.City | EMPLOYEE(T) $\wedge$ $(\exists S)$(WORKS(S) $\wedge$ T.Empname=S.Empname $\wedge$ S.Companyname="First Bank Corporation" $\wedge$ S.Salary>200000)}

(c) {T.Empname | EMPLOYEE(T) $\wedge$ $((\exists R)(\exists S)$(WORKS(R) $\wedge$ COMPANY(S) $\wedge$ T.Empname=R.Empname $\wedge$ R.Companyname=S.Companyname $\wedge$ T.City=S.City))}

Expression in domain calculus

(a) $\{w_1 | (\exists w_2)$(WORKS$(w_1, w_2, w_3) \wedge w_2=$"First Bank Corporation")$\}$

(b) $\{e_1, e_2, e_3 | (\exists w_1)(\exists w_2)(\exists w_3)$ (EMPLOYEE$(e_1, e_2, e_3) \wedge$ WORKS$(w_1, w_2, w_3) \wedge e_1=w_1 \wedge w_2=$"First Bank Corporation" $\wedge w_3>200000)\}$

(c) $\{e_1 | (\exists w_1)(\exists w_2)(\exists e_3)(\exists c_1)(\exists c_2)$ (EMPLOYEE$(e_1, e_2, e_3) \wedge$ WORKS$(w_1, w_2, w_3) \wedge$ COMPANY$(c_1, c_2) \wedge e_1=w_1 \wedge w_2=c_1 \wedge e_3=c_2)\}$

25. Consider the following relation schema for the BANK database:

BRANCH(BranchID, Bname, City, Phone)

ACCOUNT(AccountNo, Aname, AType, BranchID, Balance)

TRANSACTION(TID, T_Date, T_Type, AccountNo, Amount)

On the basis of this relational schema, write the following queries in relational algebra, tuple calculus ((a) to (e)) and domain calculus ((a) to (e)):

(a) Retrieve the ID and name of all the branches located in *Seattle* city.

(b) Retrieve the ID, type and amount of all the transactions of withdrawal type.

(c) List the number and type of all accounts opened in the branch having ID *B010*.

(d) List the number and name of account holders withdrawing an amount greater than 10,000 on 31st March, 2007.

(e) List the number and name of account holders having savings account in the city *Los Angeles.*

(f) Calculate the average balance of accounts present in the *AX International Bank* in *New York.*

(g) Calculate the maximum and minimum balance of accounts in each city.

Ans:

Queries in relational algebra

(a) $\pi_{\text{BranchID, Bname}}(\sigma_{\text{City="Seattle"}}(\text{BRANCH}))$

(b) $\pi_{\text{TID, T\_Type, Amount}}(\sigma_{\text{T\_TYPE="Withdrawal"}}(\text{TRANSACTION}))$

(c) $\pi_{\text{AccountNo,AType}}(\sigma_{\text{BranchID="B010"}}(\text{ACCOUNT}))$

(d) $\pi_{\text{ACCOUNT.AccountNo,Aname}}(\sigma_{\text{T\_Type="Withdrawal"} \wedge \text{Amount>10000} \wedge \text{T\_Date="31 march 2007"}}(\text{ACCOUNT} \bowtie_{\text{ACCOUNT.AccountNo=TRANSACTION.AccountNo}} \text{TRANSACTION}))$

(e) $\pi_{\text{AccountNo,Aname}}(\sigma_{\text{AType="Savings"} \wedge \text{City="Los Angeles"}}(\text{BRANCH} \bowtie_{\text{BRANCH.BranchID=ACCOUNT.BranchID}} \text{ACCOUNT}))$

(f) $\Im_{\text{AVG(Balance)}}(\text{ACCOUNT} \bowtie_{\text{ACCOUNT.BranchID=BRANCH.BranchID} \wedge \text{Bname="AXInternationalBank"} \wedge \text{City="New York"}} \text{BRANCH})$

(g) ${}_{\text{City}}\Im_{\text{MAX(Balance),MIN(Balance)}}(\text{ACCOUNT} \bowtie_{\text{ACCOUNT.BranchID=BRANCH.BranchID}} \text{BRANCH})$

Queries in tuple calculus

(a) {T.BranchID, T.Bname | BRANCH(T) ∧ T.City="Seattle"}

(b) {T.TID,T.T_Type,T.Amount|TRANSACTION(T)∧ T.T_Type="Withdrawal")}

(c) {T.AccountNo, T.Atype | ACCOUNT(T)∧ T.BranchID="B010"}

(d) {T.AccountNo, T.AName | ACCOUNT(T)∧ (∃R) (TRANSACTION(R)∧ T.AccountNo= R.AccountNo ∧ R.T_Type="Withdrawal" ∧ R.Amount > 10000 ∧ R.T_Date="31 March 2007")}

(e) {T.AccountNo, T.Name | ACCOUNT(T)∧ (∃R) (BRANCH(R)∧ R.BranchID= T.BranchID ∧ R.City="Los Angeles" ∧ T.AType="Savings")}

Queries in domain calculus

(a) $\{b_1, b_2 \mid (\exists b_3)\ (\text{BRANCH}(b_1, b_2, b_3, b_4) \wedge b_3=\text{"Seatle"})\}$

(b) $\{t_1, t_3, t_5 \mid (\exists t_3)\ (\text{TRANSACTION}(t_1, t_2, t_3, t_4, t_5) \wedge t_3=\text{"Withdrawal"})\}$

(c) $\{a_1, a_3 \mid (\exists a_4)\ (\text{ACCOUNT}(a_1, a_2, a_3, a_4, a_5) \wedge a_4=\text{"B010"})\}$

(d) $\{a_1, a_2 \mid (\exists t_2)(\exists t_4)(\exists t_5)(\text{ACCOUNT}(a_1, a_2, a_3, a_4, a_5) \wedge \text{TRANSACTION}(t_1, t_2, t_3, t_4, t_5) \wedge a_1=t_4 \wedge t_5>10000 \wedge t_2=\text{"31 March 2007"} \wedge t_3=\text{"Withdrawal"})\}$

(e) $\{a_1, a_2 | (\exists a_3)(\exists b_3)(\exists b_1)(\exists a_4)(BRANCH(b_1, b_2, b_3, b_4) \wedge ACCOUNT(a_1, a_2, a_3, a_4, a_5) \wedge b_1 = a_4 \wedge b_3 = \text{"Los Angeles"} \wedge a_3 = \text{"Savings"})\}$

26. R_1 and R_2 are two given relations:

R1

A	B
A1	B1
A2	B2
A3	B3
A4	B4

R2

A	B
A1	B1
A7	B7
A2	B2
A4	B4

Find the union, intersection and set difference.

Ans:

Union operation

R1 ∪ R2

A	B
A1	B1
A2	B2
A3	B3
A4	B4
A7	B7

Intersection operation

R1 ∩ R2

A	B
A1	B1
A2	B2
A4	B4

Set difference

R1 – R2

A3	B3

R2 – R1

A7	B7

Multiple-choice Questions

1. Which of the following is the operation developed specifically for the relational databases?
(a) Union (b) Cartesian product (c) Division (d) Difference
2. Which of the following is the set-oriented operation?
(a) Select (b) Difference (c) Division (d) Project
3. Which of the following is the binary operation?
(a) Union (b) Join (c) Cartesian product (d) All of these
4. Which of the following is true for a right outer join?
(a) It includes all the tuples from both the relations satisfying the join condition along with all the tuples in the right relation that do not have a corresponding tuple in the left relation.
(b) It includes all the tuples from both the relations satisfying the join condition along with all the tuples in the left relation that do not have a corresponding tuple in the right relation.
(c) It selects all the tuples satisfying the join condition along with the tuples for which no tuples from the other relation satisfy the join condition.
(d) None of these
5. Which of the following aggregate functions is used for counting tuples or values in a relation?
(a) `Avg` (b) `Count` (c) `Max` (d) `Min`
6. Which of the following is the component of a tuple relational calculus expression?
(a) The relation `R` for which tuple variable `T` is defined.
(b) A condition `P(T)` on the basis of which a set of tuples is to be retrieved.
(c) An attribute list specifying the required attributes to be retrieved for the tuples satisfying the given condition.
(d) All of these
7. The truth value of a formula can be derived as ________.
(a) $\neg F$ is *true* if F is *false*, and it is *false* if F is *true*.
(b) $F_1 \wedge F_2$ is *true* if both F_1 and F_2 are *true*; otherwise, it is *false*.
(c) $F_1 \vee F_2$ is *false* if both F_1 and F_2 are *false*; otherwise, it is *true*.
(d) All of these
8. Which of the following is the symbol for an existential quantifier?
(a) $\forall$ (b) $\exists$ (c) $\neg$ (d) $\equiv$
9. Which of the following statements is true?
(a) $(\forall T)\ (F) \equiv \neg(\exists T)\ (F)$ (b) $(\exists T)\ (F_1 \wedge F_2) \equiv \neg(\forall T)\ (\neg F_1 \vee \neg F_2)$
(c) $(\forall T)\ (F_1 \vee F_2) \equiv (\exists T)\ (\neg F_1 \wedge \neg F_2)$ (d) $(\forall T)\ (F_1 \wedge F_2) \equiv \neg(\exists T)\ (F_1 \vee F_2)$
10. Which of the following is not a rule for forming formula in domain relational calculus?
(a) An atom is a formula.
(b) If F is a formula, then so is $\neg F$.
(c) If F_1 and F_2 are formulae, then so are $F_1 \wedge F_2$, $F_1 \vee F_2$ and $F_1 \Rightarrow F_2$.
(d) If F is a formula, then so is $\exists T(F)$, where T is a tuple variable.
11. Which of the following operation requires two tables as input and the two tables must have one common column?
(a) Join (b) Division
(c) Cartesian product (multiplication) (d) Projection

12. Which of the following is not a valid aggregate function?
(a) COUNT (b) COMPUTE (c) AVG (d) MAX
13. If relation R has *m* tuples and relation S has *n* tuples, then the result of join on relations R and S will have up to __________ tuples.
(a) m * n (b) m / n (c) m + n (d) m – n
14. The result of $R(A_1, A_2, ..., A_m) X S(B_1, B_2, ..., B_n)$ is a relation with __________ attributes.
(a) m + n (b) m – n (c) m * n (d) n – m
15. The join operation where only matching tuples are kept in the result is called __________.
(a) Outer join (b) Left outer join (c) Inner join (d) Right outer join
16. Which of the following relational algebra operations require two tables as input with exactly the same attributes?
(a) Join, cartesian product (multiplication), division
(b) Project, restriction, union
(c) Union, intersection, minus
(d) Update, insert, delete
17. Which of the following operations is used to select some required attributes from a relation while discarding the other attributes?
(a) Select operation (b) Project operation (c) Rename operation (d) None of these
18. Intersection operation is __________.
(a) Commutative (b) Associative (c) Both (a) and (b) (d) None of these

Answers

1. (b)	2. (b)	3. (d)	4. (a)	5. (b)	6. (d)	7. (d)
8. (b)	9. (b)	10. (d)	11. (a)	12. (b)	13. (a)	14. (a)
15. (c)	16. (c)	17. (b)	18. (c)			

5

Structured Query Language

1. What is SQL? What are the two major categories of SQL commands? Explain them.

Ans: SQL stands for structured query language. It is a language that can be used for retrieval and management of data stored in relational database. It is a non-procedural language as it specifies what is to be retrieved rather than how to retrieve it. It can be used for defining the structure of data, modifying data in the database and specifying the security constraints.

The two major categories of SQL commands are Data Definition Language (DDL) and Data Manipulation Language (DML). **DDL** provides commands that can be used to create, modify and delete database objects. **DML** provides commands that can be used to access and manipulate the data, that is, to retrieve, insert, delete and update data in a database.

2. What is data type? What are the various data types supported by standard SQL?

Ans: Data type identifies the type of data to be stored in an attribute of a relation and also specifies associated operations for handling the data. The common data types supported by standard SQL are as follows:

- `NUMERIC(p, s)`: used to represent data as floating-point number. The number can have `p` significant digits (including sign) and `s` number of the `p` digits can be present on the right of decimal point. For example, the data type specified as `NUMERIC(5, 2)` indicates that the value of an attribute can be of form 332.32 .
- `INT` or `INTEGER`: used to represent data as a number without a decimal point.
- `SMALLINT`: used to represent data as a number without a decimal point. It is a subset of the `INTEGER`; so the default size is usually smaller than `INT`.
- `CHAR(n)` or `CHARACTER(n)`: used to represent data as a fixed-length string of characters of size `n`. In case of fixed-length strings, a shorter string is padded with blank characters to the right. For example, if the value *ABC* is to be stored for an attribute with data type `CHAR(8)`, the string is padded with five blanks to the right.
- `VARCHAR(n)` or `CHARACTER VARYING`: used to represent data as a variable length string of characters of maximum size `n`. In case of variable length string, a shorter string is not padded with blank characters.
- `DATE` and `TIME`: used to represent data as date or time. The `DATE` data type has three components, namely *year*, *month* and *day* in the form `YYYY-MM-DD`. The `TIME` data type also has three components, namely *hours*, *minutes* and *seconds* in the form `HH:MM:SS`.

- BOOLEAN: used to represent the third value *unknown,* in addition to *true* and *false* values, because of the presence of *null* values in SQL.
- TIMESTAMP: used to represent data consisting of both date and time. The TIMESTAMP data type has six components, *year*, *month*, *day*, *hour*, *minute* and *second* in the form YYYY-MM-DD-HH:MM:SS[.sF], where F is the fractional part of the *second* value.

3. Which command is used for creating user-defined data types?

Ans: The user-defined data types can be created using the CREATE DOMAIN command. For example, to create user-defined data type Vchar, the command can be specified as

```
CREATE DOMAIN Vchar AS VARCHAR (15);
```

Vchar can be used as data type for any attribute for which data type VARCHAR(15) is to be defined.

4. Explain the CREATE TABLE and DESCRIBE command.

Ans: The CREATE TABLE command is used to define a new relation, its attributes and its data types. Various constraints like key, entity integrity and referential integrity constraints can also be specified. The syntax for CREATE TABLE command is shown here.

```
CREATE TABLE <table_name> (<attribute1><data_type1> [constraint1],
                           <attribute2><data_type2> [constraint2],
                           :
                           <attributen><data_typen> [constraintn],
                           [table_constraint1]
                           :
                           [table_constraintn]
                          );
```

where table_name is the name of new relation, $attribute_i$ the attribute of relation, $data\_type_i$ the data type of values of the attribute, $constraint_i$ any of the column-level constraints defined on the corresponding attribute and $table\_constraint_i$ any of the table-level constraints.

For example, the command to create BOOK relation whose schema is BOOK(ISBN, Book_title, Category, Price, Copyright_date, Year, Page_count, P_ID) can be specified as

```
CREATE TABLE BOOK (   ISBN             VARCHAR(15),
                      Book_title       VARCHAR(50),
                      Category         VARCHAR(20),
                      Price            NUMERIC(6,2),
                      Copyright_date   NUMERIC(4),
                      Year             NUMERIC(4),
                      Page_count       NUMERIC(4),
                      P_ID             VARCHAR(4)
                  );
```

The DESCRIBE (or DESC) command is used to view the structure of an already existing relation. For example, the command to view the structure of the BOOK relation can be specified as

```
DESCRIBE BOOK
OR
DESC BOOK
```

5. What is the use of constraints? What are the different types of constraints that can be specified? Explain with examples.

Ans: Constraints are required to maintain the integrity of the data, which ensures that the data in the database are consistent, correct and valid. The different types of constraints that can be specified while creating a relation in SQL are PRIMARY KEY Constraint, UNIQUE Constraint, CHECK Constraint, NOT NULL Constraint and FOREIGN KEY Constraint.

- **PRIMARY KEY constraint:** This constraint ensures that the attribute declared as a primary key cannot have a *null* value, and no two tuples can have the same value for a primary key attribute. In other words, the values in the primary key attribute are not *null* and are unique. If a primary key has a single attribute, the `PRIMARY KEY` can be applied as a column-level as well as table-level constraint. For example, the attribute `ISBN` of the `BOOK` relation can be declared as a primary key as

```
ISBN VARCHAR (15) PRIMARY KEY
```
OR
```
PRIMARY KEY (ISBN)
```

  If a primary key has more than one attribute, the `PRIMARY KEY` constraint is specified as a table-level constraint. For example, attributes `ISBN` and `R_ID` of the `REVIEW` relation can be declared as a composite primary key as

```
PRIMARY KEY (ISBN, R_ID)
```

- **UNIQUE constraint:** This constraint ensures that the set of attributes has unique values, that is, no two tuples can have the same value in the specified attributes. `UNIQUE` constraint, like the primary key can be applied as a column-level as well as table-level constraint. For example, the `UNIQUE` constraint on attribute `Pname` of the relation `PUBLISHER` can be specified as

```
Pname VARCHAR (50) UNIQUE
```
OR
```
UNIQUE (Pname)
```

  When a `UNIQUE` constraint is applied on more than one attribute, it is specified as a table-level constraint. For example, the `UNIQUE` constraint on attributes `Pname` and `Address` of relation `PUBLISHER` can be specified as

```
UNIQUE (Pname, Address)
```

- **CHECK constraint:** This constraint ascertains that the value inserted in an attribute must satisfy a given expression. In other words, it is used to specify the valid values for a certain attribute. For example, the `CHECK` constraint for ensuring that the value of attribute `Price` of the relation `BOOK` is greater than $*20* can be specified as

```
Price NUMERIC(6,2) CHECK(Price>20)
```

  The `CHECK` constraint when specified as a table-level constraint can be given a separate name that allows referring to the constraint whenever needed. For example, the constraint on the attribute `Price` of the `BOOK` relation can be given a name as

```
CONSTRAINT Chk_price CHECK(Price > 20)
```

  Constraints can also be applied on more than one attribute simultaneously. For example, the constraint that the `Copyright_date` must be either less than or equal to the `Year` (publishing year) can be specified as

```
CONSTRAINT Chk_date CHECK (Copyright_date <= Year)
```

- **NOT NULL constraint:** This constraint is used to specify that an attribute will not accept *null* values. For example, the `NOT NULL` constraint for the attribute `Page_count` of `BOOK` relation can be specified as

```
Page_count Numeric (4) NOT NULL
```

The `NOT NULL` constraint can be specified only as a column-level constraint and not as a table-level constraint. This constraint can also be specified using the `CHECK` constraint.

- **FOREIGN KEY constraint:** This constraint ensures that the foreign key value in the referencing relation must exist in the primary key attribute of the referenced relation, that is, foreign key references the primary key attribute of a referenced relation. For example, the attribute `P_ID` of the relation `BOOK` can be specified as a foreign key, which refers to the primary key `P_ID` of relation `PUBLISHER` as

```
P_ID VARCHAR(4) REFERENCES PUBLISHER(P_ID)
```

When `FOREIGN KEY` constraint is applied on more than one attribute, it is specified as a table-level constraint. For example, attributes `ISBN` and `R_ID` of relation `REVIEW` can be declared as foreign keys as

```
FOREIGN KEY (ISBN) REFERENCES BOOK(ISBN)
FOREIGN KEY (R_ID) REFERENCES AUTHOR(A_ID)
```

6. Write appropriate DDL commands to define PUBLISHER, BOOK, AUTHOR, AUTHOR_BOOK and REVIEW relations of the *Online Book* database.

Ans: DDL commands to define PUBLISHER, BOOK, AUTHOR, AUTHOR_BOOK and REVIEW relations of *Online Book* database are as follows:

```
CREATE TABLE PUBLISHER
    (   P_ID            VARCHAR(4),
        Pname           VARCHAR(50)      NOT NULL,
        Address         VARCHAR(50),
        State           VARCHAR(15),
        Phone           VARCHAR(20),
        Email_id        VARCHAR(30),
        PRIMARY KEY(P_ID)
    );
CREATE TABLE BOOK
    (   ISBN            VARCHAR(15),
        Book_title      VARCHAR(50)      NOT NULL,
        Category        VARCHAR(20),
        Price           NUMERIC(6,2),
        Copyright_date  NUMERIC(4),
        Year            NUMERIC(4),
        Page_count      NUMERIC(4),
        P_ID            VARCHAR(4)       NOT NULL,
        CONSTRAINT Chk_price CHECK (Price BETWEEN 20 AND 200),
        PRIMARY KEY(ISBN),
        FOREIGN KEY(P_ID) REFERENCES PUBLISHER(P_ID)
    );
```

```
CREATE TABLE AUTHOR
    (   A_ID            VARCHAR(4),
        Aname           VARCHAR(30)     NOT NULL,
        State           VARCHAR(15),
        City            VARCHAR(15),
        Zip             VARCHAR(10),
        Phone           VARCHAR(20),
        URL             VARCHAR(30),
        PRIMARY KEY(A_ID)
    );
CREATE TABLE AUTHOR_BOOK
    (   A_ID            VARCHAR(4)      NOT NULL,
        ISBN            VARCHAR(15)     NOT NULL,
        FOREIGN KEY(A_ID) REFERENCES AUTHOR(A_ID),
        FOREIGN KEY(ISBN) REFERENCES BOOK(ISBN)
    );
CREATE TABLE REVIEW
    (   R_ID            VARCHAR(4)      NOT NULL,
        ISBN            VARCHAR(15)     NOT NULL,
        Rating          NUMERIC(2),
        PRIMARY KEY(R_ID, ISBN),
        CONSTRAINT Chk_rating CHECK (Rating BETWEEN 1 AND 10),
        FOREIGN KEY(R_ID) REFERENCES AUTHOR(A_ID),
        FOREIGN KEY(ISBN) REFERENCES BOOK(ISBN)
    );
```

7. Explain the following commands with examples:

(a) ALTER TABLE **(b) DROP TABLE** **(c) SELECT**

Ans(a): This command is used to make changes in the structure of a relation in the form of adding a new attribute, redefining an attribute or dropping attributes from a relation. The ALTER TABLE command can be used for the following purposes:

- to add an attribute
- to modify the definition of an attribute
- to drop an attribute
- to add a constraint
- to drop a constraint
- to rename an attribute and relation

Adding an attribute

The new attribute can be added to the relation by using the ADD clause of the ALTER TABLE command. For example, the command to add a new attribute Pname in the relation BOOK can be specified as

```
ALTER TABLE BOOK ADD Pname VARCHAR(10);
```

Modifying an attribute

Any attribute of a relation can be modified by using the MODIFY clause of the ALTER TABLE command. It can be used to change either its data type or size or both. The attribute to be modified must be empty before modification. For example, the command to change the data type and size of the attribute Pname can be specified as

```
ALTER TABLE BOOK MODIFY Pname VARCHAR(50);
```

Dropping an attribute

Sometimes, it is required to remove an attribute, which is no longer required from a relation. The DROP COLUMN clause of the ALTER TABLE command can be used to remove undesirable attributes from a relation. For example, the command to remove the attribute Pname from the relation BOOK can be specified as

```
ALTER TABLE BOOK DROP COLUMN Pname;
```

Adding a constraint

Different types of constraints can be added to the definition of an already existing relation. For example, the commands to add different types of constraints for the different attributes of the BOOK relation are as follows:

```
ALTER TABLE BOOK ADD CHECK(Book_title <> '');
ALTER TABLE BOOK ADD CONSTRAINT Cons_1 UNIQUE(ISBN);
ALTER TABLE BOOK ADD FOREIGN KEY(P_ID) REFERENCES PUBLISHER;
```

Dropping a constraint

Any of the constraint defined can be dropped, provided it is given a name when specified. For example, the constraint Cons_1 specified on attribute ISBN can be dropped as

```
ALTER TABLE BOOK DROP CONSTRAINT Cons_1;
```

In addition, the DEFAULT and NOT NULL constraint can be dropped as

```
ALTER TABLE BOOK ALTER COLUMN Category DROP DEFAULT;
ALTER TABLE BOOK ALTER COLUMN Page_count DROP NOT NULL;
```

Renaming an attribute

The name of an attribute of a relation can be modified by using the RENAME COLUMN … TO clause. For example, the command to modify the name of an attribute Page_count can be specified as

```
ALTER TABLE BOOK RENAME COLUMN Page_count TO P_count;
```

Renaming a relation

In addition to renaming an attribute, the name of a relation can also be modified using the RENAME TO clause. For example, the command to rename the relation BOOK to a new name can be specified as

```
ALTER TABLE BOOK RENAME TO Book_detail;
```

Ans(b): This command is used to remove an already existing relation, which is no more required as a part of a database. For example, the command to remove the relation Book_detail can be specified as

```
DROP TABLE Book_detail;
```

The two clauses that can be used with the DROP TABLE command are CASCADE and RESTRICT. If the CASCADE clause is used, all constraints and views that reference the relation to be removed are also dropped automatically. On the other hand, the RESTRICT clause, prevents a relation to be dropped if it is referenced by any of the constraints or views. These clauses can be used with the DROP TABLE command as

```
DROP TABLE Book_detail CASCADE;
DROP TABLE Book_detail RESTRICT;
```

Ans(c): This command is used to retrieve a subset of tuples or attributes from one or more relations. For example, the command to retrieve the attributes ISBN, Book_title and Category from the relation BOOK can be specified as

```
SELECT ISBN, Book_title, Category FROM BOOK;
```

Note that the order of the attributes appearing in the command can be different from the order of attributes in the relation. When all the attributes of a relation has to be retrieved, then instead of specifying a list of all attributes in the SELECT command, the symbol asterisk (*) denoting 'all attributes' can be used as

```
SELECT * FROM BOOK;
```

To eliminate duplicate tuples from the resultant relation, the keyword DISTINCT is used in the SELECT command. Hence, the command to display only the unique values for the attribute Category can be specified as

```
SELECT DISTINCT Category FROM BOOK;
```

The SELECT command can be used to perform simple numeric computations on the data stored in a relation. SQL allows using scalar expressions and constants along with the attribute list. For example, the command to display the incremented value of the price of books by 10% along with the attributes Book_title, Category and Price can be specified as

```
SELECT Book_title, Category, Price, Price+Price*.10
FROM BOOK;
```

WHERE clause: The WHERE clause is used when we want to retrieve the tuples based on a certain condition. A particular tuple is retrieved only if it satisfies the condition in the WHERE clause.

For example, the command to retrieve the attributes Book_title, Category and Price of those books from the BOOK relation whose Category is *Novel* can be specified as

```
SELECT Book_title, Category, Price FROM BOOK
WHERE Category = 'Novel';
```

8. Explain the concept of aliasing and tuple variables in SQL.

Ans: The attributes of a relation can be given an alternate name using an AS clause in a SELECT command. Note that the alternate name is provided within the query only. For example, consider the command given here.

```
SELECT Book_title AS Title, P_ID AS Publisher_ID
FROM BOOK;
```

In this command, the attribute Book_title is renamed as Title and P_ID as Publisher_ID. An AS clause can also be used to define tuple variables. A tuple variable is associated with a particular relation and is defined in the FROM clause. For example, to retrieve details of publishers publishing books of the language book category, the command can be specified as

```
SELECT P.P_ID, Pname, Address, Phone
FROM BOOK AS B, PUBLISHER AS P
WHERE P.P_ID = B.P_ID AND Category = 'Language Book';
```

In this command, tuple variables B and P are defined, which are associated with the relations BOOK and PUBLISHER, respectively.

9. What is the purpose of the BETWEEN operator and the IN operator? Explain with examples.

Ans: BETWEEN operator: The BETWEEN comparison operator can be used to simplify the condition in the WHERE clause that specifies numeric values based on ranges. For example, the command to retrieve details of all the books with a price between *20* and *30* can be specified as

```
SELECT * FROM BOOK
WHERE Price BETWEEN 20 AND 30;
```

Similarly, the NOT BETWEEN operator can also be used to retrieve tuples that do not belong to the specified range.

IN operator: The IN operator is used to specify a list of values. The IN operator selects values that match any value in a given list of values. For example, the command to retrieve the book details belonging to the categories *Textbook* or *Novel* can be specified as

```
SELECT *
FROM BOOK
WHERE Category IN ('Textbook', 'Novel');
```

Similarly, the NOT IN operator can also be used to retrieve tuples that do not belong to the specified list.

10. Which operator of SQL is used to specify string patterns in the queries? Explain in detail with examples.

Ans: In SQL, the LIKE operator is used to specify string patterns in the queries. Different string patterns are specified by using two special wildcard characters, *percent* (%) and *underscore* (_). The % character is used to match the substring with any number of characters, whereas, _ is used to match the substring with only one character. Pattern matching is case-sensitive as uppercase characters are considered different from lowercase characters. Some of the examples are:

- 'A%' matches any string beginning with character *A*
- '%A' matches any string ending with character *A*
- 'A%A' matches any string beginning and ending with character *A*
- '%AO%' matches any string with character *AO* appearing anywhere in a string as substring.
- 'A__' matches any string beginning with character *A* and is followed by exactly two characters
- '__A' matches any string ending with character *A* and is preceded by exactly two characters
- 'A___D' matches any string beginning with character *A*, ending with the character *D* and with exactly three characters in between

Consider the following queries to illustrate the use of the LIKE operator:

The command to retrieve details of all the authors, whose name begins with the characters *Jo* can be specified as

```
SELECT * FROM AUTHOR WHERE Aname LIKE 'Jo%';
```

The command to retrieve details of all the authors, whose name begins with the characters *James* followed by exactly five characters, can be specified as

```
SELECT * FROM AUTHOR WHERE Aname LIKE 'James_____';
```

The special pattern characters (`%` and `_`) can be included as a literal in the string by preceding the character by an escape character. The escape character is specified after the string using the `ESCAPE` keyword. Any character not appearing in a string to be matched can be defined as an escape character. For example, consider the following pattern, in which backslash (\) is used as an escape character:

`LIKE 'A\%b%' ESCAPE '\'`, searches the strings beginning with the characters *A%b*

11. Explain various set operations available in SQL with examples.

Ans: In SQL, the set operations like union, intersection and difference are implemented by using `UNION`, `INTERSECT` and `MINUS` operations, respectively.

`UNION` operation: It is used to retrieve tuples from more than one relation and it also eliminates duplicate tuples. For example, the command to find the union of all the tuples with `Price` less than *40* and all the tuples with `Price` greater than *30* from the `BOOK` relation can be specified as

```
(SELECT * FROM BOOK WHERE Price<40)
UNION
(SELECT * FROM BOOK WHERE Price>30);
```

`INTERSECT` operation: It is used to retrieve common tuples from more than one relation. For example, the command to find the intersection of all the tuples with `Price` less than *40* and all the tuples with `Price` greater than *30* from the `BOOK` relation can be specified as

```
(SELECT *
FROM BOOK
WHERE Price<40)
INTERSECT
(SELECT *
FROM BOOK
WHERE Price>30);
```

`MINUS` operation: It is used to retrieve those tuples present in one relation, which are not present in other relations. For example, the command to find the difference (using `MINUS` operation) of all the tuples with `Price` less than *40* and all the tuples with `Price` greater than *30* from the `BOOK` relation can be specified as

```
(SELECT * FROM BOOK WHERE Price<40)
MINUS
(SELECT * FROM BOOK WHERE Price>30);
```

The `UNION`, `INTERSECT` and `MINUS` operations automatically eliminate the duplicate tuples from the result. However, if all the duplicate tuples are to be retained, the `ALL` keyword can be used with these operations.

12. Which clause of the `SELECT` command can be used to change the order of tuples in a relation? Explain with examples.

Ans: The `ORDER BY` clause can be used with the `SELECT` command to change the order of tuples in a relation. The tuples can be arranged on the basis of the values of one or more attributes.

For example, the command to display the tuples of the relation `BOOK`, on the basis of `Price` attribute can be specified as

```
SELECT * FROM BOOK ORDER BY Price;
```

By default, the `ORDER BY` clause arranges the tuples in an ascending order on the basis of values of the specified attribute. However, the tuples can be sorted in a descending order by using the `DESC` keyword. For example, the command to sort tuples of the relation `BOOK` on the basis of the `Price` attribute in the descending order can be specified as

```
SELECT * FROM BOOK ORDER BY Price DESC;
```

Tuples can also be sorted on the basis of more than one attribute. This can be done by specifying more than one attribute in the `ORDER BY` clause.

13. Explain the following commands with examples:
(a) INSERT (b) UPDATE (c) DELETE

Ans(a): This command is used to insert tuples in a relation. This command adds a single tuple at a time in a relation. The syntax to add a tuple in a relation is

```
INSERT INTO <table_name> [(<attribute_list>)] VALUES
(<value_list>);
```

where `value_list` is the list of values to be inserted in the corresponding attributes listed in `attribute_list`.

For example, the command to add a tuple in the relation `BOOK` can be specified as

```
INSERT INTO BOOK (ISBN, Book_title, Category, Price, Copyright_
date, Year, Page_count, P_ID)
VALUES ('001-987-760-9','C++', 'Textbook', 40, 2004, 2005, 800,
'P001');
```

Tuples can be inserted into a relation by omitting the attribute list from the command. That is, the tuple can also be inserted as

```
INSERT INTO BOOK
VALUES ('001-987-760-9', 'C++', 'Textbook', 40, 2004, 2005, 800,
'P001');
```

Ans(b): This command is used to make changes in the values of attributes of the relation. The syntax for update command is

```
UPDATE <table_name> SET <attribute> = New_value [WHERE Clause]
```

The `SET` clause in the `UPDATE` command specifies the attributes to be modified and the new values to be assigned to them. The `WHERE` clause is also required to specify the tuples for which the attributes are to be modified, otherwise the value for all the tuples in the relation will be modified. For example, the command to modify the `City` to *New York* for the author whose name is *Lewis Ian* can be specified as

```
UPDATE AUTHOR SET City = 'New York'
WHERE Aname = 'Lewis Ian';
```

The command to modify `State` and `Phone` for the publisher *Bright Publications* can be specified as

```
UPDATE PUBLISHER
SET State = 'Georgia', Phone = '27643676'
WHERE Pname = 'Bright Publications';
```

Ans(c): This command is used to remove tuples, which are no more required as a part of a relation. Tuples can be deleted from only one relation at a time. The syntax for the DELETE command is

```
DELETE FROM <table_name> [WHERE Clause]
```

The condition in the WHERE clause of the DELETE command is used to specify the tuples to be deleted. If the WHERE clause is omitted, all the tuples of a relation are deleted; however, the relation remains in the database as an empty relation. For example to delete those tuples from the BOOK relation, whose category is *Novel*, the command can be specified as

```
DELETE FROM BOOK WHERE Category = 'Novel';
```

14. Explain the concept of *null* values in SQL.

Ans: SQL allows an attribute to have *null* values. The *null* value usually represents a missing value having one of the three interpretations—value is unknown, value is not available or the attribute is not applicable for a particular tuple. However, SQL does not distinguish between the different meanings of *null*. The *null* value in an attribute for a relation can be searched using the IS NULL predicate in the WHERE clause. For example, the command to retrieve the details of publishers not having an email ID can be specified as

```
SELECT * FROM PUBLISHER WHERE Email_id IS NULL;
```

The predicate IS NOT NULL can be used to check whether an attribute contains a non-null value. For example, to retrieve the details of publishers having an email ID, the command can be specified as

```
SELECT * FROM PUBLISHER WHERE Email_id IS NOT NULL;
```

15. What is the role of aggregate functions in SQL queries?

Ans: **Aggregate functions** process a set of values taken as the input and return a single value as a result. The SQL provides five built-in aggregate functions, namely AVG, MIN, MAX, SUM and COUNT. The SUM and AVG functions work for numeric values only, whereas other functions can work for numeric as well as non-numeric values, like strings, date, time, etc.

For example, the command to find the average price, maximum price and minimum price of books in the BOOK relation can be specified as

```
SELECT AVG(Price), MAX(Price), MIN(Price) FROM BOOK;
```

The COUNT(*) function is used to count the total number of tuples in the resultant relation, whereas, COUNT() is used to count the number of non-null values in a particular attribute. For example, the command to find the total number of tuples in the relation PUBLISHER can be specified as

```
SELECT COUNT(*) FROM PUBLISHER;
```

To find the number of non-null values in the attribute Category of the Book relation, the command can be specified as

```
SELECT COUNT(Category) FROM PUBLISHER;
```

If duplicate values are to be eliminated, the DISTINCT keyword can be used and the command can be specified as

```
SELECT COUNT(DISTINCT Category) FROM BOOK;
```

16. Explain how the GROUP BY clause works. What is the difference between WHERE and HAVING clauses? Explain with the help of an example.

Ans: The GROUP BY clause when used in a SELECT command divides the relation into groups on the basis of values of one or more attributes. After dividing the relation into groups, the aggregate functions can be applied on the individual group independently. The aggregate functions are performed separately for each group and return the corresponding result value separately. For example, the command to calculate the average price for each category of book in the BOOK relation can be specified as

```
SELECT AVG(Price) FROM BOOK GROUP BY Category;
```

To calculate the maximum, minimum and average price of the books published by each publisher, the command can be specified as

```
SELECT MAX(Price), MIN(Price), AVG(Price) FROM BOOK GROUP BY P_ID;
```

Conditions can be placed on the groups using the HAVING clause. For example, the command to retrieve the book categories for which the number of books published is less than *5* can be specified as

```
SELECT Category, COUNT(*)FROM BOOK GROUP BY Category HAVING
COUNT(*)<5;
```

More than one condition can be specified in the HAVING clause by using logical operators.

For example, the command to retrieve the average price and the average page count for each category of books with an average price greater than *30* and an average page count less than *900* can be specified as

```
SELECT Category, AVG(Price), AVG(Page_count)
FROM BOOK
GROUP BY Category
HAVING AVG(Price)>30 AND AVG(Page_count)<900;
```

Difference between WHERE and HAVING clauses: The HAVING clause places conditions on groups, whereas the WHERE clause is used to place conditions on the individual tuples. Another difference between the WHERE and HAVING clause is that conditions specified in the WHERE clause cannot include aggregate functions, whereas the HAVING clause can.

17. How are queries based on joins expressed in SQL? Explain the various join conditions.

Ans: Queries based on joins are those queries that combine the tuples from two or more relations. In SQL, such types of queries are expressed by specifying more than one relation in the FROM clause of the SELECT command. The condition on the basis of which relations are joined is known as the **join condition**. For example, the command to retrieve details of both book and publishers, where P_ID attribute in both the relations has identical values can be specified as

```
SELECT * FROM BOOK, PUBLISHER WHERE BOOK.P_ID=PUBLISHER.P_ID;
```

Alias names can also be used for the relations to make the command simple as

```
SELECT * FROM BOOK AS B, PUBLISHER AS P WHERE B.P_ID=P.P_ID;
```

This type of join query in which tuples are concatenated on the basis of the equality condition is known as an **equi-join query**. The resultant relation of this query consists of two columns for the attribute P_ID having identical values, one from the BOOK relation and another from the PUBLISHER relation. This can be avoided by explicitly specifying the name of attributes to be included in the resultant relation. Such a type of command can be specified as

```
SELECT ISBN, Book_title, Price, B.P_ID, Pname
FROM BOOK AS B, PUBLISHER AS P
WHERE B.P_ID=P.P_ID;
```

As a result of this command only one column for the attribute P_ID from the relation BOOK is displayed in the result. This type of query is known as a **natural join query**. In addition, some additional conditions can also be given apart from the join condition to make the selection of tuples more specific.

18. Explain the concept of nested queries with examples.

Ans: When a query is defined in the WHERE clause of another query, it is known as a **nested query** or **subquery**. The query in which another query is nested is known as an **enclosing query**. The result returned by the subquery is used by the enclosing query for specifying the conditions. Several levels of nested queries can be defined. That is, the query can be defined inside another query a number of times. For example, the command to retrieve ISBN, Book_title and Category of a book with minimum price can be specified as

```
SELECT ISBN, Book_title, Category FROM BOOK
WHERE PRICE = (SELECT MIN (Price) FROM BOOK);
```

In this command, first the nested query returns a minimum Price from the BOOK relation, which is used by the enclosing query to retrieve the required tuples.

19. Discuss the different operators in SQL, which are used with subqueries/nested queries.

Ans: SQL provides three useful operators that are generally used with subqueries. These are ANY, ALL and EXISTS.

- The **ANY operator** compares a value with any of the values in a list or returned by the subquery. This operator returns a *false* value if the subquery returns no tuple.
  For example, the command to retrieve details of books with a price equal to any of the books belonging to the *Novel* category can be specified as

```
SELECT ISBN, Book_title, Price
FROM BOOK
WHERE Price = ANY (SELECT Price
                   FROM BOOK
                   WHERE Category = 'Novel');
```

  In addition to the ANY operator, the **IN** operator can also be used to compare a single value to the set of multiple values. For example, the command to retrieve the details of books belonging to a category with a page count greater than *300* can be specified as

```
SELECT *
FROM BOOK
WHERE Category IN (SELECT Category
                   FROM BOOK
                   WHERE Page_count >300);
```

  In case the nested query returns a single attribute and a single tuple, the query result will be a single value. In such a situation, the = can be used instead of the IN operator for the comparison.
- The **ALL operator** compares a value to every value in a list returned by the subquery. For example, the command to retrieve details of books with price greater than the price of all the books belonging to *Novel* category can be specified as

```
SELECT ISBN, Book_title, Price
FROM BOOK
WHERE Price > ALL (SELECT Price
```

```
        FROM BOOK
        WHERE Category = 'Novel');
```

- The **EXISTS operator** evaluates to *true* if a subquery returns at least one tuple as a result; otherwise, it returns a *false* value. For example, the command to retrieve the details of publishers having at least one book published can be specified as

```
SELECT P_ID, Pname, Address
FROM PUBLISHER
WHERE EXISTS (SELECT *
              FROM BOOK
              WHERE PUBLISHER.P_ID = BOOK.P_ID);
```

On the other hand, the **NOT EXISTS operator** evaluates to *true* if a subquery returns no tuple as a result. For example, the command to retrieve the details of publishers having not published any book can be specified as

```
SELECT P_ID, Pname, Address
FROM PUBLISHER
WHERE NOT EXISTS (SELECT *
                  FROM BOOK
                  WHERE PUBLISHER.P_ID = BOOK.P_ID);
```

20. What are assertions? Why are they necessary?

Ans: There are some data integrities, which cannot be specified using the constraints like PRIMARY KEY, NOT NULL, UNIQUE, CHECK, etc. Such a type of constraints can be specified using the assertions. The DBMS enforces the assertion on the database and the constraints specified in assertion must not be violated. Assertions are always checked whenever modifications are done in corresponding relation. The syntax to create an assertion can be specified as

```
CREATE ASSERTION <assertion_name>
CHECK (<condition>);
```

The assertion name is used to identify the constraints specified by the assertion and can be used for modification and deletion of assertion, whenever required. DBMS tests the assertion for its validity when it is created. An assertion is implemented by writing a query that retrieves any tuple that violates the specified condition. Then this query is placed inside a NOT EXISTS clause, which indicates that the result of this query must be empty. Hence, the assertion is violated whenever the result of this query is not empty. For example, the price of textbook must not be less than the minimum price of a novel, the assertion for this requirement can be specified as

```
CREATE ASSERTION price_constraint
CHECK(NOT EXISTS(
          SELECT *
          FROM BOOK
          WHERE Category= 'Textbook' AND
                   (Price<(SELECT MIN(Price)
                   FROM BOOK
                   WHERE Category='Novel')
                   )
          )
);
```

21. What is the purpose of view in SQL? How can you create a view?

Ans: A view is a virtual relation, whose contents are derived from already existing relations and it does not exist in physical form. The contents of view are determined by executing a query based on any relation and it does not form the part of database schema. Each time a view is referred to, its contents are derived from the relations on which it is based. A view can be used like any other relation, which is, it can be queried, inserted into, deleted from and joined with other relations or views, though with some limitations on update operations. For example, the command to create a view containing details of books, which belong to Textbook and Language Book categories, can be specified as

```
CREATE VIEW BOOK_1
AS SELECT * FROM BOOK
WHERE Category IN ('Textbook', 'Language Book');
```

This command creates a view, named as BOOK_1, having details of books satisfying the condition specified in the WHERE clause.

Views can be based on more than one relation and such views are known as **complex views**. For example, the command to create a view consisting of attributes Book_title, Category, Price and P_ID of the BOOK relation, Pname and State of the PUBLISHER relation can be specified as

```
CREATE VIEW BOOK_3
AS SELECT Book_title, Category, Price, BOOK.P_ID, Pname, State
FROM BOOK, PUBLISHER
WHERE BOOK.P_ID = PUBLISHER.P_ID;
```

22. What are the conditions under which views can be updated? How can a view be made non-updateable?

Ans: A view is updateable if it is based on a single relation and the update query can be mapped on to the already existing relation successfully under certain conditions. Any view can be made non-updateable by adding the WITH READ ONLY clause. That is, no INSERT UPDATE or DELETE command can be carried over that view.

23. What are stored procedures? When are they beneficial? Give the syntax and example of creating a procedure and function in SQL.

Ans: Stored procedures are procedures or functions that are stored and executed by the DBMS at the database server machine. In SQL standard, stored procedures are termed as **persistent stored modules** (PSM), as these procedures, like data, are persistently stored by the DBMS. Stored procedures improve performance, as these procedures are compiled only at the time of their creation or modifications. Hence, whenever these procedures are called for the execution, the time for compilation is saved.

Stored procedures are beneficial when a procedure is required by different applications located at remote sites, as stored procedures are located at the server site and can be invoked by any of the applications. This eliminates duplication of efforts in writing the SQL application logic and makes code maintenance easy.

The syntax for creating a stored procedure is given as

```
CREATE PROCEDURE <name> (<parameters_1, ..., parameters_n>)
<local_declarations>
<body of procedure>;
```

Parameters and local declarations are optional and if declared must be of valid SQL data types. Parameters declared must have one of the three modes, namely `IN`, `OUT` or `INOUT` specified for it. Parameters specified with the `IN` mode are arguments passed to the stored procedure and act like a constant, whereas `OUT` parameters act like an un-initialized variables and they cannot appear on the right-hand side of the = symbol. Parameters with the `INOUT` mode have combined properties of both the `IN` and `OUT` mode. For example, the procedure to update the value of the price of a book with a given `ISBN` of the relation `BOOK` can be specified as

```
CREATE PROCEDURE Update_price (IN B_ISBN VARCHAR(15),
IN New_Price NUMERIC(6,2))
UPDATE BOOK
SET Price = New_Price
WHERE ISBN = B_ISBN;
```

Procedures cannot return a value; thus, when a value is required to be returned to the calling program, functions are required. The syntax for creating a function is

```
CREATE FUNCTION <name> (<parameters1, ..., parametersn>)
RETURNS <return_type>
<local_declarations>
<body of function>;
```

For example, the function returning the rating of a book with a given `ISBN` and author ID can be specified as

```
CREATE FUNCTION Book_rating (IN B_ISBN VARCHAR(15),
IN Au_ID VARCHAR(4))
RETURNS NUMERIC(2)
DECLARE B_rating NUMERIC(2)
SET B_rating=(SELECT Rating FROM REVIEW WHERE ISBN=B_ISBN AND
R_ID = Au_ID);
RETURN B_rating;
```

24. What are triggers? How are they created? Explain with an example how triggers offer a powerful mechanism for dealing with the changes to database.

Ans: A trigger is a type of stored procedure that is executed automatically when some database-related events like, insert, update, delete, etc. occur. Triggers, unlike procedures, do not accept any arguments. The main aim of triggers is to maintain data integrity and also one can design a trigger for recording information, which can be used for auditing purposes. The trigger can be created as

```
CREATE TRIGGER <trigger_name>
[BEFORE or AFTER][INSERT or UPDATE or DELETE]ON <relation_name>
[FOR EACH ROW]
WHEN <condition>
<statements>;
```

For example, when the value in the `Phone` attribute of a new inserted tuple of a relation `AUTHOR` is empty, indicating the absence of a phone number, the trigger to insert a *null* value in this attribute can be specified as

```
CREATE TRIGGER Setnull_phone BEFORE INSERT ON AUTHOR
REFERENCING NEW ROW AS nr
```

```
FOR EACH ROW
WHEN nr.Phone = ' '
SET nr.Phone = NULL;
```

The FOR EACH ROW clause makes sure that a trigger is executed for every single tuple processed. Such a type of trigger is known as the **row-level trigger**, whereas the trigger that is executed only once for a specified statement, regardless of the number of tuples being effected as a result of that statement, is known as a **statement-level trigger**. The FOR EACH STATEMENT clause specifies the trigger as a statement-level trigger. Triggers can be enabled and disabled by using the ALTER TRIGGER command, and the triggers that are not required can be removed by using the DROP TRIGGER command.

Triggers offer a powerful mechanism for dealing with the changes made to the database as they can be used for the following purposes:

- Implementing and maintaining complex integrity constraints.
- Recording the changes for auditing purposes.
- Automatically passing a signal to other programs that action needs to be taken whenever specific changes are made to a relation.

25. What do you understand by an active database? What are the three parts of triggers?

Ans: A database having triggers associated with it is known as an **active database**. A trigger consists of three parts:

- **Event:** Any change in the database that activates the trigger.
- **Condition:** When the trigger is activated, the condition is checked.
- **Action:** A procedure that is to be executed whenever the trigger is activated and the corresponding condition is satisfied.

In other words, a trigger is an event–condition–action rule that states that whenever a specified event occurs and the condition is satisfied, the corresponding action must be executed.

26. What do you understand by an embedded SQL? How are variables declared and used in an embedded SQL? Explain with examples.

Ans: Embedded SQL refers to the use of SQL statements within a host language program. For accessing a database from any application program, the SQL statements are embedded within an application program written in host language. These statements are also known as static, that is, they do not change at the run-time.

Variables of host language can be referred in SQL statements. Such variables are also known as **host variables** and are prefixed by a colon (:) when they appear in SQL statements and are declared between the commands EXEC SQL BEGIN DECLARE SECTION and EXEC SQL END DECLARE SECTION.

For example, the declaration of variables corresponding to the attributes of the relation BOOK is given below:

```
EXEC SQL BEGIN DECLARE SECTION;
    varchar c_ISBN[15], c_book_title[50], c_category[20];
    char c_p_id[4];
    int c_copyright_date, c_year, c_page_count;
    float c_price;
    int SQLCODE;
    char SQLSTATE[6];
EXEC SQL END DECLARE SECTION;
```

Before executing any SQL statements, the host program must establish a connection with the database as

```
EXEC SQL CONNECT TO <server_name> AS <connection_name>
AUTHORIZATION <user_name and password>;
```

In this command, `server_name` identifies the server to which a connection is to be established and the `connection_name` is the name provided to the connection. In addition, `user_name` and `password` identify the authorized user. While programming, more than one connection can be established with only one connection active at a time. When a connection is no longer needed, it can be ended by using the command

```
EXEC SQL DISCONNECT <connection_name>;
```

Assuming that the required connection is already established, the command to insert a tuple in a relation using host variables can be specified as

```
EXEC SQL
INSERT INTO BOOK
VALUES(:c_ISBN, :c_book_title, :c_category, :c_price, :c_copy-
right_date, :c_year, :c_page_count, :c_p_id);
```

27. What problem is faced while using an embedded SQL and how is it addressed by cursors? Explain with examples.

Ans: In an embedded SQL, only a single tuple can be retrieved. However, while programming, more than one tuple satisfying the condition may also be retrieved. To deal with such a situation, the concept of cursors can be used. **Cursor** is a mechanism that provides a way to retrieve multiple tuples from a relation and then process each tuple individually in a host program. The cursor is first opened, then processed and then closed. The cursor can be declared on any relation or any SQL statement that returns a set of tuples.

For example, the program segment to increment the price of books belonging to a given category from the relation `BOOK` by the value entered by the user can be written as

```
printf("Enter the category of the book :");
scanf("%s",c_category);
EXEC SQL DECLARE Cur1 CURSOR FOR
SELECT Book_title, Price, Year
FROM BOOK
WHERE Category=:c_category
ORDER BY Book_title
FOR UPDATE OF Price;
EXEC SQL OPEN Cur1;
EXEC SQL FETCH FROM Cur1 INTO :c_Book_title, :c_Price, :c_Year
while(SQLCODE==0)
{
    printf("Enter the increment amount :");
    scanf("%f",&inc);
    EXEC SQL
        UPDATE BOOK
        SET Price=Price+ :inc
        WHERE CURRENT OF Cur1;
```

```
    EXEC SQL FETCH FROM Curl INTO :c_Book_title, :c_Price,
    :c_Year;
}
EXEC SQL CLOSE Curl;
```

28. Differentiate between a dynamic SQL and an embedded SQL.

Ans: Dynamic SQL statements are SQL statements that are generated at run-time and it is placed as a string in the host variable.

Dynamic SQL is slower than an embedded SQL as it involves time to generate a query during run-time. However, it is more powerful than the embedded SQL, as queries can be generated at the run-time as per varying user requirements. For example, this sample program allows users to enter the update SQL query to be executed.

```
EXEC SQL BEGIN DECLARE SECTION;
    char sqlquerystring[200];
EXEC SQL END DECLARE SECTION;
printf("Enter the required update query : \n");
scanf("%s", sqlquerystring);
EXEC SQL PREPARE sqlcommand FROM :sqlquerystring;
EXEC SQL EXECUTE sqlcommand;
```

29. What is the purpose of ODBC in SQL? How is it implemented? Explain with examples.

Ans: Open Database Connectivity (ODBC) is a standard that provides an application programming interface (API), which is used by the application programs to establish a connection with the database. Once the connection is established, the application program can communicate with the database through queries.

An application program from the client site can access several DBMSs by making an ODBC API call. The requests from the client program are then processed at the server sites, and the results are sent back to the client program. Consider an example of C code using ODBC API given below:

```
void Example()
{
    HENV En1; //environment
    HDBC Cn; //to establish connection
    RETCODE Err;
    SQLAllocEnv(&En1);
    SQLAllocConnect(En1,&Cn);
    SQLConnect(Cn, "db.onlinebook.edu", SQL_NTS, "John", SQL_
    NTS, "Passwd", SQL_NTS);
    int c_Price1, c_Price2;
    int L1, L2;
    HSTMT st;
    char *Query = "SELECT MAX(Price), MIN(Price) FROM BOOK
                   GROUP BY Category";
    SQLAllocStmt(Cn, &st);
    Err = SQLExecDirect(st, Query, SQL_NTS);
    if (Err == SQL_SUCCESS)
```

```
    {
        SQLBindCol(st, 1, SQL_C_INT, &c_Price1, 0, &L1);
        SQLBindCol(st, 2, SQL_C_INT, &c_Price2, 0, &L2);
        while(SQLFetch(st)== SQL_SUCCESS)
        {
            printf("Maximum Price is %d", c_Price1);
            printf("Minimum Price is %d", c_Price2);
        }
    }
    SQLFreeStmt(st, SQL_DROP);
    SQLDisconnect(Cn);
    SQLFreeConnect(Cn);
    SQLFreeEnv(En1);
}
```

In the beginning of the program, the variables `En1`, `Cn` and `Err` of types `HENV`, `HDBC` and `RETCODE`, respectively, are declared. The variables `En1` and `Cn` are used to allocate an SQL environment and database connection handle, respectively. The variable `Err` is used for error detection. Further, the program establishes a connection with the database by using the `SQLConnect()` function, which accepts parameters, database connection handle (`Cn`), server (`db.onlinebook.edu`), user identifier (`John`) and the password (`Passwd`). Notice the use of constant `SQL_NTS`, which denotes that the previous argument is a null-terminated string.

After establishing a connection, the program communicates with the database by sending a query to the `SQLExecDirect()` function. The attributes of the query result are bounded to corresponding C variables by using the `SQLBindCol()` function. The parameters passed to the `SQLBindCol()` are as follows:

- **First parameter (`st`)**: Stores the result of the query
- **Second parameter (1 or 2)**: Determines the location of an attribute in the result of a query
- **Third parameter (`SQL_C_INT`)**: Specifies the required data type conversion of an attribute from SQL to C.
- **Fourth parameter (`&c_Price1` or `&c_Price2`)**: specifies the address of the C variable where the attribute value is to be stored. Note that the values of the last two parameters passed to the `SQLBindCol()` function depends on the data type of an attribute. For example, in case of fixed-length types, such as float or integer the fifth parameter is ignored and the negative value in the last parameter indicates a *null* value in an attribute.

When the resultant tuple is fetched using the `SQLFetch()` function, the attribute values of the query are stored in corresponding C variables. The `SQLFetch()` function executes the statement `st` as long as it returns the value `SQL_SUCCESS`. In each iteration of the `while` loop, the attribute values for each category are stored in corresponding C variables and are displayed through `printf` statements. The connection must be closed when it is no more required using the `SQLDisconnect()` function. Also, all the resources that are allocated must be freed.

30. What is the purpose of JDBC in SQL? Explain with examples.

Ans: JDBC provides a standard API that is used to access databases, through Java, regardless of the DBMS. The four main components required for the implementation of JDBC are application, driver manager, data source-specific drivers and corresponding data sources.

An application establishes and terminates the connection with a data source. The main goal of the driver manager is to load JDBC drivers and pass JDBC function calls from the application to the corresponding driver. The driver establishes the connection with the data source. The driver performs various basic functions like submitting requests and returning results. In addition, the driver translates data, error formats and error codes from a form that is specific to the data source into the JDBC standard. The data source processes commands from the driver and returns the results.

For understanding the connectivity of the Java program with JDBC, consider the sample program segment given below:

```
public static void Sample(String DB_id, String U_id, String
Pword)
{
    String URL="jdbc:oracle:oci8:@db.onlinebook.
      edu:100:onbook_db";
    Class.forName("oracle.jdbc.driver.OracleDriver");
    Connection Cn=DriverManager.getConnection(URL,U_id, Pword);
    Statement st = Cn.createStatement();
    try
    {
        st.executeUpdate("INSERT INTO AUTHOR VALUES('A010',
        'Smith Jones', 'Texas')");
    }
    catch(SQLException se)
    {
        System.out.println("Tuple cannot be inserted."+se);
    }
    ResultSet rs = st.executeQuery("SELECT Aname, State from AUTHOR
    WHERE City = 'Seattle'");
    while(rs.next())
    {
        System.out.println(rs.getString(1)+" "+rs.getString(2));
    }
    st.close();
    Cn.close();
}
```

In this program, the following steps are taken when writing a Java application program accessing database through JDBC function calls:

1. Appropriate drivers for the database are loaded by using `Class.forName`.
2. The `getConnection()` function of the `DriverManager` class of JDBC is used to create the connection object. The first parameter (`URL`) specifies the machine name (`db.onlinebook.edu`) where the server runs, the port number (`100`) used for communication, schema (`onbook_db`) to be used and the protocol (`jdbc:oracle:oci8`) used to communicate with the database. To connect to the database, username and password are also required, which are specified by the strings `U_id` and `Pword`, respectively, the other two parameters of the `getConnection()` function.

3. A statement handle is created for the connection established, which is used to execute an SQL statement. In this example, `st.executeUpdate` is used to execute an `INSERT` statement of SQL. The `try {..}catch{..}` is used to catch any exceptions that may arise as a result of executing this query statement.
4. Another query is executed using the statement `st.executeQuery`. The result of this may consist of a set of tuples, which is assigned to `rs` of type `ResultSet`.
5. The `next()` function is used to fetch one tuple at a time from the result set `rs`. The value of an attribute of a tuple is retrieved by using the position of the attribute. The attribute `Aname` is at first (1) position and `State` is at second (2) position. The value for the attribute can also be retrieved by using its name as shown here.

```
System.out.println(rs.getString("Aname")+" "
                        +rs.getString("State"));
```

6. The connection must be closed after it is no more required at the end of the procedure.

31. What is SQLJ? What is the significance of using SQLJ? Explain with examples.

Ans: SQLJ is a standard that has been used for embedding SQL statements in Java programming language, which is object-oriented language. In SQLJ, a pre-processor called **SQLJ translator** converts SQL statements into Java, which can be executed through the JDBC interface. Hence, it is essential to install the JDBC driver while using SQLJ. When writing SQLJ applications, regular Java code is written and SQL statements are embedded into it using a set of rules. SQLJ applications are pre-processed using the SQLJ translation program that replaces the embedded SQLJ code with calls to an SQLJ library. Any Java compiler can then compile this modified program code. The SQLJ library calls the corresponding driver, which establishes the connection with the database system. The use of SQLJ improves the productivity and manageability of the JAVA code as the code becomes compact and no run-time syntax errors occur as SQL statements are checked at the compile time. Moreover, it allows sharing of Java variables with SQL statements.

For understanding the working of SQLJ, consider a sample SQLJ program segment given here. This program retrieves the book details belonging to a given category:

```
String Book_title; float Price; String Category;
#sql iterator Bk(String Book_title, float Price);
Bk book = {SELECT Book_title, Price INTO :Book_title, :Price
FROM BOOK WHERE Category = :Category};
while(book.next())
{
    System.out.println(book.Book_title()+ ", " + book.Price());
}
book.close();
```

SQLJ statements always begin with the `#sql` keyword. The result of SQL queries is retrieved through the objects of an **iterator**, which is a type of cursor. The iterator is associated with the tuples and attributes appearing in the query result. An iterator is declared as an instance of iterator class.

32. Give steps involved in the implementation of iterators in SQLJ. Discuss two types of iterators available in SQLJ.

Ans: The implementation of an iterator in SQLJ basically goes through following four steps:

1. **Declaration of the iterator class:** In the previous example, the iterator class `Bk` is declared by using the statement

```
#sql iterator Bk(String Book_title, float Price);
```

2. **Creation and initialization of iterator object:** An object of the iterator class is created and initialized with a set of tuples returned as a result of the SQL query statement.
3. **Accessing the tuples with the help of an iterator object:** An iterator is set to the position just before the first row in the result of the query, which becomes the current tuple for the iterator. The `next()` **function** is then applied on the iterator repeatedly to retrieve the subsequent tuples from the result.
4. **Closing the iterator object:** An object of iterator is closed after all the tuples associated with the **result** of SQL query are processed.

There are two types of iterator classes, namely *named* and *positional* iterators. In case of **named iterators** both the variable types and the name of each column of the iterator is specified. This helps in retrieving the individual columns by their name. Similar to the previous example, the sample program to retrieve `Book_title` from the iterator `book`, the expression `book.Book_title()` is used. While, in case of **positional iterators**, only the variable type for each column of iterator is specified. The individual columns of the iterator are accessed using the `FETCH . . INTO` statement like embedded SQL. Both types of iterators have the same performance and can be used according to the user requirement.

33. Write SQL queries for the following based on the *Online Book* database:

(a) Retrieve the city, phone and url of the author whose name is *Lewis Ian*.

(b) Retrieve the name, address and phone of all the publishers located in *New York* state.

(c) Retrieve the title and price of all textbooks with a page count greater than *600*.

(d) Retrieve the ISBN, title and price of the books belonging to either novel or language book category.

(e) Retrieve the title and price of all books published by *Hills Publications*.

(f) Retrieve the book title, reviewers ID and rating of all textbooks.

(g) Retrieve the ID, name, url of author and category of the book *C++*.

(h) Retrieve the book title, price, author name and url for the publishers *Bright Publications*.

Ans:

(a)
```
SELECT City, Phone, URL FROM AUTHOR
WHERE Aname = 'Lewis Ian';
```
(b)
```
SELECT Pname, Address, Phone FROM PUBLISHER
WHERE State = 'New York';
```
(c)
```
SELECT Book_title, Price FROM BOOK
WHERE Category = 'Textbook' AND Page_count>600;
```
(d)
```
SELECT ISBN, Book_title, Price FROM BOOK
WHERE Category = 'Novel' OR Category = 'Language Book';
```
(e)
```
SELECT Book_title, Price FROM BOOK AS B, PUBLISHER AS P
WHERE B.P_ID=P.P_ID AND Pname='Hills Publications';
```
(f)
```
SELECT Book_title, R_ID, Rating FROM BOOK AS B, REVIEW AS R
WHERE B.ISBN=R.ISBN AND Category = 'Textbook';
```

(g) **SELECT** AB.A_ID, Aname, URL, Category **FROM** BOOK **AS** B, AUTHOR **AS** A, AUTHOR_BOOK **AS** AB **WHERE** A.A_ID=AB.A_ID **AND** AB.ISBN=B.ISBN **AND** Book_title= 'C++';

(h) **SELECT** Book_title, Price, Aname, URL **FROM** BOOK **AS** B, AUTHOR_BOOK **AS** AB, AUTHOR **AS** A, PUBLISHER **AS** P **WHERE** B.ISBN=AB.ISBN **AND** AB.A_ID=A.A_ID **AND** B.P_ID=P.P_ID **AND** Pname='Bright Publications';

34. Specify the following queries on the *Online Book* database in SQL:

(a) In the BOOK relation, increase the price of all books belonging to novel category by 10%.

(b) In the PUBLISHER relation, change the phone of *Wesley Publications* to *9256774.*

(c) Calculate and display the average, maximum and minimum price of a book from each category.

(d) Calculate and display the average, maximum and minimum price of a book from each publisher.

(e) Delete details of all the books having a page count less than *100.*

(f) Retrieve details of all the books whose name begins with character *D.*

(g) Retrieve details of all the publishers located in state *Georgia*.

(h) Retrieve details of all the authors residing in the city *New York* and whose name begins with character *J.*

(i) Retrieve the book title, name of publisher and author name of all language books.

(j) Retrieve the book details having a price that equals the average price of all the books.

(k) Retrieve details of authors residing in the same city as *Lewis Ian.*

Ans:

(a) **UPDATE** BOOK **SET** Price=Price + 0.10 * Price **WHERE** Category='Novel';

(b) **UPDATE** PUBLISHER **SET** Phone='9256774' **WHERE** Pname='Wesley Publications';

(c) **SELECT AVG**(Price), **MAX**(Price), **MIN**(Price) **FROM** BOOK **GROUP BY** Category;

(d) **SELECT AVG**(Price), **MAX**(Price), **MIN**(Price) **FROM** BOOK, PUBLISHER **WHERE** BOOK.P_ID=PUBLISHER.P_ID **GROUP BY** Pname;

(e) **DELETE FROM** BOOK **WHERE** Page_count<100;

(f) **SELECT** * **FROM** BOOK **WHERE** Book_title **LIKE** 'D%';

(g) **SELECT** * **FROM** PUBLISHER **WHERE** State='Georgia';

(h) **SELECT** * **FROM** AUTHOR **WHERE** City='New York' **AND** Aname **LIKE** 'J%';

(i) **SELECT** Book_title, Pname, Aname **FROM** BOOK, PUBLISHER, AUTHOR_BOOK, AUTHOR **WHERE** BOOK.P_ID=PUBLISHER.P_ID **AND** Book.ISBN=AUTHOR_BOOK.ISBN **AND** AUTHOR_BOOK.A_ID=AUTHOR.A_ID **AND** Category='Language BOOK';

(j) **SELECT** * **FROM** BOOK **WHERE** Price=(**SELECT AVG**(Price) **FROM** BOOK);

(k) **SELECT** * **FROM** AUTHOR **WHERE** City **IN** (**SELECT** City **FROM** AUTHOR **WHERE** Aname='Lewis Ian');

35. Give commands to create views based on the following queries of the *Online Book* database.

(a) A view containing details of all the books belonging to the textbook category.

(b) A view containing details of all the books published by the publisher *Bright Publications* and price greater than $*30*.

(c) A view containing details of all the textbooks written by author *Charles Smith*.

(d) A view containing details of all the books having page count *600* and published in the year *2004*.

Ans:

(a)
```
CREATE VIEW BOOK_1 AS SELECT * FROM BOOK
WHERE Category='Textbook';
```
(b)
```
CREATE VIEW BOOK_2 AS SELECT * FROM BOOK, PUBLISHER
WHERE BOOK.P_ID=PUBLISHER.P_ID AND Pname='Bright Publications'
AND Price>30
```
(c)
```
CREATE VIEW Textbook_Charles
AS SELECT * FROM BOOK, AUTHOR, AUTHOR_BOOK WHERE BOOK.
ISBN=AUTHOR_BOOK.ISBN AND AUTHOR_BOOK.A_ID=AUTHOR.A_ID AND
Aname='Charles Smith' AND Category='Textbook'
```
(d)
```
CREATE VIEW BOOK_3 AS SELECT * FROM BOOK
WHERE Page_count=600 AND Year=2004
```

36. Express queries given in Question 23 of Chapter 4 in SQL using various DML commands.

Ans:

(a)
```
SELECT OrderNo, OrderDate FROM CUSTOMER AS P, ORDER AS Q WHERE
P.CustNo=Q.CustNo AND City='Atlanta';
```
(b)
```
SELECT S.ItemNo, UnitPrice FROM ORDER_ITEM AS R, ITEM AS S
WHERE R.ItemNo=S.ItemNo AND Qty>50;
```
(c)
```
SELECT Q.OrderNo, OrderDate, S.ItemNo FROM ORDER AS Q, ORDER_
ITEM AS R, ITEM AS S WHERE Q.OrderNo=R.OrderNo AND R.ItemNo=S.
ItemNo AND UnitPrice>20;
```
(d)
```
SELECT P.CustNo, CName, City FROM CUSTOMER AS P, ORDER AS
Q, ORDER_ITEM AS R WHERE P.CustNo=Q.CustNo AND Q.OrderNo=R.
OrderNo AND ItemNo='I010';
```
(e)
```
SELECT R.ItemNo, UnitPrice FROM ORDER AS Q, ORDER_ITEM AS R,
ITEM AS S WHERE Q.OrderNo=R.OrderNo AND R.ItemNo=S.ItemNo AND
CustNo='C001';
```

37. Express queries given in Question 24 of Chapter 4 in SQL using various DML commands.

Ans:

(a)
```
SELECT Empname FROM WORKS WHERE Companyname='First Bank
Corporation';
```
(b)
```
SELECT P.Empname, Street, City FROM EMPLOYEE AS P, WORKS
AS Q WHERE P.Empname=Q.Empname AND Companyname='First Bank
Corporation' AND Salary>200000;
```
(c)
```
SELECT P.Empname FROM EMPLOYEE AS P, WORKS AS Q, COMPANY AS R
WHERE P.Empname=Q.Empname AND P.City=R.City AND Q.Companyname=R.
Companyname;
```

(d) **SELECT COUNT**(Empname) **FROM** WORKS **GROUP BY** Companyname;

(e) **SELECT AVG**(Salary), **MAX**(Salary), **MIN**(Salary) **FROM** WORKS **GROUP BY** Companyname;

38. Express queries given in Question 25 of Chapter 4 in SQL using various DML commands.

Ans:

(a) **SELECT** BranchID, Bname **FROM** BRANCH **WHERE** City='Seattle';

(b) **SELECT** TID, T_Type, Amount **FROM** TRANSACTION **WHERE** T_Type='Withdrawal';

(c) **SELECT** AccountNo, AType **FROM** ACCOUNT **WHERE** BranchID='B010' ;

(d) **SELECT** P.AccountNo, Aname **FROM** ACCOUNT AS P, TRANSACTION AS Q **WHERE** P.AccountNo=Q.AccountNo **AND** T_Type='Withdrawal' **AND** Amount>10000 **AND** T_Date='31 March 2007';

(e) **SELECT** AccountNo, Aname **FROM** BRANCH AS P, ACCOUNT AS Q **WHERE** P.BranchID=Q.BranchID **AND** AType='Savings' **AND** City='Los Angeles';

(f) **SELECT AVG**(Balance) **FROM** ACCOUNT AS P, BRANCH AS Q **WHERE** P.BranchID=Q.BranchID **AND** BName='AX International Bank' **AND** City='New York';

(g) **SELECT MAX**(Balance), **MIN**(Balance) **FROM** ACCOUNT AS P, BRANCH AS Q **WHERE** P.BranchID=Q.BranchID **GROUP BY** City;

39. Create a procedure to update the value of the page count of a book with a given ISBN.

Ans:

```
CREATE PROCEDURE Update_Pagecount (IN B_ISBN VARCHAR(15),
IN New_Pagecount INT ) UPDATE BOOK
SET Page_count=New_Pagecount
WHERE ISBN=B_ISBN;
```

40. Create a procedure to update the value of the phone of a publisher with a given publisher ID.

Ans:

```
CREATE PROCEDURE Update_Phone (IN New_Phone VARCHAR(20), IN PID
VARCHAR(4))
UPDATE PUBLISHER
SET Phone=New_Phone
WHERE P_ID=PID;
```

41. Create a function that returns the price of a book with a given ISBN.

Ans:

```
CREATE FUNCTION Book_price (IN B_ISBN VARCHAR(15))
RETURNS NUMERIC(6,2)
DECLARE B_price NUMERIC(6,2);
SET B_price=(SELECT Price FROM BOOK WHERE ISBN=B_ISBN);
RETURN B_price;
```

42. Create a function that searches a book with a given `ISBN` and returns the value *Old* if it is published before year *2000* and *New* if it is published in or after year *2000*.

Ans:

```
CREATE FUNCTION B_published(IN B_ISBN VARCHAR(15))
RETURNS VARCHAR(4)
DECLARE B_published NUMERIC(4)
SET B_published=(SELECT Year FROM BOOK WHERE ISBN=B_ISBN);
If B_published<2000 THEN RETURN 'Old'
    ELSE RETURN 'New'
END IF;
```

43. Create a trigger for changing the value of `Page_count` attribute to a default value *100* if the value entered by the user exceeds the upper limit of *1500* in case of insertion in the relation BOOK.

Ans:

```
CREATE TRIGGER New_Pagecount BEFORE INSERT ON BOOK
FOR EACH ROW WHEN (new.Page_count>1500)
BEGIN
new.Page_count=100;
END
```

44. Specify an embedded SQL statement to retrieve the details of author with `A_ID` value stored in the variable `C_AID`.

Ans:

```
EXEC SQL BEGIN DECLARE SECTION;
    VARCHAR C_Aname[30],C_State[15],C_City[15],C_URL[30],
      C_AID[4];
    char C_Zip[10], C_Phone[20];
EXEC SQL END DECLARE SECTION;
EXEC SQL
SELECT A_ID,Aname,State,City,Zip,Phone,URL
INTO :C_AID,:C_Aname,:C_State,:C_City,:C_Zip,:C_Phone,:C_URL
FROM AUTHOR
WHERE A_ID=C_AID;
```

45. Write a program segment that uses a cursor to update the page count of books belonging to a given publisher ID from the relation BOOK by the value entered by the user.

Ans:

```
printf("Enter the publisher ID : ");
scanf("%s", c_PID);
EXEC SQL DECLARE Cur1 CURSOR FOR
SELECT Book_title, Price, Year, Page_count
FROM BOOK
WHERE P_ID=:c_PID
```

```
ORDER BY Book_title
FOR UPDATE OF Page_count;
EXEC SQL OPEN Cur1;
EXEC SQL FETCH FROM Cur1 INTO :c_Book_title, :c_Price, :c_Year,
:c_Page_count;
while(SQLCODE ==0)
{
    printf("Enter the new page count: ");
    scanf("%d", &pg_count);
    EXEC SQL
        UPDATE BOOK
        SET Page_count =:pg_count
        WHERE CURRENT OF Cur1;
    EXEC SQL FETCH FROM Cur1 INTO :c_Book_title, :c_Price, :c_
Year, :c_Page_count;
}
EXEC SQL CLOSE Cur1;
```

46. Write an ODBC code for displaying the publisher along with the maximum price of books published by them from the BOOK relation.

Ans:

```
void Example()
{
    HENV En1; //environment
    HDBC Cn; //to establish connection
    RETCODE Err;
    SQLAllocEnv(&En1);
    SQLAllocConnect(En1,&Cn);
    SQLConnect(Cn, "db.onlinebook.edu", SQL_NTS, "John",
    SQL_NTS, "Passwd", SQL_NTS);
    char c_Pname[50]; float c_Price;
    int L1, L2;
    HSTMT st;
    char *Query = "SELECT Pname, MAX(Price) FROM BOOK, PUBLISHER
                   GROUP BY Pname HAVING BOOK.P_ID=PUBLISHER.P_ID";
    SQLAllocStmt(Cn, &st);
    Err = SQLExecDirect(st, Query, SQL_NTS);
    if (Err == SQL_SUCCESS)
    {
        SQLBindCol(st, 1, SQL_C_CHAR, &c_Pname, 0, &L1);
        SQLBindCol(st, 2, SQL_C_FLOAT, &c_Price, 0, &L2);
        while(SQLFetch(st)== SQL_SUCCESS)
        {
            printf("Publisher Name is %s", c_Pname);
            printf("Maximum Price is %f", c_Price);
        }
```

```
    }
    SQLFreeStmt(st, SQL_DROP);
    SQLDisconnect(Cn);
    SQLFreeConnect(Cn);
    SQLFreeEnv(En1);
}
```

47. Write the JDBC code for displaying the title, price and page count of books belonging to the language book category.

Ans:

```
public static void Sample(String DB_id, String U_id, String
Pword)
{
String URL = "jdbc:oracle:oci8:@db.onlinebook.edu:100:onbook_db";
Class.forName("oracle.jdbc.driver.OracleDriver");
Connection Cn=DriverManager.getConnection(URL,U_id, Pword);
Statement st = Cn.createStatement();
ResultSet rs = st.executeQuery("SELECT Book_title, Price,
    Page_count FROM BOOK WHERE Category = 'Language Book'");
  while(rs.next())
    {
        System.out.println(rs.getString(1)+ " "+ rs.getString(2)+
" " + rs.getString(3));
    }
    st.close();
    Cn.close();
}
```

48. Write the SQLJ code for retrieving the book details belonging to a given publisher.

Ans:

```
String Book_title; float Price; String Category; String Pname;
#sql iterator Bk(String Book_title, float Price, String Category);
Bk book = {SELECT Book_title, Price, Category INTO :Book_title,
:Price, :Category FROM BOOK, PUBLISHER WHERE Pname=:Pname and
BOOK.P_ID=PUBLISHER.P_ID};
while(book.next())
{
    System.out.println(book.Book_title()+", "+book.Price()
                              +", "+book.Category());
}
book.close();
```

Multiple-choice Questions

1. Which of the following constraints ensures that the foreign key value in the referencing relation must exist in the primary key attribute of the referenced relation?
   (a) Unique Key (b) Reference Key (c) Foreign key (d) Primary key

2. Which of the following SQL statements will return all the tuples from a relation named `Employee` sorted in the descending order of `Name`?
   (a) `SELECT * FROM Employee SORT BY 'Name' DESC;`
   (b) `SELECT * FROM Employee ORDER BY Name DESC;`
   (d) `SELECT * FROM Employee ORDER Name DESC;`
   (c) `SELECT * FROM Employee SORT 'Name' DESC;`
3. Which of these keywords is used to eliminate duplicate tuples from the resultant relation?
   (a) `DELETE` (b) `DISTINCT` (c) `NON DUPLICATE` (d) `EXISTS`
4. Which of these operators selects values that match any value in a given list of values?
   (a) `BETWEEN` (b) `LIKE` (c) `IN` (d) None of these
5. Which of these characters is used to match a substring with any number of characters?
   (a) `%` (b) ? (c) _ (d) `*`
6. The operation that is used to retrieve those tuples present in one relation, and not present in another relation is __________.
   (a) `UNION` (b) `INTERSECT` (c) `MINUS` (d) `DIFFERENCE`
7. Which of these is the correct command for inserting values in the `Employee` relation?
   (a) `INSERT VALUES ('John', 2000) INTO Employee;`
   (b) `INSERT ('John', 2000) INTO Employee;`
   (c) `INSERT INTO Employee VALUES ('John', 2000);`
   (d) None of these
8. The command that can be used to make changes in the name of publishers in a relation `PUBLISHER` is __________.
   (a) `UPDATE` (b) `ALTER` (c) `MODIFY` (d) None of these
9. Which of these is the correct command to change "Jon" into "John" in the `Name` attribute of the `Employee` relation?
   (a) `UPDATE Employee SET` Name = ' John' `WHERE` Name = ' Jon' ;
   (b) `ALTER Employee SET` Name = ' Jon' `INTO` Name = ' John' ;
   (c) `UPDATE Employee SET` Name = ' Jon' `INTO` Name = ' John' ;
   (d) `ALTER Employee SET Name='John' WHERE Name='Jon';`
10. Consider the following SQL statements:
    (I) DELETE FROM Customer; (II) DROP TABLE Customer;
    (a) Only statement (I) permanently removes the relation Customer
    (b) Only statement (II) permanently removes the relation Customer
    (c) Both statements (I) and (II) permanently remove the relation Customer
    (d) None of these
11. Which of the following is the valid SQL statement?
    (a) `SELECT * FROM Employee WHERE email_id IS NULL;`
    (b) `SELECT * FROM Employee WHERE IS NULL (email_id);`
    (c) `SELECT * FROM Employee WHERE email_id NULL;`
    (d) All of these
12. Which of the following will return the number of tuples in the `Employee` relation?
    (a) `SELECT COLUMNS(*) FROM Employee;`
    (b) `SELECT COUNT() FROM Employee;`

(c) `SELECT COUNT(*) FROM Employee;`
(d) All of these

13. Which of these statements is true?
    (i) The contents of view are derived from already existing relations
    (ii) View like any other relation forms the part of database schema
    (iii) A view can be queried, inserted into, deleted from and joined with other relations or views
    (a) Only (i) is true (b) Only (i) and (iii) are true
    (c) Only (ii) and (iii) are true (d) (i), (ii) and (iii) are true
14. Which of these mechanisms provides a way to retrieve multiple tuples from a relation and then process each tuple individually in a host program?
    (a) Triggers (b) Cursors (c) Assertions (d) None of these
15. Which of the following clauses is used to restrict groups returned by the `GROUP BY` clause?
    (a) `DISTINCT` (b) `WHERE` (c) `EXISTS` (d) `HAVING`

Answers

1. (c) 2. (b) 3. (b) 4. (c) 5. (a) 6. (c) 7. (c)
8. (a) 9. (a) 10. (b) 11. (a) 12. (c) 13. (b) 14. (b)
15. (d)

Relational Database Design

1. What are the features of a good relational database design?

Ans: The goal of the relational database design is to generate a set of relations having no duplicate tuples, tuples having no particular ordering associated with them and each element in the relation being atomic. To qualify as a good relational database design, it should also have the following features:

- **Minimum redundancy:** A relational database should be designed in such a way that it should have minimum redundancy. Redundancy refers to the storage of the same data in more than one location. That is, the same data are repeated in multiple tuples in the same relation or multiple relations. The main disadvantage of redundancy is the wastage of storage space. In addition, due to redundancy, certain update anomalies, such as insertion, deletion and modification anomaly, can arise.
- **Fewer null values in tuples:** Sometimes, there may be a possibility that some attributes do not apply to all tuples in a relation. That is, values of all the attributes of a tuple are not known. In that case, the *null* value can be stored in those tuples. However, *null* values do not provide a complete solution as they cannot be inserted in the primary key attributes and the attributes for which the `NOT NULL` constraint is specified. Moreover, *null* values waste storage space and may lead to some other problems such as interpreting them, accounting for them while applying aggregate functions such as `COUNT` or `AVG`, etc. Thus, in a good database, the attributes whose values may frequently be *null* are avoided. If *null* values are unavoidable, they are applied in exceptional cases only.

2. Explain various update anomalies that can arise in a relational database with examples.

Ans: In a database, certain update anomalies can arise, which are as follows:

- **Insertion anomaly:** It leads to a situation in which certain information cannot be inserted in a relation unless some other information is stored. To understand, consider a relation `BOOK_PUBLISHER` defined on schema `BOOK_PUBLISHER(ISBN, Book_title, P_ID, Pname, Phone)` and having `ISBN` as its primary key. An instance of the `BOOK_PUBLISHER` relation is shown in Figure 6.1.

  This relation suffers from insertion anomaly as the information of a new publisher cannot be inserted unless he has not published any book. Similarly, information of a new book cannot be inserted unless information regarding the publisher is not known.

ISBN	Book_title	P_ID	Pname	Phone
001-987-760-9	C++	P001	Hills Publications	7134019
001-354-921-1	Ransack	P001	Hills Publications	7134019
001-987-650-5	Differential Calculus	P001	Hills Publications	7134019
002-678-980-4	DBMS	P002	Sunshine Publishers Ltd.	6548909
002-678-880-2	Call Away	P002	Sunshine Publishers Ltd.	6548909
004-765-409-5	UNIX	P003	Bright Publications	7678985
004-765-359-3	Coordinate Geometry	P003	Bright Publications	7678985
003-456-433-6	Introduction to German Language	P004	Paramount Publishing House	9254834
003-456-533-8	Learning French Language	P004	Paramount Publishing House	9254834

Figure 6.1 Instance of the Relation BOOK_PUBLISHER

- **Deletion anomaly:** It leads to a situation in which deletion of data representing certain information results in losing data representing some other information that is associated with it. For example, in the `BOOK_PUBLISHER` relation if the tuple with a given `ISBN`, say, *003-456-433-6* is deleted, the only information about the publisher *P004* associated with that `ISBN` is also lost.
- **Modification anomaly:** It leads to a situation in which repeated data changed at one place results in inconsistency unless the same data are also changed at other places. For example, in the `BOOK_PUBLISHER` relation, change in the name of a publisher say, *Hills Publications* to *Hills Publishers Pvt. Ltd.* needs modification in multiple tuples. If the name of a publisher is not modified at all places, the same `P_ID` will show two different values for the publisher name in different tuples.

3. What do you mean by decomposition of a relation? Why is it required? Explain by giving an example.

Ans: While designing a relational database schema, certain problems that are confronted due to redundancy and *null* values can be resolved by decomposing a relation. In decomposition, a relation is replaced with a collection of smaller relations with specific relationship between them. Formally, the **decomposition** of a relation schema `R` is defined as its replacement by a set of relation schemas such that each relation schema contains a subset of the attributes of `R`.

For example, the relation schema `BOOK_PUBLISHER` (described in Question 2) has redundancy and *null* values; thus, the schema of this relation requires to be modified so that it has less redundancy of information and fewer null values. The undesirable features from the relation schema `BOOK_PUBLISHER` can be eliminated by decomposing it into two relation schemas as given here:

`BOOK_DETAIL(ISBN, Book_title, P_ID)` and
`PUBLISHER_DETAIL(P_ID, Pname, Phone)`

Figure 6.2 illustrates the decomposition of the `BOOK_PUBLISHER` relation and shows the instances corresponding to decomposed relation schemas `BOOK_DETAIL` and `PUBLISHER_DETAIL`.

BOOK_PUBLISHER

ISBN	Book_title	P_ID	Pname	Phone
001-987-760-9	C++	P001	Hills Publications	7134019
001-354-921-1	Ransack	P001	Hills Publications	7134019
001-987-650-5	Differential Calculus	P001	Hills Publications	7134019
002-678-980-4	DBMS	P002	Sunshine Publishers Ltd.	6548909
.	.	.	.	.

BOOK_DETAIL

ISBN	Book_title	P_ID
001-987-760-9	C++	P001
001-354-921-1	Ransack	P001
001-987-650-5	Differential Calculus	P001
002-678-980-4	DBMS	P002
002-678-880-2	Call Away	P002
004-765-409-5	UNIX	P003
004-765-359-3	Coordinate Geometry	P003
003-456-433-6	Introduction to German Language	P004
003-456-533-8	Learning French Language	P004

PUBLISHER_DETAIL

P_ID	Pname	Phone
P001	Hills Publications	7134019
P002	Sunshine Publishers Ltd.	6548909
P003	Bright Publications	7678985
P004	Paramount Publishing House	9254834

Figure 6.2 Decomposition

Now, a tuple for a new publisher can be inserted easily in relation PUBLISHER_DETAIL, even if no book is associated with that particular P_ID in relation BOOK_DETAIL. Similarly, a tuple for a particular P_ID in relation PUBLISHER_DETAIL can be deleted without losing any information (taking foreign key constraint into account). Moreover, name or phone for a particular P_ID can be changed by updating a single tuple in relation PUBLISHER_DETAIL. This is more efficient than updating several tuples and the scope for inconsistency is also eliminated.

4. Name three desirable properties of decomposition. Describe attribute preservation property of decomposition.

Ans: Three essential properties of decomposition include the following:

- Attribute preservation
- Lossless join
- Dependency preservation

According to the **attribute preservation property**, the decomposition of a relation schema say R into a set of relation schemas $R_1, R_2, \ldots, R_n$ must ensure that each attribute in R appears in at least one relation schema R_i (where i=1,2,...,n) so that no attributes are lost. Formally,

$$\cup R_i = R$$

5. What is functional dependency? Give examples.

Ans: Functional dependencies are the special forms of integrity constraints that generalize the concept of keys. They play a key role in developing a good database schema.

Definition: Let X and Y be the arbitrary subsets of a set of attributes of a relation schema R, then an instance r of R satisfies functional dependency (FD) X→Y, if and only if for any two tuples t_1 and t_2 in r that have $t_1[X] = t_2[X]$, they must also have $t_1[Y] = t_2[Y]$. That means, whenever two tuples of r agree on their X value, they must also agree on their Y value. Less formally, Y is functionally dependent on X, if and only if each X value in r is associated with it precisely one Y value.

The statement X→Y is read as Y is functionally dependent on X or X determines Y. The left and right sides of a functional dependency are called **determinant** and **dependent**, respectively.

Consider the relation schema BOOK_REVIEW_DETAIL(ISBN, Price, Page_count, R_ID, City, Rating) that represents review details of the books by the reviewers. The primary key of this relation is the combination of ISBN and R_ID. Note that the same book can be reviewed by different reviewers and the same reviewer can review different books. An instance of this relation schema is shown in Figure 6.3.

In this relation, the attribute Price is functionally dependent on the attribute ISBN (ISBN → Price), as tuples having the same value for the ISBN have the same value for the Price. For

ISBN	Price	Page_count	R_ID	City	Rating
001-987-760-9	25	800	A002	Atlanta	6
001-987-760-9	25	800	A008	Detroit	7
001-354-921-1	22	200	A006	Albany	7
002-678-980-4	35	860	A003	Los Angeles	5
002-678-980-4	35	860	A001	New York	2
002-678-980-4	35	860	A005	Juneau	7
004-765-409-5	26	550	A003	Los Angeles	4
004-765-359-3	40	650	A007	Austin	3
003-456-433-6	30	500	A010	Virginia Beach	5
001-987-650-5	35	450	A009	Seattle	8
002-678-880-2	25	400	A006	Albany	4
003-456-533-8	30	500	A004	Seattle	9

Figure 6.3 An Instance of BOOK_REVIEW_DETAIL Relation

example, the tuples having ISBN *001-987-760-9* have the same value *25* for Price. Similarly, the tuples having ISBN 002-678-980-4 have the same value *35* for Price. Other FDs such as ISBN → Page_count, Page_count → Price, R_ID → City are also satisfied. In addition, one more functional dependency {ISBN, R_ID}→Rating is also satisfied. That is, the attribute Rating is functionally dependent on the composite attribute {ISBN, R_ID}.

6. Define trivial and non-trivial functional dependency.

Ans: A dependency is said to be a **trivial dependency** if it is satisfied by all relations. For example, X→X is satisfied by all relations having attribute X. Similarly, XY→X is satisfied by all relations having attributes X and Y. Generally, an FD A→B is trivial, if and only if $B \subseteq A$. For example, in BOOK_REVIEW_DETAIL relation (shown in Figure 6.3), the FDs like ISBN→ISBN and {R_ID, ISBN}→ISBN are trivial dependencies.

The dependencies that are not trivial are called **non-trivial dependencies**. These are the dependencies that correspond to the essential integrity constraints.

7. Define the closure of a set of FDs.

Ans: For a given set F of functional dependencies, some other dependencies also hold. That is, some functional dependencies are implied by F. For example, consider a relation schema R (A,B,C), such that both the FDs A→B and B→C hold for R. Then, FD A→C also holds on R as C is dependent on A transitively, via B. Thus, it can be said that FD A→C is implied. The set of all FDs that are implied by a given set F of FDs is called the **closure of F**, denoted as $\mathbf{F^+}$. For a given F (if it is small), F^+ can be computed directly. However, if F is large, then some inference rules for functional dependencies are used to compute F^+.

8. Explain the inference rules for functional dependencies.

Ans: While computing the closure of a given set of FDs (say F), certain inference rules are required to find FDs that are logically implied by F. Armstrong proposed a set of inference rules or axioms (also known as **Armstrong's axioms**) to find logically implied functional dependencies. These rules are applied repeatedly for a given set F of functional dependencies so that all of F^+ can be inferred. Let A, B, C and D be the arbitrary subsets of the set of attributes of a relation schema R and A U B is denoted by AB, then Armstrong's axioms can be stated as:

- **Reflexivity rule:** If $B \subseteq A$, then A→B holds.
- **Augmentation rule:** If A→B holds, then AC→BC holds.
- **Transitivity rule:** If both A→B and B→C hold, then A→C holds.

Computing F^+ using Armstrong's axioms directly is quite complicated. Thus, to simplify the task of computing F^+ from F, additional inference rules are derived from Armstrong's axioms. These rules are as follows:

- **Decomposition rule:** If A→BC then A→B holds and A→C holds.
- **Union rule:** If A→B and A→C hold, then A→BC holds.
- **Pseudotransitivity rule:** If A→B holds and BC→D holds, then AC→D holds.

9. Why are Armstrong's inference rules considered complete and sound?

Ans: Armstrong's inference rules are considered complete as for a given set F of FDs, all FDs implied by F can be inferred. The axioms are also sound as no additional FDs or incorrect FDs can be deduced from F using the rules.

10. What do you understand by the closure of a set of attribute? How it can be determined?

Ans: The closure of a set of attributes implies a certain subset of the closure that consists of all FDs with a specified set Z of attributes as determinant. For a given relation schema R, a set Z of attributes of R and the set F of functional dependencies that hold on R, the set of all attributes of R that are functionally dependent on Z (known as **the closure of Z under F**, denoted by **Z^+**) can be determined using the following algorithm:

```
Z+:= Z;                     //Initialize result to Z
while(change in Z+) do //until change in result
   for each FD X→Y in F do //inner loop
begin
       if X ⊆ Z+           //check if left hand side is subset
                          //of closure (result)
       then Z+:= Z+ U Y; //include the value on right
                             //hand side in result
end
```

11. What are the uses of the closure algorithm?

Ans: Besides computing the subset of closure, the closure algorithm has some other uses that are as follows:

- To determine if a particular FD, say X→Y is in the closure F^+ of F, without computing the closure F^+. This can be done by simply computing X^+ by using the closure algorithm and then checking if $Y \subseteq X^+$.
- To test if a set of attributes A is a superkey of R. This can be done by computing A^+ and checking if A^+ contains all the attributes of R.

12. When are two sets of functional dependencies said to be equivalent? How can we determine their equivalence?

Ans: Two sets F_1 and F_2 of FDs are said to be equivalent if $F_1^+ = F_2^+$, that is, every FD in F_1 is implied by F_2 and every FD in F_2 is implied by F_1. In other words, F_1 is equivalent to F_2, if both the conditions F_1 covers F_2 and F_2 covers F_1 hold. A set F_2 of FDs is covered by another set F_1 or F_1 is the cover of F_2 if every FD in F_2 can be inferred from F_1, that is, if every FD in F_2 is also in F_1^+. If F_1 and F_2 are equivalent and the FDs in F_1 are enforced by any database system, then the FDs in F_2 will be enforced automatically and vice versa.

To determine whether F_1 covers F_2, compute X^+ under F_1 for each FD X→Y in F_2. If X^+ includes all attributes in Y for all FDs in F_2, then we can say that F_1 covers F_2. Similarly, it can also be determined whether F_2 covers F_1. If both F_1 and F_2 cover each other, then they are said to be equivalent.

13. Define the canonical cover of a set of FDs. How can it be computed?

Ans: For a given a set of FDs F, the canonical cover F_c of F is a set of FDs derived from F in such a way that

- F_c contains no extraneous attributes. Consider a functional dependency X→Y in F.
  - Attribute A is extraneous in X if A ∈ X, and F logically implies (F-{X→Y}) U {(X-A→Y}.
  - Attribute A is extraneous in Y if A ∈ Y, and the set of FDs (F-{X→Y}) U{X→(Y-A)} logically implies F.
- The determinant of each FD in F_c is unique, that is, there are no two dependencies like X→Y and X→Z in F_c.

A canonical cover for a set of functional dependencies can be computed by using the following algorithm:

```
Fc := F;
while(change in Fc) do
begin
    replace any FD in Fc of the form X→A, X→B
        with X→AB (Use union rule)
    for(each FD X→Y in Fc) do
    begin
        if(extraneous attribute is found either in X or in Y)
        then remove it from X→Y
    end
end
```

14. What is normalization? Define normal forms.

Ans: **Normalization** is the process of modifying a relation schema based on its FDs and primary keys so that it conforms to certain rules called **normal forms**. It is conducted by evaluating a relation schema to check whether it satisfies particular rules and if not, then decomposing the schema into a set of smaller relation schemas that do not violate those rules. Normalization can be considered as fundamental to the modelling and design of a relational database, the main purpose of which is to eliminate data redundancy and avoid data update anomalies.

A relation is said to be in a particular normal form if it satisfies certain specified constraints. Each of the normal forms is stricter than its predecessors. The normal forms are used to ensure that various types of anomalies and inconsistencies are removed from the database.

15. Define the following:

(a) Full functional dependency

(b) Partial dependency

Ans: **(a)** A dependency X→Y in a relation schema R is said to be a **fully functionally dependency** if there is no A, where A is the proper subset of X such that A→Y. It implies removal of any attribute from X means that the dependency does not hold any more.

(b) A dependency X →Y in a relation schema R is said to be a **partial dependency** if there is any attribute A where A is the proper subset of X such that A →Y. The attribute Y is said to be partially dependent on the attribute X.

16. Explain first normal form (1NF) and second normal form (2NF) with the help of an example.

Ans: **First Normal Form (1NF):** The first normal form states that every tuple must contain exactly one value for each attribute from the domain of that attribute. That is, multi-valued attributes, composite attributes and their combinations are not allowed in 1NF.

Definition: A relation schema R is said to be in the **first normal form (1NF)** if and only if the domains of all attributes of R contain atomic (or indivisible) values only.

To understand, consider a relation schema BOOK_INFO{ISBN, Price, Page_count, P_ID, R_ID, rating} that represents the information regarding books and reviews. The functional dependencies that hold on relation schema BOOK_INFO are {ISBN→Price, Page_count,

`P_ID}` and `{ISBN, R_ID→Rating}`. The only key of the relation `BOOK_INFO` is the combination of `ISBN` and `R_ID`. Further suppose, an additional constraint `Page_count→Price` is also introduced in this relation, which implies that the price of a book is determined by the number of pages in the book.

The `BOOK_INFO` relation (shown in Figure 6.4) contains non-atomic values; hence, it is unnormalized. However, it can be normalized into 1NF by creating one tuple for each value in multi-valued attributes as shown in Figure 6.5.

ISBN	Price	Page_count	P_ID	R_ID	Rating
001-987-760-9	25	800	P001	A002 A008	6 7
001-354-921-1	22	200	P001	A006	7
002-678-980-4	35	860	P002	A001 A003 A005	2 5 7
004-765-409-5	26	550	P003	A003	4
004-765-359-3	40	650	P003	A007	3
003-456-433-6	30	500	P004	A010	5
001-987-650-5	35	450	P001	A009	8
002-678-880-2	25	400	P002	A006	4
003-456-533-8	30	500	P004	A004	9

Figure 6.4 Unnormalized Relation BOOK_INFO

ISBN	Price	Page_count	P_ID	R_ID	Rating
001-987-760-9	25	800	P001	A002	6
001-987-760-9	25	800	P001	A008	7
001-354-921-1	22	200	P001	A006	7
002-678-980-4	35	860	P002	A001	2
002-678-980-4	35	860	P002	A003	5
002-678-980-4	35	860	P002	A005	7
004-765-409-5	26	550	P003	A003	4
004-765-359-3	40	650	P003	A007	3
003-456-433-6	30	500	P004	A010	5

Figure 6.5 Relation BOOK_INFO in 1NF

ISBN	Price	Page_count	P_ID	R_ID	Rating
001-987-650-5	35	450	P001	A009	8
002-678-880-2	25	400	P002	A006	4
003-456-533-8	30	500	P004	A004	9

Figure 6.5 (...Contd)

Second Normal Form (2NF): The second normal form is based on the concept of full functional dependency.

Definition: A relational schema `R` is said to be in the **second normal form (2NF)** if every non-key attribute `A` in `R` is fully functionally dependent on the primary key. An attribute is **non-key** or **non-prime** attribute, if it is not a part of the candidate key of `R`.

For example, consider once again, the relation schema `BOOK_INFO` in which the attributes `ISBN` and `R_ID` together form the key. In this schema, the attribute `Rating` is fully functionally dependent on the key `{ISBN, R_ID}` as `Rating` is not dependent on any subset of the key. That is, neither `ISBN→Rating` nor `R_ID→Rating` holds. However, the attributes `Price, Page_count, P_ID` are partially dependent on the key since they are dependent on `ISBN`, which is a subset of the key `{ISBN, R_ID}`. Thus, this schema is not in 2NF. However, it can be normalized to 2NF by eliminating all partial dependency between a non-key attribute and the key. This can be achieved by decomposing `BOOK_INFO` into two relation schemas (see Figure 6.6) as follows:

```
BOOK{ISBN,Price, Page_count, P_ID}
REVIEW {ISBN,R_ID, Rating}
```

BOOK

ISBN	Price	Page_count	P_ID
001-987-760-9	25	800	P001
001-354-921-1	22	200	P001
002-678-980-4	35	860	P002
004-765-409-5	26	550	P003
004-765-359-3	40	650	P003
003-456-433-6	30	500	P004
001-987-650-5	35	450	P001
002-678-880-2	25	400	P002
003-456-533-8	30	500	P004

REVIEW

ISBN	R_ID	Rating
001-987-760-9	A002	6
001-987-760-9	A008	7
001-354-921-1	A006	7
002-678-980-4	A001	2
002-678-980-4	A003	5
002-678-980-4	A005	7
004-765-409-5	A003	4
004-765-359-3	A007	3
003-456-433-6	A010	5
001-987-650-5	A009	8
002-678-880-2	A006	4
003-456-533-8	A004	9

Figure 6.6 Relations in 2NF

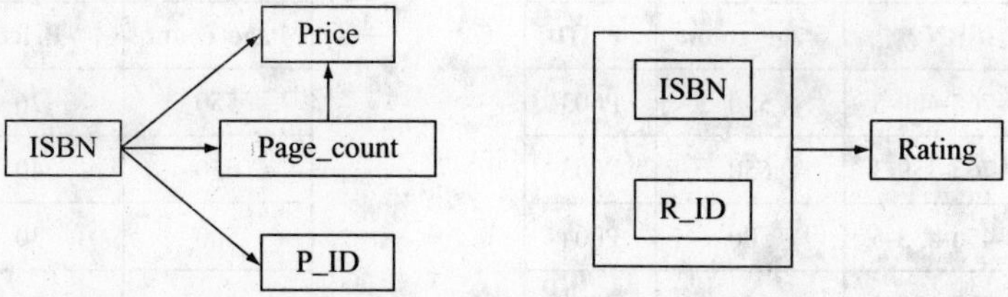

(a) FD Diagram for BOOK (b) FD Diagram for REVIEW

Figure 6.7 FDs in 2NF

The relation schemas BOOK and REVIEW do not have any partial dependencies. Each of the non-key attributes of relation schemas BOOK and REVIEW is fully functionally dependent on key attributes namely, ISBN and (ISBN, R_ID), respectively. Hence, both the schemas are in 2NF. The FDs corresponding to these relation schemas are shown in Figure 6.7.

17. What is transitive dependency? Explain the normal form based on the concept of transitive dependency.

Ans: An attribute Y of a relation schema R is said to be **transitively dependent** on attribute X (X→Y), if there is a set of attributes A that is neither a candidate key nor a subset of any key of R and both X→A and A→Y hold. For example, the dependency ISBN→Price is transitive through Page_count in relation schema BOOK (see Figure 6.7). This is because both the dependencies ISBN→Page_count and Page_count→Price hold and Page_count is neither a candidate key nor a subset of the candidate key of BOOK.

The normal form that is based on the concept of transitive dependency is the third normal form (3NF).

Definition: A relation schema R with a set F of functional dependencies is in the **third normal form (3NF)** if, for every FD X→Y in F, where X is any subset of attributes of R and Y is any single attribute of R, at least one of the following statements hold:

- X→Y is a trivial FD, that is, Y ⊆ X.
- X is a superkey for R.
- Y is contained in a candidate key for R.

It can also be stated as: A relation schema R is in the third normal form (3NF) if and only if it satisfies 2NF and every non-key attribute is non-transitively dependent on the primary key.

For example, the schema BOOK (shown in Figure 6.6) can be decomposed into two relation schemas say, BOOK_PAGE and PAGE_PRICE, to eliminate transitive dependency between the attributes ISBN and Price. Hence, the schemas BOOK_PAGE and PAGE_PRICE are in 3NF. The instances of these schemas are shown in Figure 6.8, and Figure 6.9 shows FD diagrams of these schemas.

BOOK_PAGE

ISBN	Page_count	P_ID
001-987-760-9	800	P001
001-354-921-1	200	P001
002-678-980-4	860	P002

PAGE_PRICE

Page_count	Price
800	25
200	22
860	35

Figure 6.8 Relations in 3NF

ISBN	Page_count	P_ID
004-765-409-5	550	P003
004-765-359-3	650	P003
003-456-433-6	500	P004
001-987-650-5	450	P001
002-678-880-2	400	P002
003-456-533-8	500	P004

Page_count	Price
550	26
650	40
500	30
450	35
400	25

Figure 6.8 (...Contd)

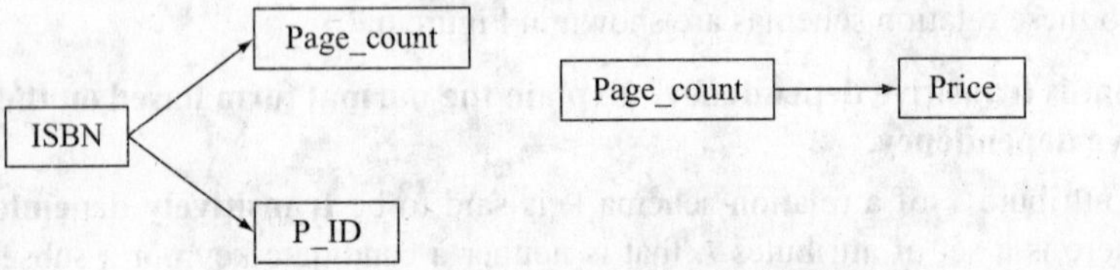

Figure 6.9 FD Diagram for BOOK_PAGE and PAGE_PRICE

18. Define the Boyce–Codd normal form. Give an example also.

Ans: The Boyce–Codd normal form was proposed to deal with the relations having two or more candidate keys that are composite and that overlap.

Definition: A relation schema `R` is in a Boyce–Codd normal form (BCNF) if, for every FD `X`→`A` in `F`, where `X` is the subset of the attributes of `R`, and `A` is an attribute of `R`, one of the following statements holds:

- `X`→`Y` is a trivial FD, that is, `Y` ⊆ `X`.
- `X` is a super key.

In simple terms, it can be stated as: A relation schema `R` is in **BCNF** if and only if every non-trivial FD has a candidate key as its determinant.

For example, consider a relation schema `BOOK(ISBN, Book_title, Price, Page_count)` with two candidate keys, namely, `ISBN` and `Book_title`. The FD diagram for this relation schema is shown in Figure 6.10.

As shown in Figure 6.10, there are two determinants, namely `ISBN` and `Book_title` and both of them are candidate keys. Thus, this relation schema is in BCNF.

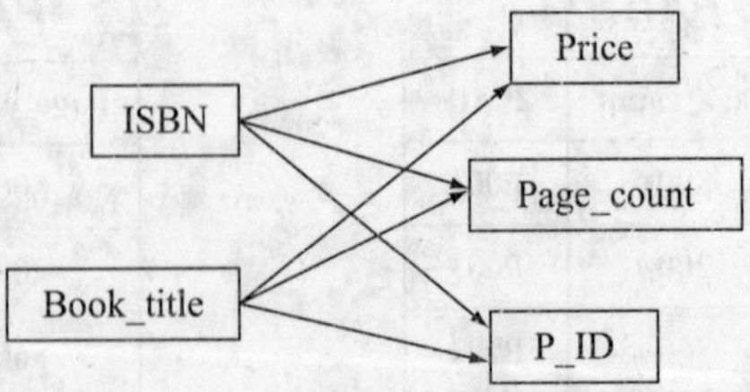

Figure 6.10 FD Diagram for BOOK with Book_title as Candidate Key

19. Why is BCNF considered simpler as well as stronger than 3NF?

Ans: BCNF is the simpler form of 3NF as it makes explicit reference to neither the first and second normal forms nor to the concept of transitive dependence.

In addition, it is stronger than 3NF as every relation that is in BCNF is also in 3NF but the vice versa is not necessarily true. For example, the relation schema BOOK (described in Question 18), which is in BCNF, does not include any transitive dependency and thus, is in 3NF as well.

Now, consider another relation schema BOOK_RATING(ISBN, Book_title, R_ID, Rating). Assuming that book titles are also unique, the relation has two candidate keys (ISBN, R_ID) and (Book_title, R_ID). This relation schema is not in BCNF since it contains two determinants, namely ISBN and Book_title, which determine each other and neither of them is a candidate key. However, this relation is in 3NF.

20. Are normal forms alone sufficient as a condition for a good schema design? Explain.

Ans: No, normal forms alone are not sufficient as a condition for a good schema design. There are two additional properties, namely *lossless–join* property and *dependency preservation* property that must hold on decomposition to qualify it as a good design. Out of these two properties, lossless–join property is an indispensable requirement of decomposition that must be achieved at any cost, whereas the dependency preservation property, though desirable, can be sacrificed sometimes.

21. State the lossless–join property of decomposition. What is its significance?

Ans: Let R be a relation schema with a given set F of functional dependencies. Then decomposition $D = \{R_1, R_2, \ldots, R_n\}$ on R is said to be **lossless (lossless–join)**, if for every legal relation (that is, relation that satisfies the specified functional dependencies and other constraints), the following statement holds:

$$\pi_{R1}(R) \bowtie \pi_{R2}(R) \bowtie \ldots \bowtie \pi_{Rn}(R) = R$$

In other words, if the original relation can be reconstructed by combining the projections of a relation using natural join (or the process of decomposition is reversible), decomposition is **lossless decomposition**, otherwise, it is a **lossy (lossy–join) decomposition.**

For example, consider the relation schema BOOK(ISBN, Price, Page_count) with the functional dependencies ISBN → Price and Page_count → Price. An instance of this relation schema is shown in Figure 6.11.

ISBN	Price	Page_count
001-987-760-9	25	800
001-354-921-1	22	200
002-678-745-2	25	810

Figure 6.11 An Instance of BOOK Relation

The relation schema BOOK(ISBN, Price, Page_count) can be decomposed in two different ways, say decomposition A and decomposition B (refer Figure 6.12). The schemas corresponding to decomposition A and decomposition B are given as follows:

Decomposition A

BOOK_PRICE(ISBN, Price)
and BOOK_PAGES(ISBN, Page_count)

Decomposition B

BOOK_PRICE(ISBN, Price)
and PRICE_PAGE(Price, Page_count)

Decomposition A

BOOK_PRICE

ISBN	Price
001-987-760-9	25
001-354-921-1	22
002-678-745-2	25

BOOK_PAGES

ISBN	Page_count
001-987-760-9	800
001-354-921-1	200
002-678-745-2	810

Decomposition B

BOOK_PRICE

ISBN	Price
001-987-760-9	25
001-354-921-1	22
002-678-745-2	25

PRICE_PAGE

Page_count	Price
800	25
200	22
810	25

Figure 6.12 Decompositions of Relation BOOK

In Decomposition A (refer Figure 6.12), the price and the number of pages for all the books can be determined easily. Since no information is lost in this decomposition, decomposition A is lossless. On the other hand, in Decomposition B, it can be determined that the price of the books having ISBN *001-987-760-9* and *002-678-980-4* is *25*. However, the number of pages in these books cannot be determined as there are two values for Page_count in relation PRICE_PAGE corresponding to the price *25*. Thus, this decomposition is lossy.

The notion of the lossless join (also known as **non-additive join**) property is crucial as it ensures that the original relation can be recovered from the smaller relations that result after decomposition. That is, it ascertains that no information is lost after decomposition.

22. How would you test decomposition for having a lossless–join property?

Ans: Let R be a relation schema with F a set of FDs over R. The decomposition D of R into multiple relations R_1, R_2,..., R_n can be tested for having a lossless–join property using the following algorithm:

1. Create a matrix M[m,n]with m equal to number of decomposed relations and n equal to number of attributes in R. The ith row of matrix M corresponds to the decomposed relation R_i and jth column corresponds to the attribute A_j of R.
2. for(i= 1 to m) do
```
    for(j= 1 to n) do
        M[i,j]:= a_ij;
```

```
3. for(i=1 to m) do
   begin
     for(j= 1 to n) do
     begin
        if(Aj ∈ Ri) then
             M[i,j]:= bj;
     end
   end
4. while(change in M) do
   begin
     for(each X → Y in F) do
     begin
        for(all rows in M having same value in the columns corre-
        sponding to attributes in X) do
        begin
           if (any row has 'b' value for a column corresponding to
                an attribute in Y) then
              set other rows to that same 'b' value in the column
           else
              choose one of the 'a' values that appears in one of
              the rows for the attribute and set other rows to that
              same 'a' value in the column
        end
     end
   end
5. if(any row has 'b' value for each column) then
     decomposition is lossless
   else
     decomposition is lossy.
```

If the decomposition is binary, that is, a relation is decomposed into two relations, then a simpler test (rather than the above algorithm) can be applied to test the lossless–join property. Let R be a relation schema with F a set of FDs over R. The decomposition of R into two relations R_1 and R_2 form a lossless decomposition if at least one of the following dependencies is in F^+:

$$R_1 \cap R_2 \rightarrow R_1 - R_2$$

$$R_1 \cap R_2 \rightarrow R_2 - R_1$$

23. Explain the dependency preservation property. How can it be tested?

Ans: Dependency preservation is a property that is desired while decomposition, that is, no FD of the original relation is lost. Consider a relation schema R with set F of FDs $\{X \rightarrow Y,\ Y \rightarrow Z\}$. Another dependency that is implied from F is $X \rightarrow Z$. Let R be decomposed into two relation schemas, namely $R_1\ \{X, Y\}$ with FD $X \rightarrow Y$ and $R_2\{Y, Z\}$ with FD $Y \rightarrow Z$. Here, $X \rightarrow Z$ is enforced automatically since it is implied from FDs of R_1 and R_2. Hence, this decompostion is dependency preserving.

The dependency preservation property ensures that each FD represented by the original relation is enforced by examining any single relation resulted from decomposition or can be inferred from the FDs in some decomposed relation. Thus, it prevents computation of a join. To understand this property, let us first understand the term projection. Given a relation schema R with set F of FDs and

R_1, R_2, ... R_n is the decomposition of R, the **projection** of F to R_i is the set F_i of all FDs in F^+ (not just F) that include only attributes of R_i. For example, once again consider the decomposition of R_1 {X, Y} and R_2 {X, Z} of R. The projection of F to R_1, denoted by F_{R1} is X→Z, since X→Z in F^+, even though it is not in F. This FD can be tested by examining relation R_2 only. Similarly, FDs in each projection can be tested by analyzing only one relation in the decomposed set.

However, testing each projection is not sufficient to determine whether the decomposition is dependency preserving. It is not always necessary that all the dependencies in the original relation appear directly in an individual decomposed relation. That is, there may be FDs in F^+ that are not the projections. Thus, we also need to examine the FDs that are inferred from the projections. Formally, the decomposition of relation schema R with a given set F of FDs into relations R_1, R_2, ... R_n is **dependency preserving** if $F'^+ = F^+$, where $F' = F_{R1} \cup F_{R2} \cup ... \cup F_{Rn}$.

24. "If a relation is broken into BCNF, it will be dependency preserving". Prove or disprove this statement with the help of an example.

Ans: Whenever a relation is broken into BCNF, it is always not possible to preserve all the dependencies of the relation. To illustrate this, consider a relation schema `CITY_ZIP(City, Street, Zip)` with FDs `{City, Street}→Zip` and `Zip→City` is decomposed into two relation schemas, namely R_1 `(Street, Zip)` and R_2 `(City, Zip)`. It is observed that both these schemas are in BCNF. In R_1, there is only trivial dependency and in R_2, the dependency `Zip→City` holds. It can be seen clearly that the FD `{City, Street}→Zip` is not implied from the decomposed relation schemas. Thus, this decomposition does not preserve dependency, that is, $(F_1 \cup F_2)^+ \neq F^+$, where F_1 and F_2 are the restrictions of R_1 and R_2, respectively.

25. What is multi-valued dependency? What is the difference between functional dependency and multi-valued dependency?

Ans: Multi-valued dependencies (MVDs) are the generalization of functional dependencies.
Definition: In a relation schema R, an attribute Y is said to be **multi-dependent** on attribute X (X→→Y) if and only if for a particular value of X, the set of values of Y is completely determined by the value of X alone and is independent of the values of Z where X, Y and Z are the subsets of the attributes of R. X→→Y is read as Y is **multi-dependent** on X or X **multi-determines** Y.

Let us understand the notion of multi-valued dependencies with the help of an example. Consider the relation `BOOK_AUTHOR_DETAIL` as shown in Figure 6.13.

ISBN	A_ID	Phone
001-987-760-9	A001	923673
001-987-760-9	A001	923743
001-987-760-9	A003	419456
001-987-760-9	A003	419562
001-354-921-1	A005	678654
001-354-921-1	A005	678655
001-354-921-1	A005	678657

Figure 6.13 An Instance of BOOK_AUTHOR_DETAIL

ISBN	A_ID	Phone
002-678-980-4	A002	376045
002-678-980-4	A008	765490
004-765-409-5	A008	765490

Figure 6.13 (...Contd)

In this relation, each ISBN has a well-defined set of corresponding A_ID. Similarly, for a particular A_ID, a well-defined set of Phone exists. In addition, book is independent of the phone numbers of authors, due to which there is a lot of redundancy in this relation. Thus, the multi-valued dependencies that hold in this relation can be represented as follows:

ISBN→→A_ID

A_ID→→Phone

Functional dependencies prevent the existence of certain tuples in a relation. For example, if an FD X→Y holds in R, then any r(R) cannot have two tuples having the same X value but different Y values. On the contrary, multi-valued dependencies do not rule out the presence of those tuples, rather, they require the presence of other tuples of a certain form in the relation.

26. State the inference rules for multi-valued dependencies.

Ans: The set of inference rules for multi-valued dependencies consists of three Armstrong axioms (discussed in Question 8) and five additional rules, which are as follows:

- **Complementation rule for MVDs:** If X →→ Y, then X →→ R-XY.
- **Augmentation rule for MVDs:** If X →→ Y and W ⊇ Z, then WX →→ YZ.
- **Transitive rule for MVDs:** If X →→ Y and Y →→ Z, then X →→ (Z-Y).
- **Replication rule for FD to MVD:** If X → Y, then X →→ Y.
- **Coalescence rule for FD to MVD:** If X →→ Y and there exists W such that W ∩ Y is empty, W → Z and Y ⊇ Z, then X → Z.

27. Define the fourth normal form. Explain why it is more desirable than BCNF.

Ans: The fourth normal form is based on the concept of multi-valued dependency. It is required when undesirable multi-valued dependencies occur in a relation.

Definition: A relation schema R is in the **fourth normal form (4NF)** with respect to a set F of functional and multi-valued dependencies if, for every non-trivial multi-valued dependency X →→ Y in F^+, where X ⊆ R and Y⊆R, X is a superkey of R.

For example, consider the relation BOOK_AUTHOR_DETAIL shown in Figure 6.13. A problem arises due to the fact that book is independent of the phone number of authors. This problem can be resolved by eliminating this undesirable dependency, that is, by decomposing this relation into two relations BOOK_AUTHOR and AUTHOR_PHONE as shown in Figure 6.14. Since, the relations BOOK_AUTHOR and AUTHOR_PHONE do not involve any MVD, they are in 4NF.

4NF is more desirable than BCNF as any relation in 4NF is necessarily in BCNF but the converse is not true. For example, the 4NF relations BOOK_AUTHOR and AUTHOR_PHONE satisfy only trivial dependencies. In addition, each of them is an **all key relation** (a relation in which key is the combination of all the attributes taken together) and any all key relation must necessarily be in BCNF. Thus, the relations BOOK_AUTHOR and AUTHOR_PHONE are in 4NF as well as BCNF. On the other hand,

BOOK_AUTHOR

ISBN	A_ID
001-987-760-9	A001
001-987-760-9	A003
001-354-921-1	A005
002-678-980-4	A002
002-678-980-4	A008
004-765-409-5	A008

AUTHOR_PHONE

A_ID	Phone
A001	923673
A001	923743
A003	419456
A003	419562
A005	678654
A005	678655
A005	678657
A002	376045
A008	765490

Figure 6.14 Relations in 4NF

consider the relation BOOK_AUTHOR_DETAIL shown in Figure 6.13. This relation satisfies only trivial dependencies and an all key relation, thus it is in BCNF. However, as it involves multi-valued dependencies, it is not in 4NF.

28. Discuss join dependencies and the fifth normal form with examples.

Ans: Join dependency is the most general form of dependency possible.

Definition: Let R be a relation schema and $R_1, R_2, ..., R_n$ be the decomposition of R, R is said to satisfy the **join dependency** $*(R_1, R_2, ..., R_n)$, if and only if

$$\pi_{R1}(R) \bowtie \pi_{R2}(R) \bowtie \ldots \bowtie \pi_{Rn}(R) = R$$

In other words, relation schema R satisfies the JD $*(R_1, R_2 \ldots R_n)$ if and only if every legal instance r(R) is equal to the join of its projections on $R_1, R_2, ..., R_n$.

For example, consider the relation AUTHOR_BOOK_PUBLISHER (see Figure 6.15), which is all key relation (all the attributes form key). If this relation is decomposed exactly into any two relations and joined back, a spurious tuple is created (see Figure 6.15), however, if it is decomposed into three relations and joined back as shown in Figure 6.15, the original relation is obtained. It is because it specifies another constraint according to which, whenever an author *a* writes book *b*, and a publisher *p* publishes book *b*, and the author *a* writes at least one book for publisher *p*, then author *a* will also be writing book *b* for publisher *p*. Since this constraint is satisfied if and only if the relation is joining of certain projections, this constraint is referred to as join dependency (JD).

The fifth normal form also called **project–join normal form (PJ/NF)** is based on the concept of join dependencies.

Definition: A relation schema R is in the fifth normal form (5NF) with respect to a set F of functional, multi-valued and join dependencies if, for every non-trivial join dependency $*(R_1, R_2, ..., R_n)$ in F+, every R_i is a superkey of R.

For example, consider once again the AUTHOR_BOOK_PUBLISHER relation (shown in Figure 6.15) which satisfies join dependency that is not implied by its sole superkey (that key being the combination of all its attributes). Thus, it is not in 5NF. In addition, this relation suffers from a

AUTHOR_BOOK_PUBLISHER

A_ID	Book_title	P_ID
A001	C++	P002
A001	Unix	P001
A002	C++	P001
A001	C++	P001

AUTHOR_BOOK

A_ID	Book_title
A001	C++
A001	Unix
A002	C++

BOOK PUBLISHER

Book_title	P_ID
C++	P002
Unix	P001
C++	P001

PUBLISHER AUTHOR

P_ID	A_ID
P002	A001
P001	A001
P001	A002

Join over Book title

Join over P_ID and A_ID

Original relation

A_ID	Book_title	P_ID
A001	C++	P002
A001	Unix	P001
A002	C++	P001
A002	C++	P002
A001	C++	P001

← Spurious tuple (row A002, C++, P002)

Figure 6.15 Non-loss Decomposition of a Relation into Three Projections

number of update anomalies. These anomalies can be eliminated if it is decomposed into three relations AUTHOR_BOOK, BOOK_PUBLISHER and PUBLISHER_AUTHOR. Each of these relations is in 5NF since they do not involve any join dependency.

29. Consider a relation schema R(A, B, C, D, E, G) with set F of functional dependencies {A → B, BC → D, D → E, D → G}. Find the closure of F.

Ans: Using the inference rules explained in Question 8, the members of F^+ of the given set F are:

1. Since A → B and BC→ D, A C→ D (Pseudotransitivity rule)
2. Since BC → D and D → E, BC→ E (Transitivity rule)

3. Since BC → D and D → G, BC→ G (Transitivity rule)
4. Since AC → D (from 1), D → E, and D→ G, AC→ E and AC→ G (Transitivity rule)
5. Since D→E and D → G, D→EG (Union rule)
6. Since AC→ D, AC→ E, and AC→ G, AC→DEG (Union rule)
7. From 2 and 3 BC→ DEG (Union rule)

30. A relation R (A, B, C, D, E, F, G) satisfies the following FDs:

A → B

BC → DE

AEF → G

Find the closure $\{A,C\}^+$ under this set of FDs. Is FD ACF→ DG implied by F?

Ans: Using the algorithm explained in Question 10, the closure $\{A, C\}^+$ of the set of attributes {A,C} under the set F of FDs is found as follows:

1. Let Z= (A,C). Then, Z^+ = {A, C}.
2. For A → B, since A ⊆ Z^+, thus, Z^+ = {A, B, C}.
3. For BC → DE, since BC ⊆ Z^+, thus, Z^+ = {A, B, C, D, E}.
4. For AEF → G, Z^+ remains unchanged, since AEF is not a subset of Z^+.
5. On repeating the same procedure again, no new attribute is added in Z^+; hence, the algorithm terminates.

Thus, $\{A,C\}^+$ = {A, B, C, D, E}.

To check whether ACF→DG implied by F, we need to compute $\{ACF\}^+$, which is equal to {A, B, C, D, E, F, G}. Since DG ⊆ $\{ACF\}^+$, the FD ACF→DG is implied by F.

31. Consider a relation R(A,B,C,D,E) with the following functional dependencies AB→ C, CD→ E and DE→ B. Is AE a candidate key of this relation? If not, which is the candidate key? Explain.

Ans: To check whether AE is the candidate key of R, we need to compute the $\{AE\}^+$, which is equal to {A, E}. Since $\{AE\}^+$ does not contain all attributes of R, it is not the candidate key of R.

The candidate keys of R are computed as follows:

1. Since AB→C, ABD→CD (Augmentation rule)
2. Since ABD→CD and CD→E, ABD→E (Transitivity rule)
3. Since ABD→CD, ABD→ABCD (Reflexive rule)
4. From 1, 2 and 3, ABD→ABCDE (Union rule)
5. Since DE→B, ADE→AB (Augmentation rule)
6. Since ADE→AB and AB→C, ADE→C (Transitive rule)
7. Since ADE→AB and ADE→C, ADE→ABCDE (Reflexive and union rule)
8. Since CD→E and DE→B, CD→B (Reflexive and transitive rule)
9. Since CD→E and CD→B, CD→BE (Union rule)
10. Since CD→BE, ACD→ABCDE (Reflexive and Augmentation rule)

From 4, 7 and 10, it is clear that the possible candidate keys for R include {ABD}, {ADE} and {ACD}.

32. Consider two sets of functional dependencies F_1 = {A → C, AC → D, E → AD, E → H} and F_2 = {A → CD, E → AH}. Are they equivalent?

Ans: As explained in Question 12, F_1 and F_2 will be equivalent if $F_1^+ = F_2^+$. To determine the equivalence of F_1 and F_2, we need to determine whether F_1 and F_2 cover each other.

Checking whether F_1 covers F_2

1. For A → CD in F_2, the closure of A (A^+) under F_1, which is equal to {A,C,D} contains all attributes on the right-hand side of FD (that is, C and D).
2. For E → AH in F_2, the closure of E (E^+) under F_1, which is equal to {A,D,H} contains all attributes on the right-hand side of FD (that is, A and H).

From 1 and 2, it is clear that F_1 covers F_2.

Checking whether F_2 covers F_1

1. For A → C in F_1, the closure of A (A^+) under F_2, which is equal to {A,C,D}, contains all attributes on the right-hand side of FD (that is, C).
2. For AC → D in F_1, the closure of AC ($\{AC\}^+$) under F_2, which is equal to {A,C,D}, contains all attributes on the right-hand side of FD (that is, D).
3. For E → AD in F_1, the closure of E (E^+) under F_2, which is equal to {E,A,H,C,D}, contains all attributes on the right-hand side of FD (that is, A and D).
4. For E → H in F_1, the closure of E (E^+) under F_2, which is equal to {E,A,H,C,D}, contains all attributes on the right-hand side of FD (that is, H).

From 1, 2, 3 and 4, it is clear that F_2 covers F_1. Since F_1 and F_2 cover each other, they are equivalent.

33. A relation R (A, C, D, E, H) satisfies the following FDs:

A→C

AC→D

E→AD

E→H

Find the canonical cover for this set of FDs.

Ans: Given F= {A→C, AC→D, E→AD, E→H}. Using the algorithm explained in Question 13, the canonical cover F_c is found as follows:

1. Initially F_c= {A→C, AC→D, E→AD, E→H}.
2. Replace FDs E→AD and E → H with E→ADH, as both these FDs have the same set of attributes in determinant. Thus, F_c = {A →C, AC→D, E→ADH}.
3. In FD AC →D, C is extraneous because F logically implies (F-{AC →D}) U {A→D}. Thus, F_c = {A →C, A→D, E→ADH}.
4. Replace FDs A→C and A→D with A→CD. Now, F_c = {A→CD, E→ADH}.
5. In FD A→CD, no attribute is extraneous. Thus, F_c remains the same.
6. In FD E→ADH, D is extraneous. Thus, F_c = {A →CD, E→AH}.
7. Since the determinant of each FD is unique and no extraneous attribute is there. Thus, F_c = {A→CD,E→AH}.

34. Examine the relation shown here:

Employee ID	Branch No	Branch Address	Name	Position	Hrs/Week
E101	B02	Sun Plaza, Atlanta, 46227	Steve	Assistant	15
E101	B04	2/3 UT, New York, 46238	Steve	Assistant	10
E122	B02	Sun Plaza, Atlanta, 46227	John	Assistant	14
E122	B04	2/3 UT, New York, 46238	John	Assistant	9

(i) Is this relation in 2NF? If not, why?
(ii) Normalize the relation to 2NF and 3NF.
(iii) Identify the primary and foreign keys in 3NF relations.

Ans: (i) The primary key for the given relation is `{Employee ID, Branch No}` and to be in 2NF, all non-key attributes must be fully functionally dependent on the primary key. However, in this relation, only `Hrs/Week` attribute is fully functionally dependent on the key. The attributes `Name` and `Position` are partially dependent on `Employee ID` while the attribute `Branch Address` is partially dependent on `Branch No`. Thus, this relation is not in 2NF.

Ans: (ii) The set of FDs that must hold on the given relation schema include:

```
Employee ID→{Name, Position}
Branch No→Branch Address
{Employee ID, Branch No}→Hrs/Week
```

The FD diagram of the given relation schema is shown in Figure 6.16.

To normalize the relation to 2NF, the given relation schemas will be decomposed into three relations: `Emp_Detail(Employee ID, Name, Position)`, `Emp_Branch(Employee ID, Branch No, Hrs/Week)`, and `Branch_Detail(Branch No, Branch Address)`. The instances of these relation schemas are shown in Figure 6.17.

Now, each of the `Emp_Detail`, `Emp_Branch` and `Branch_ Detail` relations is in 3NF also since every non-key attribute is non-transitively dependent on the primary key.

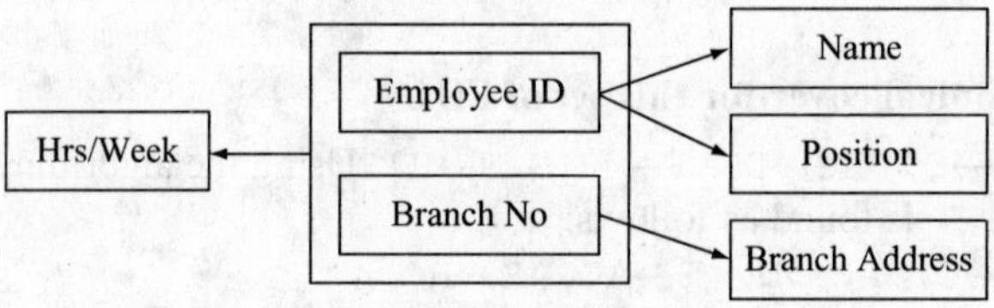

Figure 6.16 FD Diagram

Emp_Detail

Employee ID	Name	Position
E101	Steve	Assistant
E122	John	Assistant

Emp_Branch

Employee ID	Branch No	Hrs/Week
E101	B02	15
E101	B04	10
E122	B02	14
E122	B04	9

Branch_Detail

Branch No	Branch Address
B02	Sun Plaza, Atlanta, 46227
B04	2/3 UT, New York, 46238

Figure 6.17 Relations in 2NF and 3NF

Ans: (iii) The primary key of the relations `Emp_Detail`, `Emp_Branch`, and `Branch_Detail` is `Employee ID`, `{Employee ID, Branch No}`, and `Branch No` respectively. There is no foreign key in the `Emp_Detail` and `Branch_Detail` relation. There are two foreign keys in `Emp_Branch` relation, namely `Employee ID` and `Branch No` referring to `Employee ID` attribute of `Emp_Detail` relation and `Branch No` attribute of `Branch_Detail` relation, respectively.

35. A relation `R(A, B, C, D, E, F)` has the following set of functional dependency:

A → CD
B → C
F → DE
F→ A

Is the decomposition of R in `R1(A, B, C)`, `R2(A, F, D)` and `R3(E, F)` dependency preserving and lossless decomposition?

Ans: The decomposition of R into R1, R2 and R3 over a set of FDs F is dependency preserving, if $F'^+ = F^+$, where $F' = F_{R1} \cup F_{R2} \cup F_{R3}$. Here,

F_{R1} = {A→C, B→C}
F_{R2} = {A→D, F→A, F→D}
F_{R3} = {F→E}

Thus, F′ = {A→C, B→C, A→D, F→A, F→D, F→E}

Now, as explained in Question 32, it can be easily proved that the set of FDs F′ and F are equivalent, that is, $F'^+ = F^+$. Thus, the given decomposition is dependency preserving.

Using the algorithm explained in Question 22, the given decomposition is tested for lossless–join as follows: The initial contents of matrix M are as shown below:

	A	B	C	D	E	F
R1	a_{11}	a_{12}	a_{13}	a_{14}	a_{15}	a_{16}
R2	a_{21}	a_{22}	a_{23}	a_{24}	a_{25}	a_{26}
R3	a_{31}	a_{32}	a_{33}	a_{34}	a_{35}	a_{36}

Since R1=(A, B, C), R2=(A, F, D) and R3=(E, F), the contents of matrix M are:

	A	B	C	D	E	F
R1	b_1	b_2	b_3	a_{14}	a_{15}	a_{16}
R2	b_1	a_{22}	a_{23}	b_4	a_{25}	b_6
R3	a_{31}	a_{32}	a_{33}	a_{34}	b_5	b_6

Now, F={A→CD, B→C, F→DE, F→A}.

For A→CD, the rows corresponding to R1 and R2 have the same value b_1 in the column corresponding to attribute A. Further, the row corresponding to R1 has value b_3 in the column corresponding to attribute C. Thus, the value a_{23} will be replaced with b_3. In addition, the row corresponding to R2 has value b_4 in the column corresponding to attribute D. Thus, the value a_{14} will be replaced with b_4. Similarly, other FDs in F can be checked. After repeating this process for all FDs in F, until there is no change in M, the final contents of matrix M are:

$$\begin{array}{c} \\ R1 \\ R2 \\ R3 \end{array}\begin{array}{c} \begin{array}{cccccc} A & B & C & D & E & F \end{array} \\ \begin{pmatrix} b_1 & b_2 & b_3 & a_4 & a_{15} & a_{16} \\ b_1 & a_{22} & b_3 & b_4 & a_5 & b_6 \\ b_1 & a_{32} & b_3 & a_4 & b_5 & b_6 \end{pmatrix} \end{array}$$

Since no row in matrix M has 'b' value for each column, the decomposition is not lossless.

36. Consider the universal relation R(A,B,C,D,E,F,G,H,I,J) and the set of functional dependencies:

AB→C

A→DE

B→F

F→GH

D→IJ

What is the key for R? Decompose R into 2NF and 3NF relations.

Ans: Using the inference rules (see Question 31), it can be determined that the candidate key of R is {AB}. The FD diagram of R is shown in Figure 6.18.

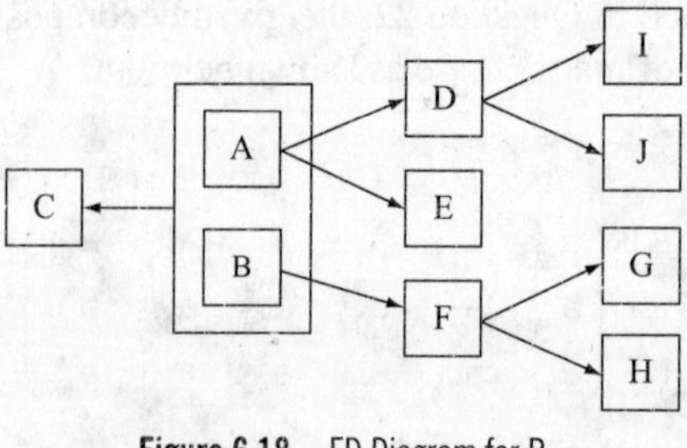

Figure 6.18 FD Diagram for R

From the figure, it is clear that only attribute C is fully functionally dependent on the primary key {AB}. Thus, the 2NF decomposition of relation schema R is R_1(<u>A</u>, <u>B</u>, C), R_2(<u>A</u>, D, E, I, J) and R_3(<u>B</u>, F, G, H).

Now, out of R_1, R_2 and R_3, the relation schema R_1 is in 3NF also as it does not include any transitivity dependency. However, relation schemas R_2 and R_3 are not in 3NF and thus, required to be decomposed. The 3NF decomposition of R_2 is R_{21}(<u>A</u>, D, E) and R_{22}(<u>D</u>, I, J) and of R_3 is R_{31}(<u>B</u>, F) and R_{32}(<u>F</u>, G, H).

37. Prove or disprove the following inference rules for functional dependencies:

(a) If {W→Y, X→Z} then {WX→Y}.

(b) If {X→Y, Y→Z} then {X→YZ}.

(c) If {X→Z, Y→Z} then {X→Y}.

Ans: **(a)** Given {W→Y, X→Z}

(i) Since W→Y, WX→XY (Augmentation rule)

(ii) Since WX→XY, WX→Y (Decomposition rule)

Hence, WX→Y proved.

(b) Given {X→Y, Y→Z}

(i) Since Y→Z, Y→YZ (Augmentation rule)

(ii) Since X→Y and Y→YZ, X→YZ (Transitive rule)

Hence, X→YZ proved.

(c) Given {X→Z, Y→Z}

(i) Since X→Z, X ⊇ Z

(ii) Since Y→Z, Y ⊇ Z

From (i) and (ii), it cannot be said that whether X ⊇ Y or Y ⊇ X. Thus, X→Y does not hold.

38. Give an example of a relation schema R and a set of functional dependencies such that R is in BCNF, but not in 4NF.

Ans: Consider a relation schema Employee(Emp_no, Proj_no, Dependent_name). Each employee can work on multiple projects and can have one or more dependents. Figure 6.19 shows an instance of this relation schema.

From this figure, it is clear that there are two MVDs in the Employee relation, which are:

Emp_no→→Proj_no

Emp_no→→Dependent_name

Thus, the Employee relation is not in 4NF. However, it is in BCNF as it is an all key relation.

Emp_no	Proj_no	Dependent_name
E001	P001	Allen
E001	P001	Barbara
E001	P003	Allen
E001	P003	Barbara
E002	P001	Chang
E002	P004	Chang
E002	P005	Chang
E003	P004	Mark
E003	P004	Smith
E004	P002	John
E004	P005	John

Figure 6.19 An Instance of Employee Relation

39. Consider the relation R as shown here:

A	B	C
a	b	c
d	b	c
e	c	c
e	c	d

Which of the following functional and multi-valued dependencies does not hold over relation R?

A→B

A→→B

B→C

B→→C

BC→A

BC→→A

Ans: The FDs B→C and BC→A do not hold over R.

40. Given a relation schema R(A,B,C,D) with primary key AB. Under which conditions is R in 2NF but not in 3NF.

Ans: R will be in 2NF but not in 3NF under the following conditions:

(i) {A, B}→C, D

(ii) A or B alone cannot determine either C or D or both.

(iii) Either C→D or D→C holds.

41. Consider a relation schema R(A, B, C) with a set of FDs {AB→C, C→A}. Show that R is in 3NF but not in BCNF.

Ans: From AB→C and C→A, AB→A (transitive rule) which is a trivial dependency. {AB} is the superkey as well as candidate key of R. Thus, R is in 3NF.

However, the determinant C is not a candidate key as it cannot determine B. Thus, R is not in BCNF.

42. Given the structure:

Proj_no	Proj_name	Emp_no	Emp_name	Job_class	Chg/hr	Hrs_ billed	Total charge
13	Banking	103	Ramesh	System Analyst	500	8	4000
		105	Ram	Programmer	300	8	2400
26	Telecom	115	Amit	Business Analyst	100	10	1000
		117	Shyam	Engineer	300	7	2100
39	Finance	113	Gopal	Team leader	1000	4	4000
		120	Suresh	DBA	800	3	2400

Normalize this relation up to the third normal form.

Ans: In the given relation, `Total_charge` is the derived attribute; thus, there is no need to store this attribute in the database. The relation is normalized to 1NF as shown in Figure 6.20.

We assume that the primary key of this relation is `Emp_no`. Since all non-key attributes are fully functionally dependent on it, the relation shown in Figure 6.20 is in 2NF also.

There is only one transitive dependency in this relation. The attribute `Proj_name` is transitively dependent on the primary key `Emp_no` via `Proj_no` attribute. Thus, to normalize the relation to 3NF, it is decomposed into two relations as shown in Figure 6.21.

Proj_no	Proj_name	Emp_no	Emp_name	Job_class	Chg/hr	Hrs_ billed
13	Banking	103	Ramesh	System Analyst	500	8
13	Banking	105	Ram	Programmer	300	8
26	Telecom	115	Amit	Business Analyst	100	10
26	Telecom	117	Shyam	Engineer	300	7
39	Finance	113	Gopal	Team Leader	1000	4
39	Finance	120	Suresh	DBA	800	3

Figure 6.20 Relation in 1NF

Proj_no	Proj_name
13	Banking
26	Telecom
39	Finance

Emp_no	Emp_name	Job_class	Chg/hr	Hrs_ billed
103	Ramesh	System Analyst	500	8
105	Ram	Programmer	300	8
115	Amit	Business Analyst	100	10
117	Shyam	Engineer	300	7
113	Gopal	Team Leader	1000	4
120	Suresh	DBA	800	3

Figure 6.21 Relations in 3NF

Multiple-choice Questions

1. A relation is in first normal form if ___________.
   (a) All the key attributes are defined
   (b) There are no repeating groups in the relation

(c) All attributes are dependent on the primary key
(d) All of these

2. A functional dependency is a relationship between/among ________.
(a) Tuples (b) Relations (c) Attributes (d) None of these
3. Given a relation R having two attributes X and Y such that X→Y holds. This implies that for each value of X in R, ________.
(a) There is only one Y value (b) There is none or one Y value
(c) There are many Y values (d) Both (a) and (b)
4. In which of the following situations, 3NF and BCNF are considered identical?
(a) If there are more than one candidate key in the relation and they overlap.
(b) If there is only one determinant upon which other attributes depend and it is a candidate key.
(c) If the candidate keys in the relation are composite keys.
(d) None of these
5. A relation in which every non-key attribute is fully functionally dependent on the primary key and which has no transitive dependencies is said to be in ________.
(a) 3NF (b) 2NF (c) BCNF (d) 4NF
6. An attribute X may be functionally dependent on ________.
(a) A single attribute Y (b) A composite attribute (X, Y)
(c) Both (a) and (b) (d) None of these
7. Which of the following is a key for relation R(P,Q,R,S,T,U) having FDs P→Q, R→U, T→P and TR→S?
(a) PS (b) PT (c) PQ (d) TR
8. Given a relation R having three attributes X, Y and Z. Which of the following statements is true according to augmentation rule?
(a) If both X→Y and Y→Z hold, then X→Z holds.
(b) If X→Y holds, then XZ→YZ holds.
(c) If X→YZ holds, then both X→Y and X→Z hold.
(d) None of these
9. The closure algorithm is used to ________.
(a) Determine whether a particular FD, say X→Y is in the closure F^+ of F without computing F^+
(b) Test whether a set of attributes A is a superkey of R
(c) Both (a) and (b)
(d) None of these
10. Which of the following defines the complementation rule for MVDs?
(a) If X→Y, then X→→Y (b) If X→→Y and W⊇Z, then WX→→YZ
(c) If X→→Y and Y→→Z, then X→→(Z-Y) (d) If X→→Y, then X→→R-XY
11. The decomposition of a relation R(X,Y,Z,W) having FDs X→Y and Z→W into R_1(X,Y) and R_2(Z,W) is ________.
(a) Lossless (b) Dependency preserving
(c) Both (a) and (b) (d) None of these
12. The essential requirement of ________ normal form is that every determinant in the relation must be a candidate key.
(a) Boyce Codd (b) Fourth (c) Fifth (d) Third

Answers

1. (b)	2. (c)	3. (a)	4. (b)	5. (a)	6. (c)	7. (d)
8. (b)	9. (c)	10. (d)	11. (c)	12. (a)		

7

Data Storage and Indexing

1. List the different types of storage media available in the computer system. Also explain how they are classified into different categories?

Ans: In a computer system, several types of storage media, such as cache memory, main memory, magnetic disk, etc. exist. On the basis of their characteristics, such as cost per unit of data and speed with which data can be accessed, they can be arranged in a hierarchical order (see Figure 7.1). In addition to the speed and cost of the various storage media, another issue is volatility.

The cost per unit of data as well as the speed of accessing data decreases while moving down in the memory hierarchy. The storage media at the top, such as cache and main memory, is the highest speed memory and is referred to as **primary storage**. The storage media in the next level consists of slower devices, such as magnetic disk, and is referred to as **secondary storage**. The storage media in the lowest level is the slowest storage devices, such as optical disk and magnetic tape, and are referred to as **tertiary storage**. The various storage devices are described as follows:

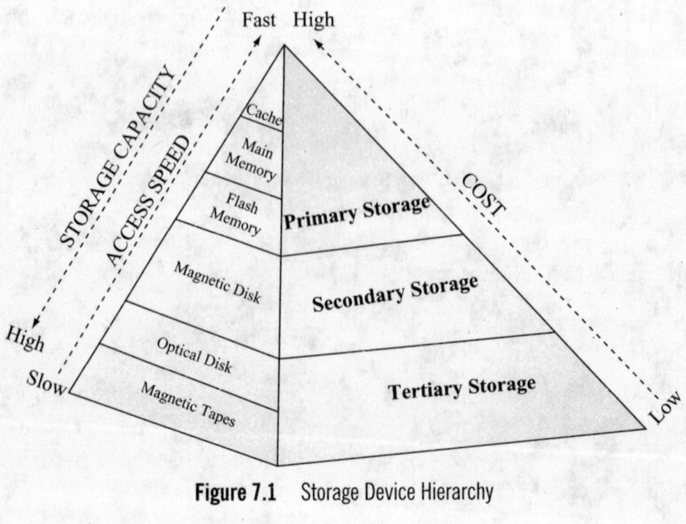

Figure 7.1 Storage Device Hierarchy

Primary storage

Primary storage generally offers limited storage capacity due to its high cost but provides very fast access to data. Primary storage is usually made up of semiconductor chips. The two basic forms of semiconductor memory are static RAM or SRAM (used for cache memory) and dynamic RAM or DRAM (used for main memory).

- **Cache memory:** Cache memory is a static RAM and is very small in size. The cache memory is the fastest; however, most expensive among all the storage media available. It is directly accessed by the CPU and is basically used to speed up the execution. A major limitation of cache is high cost and its volatility.
- **Main memory:** The main memory is a dynamic RAM (DRAM) and is used to keep the data that are currently being accessed by the CPU. It offers fast access to data as compared to other storage media except the static RAM. However, it is expensive and offers limited storage capacity. Thus, the entire database cannot be placed in the main memory at once. Moreover, it is volatile in nature.
- **Flash memory:** Flash memory uses an electrical erasing technology (like EEPROM). Reading data from flash memory is as fast as reading it from the main memory. However, it requires an entire block to be erased and written at once. This makes the writing process complicated. Flash memory is non-volatile in nature and the data survive system crashes and power failure.

Secondary storage

Secondary storage devices usually provide the bulk of storage capacity for storing data but are slower than primary storage devices. Secondary storage is non-volatile in nature, that is, the data are permanently stored and survive power failure and system crashes. Data on the secondary storage are not directly accessed by the CPU. **Magnetic disk** (generally called disk) is the primary form of secondary storage that enables storage of enormous amount of data. It is used to hold on-line data for a long term.

Tertiary storage

Removable media, such as optical discs and magnetic tapes, are considered as tertiary storage. Larger capacity and least cost are major advantages of tertiary storage. Data access speed, however, is much slower than primary storage. Since these devices can be removed from the drive, they are also termed as **off-line storage.**

- **Optical disc:** Optical disc comes in various sizes and capacities. Most commonly used optical discs are CD-ROM and DVD-ROM, which can store 600–700 MB and 8.5 GB (per side) of data, respectively. Both the CD-ROM and DVD-ROM come pre-recorded with data, which cannot be altered. However, both use laser beams for performing read operations.
- **Tape storage:** Tape storage is a cheap and reliable storage medium for organizing archives and taking backup. However, it is not suitable for data files that need to be revised or updated often because it stores data in a sequential manner and offers only **sequential-access** to the stored data.

2. Give hardware description and various features of magnetic disk. How do you measure its reliability?

Ans: A magnetic disk consists of **plate/platter**, which is made up of metal or glass material, and its surface is covered with magnetic material to store data on its surface. If the data can be stored on only one side of the platter, the disk is a **single-sided disk**, and if both sides are used to hold the data, the disk is a **double-sided disk**. The disk surface of a platter is divided into imaginary tracks and

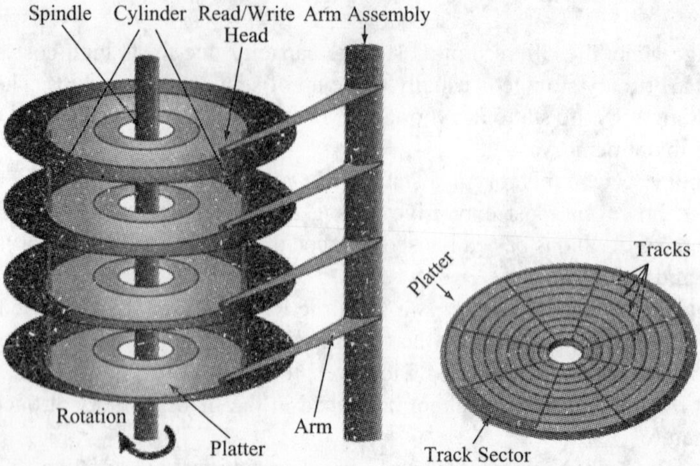

Figure 7.2 Organization of Magnetic Disk

sectors. **Tracks** are concentric circles where the data are stored, and are numbered from the outermost to the innermost ring, starting with zero. There are about 50,000 to 100,000 tracks per platter and a disk generally has 1 to 5 platters. Tracks are further subdivided into sectors (or track sector). A **sector** is just like an arc that forms an angle at the center. It is the smallest unit of information that can be transferred to/from the disk. A disk contains one **read–write head** for each surface of the platter. All the heads are attached to a single assembly called a **disk arm**. Thus, all the heads of different platters move together. The disk platters mounted on a **spindle** together with the heads mounted on a disk arm is known as **head-disk assemblies**. All the read–write heads are on the equal diameter track on different platters at one time. The tracks of equal diameter on different platters form a **cylinder**.

A magnetic disk is the most commonly used secondary storage medium. It offers high storage capacity and reliability. It can easily accommodate the entire database at once. However, if the data stored on the disk need to be accessed by the CPU, it is first moved to the main memory and then the required operation is performed. Once the operation is performed, the modified data must be copied back to the disk for consistency of the database. The system is responsible for transferring the data between the disk and the main memory as and when required. Data on the disk survive power failures and system crashes. There is a chance that the disk may sometimes fail and destroy the data; however, such failures occur rarely. The data in a magnetic disk can be erased and reused virtually infinitely. The disk is designed to reside in a protective case or cartridge to shield it from the dust and other external interference.

The **reliability** of the disk is measured in terms of **mean time to failure (MTTF)**. It is the amount of time for which the system can run continuously without any failure.

3. Explain the steps involved in accessing data from a magnetic disk.

Ans: The process of accessing data from a magnetic disk comprises three steps, which are as follows:

1. **Seek:** As soon as the disk unit receives the read/write command, the read/write heads are positioned on a specific track on the disk platter. The time taken in doing so is known as the **seek time**. It is the average time required to move the heads from one track to some other desired track on the disk. Seek times of modern disk may range between 6 and 15 milliseconds.

2. **Rotate:** Once the heads are positioned on the desired track, the head of the specific platter is activated. Since the disk is rotated constantly, the head has to wait for the required sector or cluster (desired data) to come under it. This delay is known as **rotational delay time** or **latency** of the disk. The average rotational latencies range from 4.2 to 6.7 ms.
3. **Data transfer:** After waiting for the desired data location, the read/write head transfers the data to or from the disk to primary memory. The rate at which the data are read from or written to the disk is known as the **data transfer rate**. It is measured in kilobits per second (kbps). Some of the latest hard disks have a data transfer rate of 66 MB/second. The data transfer rate depends upon the rotational speed of the disk. If the disk has a rotational speed of 6000 rpm (rotations per minute), having 125 sectors and 512 bytes/sector, the data transfer rate per revolution will be $125 \times 512 = 64{,}000$ bytes. Hence, the total transfer rate per second will be $64{,}000 \times 6000/60 = 6{,}400{,}000$ bytes/second or 6.4 MB/second.

4. Define RAID. What is the need of having RAID technology?

Ans: RAID (Redundant Arrays of Independent Disks) is a technique to improve the performance and reliability of the secondary storage. The basic idea behind RAID is to have a large array of small independent disks. The presence of multiple disks in the system improves the overall transfer rates, if the disks are operated in parallel. Parallelizing the operation of multiple disks allow multiple I/O to be serviced in parallel. This setup also offers opportunities for improving the reliability of data storage, because data can be stored redundantly on multiple disks. Thus, failure of one disk does not lead to loss of data. In other words, this large array of independent disks acts as a single logical disk with improved performance and reliability.

The technology of semiconductor memory has been advancing at a much higher rate than the technology of secondary storage. The performance and capacity of semiconductor memory is much superior to secondary storage. To match this growth in semiconductor memory, a significant development is required in the technology of secondary storage. A major advancement in secondary storage technology is the development of RAID.

5. How can the rellability and performance of disk be improved using RAID? Explain different RAID levels.

Ans: RAID employs data striping and mirroring techniques to improve the performance and reliability of a disk respectively. **Data striping** utilizes parallelism. It distributes the data transparently among `N` disks, which make them appear as a single large, fast disk. Striping of data across multiple disks improves the transfer rate as well, since operations are carried out in parallel. Data striping also balances the load among multiple disks.

In the simplest form, data striping splits each byte of data into bits and stores them across different disks. This splitting of each byte into bits is known as **bit-level data striping**. Having 8-bits per byte, an array of eight disks (or either a factor or multiple of eight) is treated as one large logical disk. In general, bit `i` of each byte is written to the `i`th disk. Since each I/O request is accomplished with the use of all disks in the array, the transfer rate of I/O requests goes to `N` times, where `N` represents the number of disks in the array. Alternatively, blocks of a file can be striped across multiple disks. This is known as **block-level striping**. Logical blocks of a file are assigned to multiple disks. Large requests for accessing multiple blocks can be carried out in parallel, thus improving the data transfer rate. However, the transfer rate for the request of a single block is the same as it is in case of one disk.

Having an array of `N` disks in a system improves the system performance; however, lowers the overall storage system reliability. The chance of failure of at least one disk out of a total of `N` disks is much higher than that of a specific single disk. Thus, some solution must be employed to increase the reliability of storage system. The most acceptable solution is to have **redundant** information so that the lost information of failed disk can be restored in case of a disk failure.

One simple technique to keep redundant information is **mirroring** (also termed as **shadowing**). In this technique, the data are redundantly stored on two physical disks. In this way every disk is duplicated, and all the data have two copies. Thus, every write operation is carried on both the disks. During read operation, the data can be retrieved from any disk. In case of failure of one disk, the second disk can be used until the first disk gets repaired. An alternative solution to increase the reliability is storing error-correcting codes such as parity bits and hamming codes. Such additional information is needed only in case of recovering the data of a failed disk. Error- correcting codes are maintained in a separate disk called **check disk**. The parity bits corresponding to each bit of N disks are stored in the check disk.

Though data striping and mirroring improve the performance and reliability of a disk, mirroring is expensive and striping does not improve reliability. Thus, several RAID organizations, referred to as **RAID levels**, have been proposed, which aims at providing redundancy at lower cost by using the combination of these two techniques. The RAID levels are classified into seven levels (from level 0 to level 6):

- **RAID level 0:** RAID level 0 uses block-level data striping but does not maintain any redundant information. Thus, the write operation has the best performance with level 0, as only one copy of data is maintained and no redundant information needs to be updated. The absence of redundant information also ensures 100 per cent space utilization for RAID level 0 systems. However, RAID level 0 does not have the best read performance among all the RAID levels. In addition, it is not fault-tolerant because failure of just one drive will result in loss of data.
- **RAID level 1:** RAID level 1 is the most expensive system as this level maintains a duplicate or redundant copy of data using mirroring. Thus, two identical copies of the data are maintained on two different disks. Every write operation needs to update both the disks, thus, the performance of RAID level 1 system degrades while writing. However, performance while read operation is improved by scheduling request to the disk with the shortest expected access time and rotational delay. With two identical copies of data, RAID level 1 system ensures only 50% space utilization.
- **RAID level 2:** RAID level 2 is known as **error-correcting-code (ECC)** organization. Two most popular error-detecting and correcting codes are parity bits and hamming codes. The use of parity bit detects all 1-bit errors in the memory system while the hamming code has the ability to detect the damaged bit. RAID level 2 requires three redundant disks to store error detecting and correcting information for four original disks. Thus, effective space utilization is about 57% in this case. However, space utilization increases with the number of data disks because check disks grow logarithmically with the number of data disks.
- **RAID level 3:** RAID level 3 maintains only a single check disk with parity bit information for error correction as well as for detection. This level is also named as **bit-interleaved parity organization**. RAID level 3 has the lowest possible overheads for reliability. This level requires only one parity disk for multiple disks, thus, increasing effective space utilization. In addition, level 3 distributes the data over multiple disks, with N-way striping of data, which makes the transfer rate for reading or writing a single block by N times faster than level 1.
- **RAID level 4:** Like RAID level 0, RAID level 4 uses block-level striping. It maintains parity block on a separate disk for each corresponding block from N other disks. This level is also named as **block-interleaved parity organization**. RAID level 4 always requires only one check

disk to hold parity information, effective space utilization increases with the number of data disks. In our example, with four data disks and one check disk, effective space utilization is 80%. However, the parity block is to be updated with each write operation, thus, only one write operation can be processed at a particular point of time.

- **RAID level 5:** Instead of placing data across N disks and parity information in one separate disk, this level distributes the **block-interleaved** parity and data among all the N + 1 disks. Such distribution has advantage in processing read/write requests. All disks can participate in processing read request so more number of read requests can be satisfied in a given amount of time. Several write requests can also be processed in parallel as the bottleneck of single check disk has been eliminated. RAID level 5 has the best performance among all the RAID levels. In our example

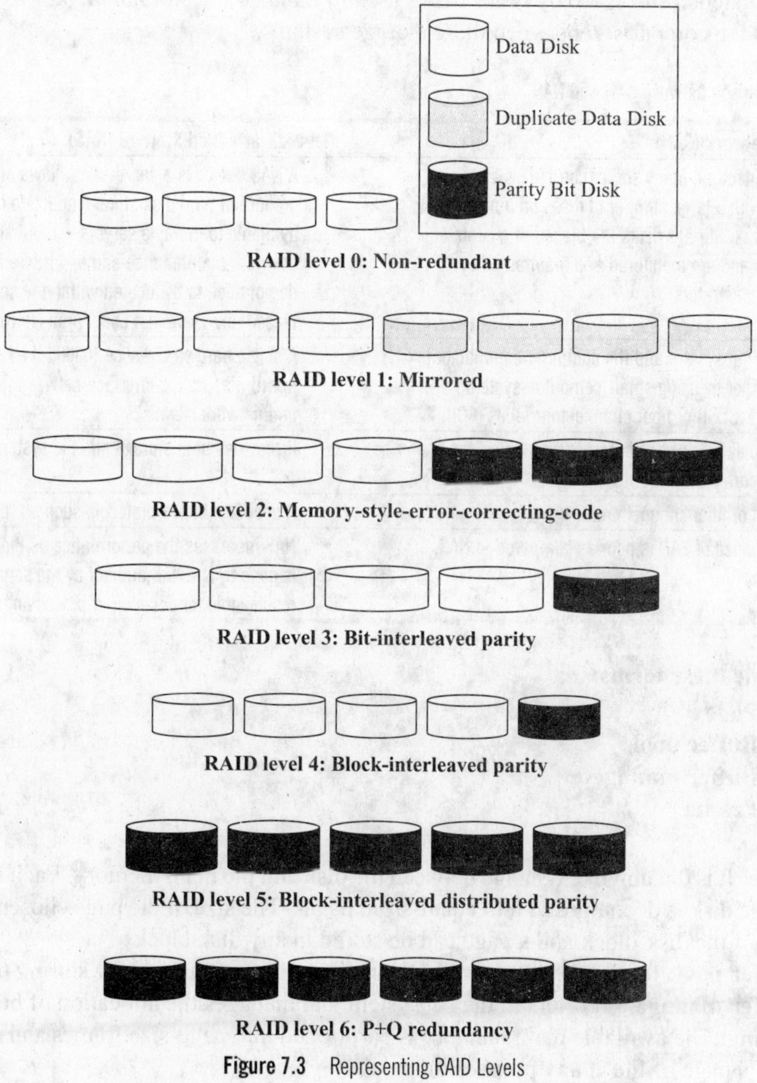

Figure 7.3 Representing RAID Levels

of four actual disks, level 5 has five disks overall, thus, effective space utilization for level 5 is the same as in levels 3 and 4.

- **RAID level 6:** RAID level 6 is an extension of RAID level 5 and applies P + Q redundancy scheme using Reed–Solomon codes. **Reed–Solomon codes** enable RAID level 6 to recover from up to two simultaneous disk failures. RAID level 6 requires two check disks; however, like RAID level 5, redundant information is distributed across all disks using block-level striping.

6. Compare SAN and NAS.

Ans: Due to increasing demand for storage of data and increase in simultaneous requests, managing all the data has become costly. Thus, new storage systems including storage area network (SAN) and network-attached storage (NAS) are being used to manage the storage in various organizations. Table 7.1 lists the comparison between these storage systems.

Table 7.1 Comparison between SAN and NAS

Storage Area Network (SAN)	Network-attached Storage (NAS)
• In SAN architecture, many server computers are connected with a large number of disks on a high-speed network. Storage disks are placed at a central server room and are monitored and maintained by system administrators.	• A NAS device is a server that allows an enormous amount of hard disk storage space to be made available to multiple servers without shutting them down for maintenance and upgrades. The NAS devices do not need to be located within the server, but can be placed anywhere in a Local Area Network (LAN).
• The storage subsystem and the computer communicate with each other by using small-computer-system interconnect (SCSI) or fiber channel interfaces (FCI).	• A single hardware device (called the **NAS box** or **NAS head**) acts as the interface between the NAS system and network clients.
• It provides only block-based storage and leaves the file system concern on the client side.	• It provides both storage and file systems.
• It uses SCSI or fiber channel protocols.	• It uses file-based protocols such as NFS or SMB.
• The performance of SAN is poor as compared to NAS.	• NAS increases the performance as the file serving is done by the NAS and not by the server, which is responsible for doing other processing.

7. Define these terms:

(a) Page
(b) Buffer pool
(c) Buffer manager
(d) Frame

Ans:

(a) Page: It is the unit of exchange between the disk and the main memory. Each file to be stored on the disk is decomposed into equal-sized pages. The size of the page chosen is equal to the size of the disk block and a page can be stored in any disk block.

(b) Buffer pool: It refers to the space in the main memory available for storing the data.

(c) Buffer manager: It refers to the subsystem that manages the allocation of buffer space.

(d) Frame: The available main memory is partitioned into page-size frames and each frame can hold a page of file at any point of time.

8. Define the role of a buffer manager.

Ans: When a request for a page is generated, the buffer manager handles it by passing the memory address of the frame that contains the requested page to its requester, if the page is already in the buffer pool. However, if the page is not available in the buffer pool, the buffer manager allocates space for that page. If no free frame is available in the buffer pool, allocation of space requires de-allocation of some other pages that are no longer needed by the system. After allocating the space in the buffer pool, the buffer manager transfers the requested page from the disk to the main memory. While de-allocating a page, the buffer manager writes back the updated information of that page on the disk if the page has been modified since its last access from the disk (see Figure 7.4).

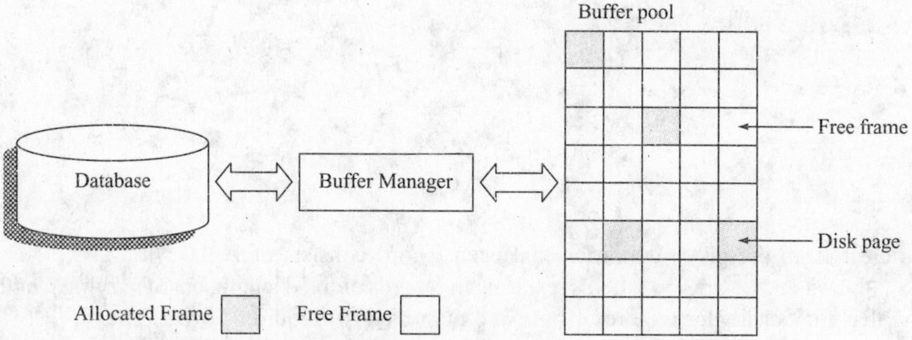

Figure 7.4 Buffer Management

9. Explain the policies used by the buffer manager to replace a page.

Ans: When a page request is generated but there is no space for a new page in the memory, the buffer manager uses a **replacement policy** to choose a page for replacement from the list of unpinned pages. The main goal of replacement policies is to minimize the number of disk accesses for the requested page. Some commonly used replacement policies include **least recently used (LRU), most recently used (MRU)** and **clock replacement**.

- **Least recently used (LRU):** This replacement policy assumes that the pages that have been referenced recently have a greater chance to be referenced again in the near future. Thus, the least recently referenced page should be chosen for replacement.
- **Most recently used (MRU) policy:** This is an optimal replacement policy, which chooses the most recently accessed page for replacement, as and when required. Note that the page currently being used by the system must be pinned and, hence, they are not eligible for replacement. After completing the processing with the page, it must be unpinned by the system so that it becomes available for replacement.
- **Clock replacement:** This replacement policy is a variant of LRU in which an additional `reference` bit is associated with each frame, which is set on as soon as `pin_count`—a variable associated with a frame indicating the number of current users of that frame—becomes 0. All the frames are considered as arranged in a circular manner. A variable `current` moves around the logical circle of frames, starting with the value 1 through `N` (total number of frames in the buffer pool). The clock replacement policy considers the `current` frame for replacement. If the considered frame is not chosen for replacement, the value of the `current` is incremented by one and the next frame is considered. The policy continues to consider the frame until some frame is chosen for replacement. If the `pin_count` of the `current` frame is greater than 0, then the

`current` frame is not a candidate for replacement. If the `current` frame has `pin_count` 0 and `reference` bit on, the algorithm turns it off. Only the frame having `pin_count` 0 and `reference` bit off can be chosen for replacement.

10. Compare and contrast fixed-length and variable-length records.

Ans: The database can be organized in the form of files containing either fixed-length records or variable-length records.

Fixed-length records

All the records in a file of fixed-length record are of the same length. Consider a relation `PUBLISHER` whose record is defined as:

```
CREATE PUBLISHER as
(P_ID           char(5)        PRIMARY KEY NOT NULL,
Pname           char(20)       NOT NULL,
Address         char(50),
State           char(20),
Phone           numeric(10),
Email_id        char(50))
```

It is clear from the given definition that each record consists of `P_ID, Pname, Address, State, Phone` and `Email_id` fields resulting in records of fixed length, but of varying length fields. Assume that each character requires 1 byte and numeric (10) requires 5 bytes, then a `PUBLISHER` record is 150 bytes long. Figure 7.5 represents a record of `PUBLISHER` relation with starting of each field within the record.

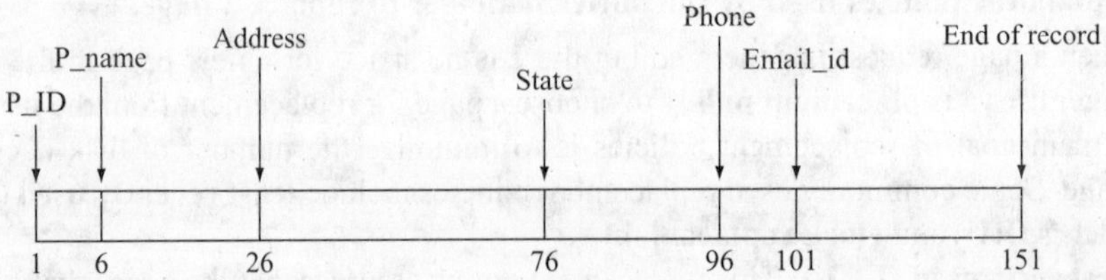

Figure 7.5 Fixed-length Record

In a file of fixed-length records, every record consists of the same number of fields, and the size of each field is fixed for every record. It ensures easy location of field values as their positions are predetermined. Since each record occupies equal memory, identifying the start and end of the record is relatively simple.

A major drawback of fixed-length records is that a lot of memory space is wasted. Since a record may contain some optional fields and space is reserved for optional fields as well—it stores *null* value if no value is supplied by the user for that field. Thus, if certain records do not have values for all the fields, memory space is wasted. In addition, it is difficult to delete a record as deletion of a record leaves a blank space in between the two records. To fill up that blank space, all the records following the deleted record need to be shifted, which is undesirable, since it requires additional disk accesses.

Variable-length Records

Variable-length records may be used to utilize memory more efficiently. In this approach, the exact length of the field is not fixed in advance. Thus, to determine the start and end of each field within the record, special separator characters, which do not appear anywhere within the field value, are required (see Figure 7.6). Locating any field within the record requires a scan of the record until the field is found.

P_ID	%	Pname	%	Address	%	State	%	Phone	%	Email_id

Figure 7.6 Organization of Variable-length Records with '%' Delimiter

Memory is utilized efficiently but processing the variable-length records requires a complicated program. Moreover, modifying the value of any field might require shifting of all the following fields, since the new value may occupy more or less space than the space occupied by the existing value.

11. What is a file header and free list?

Ans: In order to keep track of free space created by deleted or marked records, a certain number of bytes is reserved in the beginning of the file for a file header. The **file header** stores the address of a first marked record (marked for deletion), which further points to the second marked record and so on. As a result, a linked list of marked slot is formed, which is commonly termed as a **free list**.

12. Why do variable-length records require separator characters? Is there any alternative of using a separator character? Justify your answer.

Ans: In the variable-length record approach, the exact length of the field is not fixed in advance. Thus, to determine the start and end of each field within the record, special separator characters (see Figure 7.6), which do not appear anywhere within the field value, are required. Locating any field within the record requires a scan of the record until the field is found.

An alternative to the separator character is to use an array of integer offsets to indicate the starting address of fields within a record. The ith element of this array is the starting address of the ith field value relative to the start of the record. An offset to the end of the record is also stored in this array, which is used to recognize the end of the last field. Figure 7.7 shows the organization of the variable-length record shown in Figure 7.6 using an array of field offsets. For a *null* value, the pointer to the starting and end of the field is set as the same. That is, no space is used to represent a *null* value.

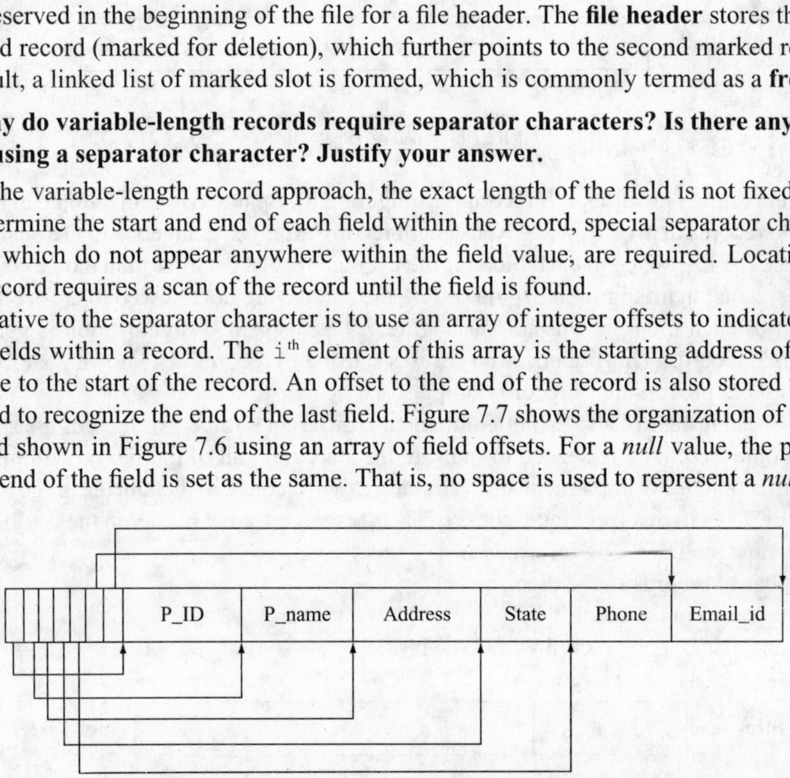

Figure 7.7 Variable-length Record Organization Using an Array of Field Offsets

This technique is a more efficient way of organizing the variable-length records and it facilitates direct access to any field of the record. However, handling such an offset array is an extra overhead.

13. Compare and contrast spanned and unspanned organization of records. What is a slotted page structure, and why is it needed?

Ans: The records of a file can be organized into disk blocks using two ways: *spanned* and *unspanned* organizations.

In **spanned organization**, records can span more than one disk block. Since the block size is not always a multiple of record size, each disk block might have some unused space. This unused space can be utilized by storing a part of a record on one block and the rest on another. In case consecutive blocks are not allocated to the file, the pointer at the end of the first block points to the block that

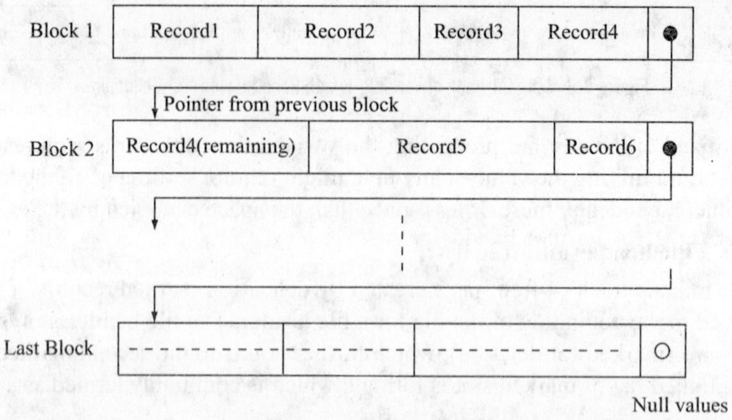

Figure 7.8 Spanned Organization

contains the remaining part of its last record (see Figure 7.8). Spanned organization can be used with variable-length records as well as with fixed-length records. It is advantageous to use spanned organization to reduce the lost space in each block if the average record is larger than a block.

On the other hand, in **unspanned organization**, the records are not allowed to cross block boundaries, thus, part of each block is wasted (see Figure 7.9). Unspanned organization is generally used with fixed-length records. This organization ensures starting of records at a known position within the block, which makes processing of records simple.

As we know that in case of a variable-length record, different numbers of records are stored in each block. Thus, some technique is needed to indicate the start and end of the record within each block. One common technique to implement the variable-length records is the **slotted page structure** as shown in Figure 7.10. In this technique, some space is reserved for the header in the beginning of each block that contains the following information:

- total number of records in the block
- end of free space in the block
- location and size of each record within the block

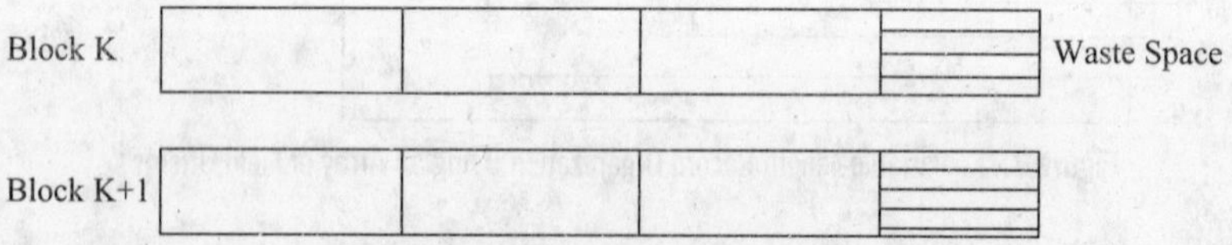

Figure 7.9 Unspanned Organization

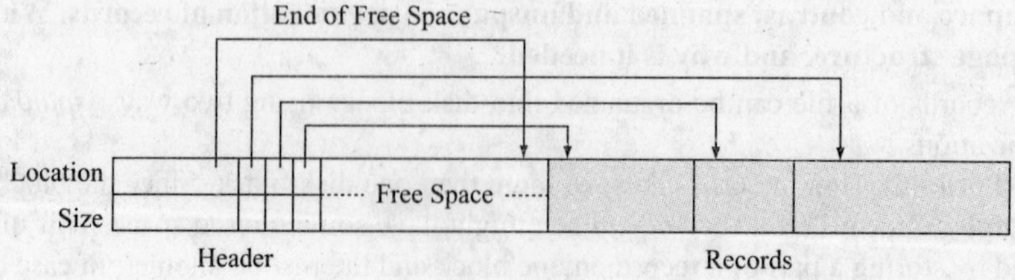

Figure 7.10 Slotted Page Structure

In the slotted page structure, starting from the end of the block, the actual records are stored contiguously and the free space is contiguous between the final entry in the header array and the first record. The space for the new record is allocated at the end of the free space, and the corresponding entry of record location and record size is included in the header. The record is deleted by removing its entry from the header and freeing the space occupied by the record. To make the free space contiguous within the block again, all the records before the records that have been deleted are shifted to their right. In addition, the header entry pointing to the end of the free space is updated as well.

In the slotted page structure, no outside pointers point directly to actual records, rather they must point to the entry in the header, which contains the location and size of each record. This support of indirect pointers to records allows records to be moved within the block to prevent fragmented free space inside a block.

14. Discuss the importance of file organization in databases. Discuss in brief various types of file organizations available.

Ans: The arrangement of the records in a file plays a significant role in accessing them. Moreover, proper organization of files on disk helps in accessing the file records efficiently. There are various methods (known as **file organization**) of organizing the records in a file while storing a file on disk. Some popular methods are *heap file organization*, *sequential file organization* and *hash file organization*.

- **Heap file organization:** It is the simplest file organization technique in which no particular order of record is maintained in the file. Instead, records can be placed anywhere in the file, where there is enough space for that record. Such an organization is generally termed as **heap file** or **pile file**. Heap file is divided into pages of equal size and every record is identified by its unique id or record id. Operations that can be carried out on a heap file include *creation* and *deletion* of files, *insertion* and *deletion* of record, *searching* a particular record and *scanning* of all records in the file. A heap file supports efficient insertion of a new record; however, scanning, searching and deletion of records are expensive processes.
- **Sequential file organization:** A file organization in which records are sorted based on the value of one of its field is called **sequential file organization**, and such a file is called a **sequential file**. In a sequential file, the field on which the records are sorted is called **ordered field**. This field may or may not be the key field. In case, the file is ordered on the basis of the key, then the field is called the **ordering key**. Searching of records is more efficient in a sequential file if the search condition is specified on the ordering field because then binary search is applicable instead of linear search. Moreover, retrieval of records with the range condition specified on the ordering field is also very efficient. In this operation, all the records starting with the first record satisfying the range selection condition till the first record that does not satisfy the condition are retrieved. However, handling deletion and insertion operations are complicated.
- **Hash file organization:** In this organization, records are organized using a technique called **hashing**, which enables very fast access to records on the basis of certain search conditions. This organization is called the **hash file** or **direct file**. In hashing, a **hash function** h is applied to a single field, called **hash field**, to determine the page to which the record belongs. The page is then searched to locate the record. In this way, only one page is accessed to locate a record. The hash field is known as the **hash key** in case the hash field is the key field of the file. Hashing is typically implemented as a **hash table** by the use of an array of records.

Given the hash field value, the hash function tells us where to look in the array for that record.

15. Explain two techniques for implementing a heap file with the help of a suitable diagram.

Ans: Heap files can be implemented using two techniques one of which is based on the linked list while the other is directory-based implementation.

In the **linked list implementation** of heap files, two linked lists of pages—one for those having no free space and another for those having some free space—are maintained (see Figure 7.11). The system only needs to keep track of first page of the file called the **header page**. When a new record is to be inserted in the file, the page with enough free space is located and the record is inserted in that page. If there is no page with enough space to accommodate that new record, a new page is allocated to the file and the record is inserted in the new page. The main disadvantage of this technique is that we sometimes may require examining several pages for inserting a new record. Moreover, in case of variable-length records, each page might always have some free space in it. Thus, all the pages allocated to the file will be on the list of free pages.

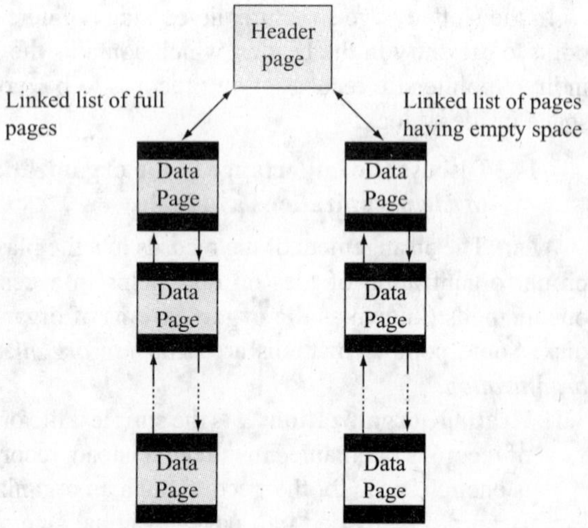

Figure 7.11 Linked List of Heap File Organization

The **directory-based implementation** of heap files addresses the disadvantage of linked list implementation and maintains a directory of pages. In this directory, each entry has a pointer to a page in the file and the amount of free space in that page. When the directory itself contains several pages, they are linked together to form a linked list. Organization of a heap file using the directory is shown in Figure 7.12.

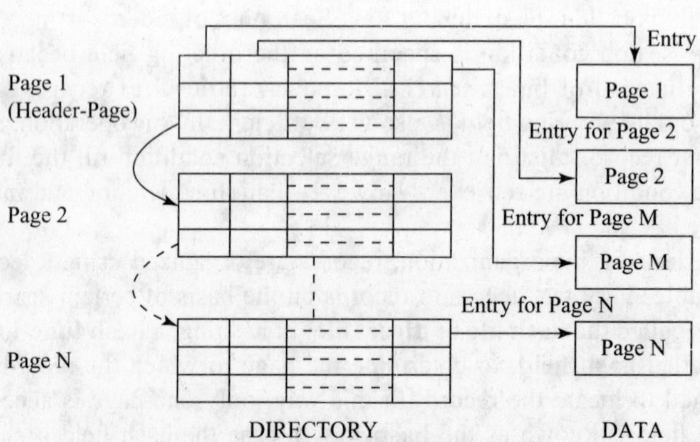

Figure 7.12 Directory-based Heap File Organization

16. Discuss the commonly used hash functions. What is the main problem associated with most of them, and how can it be resolved?

Ans: Some commonly used hash functions include cut key hashing, folded key and division-remainder hashing. These hash functions are described as follows:

- **Cut key hashing:** This hash function 'cuts' some digits from the hash field value (or simply key) and uses it as a hash address. For example, if there are 100 locations in the array, a two-digit address, say 37, may be obtained from the key 132437 by picking the highlighted digits. It is not a good algorithm because most of the key is ignored and only a part of the key is used to compute the address.
- **Folded key:** This hash function involves applying some arithmetic functions, such as *addition/subtraction* or some logical functions, such as *and/or* to the key value. The result obtained is used as the record address. For example, the key is broken down into a group of two-digit numbers from the left-most digits and they are added like 13 + 24 + 37 = 74. The sum is then used as record address. It is better than cut key hashing as the entire key is used but not good enough as records are not distributed evenly among pages.
- **Division-remainder hashing:** This hash function is commonly used and in this, the value of the hash field is divided by `N` and the remainder is used as record address.

  `Record address = (Key value) mod (N).`

  This technique works very well provided that `N` is either a prime number nor does it have a small divisor.

The main problem associated with most hashing functions is that they do not yield distinct addresses for distinct hash field values, because the number of possible values a hash field can take is much larger than the number of available addresses to store records. Thus, sometimes a problem,

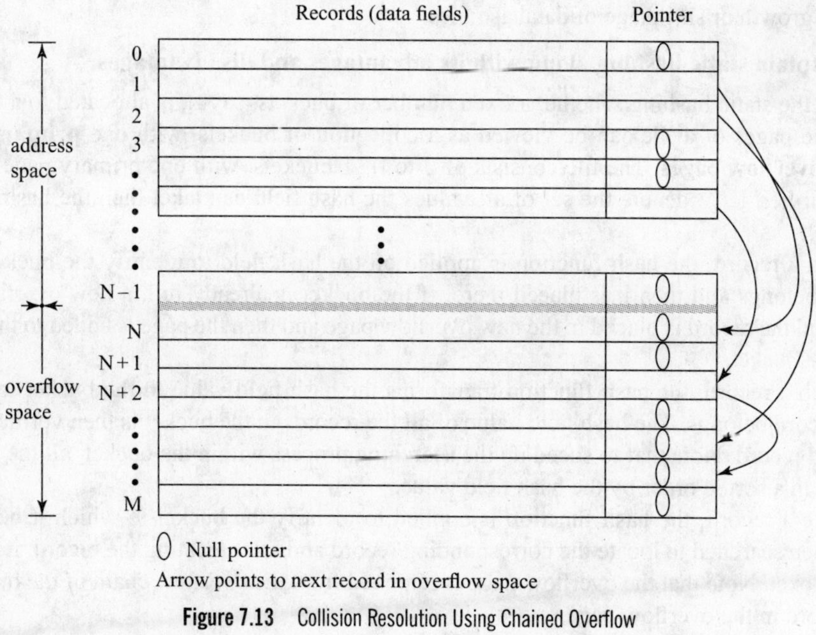

Figure 7.13 Collision Resolution Using Chained Overflow

called **collision**, occurs when the hash field value of a record to be inserted hashes to an address, which is already being occupied by another record. It should be resolved by finding some other location to place the new record. This process of finding another location is called **collision resolution**. Some popular methods for collision resolution are as follows:

- **Open addressing:** In this method, the program keeps checking the subsequent locations starting from the occupied location specified by the hash function until an unused or empty location is found.
- **Multiple hashing:** In this method, the program can use another hash function if the first hash function results in a collision. If another collision occurs, the program may apply another hash function and so on, or it can use open addressing if necessary. This technique of applying a multiple hash function is called **double hashing** or **multiple hashing**.
- **Chained overflow:** In this method, all the records whose addresses are already occupied are stored in an overflow space. In addition, a pointer field is associated with each record location. A collision is resolved by placing the new record in overflow space and the pointer field of occupied hash address location is set to that location in overflow space. In this way, a linked list of records, which hash to the same address, is maintained, as shown in Figure 7.13.

17. What is the difference between static hashing and dynamic hashing?

Ans: There are two types of hashing schemes, namely *static hashing* and *dynamic hashing*, depending on the number of buckets allocated to a file. The hashing scheme in which a fixed number of buckets, say `N`, are allocated to a file to store records is called **static hashing**. In other words, in static hashing, the number of available addresses for records is fixed in advance. This makes it unsuitable for the files that grow or shrink dynamically. An alternative to the static hashing scheme is to use **dynamic hashing** that allows the number of buckets to vary dynamically with only minor (internal) reorganization. Dynamic hashing also allows the hash function to be modified dynamically to accommodate the growth or shrinkage of database files.

18. Explain static hashing along with its advantages and disadvantages.

Ans: In the static hashing scheme, a fixed number of buckets, say `N`, is allocated to a file to store records. The pages of a file can be viewed as a collection of buckets, with one **primary** page and additional **overflow** pages. The file consists of `0` to `N-1` buckets, with one primary page per bucket initially. Further, let `V` denote the set of all values the hash field can take, then the hash function `h` maps `V` to `N`.

To insert a record, the hash function is applied on the hash field to identify the bucket to which the record belongs and then it is placed there. If the bucket is already full, a new overflow page is allocated and the record is placed in the new overflow page and then the page is added to the **overflow chain** of the bucket.

To search a record, the hash function transforms the hash field value to the bucket to which the required record belongs. The hash field value of all the records in the bucket is then verified to search the required record. Note that to speed up the searching process within the bucket, all the records are maintained in a sorted order by the hash field value.

To delete a record, the hash function is applied to identify the bucket to which it belongs. The bucket is then searched to locate the corresponding record and after locating the record, it is removed from the bucket. Note that the overflow page is removed from the overflow chain of the bucket if it is the last record in the overflow page.

Advantages

In static hashing, since the number of buckets allocated to a file is fixed when the file is created, the primary pages can be stored on consecutive disk pages. Hence, searching a record requires just one disk I/O, and other operations, such as insertion and deletion, require two I/Os (read and write the page).

Disadvantages

It is undesirable to use static hashing with files that grow or shrink a lot dynamically, since the number of buckets is fixed in advance. For example, if the file grows, long overflow chains are developed, which degrade the performance of the file, as searching a bucket requires searching all the pages in its overflow chain. Similarly, if a file shrinks greatly, a lot of space is left unused. In either case, the number of buckets allocated to the file needs to be changed dynamically and a new hash function based on the new value of N should be used for the distribution of records. However, such reorganization consumes a lot of time for large files.

19. Describe extendible hashing and linear hashing.

Ans: Extendible hashing and linear hashing are the two forms of dynamic hashing.

Extendible hashing

Extendible hashing uses a **directory** of pointers to buckets. A directory is just an array of 2^d size, where d (called **global depth)** is the number of bits of hash value used to locate the directory element. Each element of the directory is a pointer to a bucket in which the corresponding records are stored.

In this technique, the hash function is applied on the hash field value and the last d bits of hash value are used to locate the directory element. The pointer in this array position points to the bucket to which the corresponding record belongs. To understand this technique, consider a directory consisting of an array of 2^2 size (see Figure 7.14), which means an array of size 4. Here d is 2, thus, the last 2 bits of hash value are used to locate a directory element. Further, assume that each bucket can

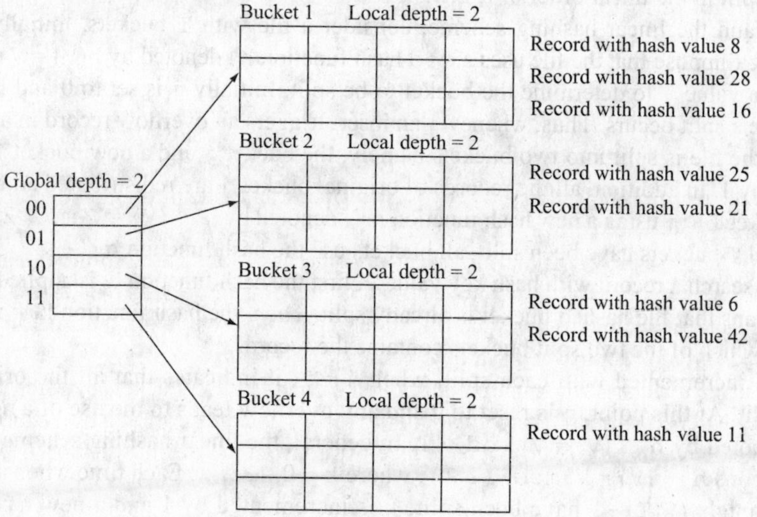

Figure 7.14 Extendible Hashed File

hold three records. The search for a key, say 21, proceeds as follows. The last 2 bits of hash value 21 (binary 10101) hash into the directory element 01, which points to bucket 2.

During the insertion of a new record, the same procedure as described above is repeated to locate the bucket where the record should be inserted. In case the searched bucket has space for the new record, the record is inserted there. However, if the bucket is full, extendible hashing splits this full bucket by allocating a new bucket and redistributes the records across the old bucket (say, Bucket 1) and its split image (named Bucket 1a). To redistribute the records among these two buckets, the last three bits of hash value are considered. The last two bits indicate the directory element and the third bit differentiates between these two buckets. Now, the contents of Bucket 1 and Bucket 1a are identified by 3 bits of hash value, whereas the contents of all the other buckets can be identified by 2 bits. To identify the number of bits on which the bucket contents are based, a **local depth** is maintained with each bucket, which specifies the number of bits required to identify its contents. Note that if the local depth of the overflowed bucket is equal to the global depth, there is a need to double the number of entries in the directory and the global depth is incremented by one. However, if the local depth of the overflowed bucket is less than the global depth, there is no need to double the directory entries.

To delete a record, first the record is located and then removed from the bucket. In case, the deletion leaves the bucket empty, the bucket can be merged with its split bucket image. The local depth is decreased if the buckets are merged. After merging, if the local depth of all the buckets becomes less than the global depth, the number of entries in the directory can be halved and the global depth is to be reduced by one.

Linear hashing

Linear hashing also allows a hash file to grow or shrink dynamically by allocating new buckets. In addition, there is no need to maintain a directory of pointers to buckets. Like static hashing, collision can be handled by maintaining overflow chains of pages; however, linear hashing solves the problem of long overflow chains. In linear hashing, overflow of any bucket in the file leads to a bucket split. Note that the bucket to be split is not necessarily the same as the overflow bucket; instead buckets are chosen to be split in the linear order 0, 1, 2,….

To understand the linear hashing scheme, consider a file with T buckets, initially numbered 0 through T - 1. Suppose that the file uses a mod hash function h_i, denoted by $h(V) = V \bmod T$. Linear hashing uses a value j to determine the bucket to be split. Initially j is set to 0 and is incremented by 1 each time a split occurs. Thus, whenever an insert triggers an overflow record in any bucket, the jth bucket in the file is split into two buckets namely, the bucket j and a new bucket T + j and j is incremented by 1. In addition, all the records of original bucket j are redistributed among the bucket j and the bucket T + j using a new hash function h_{i+1}, denoted by $h_{i+1}(V) = V \bmod 2T$. Thus, when all the original T buckets have been split, all buckets use the hash function h_{i+1}.

In order to search a record with hash key value V, first the hash function h_i is applied to V and if $h_i(V) < j$, it means that the hashed bucket is already split. Then, the hash function h_{i+1} is applied to V to determine which of the two split buckets contains the record.

Since j is incremented with each split, when j = T, it indicates that all the original buckets have been split. At this point, j is reset to 0 and any overflow leads to the use of a new hash function h_{i+2}, denoted by $h_{i+2}(V) = V \bmod 4T$. In general, the linear hashing scheme uses a family of hash functions $h_{i+k}(V) = V \bmod (2^kT)$, where k = 0, 1, 2,…. Each time when all the original buckets 0 through $(2^kT)-1$ have been split, k is incremented by 1 and a new hashing function h_{i+k} is needed.

20. List some advantages and disadvantages of extendible hashing.

Ans: Extendible hashing offers certain advantages over static hashing, which are as follows:

- The performance of the file does not degrade as the file grows dynamically. In addition, there is no space allocated in advance for future growth of the file; however, buckets can be allocated dynamically as needed.
- The size of the directory is likely to be much smaller than the file itself, since each directory element is just a page-id. Thus, the space overhead for the directory table is negligible. The directory can be extended up to 2^n, where n is the number of bits in the hash value.
- Bucket splitting requires minor reorganization in most cases.

Some disadvantages of extendible hashing are as follows:

- The reorganization is expensive when the directory needs to be doubled or halved.
- The directory must be accessed and searched before accessing the record in the bucket. Thus, most record retrievals require two block accesses, one for the directory and the other for the bucket.

21. What are the advantages of having an index on a file? List the different types of single-level indexes available? Discuss them in detail.

Ans: Once the records of a file are placed on the disk using some file organization method, the main issue is to provide a quick response to different queries. For this, an additional structure called **index** on the file can be created, which provides efficient access to the file records. Index can be created on any field of the file, and that field is called **indexing field** or **indexing attribute**. Further, more than one index can be created on a file.

Accessing records of a file using the index requires accessing the index, which helps us to locate the record efficiently. This is because the values in the index are stored in the sorted order and the size of the index file is small as compared to the original file. Thus, applying binary search on the index is efficient as compared to applying binary search on the original file.

Types of single-level indexes

Different types of single-level indexes are as follows:

- **Primary index:** It refers to the index created on the field on which the file is ordered, that is, the primary key of the relation. This index file contains two attributes—the first attribute stores the value of the attribute on which the index is created and the second attribute contains a pointer to the record in the original file. If the index contains an entry for each value of the indexing attribute, it is referred to as the **dense index**. However, if it does not include an entry for each value of the indexing attribute, it is referred to as **sparse indexes** (or **non-dense indexes**). Insertion and deletion operations on the ordered file are handled in the same way as in case of a sequential file. However, it may also require modifying the pointers in several entries of the index file.
- **Clustering index:** It refers to an index created on the ordered non-key attribute of a file and that attribute is called **clustering attribute**. This index contains an entry for each distinct value of the clustering attribute and the corresponding pointer points to the first record with that clustering attribute value. Other records with the same clustering attribute value are stored sequentially after that record since the file is ordered on that attribute. Inserting a new record in the file is easy if space is available in the block in which it has to be placed. Otherwise, a new block is allocated to the file and the new record is placed in that block. In addition, the pointer of the block to which the record actually belongs is made to point to the new block.
- **Secondary index:** It refers to an index created on the non-ordered attribute of the file. The indexing attribute may be a candidate key or a non-key attribute with duplicate values. In either

case, the secondary index must contain an entry for each value of the indexing attribute. It means the secondary index must be a dense index. This is because the file is not ordered on the indexing attribute and if some of the values are stored in the index, it is not possible to find a record whose entry does not exist in the index. The index file itself is ordered on the indexing attribute. Inserting and deleting a record is straightforward with a little modification in the index file.

22. Give any two advantages of a sparse index over a dense index.

Ans: Although the dense index provides faster access to the file records than the sparse index, the sparse index provides the following advantages over the dense index:

- A sparse index with one entry per block is advantageous in terms of disk space and maintenance overhead while updating operations.
- Once the disk block is identified and its records are brought into the memory, scanning them is almost negligible.

23. What is a multi-level index? Also give reasons for having multilevel index.

Ans: The type of index with multiple levels (two or more levels) of index is called a **multi-level index**. Generally, there are several thousands (or even lacs) of records in the database of medium or large-scale organizations. As the size of the file grows, the size of the index (even sparse index) grows as well. If the size of the index becomes too large to fit into the main memory at once, it becomes inefficient for processing, since it must be kept sequentially on the disk just like an ordinary file. It implies that searching large indexes requires several disk-block accesses.

As a solution to this problem, the index file, which we refer to as the **first** or **base level** of a multi-level index, can be viewed as just as any other sequential file, and a primary index can be created on it. This index to the first level is called the **second level** of the multi-level index. If the second-level index is too small to fit into the main memory at once, fewer blocks of the index file need to be accessed from the disk to locate a particular record. However, if the second-level index file is too large to fit into the main memory at once, another level of index can be created. In fact, this process of creating the index on an index can be repeated until the size of the index becomes small enough to fit into the main memory. Multi-level indexing reduces the number of disk accesses while searching for a record.

24. Describe a tree pointer and a data pointer.

Ans: Each node of the B-tree or B$^+$-tree can contain two types of pointers, namely *tree pointers* and *data pointers*. The **tree pointer** points to any other node of the tree and the **data pointer** points either to the block that contains the record with that index value or to the record itself. If the indexing attribute is the key attribute, the data pointer points either to the record in the file or to the disk block containing the record with that indexing attribute value. On the other hand, if the indexing attribute is not the key attribute, the data pointer points to the bucket of pointers, each of which points to the record in the file.

25. What does the order of a B-tree and B$^+$-tree indicate? Also explain the structure of both internal and external nodes of a B-tree and B$^+$-tree.

Ans: The order `n` of a B-tree indicates that there are `n` tree pointers, `n - 1` values and `n - 1` data pointers in each node. The order `n` of a B$^+$-tree indicates that there are `n - 1` values in each node, `n - 1` data pointers in each leaf node and `n` tree pointers in each internal node. Note that irrespective of the order, every leaf node of B$^+$-tree contains one tree pointer.

B-tree

In the B-tree, the structure of the leaf node and the internal node are the same except the difference that all the tree pointers in a leaf node are null. The order of information within each node is $<P_1, <V_1, R_1>, P_2, <V_2, R_2>, P_3, <V_3, R_3>, \ldots, P_{n-1}, <V_{n-1}, R_{n-1}>, P_n>$ where P_i is a tree pointer, V_i any value of the indexing attribute and R_i a data pointer (see Figure 7.15).

P_1	$<V_1,R_1>$	----------	$<V_{i-1},R_{i-1}>$	P_i	$<V_i,R_i>$	--------	$<V_{n-1},R_{n-1}>$	P_n

Figure 7.15 A Node of a B-tree

All the values in a node should be in the sorted order, it means $V_1<V_2<\ldots<V_{n-1}$ within each node of the tree. In addition, the node pointed to by any tree pointer P_i should contain all the values larger than the value V_{i-1} and less than the value V_i. Another constraint that the B-tree must satisfy is that it must be balanced; it means all the leaf nodes should be at the same level.

B⁺-tree

Unlike the B-tree, the B^+-tree includes all the values of the indexing attribute in the leaf nodes, and internal nodes contain values just for directing the search operation. All the pointers in the internal nodes are tree pointers and there is no data pointer in them. All the data pointers are included in the leaf nodes and there is one tree pointer in each leaf node that points to the next leaf node. The structure of the leaf node and internal nodes of a B^+-tree is shown in Figure 7.16.

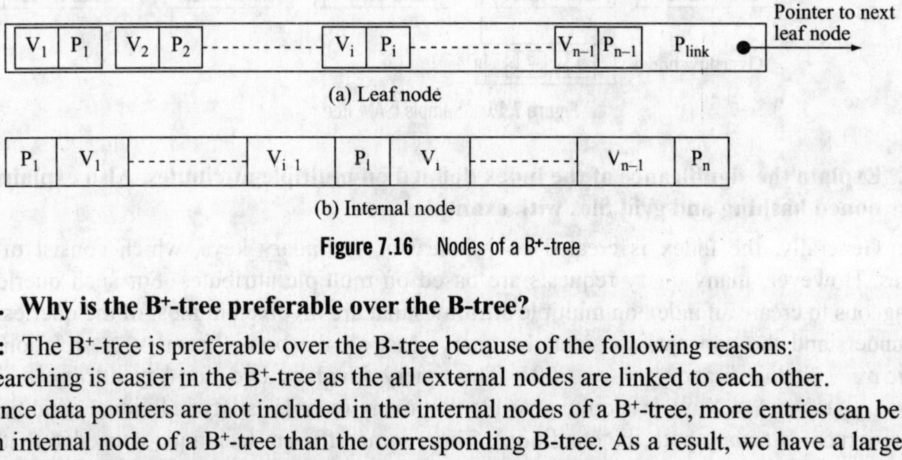

Figure 7.16 Nodes of a B^+-tree

26. Why is the B^+-tree preferable over the B-tree?

Ans: The B^+-tree is preferable over the B-tree because of the following reasons:

- Searching is easier in the B^+-tree as the all external nodes are linked to each other.
- Since data pointers are not included in the internal nodes of a B^+-tree, more entries can be fit into an internal node of a B^+-tree than the corresponding B-tree. As a result, we have a larger order for the B^+-tree than the B-tree for the same size of the disk block.

27. Write a short note on indexed the sequential access method.

Ans: Indexed Sequential Access Method (ISAM) is a variant of the B^+-tree. In ISAM, the leaf nodes and the overflow nodes (chained to some leaf nodes) contain all the values of indexing attribute and data pointers, and the internal nodes contain values and tree pointers just for directing the search operation. Unlike the B^+-tree, the ISAM index structure is static, it means the number of leaf nodes never changes; if a need arises, the overflow node is allocated and chained to the leaf node. The leaf nodes are assumed to be allocated sequentially, thus, no pointer is needed in the leaf node to point to the next leaf node.

The algorithms for insertion, deletion and search are simple. All searches start at the root node and the value in the node helps in determining the next node to search. To insert a value, first the appropriate node is determined and if there is space in the node, the value is inserted there. Otherwise, an overflow node is allocated and chained to the node, and then the value is inserted in the overflow node. To delete a value, the node containing the value is determined and the value is deleted from that node. In case it is the only value in the overflow node, the overflow node is also removed. In case, it is the only value in the leaf node, the node is left empty to handle future insertions (data from overflow nodes, if any, linked to that leaf node are not moved to the leaf node).

The ISAM structure provides the benefits of sequentially allocated leaf nodes and fast searches as in the case of B⁺-trees. However, the structure is unsuitable for situations where the file grows or shrinks much. This is because if too many insertions are made to the same leaf node, a long overflow chain can develop, which degrades the performance while searching as overflow nodes need to be searched if the search reaches that leaf node. A sample ISAM tree is shown in Figure 7.17.

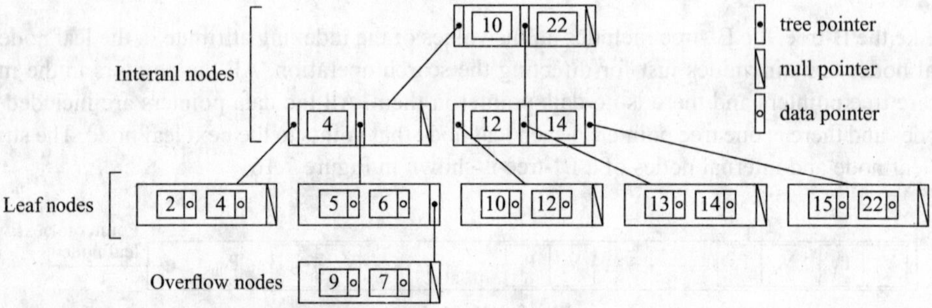

Figure 7.17 Sample ISAM Tree

28. Explain the significance of the index defined on multiple attributes. Also explain partitioned hashing and grid files with examples.

Ans: Generally, the index is created on primary or secondary keys, which consist of single attributes. However, many query requests are based on multiple attributes. For such queries, it is advantageous to create an index on multiple attributes that are involved in most of the queries.

To understand the concept, consider the query: List all the books from `BOOK` relation where `Category` = *Textbook* and `P_ID` = *P001*. This query involves two non-key attributes, namely `Category` and `P_ID`. Now, it is quite possible that many records satisfy individual conditions and only a few records satisfy both the conditions. Thus, some efficient technique is needed that would treat the combination of `Category` and `P_ID` as a search key. Two such techniques are *partitioned hashing* and *grid files*.

Partitioned hashing

It is an extension of static hashing that allows access on multiple keys. Partitioned hashing does not support range queries; however, it is suitable for equality comparisons. In partitioned hashing, for a composite search key consisting of `n` attributes, the chosen hash function produces `n` separate hash addresses. These `n` addresses are concatenated to obtain the bucket address. All the buckets, which match the part of the address, are then searched for the combined search key.

The main advantage of partitioned hashing is that it can be easily extended to any number of attributes in the search key. In addition, there is no need to maintain separate access structures for individual attributes. On the other hand, the main disadvantage of partitioned hashing is that it does not support range queries on any of the component attributes.

Grid files

In grid files, a grid array with one linear scale (or dimension) for each of the search attribute is created. Linear scales are made in order to provide a uniform distribution of attribute values in the grid array. The linear scale groups the values of one search-key attribute to each dimension. Figure 7.18 shows a grid array along with two linear scales, one is for attribute `Category` and the other is for attribute `P_ID`. Each grid cell points to some bucket address where the corresponding records are stored. The number of attributes in the search key determines the dimension of the grid array. Thus, for a search key having `n` attributes, the grid array would have `n` dimensions. In our example, two attributes are taken as search keys; thus, the grid array is of two dimensions. The linear scale is looked up to map into the corresponding grid cell. Thus, the query for `Category` = *Textbook* and `P_ID` = *P001* maps into the cell (2, 0), which further points to the bucket address where the required records are stored.

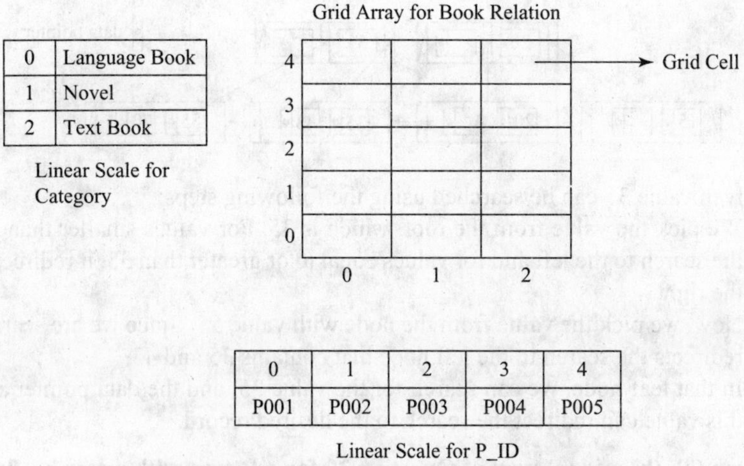

Figure 7.18 Grid Array along with Two Linear Scales

The main advantage of this method is that it can be applied for range queries. In addition, it is extended to any number of attributes in the search key. The grid file method is good for multiple-key search. On the other hand, the main disadvantage is that it represents space and management overhead in terms of the grid array because it requires frequent reorganization of grid files with dynamic files.

29. Consider an empty B⁺-tree with order $p = 3$, and perform the following.

(a) Show the tree after inserting these values: 70, 15, 20, 35, 18, 55 and 43. Assume that the values are inserted in the order given.

(b) Show the tree after deleting the node with value 18 from the tree.

(c) Show the steps involved in finding the value 35.

Ans: **(a)** After inserting the given values, the B$^+$-tree will be represented as shown in the following figure:

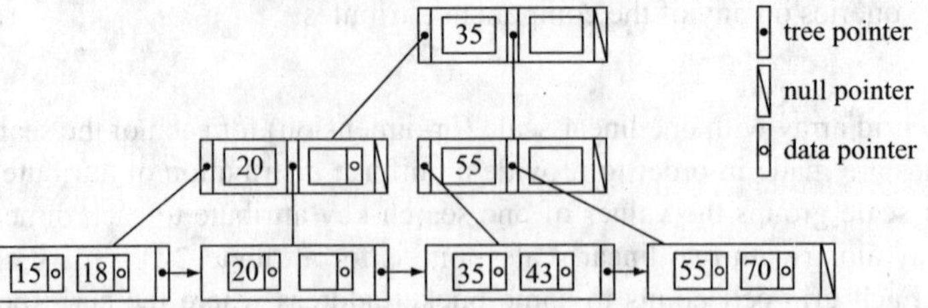

(b) After deletion of the node with value 18, the B$^+$-tree will be represented as shown in the following figure:

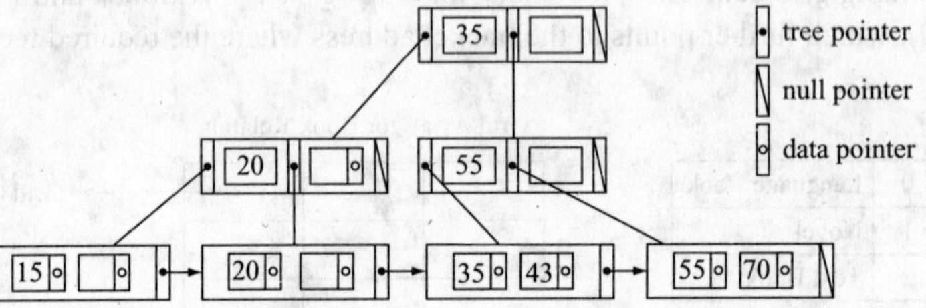

(c) The given value 35 can be searched using the following steps:

(i) We pick the value from the root, which is 35. For values smaller than 35, it redirects the search to the left and for values equal to or greater than 35, it redirects the search to the right.

(ii) Now, we pick the value from the node with value 55. Since we are searching for 35, it redirects the search to the left node that contains 35 and 43.

(iii) In that leaf node, we can search for the value 35, and the data pointer associated with this value can redirect the search to the desired record.

30. Perform (a), (b) and (c) part of Question 29 for a B-tree with order $p = 3$.

Ans: **(a)** After inserting the given values, the B-tree will be represented as shown in the following figure:

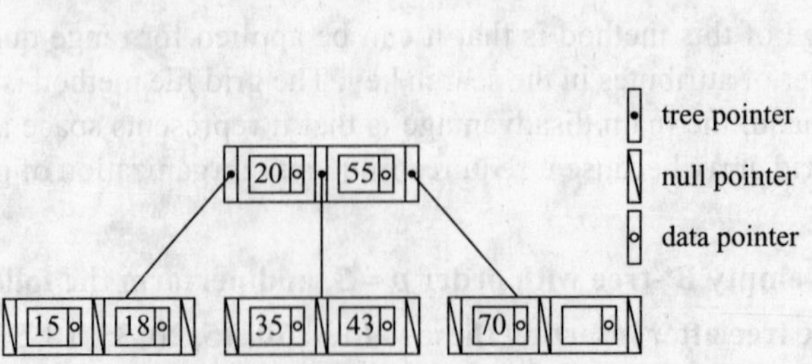

(b) After deletion of the node with value 18, the B-tree will be represented as shown in the following figure:

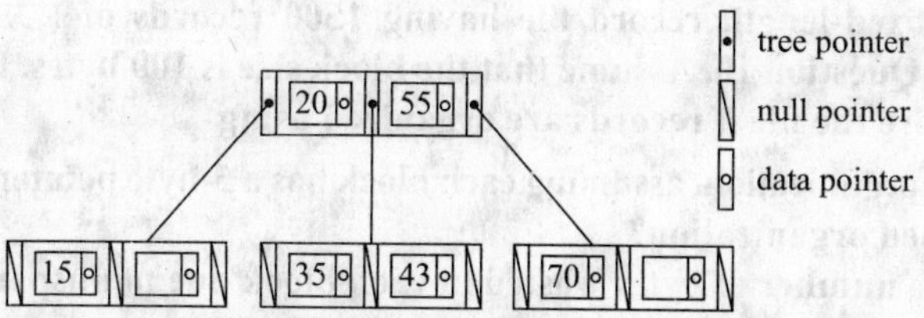

(c) Since 35 is greater than 20 and smaller than 55, the middle pointer redirects the search to the leaf node containing values 35 and 43.

31. Create a linear hash file on a file that contains records with these key values: 70, 15, 20, 35, 18, 55 and 43. Assume that the hash function used is `h(k) = k mod 5`, and each bucket can hold three records.

Ans: The linear hash file will be represented as shown in the following figure:

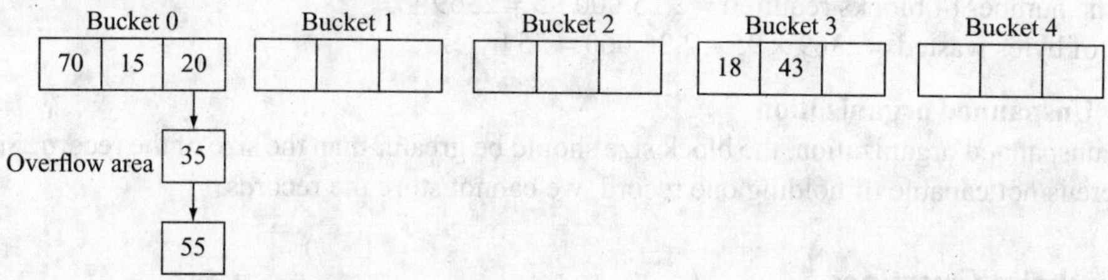

32. Show the hash file created in Question 31 when the following steps are performed on the database file:

(a) Insertion of a record with key value 12.

(b) Deletion of a record with key value 18.

Ans: **(a)** After inserting the record with key value 12, the hash file will be represented as shown in the following figure:

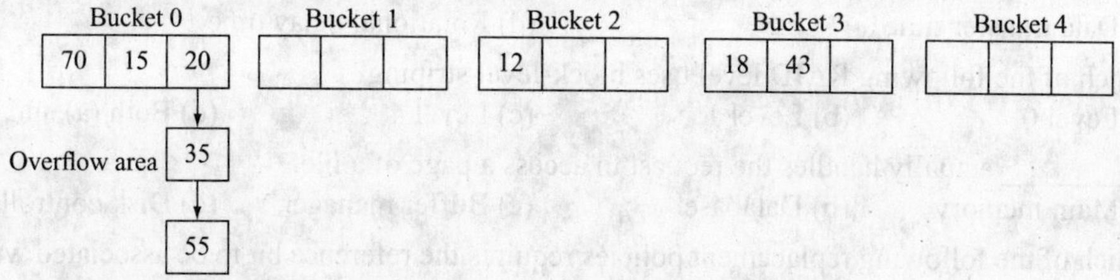

(b) After the deletion of the record with key value 18, the hash file will be represented as shown in the following figure:

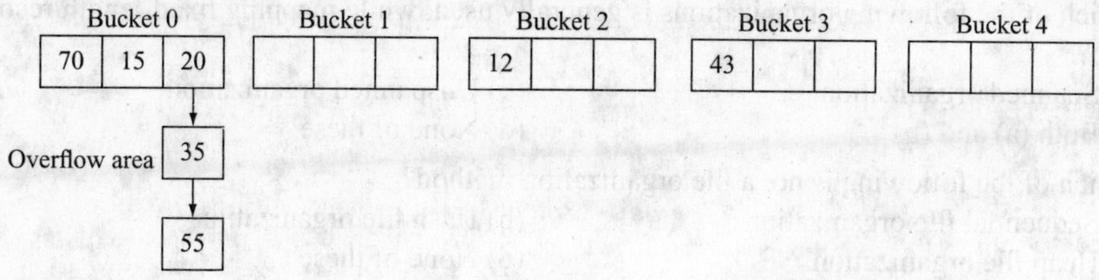

33. Consider a fixed-length record file having 1500 records of `PUBLISHER` relation as described in Question 10. Assume that the block size is 100 bytes. How many blocks are needed to store the file if records are organized using

(a) spanned organization, assuming each block has a 5-byte pointer to the next block and
(b) unspanned organization?
Calculate the number of bytes wasted in each block due to unspanned organization.

Ans: (a) Spanned organization

Given, block size = 100 bytes

As each block has a 5-byte pointer to the next block, the remaining space in each block that can be utilized = 100 - 5 = 95 bytes.

Total number of records = 1500
Size of one record = 150 bytes
Total space required by records = 1500 × 150 = 2,25,000 bytes
Hence, the number of blocks required = 2,25,000/95 = 2369
Number of bytes wasted = 2369 × 95 – 2,25,000 = 55 bytes

(b) Unspanned organization

In an unspanned organization, the block size should be greater than the size of the record. Since one block here is not capable of holding one record, we cannot store the records.

Multiple-choice Questions

1. Which of the following is not classified as primary storage?
(a) Main memory (b) Cache (c) Magnetic disk (d) Flash memory
2. Which of the following term is related to a magnetic disk?
(a) Arm (b) Cylinder (c) Platter (d) All of these
3. The time taken to position read/write heads on a specific track is known as ________.
(a) Access time (b) Seek time
(c) Data transfer time (d) Rotational delay time
4. Which of the following RAID level uses block-level striping?
(a) Level 0 (b) Level 1 (c) Level 4 (d) Both (a) and (c)
5. ________ actually handles the request to access a page of a file.
(a) Main memory (b) Database (c) Buffer manager (d) Disk controller
6. Which of the following replacement policies requires the reference bit to be associated with each frame?
(a) Least recently used (b) Most recently used
(c) Clock replacement (d) Both (a) and (b)
7. Which of the following organizations is generally used, while mapping fixed-length records to a disk?
(a) Spanned organization (b) Unspanned organization
(c) Both (a) and (b) (d) None of these
8. Which of the following is not a file organization method?
(a) Sequential file organization (b) Hash file organization
(c) Heap file organization (d) None of these

9. Which of the following hash functions never result in collision?
   (a) Cut key (b) Folded key
   (c) Division-remainder (d) None of these
10. The type of indexes that include an entry for each value of the indexing attribute is known as __________.
    (a) Secondary index (b) Sparse index (c) Dense index (d) Clustering index
11. The number of tree pointers in each node identifies the __________ of B-tree.
    (a) Order (b) Size (c) Degree (d) None of these

Answers

1. (c)	2. (d)	3. (b)	4. (d)	5. (c)	6. (c)	7. (c)
8. (d)	9. (d)	10. (c)	11. (a)			

8

Query Processing and Optimization

1. What do you mean by query processing? What are the various steps involved in query processing? Explain with the help of a block diagram.

Ans: **Query processing** includes translation of high-level queries into low-level expressions that can be used at the physical level of the file system, query optimization and actual execution of the query to get the result. It is a three-step process that consists of parsing and translation, optimization and execution of the query submitted by the user (see Figure 8.1). These steps are discussed below:

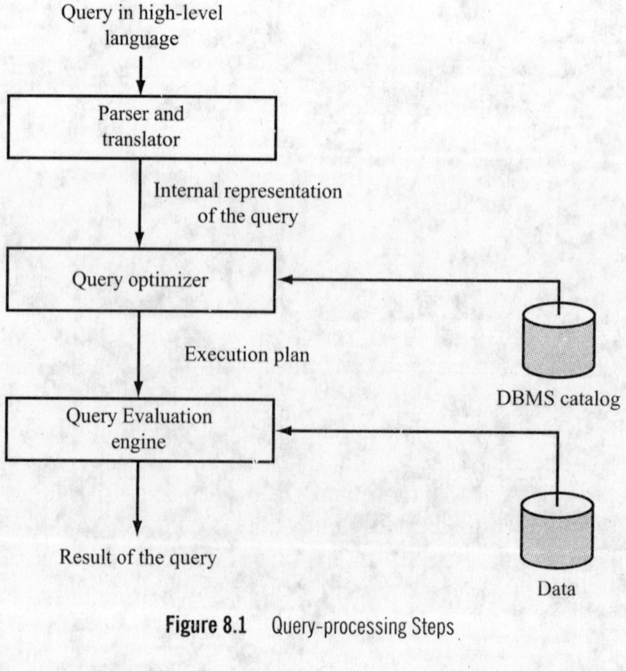

Figure 8.1 Query-processing Steps

1. **Parsing and translation:** Whenever a user submits a query in high-level language (such as SQL) for execution, it is first translated into its internal representation suitable to the system. The internal representation of the query is based on the extended relational algebra. Thus, an SQL query is first translated into an equivalent extended relational algebra expression. During translation, the parser checks the syntax of the user's query according to the rules of the query language. It also verifies that all the attributes and relation names specified in the query are the valid names in the schema of the database being queried.
2. **Optimization:** Generally, there are several possible ways of executing a query (known as execution strategies), and different execution strategies can have different costs. It is the responsibility of the **query optimizer**, a component of DBMS, to choose a least costly execution strategy. This process of choosing a suitable execution strategy for processing a query is knows as **query optimization**. The metadata stored in the special tables called **DBMS catalog** is used to find the best way of evaluating a query.
3. **Execution:** The chosen execution strategy is finally submitted to the **query-evaluation engine** for actual execution of the query to get the desired result.

2. What is a query tree? How is it different from a query evaluation plan? Explain with the help of an example.

Ans: The relational-algebra expressions are typically represented as query trees or parse trees. A **query tree** (also known as **operator tree** or **expression tree)** is a tree data structure in which the input relations are represented as the leaf nodes and the relational-algebra operations as the internal nodes. When the query tree is executed, first the internal node operation is executed whenever its operands are available. Then the internal node is replaced by the relation resulted after the execution of the operation. The execution terminates when the root node is executed and the result of the query is produced. For example, consider the following relational-algebra expression:

$$\pi_{\text{Book\_title, Price}}(\sigma_{\text{Price>30}}(\text{BOOK}))$$

The query tree representation of this expression is shown in Figure 8.2.

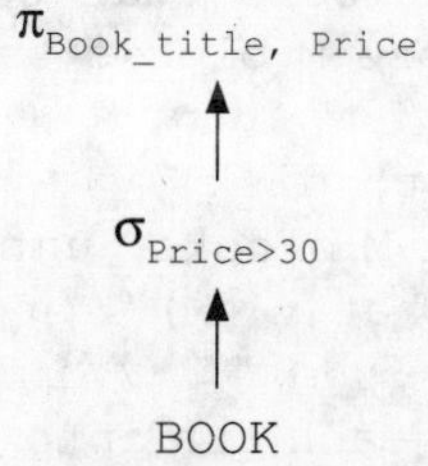

Figure 8.2 Query Tree

Each operation in the query (such as select, project, join, etc.) can be evaluated using one of the several different algorithms, which are discussed later in this chapter. The query tree representation does not specify how to evaluate each operation in the query. To fully specify how to evaluate a query, each operation in the query tree is annotated with the instructions that specify the algorithm or the index to be used to evaluate that operation. The resultant tree structure is known as the **query-evaluation plan** or **query-execution plan** or simply **plan**. One possible query-evaluation plan for our example query tree is given in Figure 8.3. In this figure, the select operator σ is annotated with the instruction `Linear Scan` that specifies a complete scan of the relation.

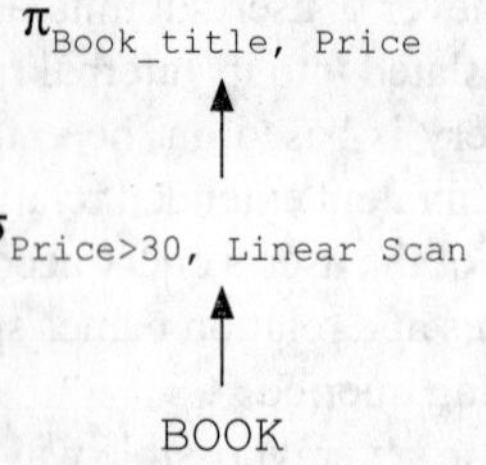

Figure 8.3 Query-evaluation Plan

3. Discuss the external sort–merge algorithm.

Ans: If a relation entirely fits in the main memory, in-memory sorting (called **internal sorting**) can be performed using any standard sorting techniques such as quick sort. If the relation does not fit entirely in the main memory, **external sorting** is required. In external sorting, some part of the relation is read in the main memory, sorted and written back to the disk. This process continues until the entire relation is sorted. The most commonly used external sorting algorithm is the external sort–merge algorithm. The external sort–merge algorithm is divided into two phases, namely *sort phase* and *merge phase*.

- **Sort phase:** In this phase, the records in the file to be sorted are divided into several groups, called **runs** such that each run can fit in the available buffer space. An internal sort is applied to each run and the resulting sorted runs are written back to the disk as temporarily sorted runs. The **number of initial runs** (n_i) is computed as $\lceil b_R/M \rceil$, where b_R is the number of blocks containing records of relation R and M is the size of available buffer in blocks.
- **Merge phase:** In this phase, the sorted runs created during the sort phase are merged into larger runs of sorted records. The merge continues until all records are in one large run. The output of merge phase is the sorted relation.

```
//Sort phase
    Load in M consecutive blocks of the relation
        //M is number of blocks that can fit in main memory
    Sort the tuples in those M blocks using some internal sorting
    technique
    Write the sorted run to disk
    Continue with the next M blocks, until the end of the relation
//Merge phase (assuming that n_i<M) //n_i is the number of
                                   //initial runs
    Load the first block of each run into the buffer page of memory.
    Choose the first tuple (with the lowest value) among all the
    runs.
    Write the tuple to an output buffer page and remove it from the
    run.
    When the buffer page of any run is empty, load the next block
    of that run
    When the output buffer page is full, write it to disk and
    start a new one.
    Continue until all buffer pages are empty.
```

Figure 8.4 External Sort–merge Algorithm

4. Define degree of merging. Explain with the help of an example.

Ans: In an external sort–merge algorithm, if the number of initial runs (n_i) is greater than the size of the available buffer space in blocks (M), then it is not possible to perform the merge operation in one pass; rather multiple passes are required. In each pass, M−1 buffer blocks are used to hold one block from each of the M−1 input runs, and one buffer block is kept for holding one block of the merge result. The number of runs that can be merged together in each pass is known as **degree of merging** (d_M). Thus, the value of d_M is the smaller of (M−1) or n_i. If two runs are merged in each pass, it is known as **two-way merging**. In general, if N runs are merged in each pass, it is known as **N-way merging**. The number of passes required can be calculate as $\lceil (\log_{dM}(n_R)) \rceil$.

Figure 8.5 shows two-way merging where we have assumed that the main memory holds at most three page frames out of which two are used as input and one for output during the merge phase. In this figure, $d_M = 2$, and $n_R = 4$; therefore, $\lceil(\log_2(4))\rceil = 2$ passes are required. In simple terms, with $d_M = 2$, 4 initial sorted runs would be merged into 2 at the end of first pass, which are then merged into 1 sorted run at the end of the second pass.

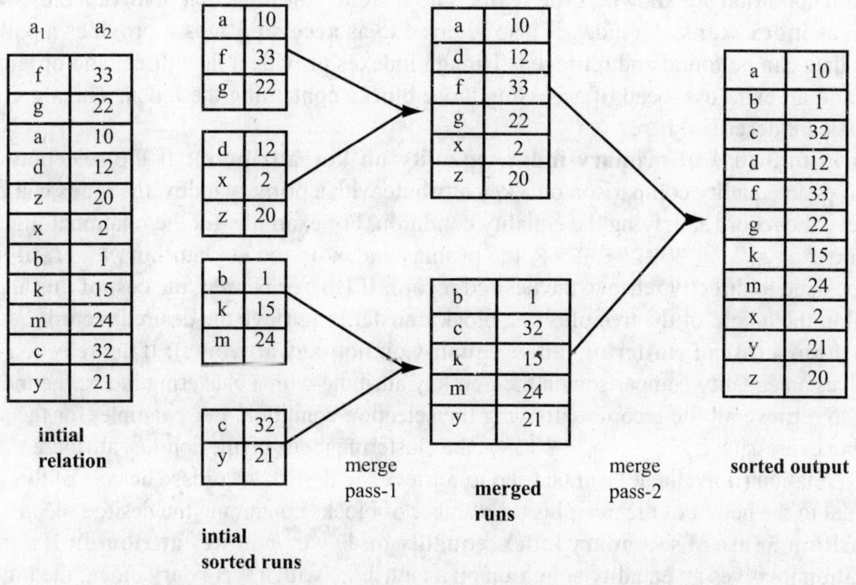

Figure 8.5 Example of Two-way Merging

5. Compare the linear search and binary search algorithms for select operation. Which one is better?

Ans: Algorithm 1 (Linear search algorithm): In linear search (also called **brute force**) algorithm, every file block is scanned and all the records are tested to see whether their attribute values satisfy the selection condition. It is the simplest algorithm and can be applied to any file, regardless of the ordering of the file or the availability of indexes. However, it may be slower than the other algorithms that are used for implementing selection. Since the linear search algorithm searches all the blocks of the file, it requires b_R block transfers, where b_R is the total number of blocks of relation R. If the selection condition involves a key attribute, the scan is terminated when the required record is found, without looking further at other records of the relation. The average cost in this case is equal to $b_R/2$ block transfers if the record is found.

In the worst case, the select operations involving the key attribute may also require the scanning of all the records (b_R block transfers) if no record satisfies the condition or the record is at the last location.

Algorithm 2 (Binary search): If the file is ordered on an attribute and the selection condition involves an equality comparison on that attribute, binary search can be used to retrieve the desired tuples. Binary search is more efficient than the linear search as it requires scanning of lesser number of file blocks. For example, for the relational-algebra operation $\sigma_{P\_ID=\text{"P002"}}$ (PUBLISHER), binary search algorithm can be applied if the PUBLISHER relation is ordered on the basis of the attribute P_ID. The cost of this algorithm is equal to $\lceil \log_2 (b_R) \rceil$ block transfers. If the selection condition involves a non-key attribute, it is possible that more than one block contains the required records.

In general, binary search algorithm is not suited for searching purposes in the database since sorted files are not used unless they have a corresponding primary index file also.

6. What are file scans and index scans? Discuss the search algorithms for select operations that involve the use of indexes.

Ans: The search algorithms that scan the records of file to locate and retrieve the records satisfying the selection condition are known as **file scans**. The search algorithms that involve the use of indexes are known as **index scans**. An index is also referred to as **access path** as it provides a path through which the data can be found and retrieved. Though indexes provide a fast, direct and ordered access, they also add an extra overhead of accessing those blocks containing the index. The algorithms that use an index are described here.

- **Algorithm 3 (use of primary index, equality on key attribute):** If the selection condition involves an equality comparison on a key attribute with a primary index, the index can be used to retrieve the record satisfying the equality condition. For example, for the relational-algebra operation $\sigma_{P\_ID=\text{"P002"}}$ (PUBLISHER), the primary index on the key attribute P_ID (if available) can be used to directly retrieve the desired record. If B^+-tree is used, the cost of this algorithm is equal to the height of the tree plus one block transfer to retrieve the desired record.
- **Algorithm 4 (use of clustering index, equality on non-key attribute):** If the selection condition involves an equality comparison on the non-key attribute with a clustering index, the index can be used to retrieve all the records satisfying the selection condition. For example, for the relational-algebra expression $\sigma_{P\_ID=\text{"P002"}}$ (BOOK), the clustering index on the non-key attribute P_ID of the BOOK relation (if available) can be used to retrieve the desired records. The cost of this algorithm is equal to the height of the tree plus the number of blocks containing the desired records, say b.
- **Algorithm 5 (use of secondary index, equality on key or non-key attribute):** If the selection condition involves an equality condition on an attribute with a secondary index, the index can be used to retrieve the desired records. This search method can retrieve a single record if the indexing field is a key (candidate key) and multiple records if the indexing field is a non-key attribute. In the first case, only one record is retrieved; thus, the cost is equal to the height of the tree plus one block transfer to retrieve the desired record. In the second case, multiple records may be retrieved and each record may reside on a different disk block; thus, the cost is equal to the height of the tree plus n block transfers, where n is the number of records fetched. For example, for the relational-algebra expression $\sigma_{Pname=\text{"Hills Publications"}}$ (PUBLISHER), the secondary index on the candidate key Pname (if available) can be used to retrieve the desired record.
- **Algorithm 6 (use of primary index, comparison):** If the selection condition involves comparisons of the form A>v, A>=v, A<v or A<=v, where A is an attribute with a primary index and v is the attribute value, the primary ordered index can be used to retrieve the desired records. The cost of this algorithm is equal to the height of the tree plus $b_R/2$ block transfers.

- For comparison conditions of the form `A>=v`, the record satisfying the corresponding equality condition `A=v` is first searched using the primary index. A file scan starting from that record up to the end of the file returns all the records satisfying the selection condition. For `A>v`, the file scan starts from the first tuple that satisfies the condition `A>v`—the record satisfying the condition `A=v` is not included.
- For the conditions of the form `A<v`, the index is not searched, rather the file is simply scanned starting from the first record until the record satisfying the condition `A=v` is encountered. For `A<=v`, the file is scanned until the first record satisfying the condition `A>v` is encountered. In both the cases, the index is not useful.

- **Algorithm 7 (use of secondary index, comparison):** The secondary ordered index can also be used for the retrievals based on comparison conditions such as `<`, `<=`, `>` or `>=`. For the conditions of the form `A<v` or `A<=v`, the lowest-level index blocks are scanned from the smallest value up to `v` and for the conditions of the form `A>v` or `A>=v`, the index blocks are scanned from `v` up to the end of the file. The secondary index provides the pointers to the records and not the actual records. The actual records are fetched using the pointers. Thus, fetching each record may require a disk access, since records may be on different blocks. This implies that using the secondary index may even be more expensive than using the linear search if the number of fetched records is large.

7. What are the various algorithms for implementing the select operations involving complex conditions?

Ans: If the select operation involves complex conditions, made up of several simple conditions connected with logical operators `AND` (conjunction) or `OR` (disjunction), some additional algorithms are used, which are discussed here.

- **Algorithm 8 (conjunctive selection using one index):** If an attribute involved in one of the simple conditions specified in the conjunctive condition has an access path (such as indexes), any one of the selection algorithms 2 to 7 can be used to retrieve the records satisfying that condition. Each retrieved record is then checked to determine whether it satisfies the remaining simple conditions. For example, for the relational-algebra operation $\sigma_{P\_ID=\text{"P001"} \wedge Category=\text{"Textbook"}}$`(BOOK)`, if a clustering index is available on the attribute `P_ID` (algorithm 4), that index can be used to retrieve the records with `P_ID="P001"`. These records can then be checked for the other condition. The records that do not satisfy the condition `Category="Textbook"` are discarded.
- **Algorithm 9 (conjunctive selection using composite index):** If a select operation specifies an equality condition on two or more attributes, the composite index (if available) on these combined attributes can be used to directly retrieve the desired records. For example, consider a relational-algebra operation $\sigma_{R\_ID=\text{"A001"} \wedge ISBN=\text{"002-678-980-4"}}$`(REVIEW)`. If an index is available on the composite key `(ISBN, R_ID)` of the `REVIEW` relation, it can be used to directly retrieve the desired records.
- **Algorithm 10 (conjunctive selection by intersection of record pointers):** If indexes or other access paths with record pointers (and not block pointers) are available on the attributes involved in the individual conditions, then each index can be used to retrieve the set of record pointers that satisfy an individual condition. The intersection of all the retrieved record pointers gives the pointers to the tuples that satisfy the conjunctive condition. For example, consider the relational-algebra expression $\sigma_{P\_ID=\text{"P001"} \wedge Category=\text{"Textbook"}}$ `(BOOK)`. If secondary indexes are available on the attributes `P_ID` and `Category` of `BOOK` relation, then these indexes can be used to retrieve the pointers to the tuples satisfying the individual condition. The intersection of these record pointers yields the record pointers of the desired tuples. These record pointers are then used to retrieve the actual tuples (see Figure 8.6).

- **Algorithm 11 (disjunctive selection by union of record pointers):** If indexes or other access paths are available on the attributes involved in the individual conditions, each index can be used to retrieve the set of record pointers that satisfy an individual condition. The union of all retrieved pointers gives the pointers to the tuples that satisfy the disjunctive condition. For example, consider the relational-algebra expression $\sigma_{\texttt{P\_ID="P001"} \vee \texttt{Category="Textbook"}}$ (BOOK). If secondary indexes are available on the attributes `P_ID` and `Category` of `BOOK` relation, then these indexes can be used to retrieve the pointers to the tuples satisfying an individual condition. The union of these record pointers yields the pointers to the desired tuples. These record pointers are then used to retrieve the actual tuples (see Figure 8.6).

Resultant relation R1: σP_ID="P001" ∧ Category="Textbook" (BOOK)

records pointers	ISBN	Book_title	Category	Price	Copy right_date	Year	Page_count	P_ID
r_1	001-354-921-1	Ransack	Novel	22	2005	2006	200	P001
r_2	001-987-650-5	Differential Calculus	Textbook	30	2003	2003	450	P001
r_3	001-987-760-9	C++	Textbook	40	2004	2005	800	P001

Resultant relation R2: σP_ID="P001" ∨ Category="Textbook" (BOOK)

	ISBN	Book_title	Category	Price	Copy right_date	Year	Page_count	P_ID
r_2	001-987-650-5	Differential Calculus	Textbook	30	2003	2003	450	P001
r_3	001-987-760-9	C++	Textbook	40	2004	2005	800	P001
r_4	002-678-980-4	DBMS	Textbook	40	2004	2006	800	P002
r_5	004-765-359-3	Coordinate Geometry	Textbook	35	2006	2006	650	P003
r_6	004-765-409-5	UNIX	Textbook	26	2006	2007	550	P003

R1 ∩ R2

	ISBN	Book_title	Category	Price	Copy right_date	Year	Page_count	P_ID
r_2	001-987-650-5	Differential Calculus	Textbook	30	2003	2003	450	P001
r_3	001-987-760-9	C++	Textbook	40	2004	2005	800	P001

R1 ∪ R2

	ISBN	Book_title	Category	Price	Copy right_date	Year	Page_count	P_ID
r_1	001-354-921-1	Ransack	Novel	22	2005	2006	200	P001
r_2	001-987-650-5	Differential Calculus	Textbook	30	2003	2003	450	P001
r_3	001-987-760-9	C++	Textbook	40	2004	2005	800	P001
r_4	002-678-980-4	DBMS	Textbook	40	2004	2006	800	P002
r_5	004-765-359-3	Coordinate Geometry	Textbook	35	2006	2006	650	P003
r_6	004-765-409-5	UNIX	Textbook	26	2006	2007	550	P003

Figure 8.6 Example of Search Algorithms 10 and 11

8. Discuss the nested-loop join and its several variations. Also analyze their respective costs in terms of block transfers.

Ans: Nested-loop join: The nested-loop join algorithm consists of a pair of nested `for` loops, one for each relation say, `R` and `S`. One of these relations, say `R` is chosen as the **outer relation** and the other relation `S` as the **inner relation**. The outer relation is scanned row by row and for each row in the outer relation the inner relation is scanned and looked for the matching rows. In other words, for each tuple `r` in `R`, every tuple `s` in `S` is retrieved and then checked whether the two tuples satisfy the join condition `r[A]=s[B]`. If the join condition is satisfied, then the values of these two tuples are concatenated, which is then added to the result. The tuple constructed by concatenating the values of the tuples `r` and `s` is denoted by `r.s`. Since this search scans the entire relation, it is also called **naïve nested-loop join**.

For natural join, this algorithm can be extended to eliminate the repeated attributes using a project operation. The nested-loop algorithms for equijoin and natural join operations are given in Figure 8.7. This algorithm is similar to the linear search algorithm for the select operation in a way that it does not require any indexes and it can be used with any join condition. Thus, it is also called the **brute force** algorithm.

An extra buffer block is required to hold the tuples resulted from the join operation. When this block is filled, the tuples are appended to the disk file containing the join result (known as **result file**). This buffer block can then be reused to hold additional result records.

```
for each tuple r in R do begin
    for each tuple s in S do begin
            if r[A]=s[B] then add r.s to the result.
    end
end
```

(a) Nested-loop Join for Equijoin Operation

```
for each tuple r in R do begin
    for each tuple s in S do begin
        if r[A]=s[B] then
        begin
            delete one of the repeated attributes from the tuple r.s
            add r.s to the result.
        end
    end
end
```

(b) Nested-loop Join for Natural Join Operation

Figure 8.7 Nested-loop Join

The two variations of nested-loop join algorithm are block nested-loop join and indexed nested-loop join algorithm, which are discussed here.

- **Block nested-loop join:** In this algorithm, the relations are processed on a per-block basis rather than on a per-tuple basis. Thus, each block in the inner relation `S` is read only once for each block in the outer relation `R` (instead of once for each tuple in `R`). The algorithm for block nested-loop join operation is given in Figure 8.8.

```
for each block B_R of R do begin
    for each block B_S of S do begin
        for each tuple r in B_R do begin
            for each tuple s in B_S do begin
                if r[A]=s[B] then
                    add r.s to the result.
            end
        end
    end
end
```

Figure 8.8 Block Nested-loop Join

- **Index nested-loop join:** If an index is available on the join attribute of one relation say S, it is taken as the inner relation, and the index scan (instead of file scan) is used to retrieve the matching tuples. In this algorithm, each tuple r in R is retrieved, and the index available on the join attribute of relation S is used to directly retrieve all the matching tuples. Indexed nested-loop join can be used with the existing as well as with a **temporary index**—an index created by the query optimizer and destroyed when the query is completed. If a temporary index is used to retrieve the matching records, the algorithm is called **temporary indexed nested-loop join**. If indexes are available on both the relations, the relation with fewer tuples can be used as the outer relation for better efficiency. The algorithm for indexed nested-loop join operation is given in Figure 8.9.

```
for each tuple r of R do begin
    probe the index on S to locate all tuples s such that
    s[B]=r[A].
    for each matching tuple s in S do
                    add r.s to the result.
end
```

Figure 8.9 Indexed Nested-loop Join

Cost analysis

To analyze the cost of these join algorithms, consider the following operation on PUBLISHER relation of the *Online Book* database:

$$\text{BOOK} \bowtie_{\text{BOOK.P\_ID = PUBLISHER.P\_ID}} \text{PUBLISHER}$$

Further, assume the following information about these two relations. This information will be used to estimate the cost of each algorithm.

number of tuples of PUBLISHER = $n_{PUBLISHER} = 2000$
number of blocks of PUBLISHER = $b_{PUBLISHER} = 100$
number of tuples of BOOK = $n_{BOOK} = 5000$
number of blocks of BOOK = $b_{BOOK} = 500$

- **Nested-loop join:** The nested-loop join algorithm is expensive, as it requires scanning of every tuple in S for each tuple in R. The pairs of tuples that need to be scanned are $n_R * n_S$, where n_R and n_S denote the number of tuples in R and S, respectively. For example, if PUBLISHER is taken as the outer relation and BOOK as the inner relation, 2000*5000 = 10^7 pairs of tuples need to be scanned.

In terms of the number of block transfers, the cost of this algorithm is equal to $b_R + (n_R * b_S)$, where b_R and b_S denote the number of blocks of R and S, respectively. For example, if PUBLISHER is taken as the outer relation and BOOK is taken as the inner relation, 100+(2000*500) = 1,000,100 block transfers are required, which is very high. On the other hand, if BOOK is taken as the outer relation and PUBLISHER as the inner relation, then 500+(5000*100) = 5,00,500 block transfers are required. Thus, by making the smaller relation as the inner relation, the overall costs of the join operation can be reduced.

If both or one of the relations fit entirely in the main memory, the cost of the join operation will be $b_R + b_S$ block transfers. This is the best-case scenario. For example, if either of the relations PUBLISHER and BOOK (or both) fits entirely in the memory, 100+500=600 block transfers are required, which is optimal.

- **Block nested-loop join:** In the worst case, when neither of the relations fit entirely in the memory, this algorithm requires $b_R + (b_R * b_S)$ block transfers. It is efficient to use the smaller relation as the outer relation. For example, if PUBLISHER is taken as the outer relation and BOOK as the inner relation, 100+(100*500) = 50,100 block transfers are required (which is much lesser than 1,000,100 or 5,00,500 block transfers as in the nested-loop join). In the best case, if one of the relations fits entirely in the main memory, the algorithm requires $b_R + b_S$ block transfers, which is the same as that of the nested-loop join. In this case, the smaller relation is chosen as the inner relation.
- **Indexed nested-loop join:** The cost of this algorithm can be computed as $b_R + n_R * c$, where c is the cost of traversing the index and retrieving all the matching tuples of S.

9. If the tuples of the relations (on which the join operation is to be performed) are physically sorted by the value of their respective join attributes, which algorithm can be used to perform the join operation? Explain with the help of an example. Also discuss its cost in terms of block transfers.

Ans: If the tuples of two relations say, R and S are physically sorted by the value of their respective join attributes, the **sort-merge join algorithm** can be used to compute equijoins and natural joins. Both the relations are scanned concurrently in the order of the join attributes to match the tuples that have the same values for the join attributes. Since the relations are in a sorted order, each tuple needs to be scanned only once and hence, each block is also read only once. Thus, if both the relations are in sorted order, the sort-merge join requires only a single pass through both the relations. The sort-merge join algorithm is given in Figure 8.10(a) and an example of sort-merge join algorithm is given in Figure 8.10(b). In this figure, the relations R and S are sorted on the join attribute a_1.

```
if R is unsorted then sort the tuples in R on the attribute A.
if S is unsorted then sort the tuples in S on the attribute B.
i:=1;
j:=1;
t:=1;
while(i<=nR) do begin
    while (R(i)[A]==S(t)[B]) do begin
        add R(i).S(t) to the result.
        t:=t+1;
    end
```

Figure 8.10 Implementing Sort-merge Join (Contd...)

```
    i:=i+1;
    if(R(i)[A]==R(i-1)[A]) then
        t=j;
    else
        j:=t;
end
```

(a) Sort-merge Join

Relation R

a_1	a_2
a	2
b	13
d	7
e	9
e	11
f	1
g	10

Relation S

a_1	a_3
b	2.5
b	7.1
c	8.2
d	9.9
e	11.0
e	2.1

Equijoin using sort-merge join

a_1	a_1	a_2	a_3
b	b	13	2.5
b	b	13	7.1
d	d	7	9.9
e	e	9	11.0
e	e	9	2.1
e	e	11	11.0
e	e	11	2.1

Natural join using sort-merge join

a_1	a_2	a_3
b	13	2.5
b	13	7.1
d	7	9.9
e	9	11.0
e	9	2.1
e	11	11.0
e	11	2.1

(b) An Example of Sort-merge Join

Figure 8.10 Implementing Sort-merge Join

The number of block transfers is equal to the sum of the number of blocks in both the relations R and S, that is, b_R+b_S. Thus, the join operation BOOK⋈PUBLISHER requires 100+500=600 block transfers. If the relations are not sorted, they can be first sorted using external sorting.

10. Explain the hash join algorithm. Analyze its cost in terms of block transfers. What is the additional optimization in hybrid hash join?

Ans: In a hash join algorithm, a hash function h is used to partition the tuples of each relation into sets of tuples with each set containing tuples that have the same hash value on the join attributes A of relation R and B of relation S. The algorithm is divided into two phases, namely, *partitioning phase* and *probing phase*. In the **partitioning** (also called **building**) phase, the tuples of relations R and S are partitioned into the hash file buckets using the same hash function h. Let $P_{r0}, P_{r1}, \ldots, P_{rn}$ be the partitions of tuples in relation R and $P_{s0}, P_{s1}, \ldots, P_{sn}$ be the partitions of tuples in relation S. Here, n is the number of partitions of relations R and S. During the partitioning phase, a single in-memory buffer with size one disk block is allocated for each partition to store the tuples that hash to this partition. Whenever the in-memory buffer gets filled, its contents are appended to a disk subfile that stores this partition. For a simple two-way join, the partitioning phase has two iterations. In the first iteration, the relation R is partitioned into n partitions, and in the second iteration, the relation S is partitioned in n partitions.

In the **probing** (also called **matching** or **joining**) phase, n iterations are required. In the ith iteration, the tuples in the partition P_{ri} are joined with the tuples in the corresponding partition P_{si}.

Cost analysis

The hash join algorithm requires $3(b_R+b_S)+4n$ block transfers. The first term $3(b_R+b_S)$ represents that the block transfer occurs three times—once when the relations are read into the main memory for partitioning, second when they are written back to the disk and third, when each partition is read again during the joining phase. The second term 4n represents an extra overhead (2n for each relation) of reading and writing of each partition to and from the disk.

Variation of the hash join technique

If the memory size is relatively large, a variation of hash join called hybrid hash join can be used for better performance. In **hybrid hash join** technique, the probing phase for one of the partitions is combined with the partitioning phase. The main objective of this technique is to join as many tuples during the partitioning phase as possible in order to save the cost of storing these tuples back to the disk and accessing them again during the joining (probing) phase.

To better understand the hybrid hash join algorithm, consider a hash function h(K)=K mod n that creates n partitions of the relation, where n<M and consider the join operation BOOK⋈PUBLISHER. In the first iteration, the algorithm divides the buffer space among n partitions such that all the blocks of first partition of the smaller relation PUBLISHER completely reside in the main memory. A single input buffer (with size one disk block) is kept for each of the other partitions, and they are written back to the disk as in the regular hash join. Thus, at the end of the first iteration of the partitioning phase, the first partition of the relation PUBLISHER resides completely in the main memory and other partitions reside in a disk subfile.

In the second iteration of the partitioning phase, the tuples of the second relation BOOK are being partitioned. If a tuple hashes to the first partition, it is immediately joined with the matching tuple of PUBLISHER relation. If the tuple does not hash to the first partition, it is partitioned normally. Thus, at the end of second iteration, all the tuples of BOOK relation that hash to the first partition have been joined with the tuples of PUBLISHER relation. Now, there are n-1 pairs of partitions on the disk. Therefore, during the joining phase, n-1 iterations are needed instead of n.

11. What do you mean by skewed partitioning? How can it be handled?

Ans: The main difficulty of the hash join algorithm is to ensure that the partitioning hash function is uniform, that is, it creates partitions of almost the same size. If the partitioning hash function is non-uniform, then some partitions may have more tuples than the average, and they might not fit in the available main memory. This type of partitioning is known as **skewed partitioning**. This problem can be handled by further partitioning the partition into smaller partitions using a different hash function.

12. Describe recursive partitioning.

Ans: If the number of partitions (n) is less than the number of page frames (M) in the main memory, the hash join algorithm is very simple and efficient to execute as both the relations can be partitioned in one pass. However, if n is greater than or equal to M, then the relations cannot be partitioned in a single pass; rather, partitions have to be done in repeated passes. In the first pass, the input relation is partitioned into M-1 partitions (one page frame is kept to be used as input buffer) using a hash function h. In the next pass, each partition created in the previous pass is partitioned again to create smaller partitions using a different hash function. This process is repeated until each partition of the input relation can fit entirely in the memory. This technique is called **recursive partitioning**.

13. What are the two techniques used to eliminate duplicates during project operation? Discuss the algorithm to implement project operation by eliminating duplicates.

Ans: A project operation of the form $\pi_{<attribute\_list>}(R)$ is easy to implement if the <attribute_list> includes the key attribute of the relation R. However, if the <attribute_list> does not contain the key attribute, duplicate tuples may exist and must be eliminated. Duplicate tuples can be eliminated by using either sorting or hashing.

- **Sorting:** The result of the operation is first sorted, and then the duplicate tuples that appear adjacent to each other are removed. If external sort-merge technique is used, the duplicate tuples can be found while creating runs, and they can be removed before writing the runs on the disk. The remaining duplicate tuples can be removed during merging. Thus, the final sorted run contains no duplicates.
- **Hashing:** As soon as a tuple is hashed and inserted into in-memory hash file bucket, it is first checked against those tuples that are already present in the bucket. The tuple is inserted in the bucket if it is not already present; otherwise, it is discarded. All the tuples are processed in the same way.

The algorithm to implement project operation by eliminating duplicates using sorting is given in Figure 8.11.

```
for each tuple r in R do
    add a tuple r[<attribute_list>] in T'
        //T' may contain duplicate tuples
if <attribute_list> includes the key attribute of R
then
    T:=T';         // T contains the projection result
                   // without duplicates
else
begin
    sort the tuples in T'
    i:=1;
    j:=2;
    while (i<=n_R) do begin
        if (T'(i)[A]==T'(j)[A]) then
            j:=j+1;
        else begin
            output the tuple T'[i] to T
            i:=j;
        end
    end
end
```

Figure 8.11 Algorithm for Project Operation

14. Discuss the algorithms for implementing union, intersection and set different operations.

Ans: The set operations, namely, *union*, *intersection*, and *set difference* can be implemented by first sorting the relations on the basis of same attribute and then scanning each sorted relation once to produce the result. For example, the operation $R \cup S$ can be implemented by concurrently scanning and merging both the sorted relations—whenever same tuple exists in both the relations, only one of them is kept in the merged result. The operation $R \cap S$ can be implemented by adding only those tuples to the merged result that exist in both the relations. Finally, the operation $R - S$ is implemented by retaining only those tuples that exist in R but are not present in S.

If the relations are initially sorted in the same order, all these operations require $b_R + b_S$ block transfers. If the relations are not sorted initially, the cost of sorting the relations has to be included. The algorithms for the operations $R \cup S$, $R \cap S$, and $R - S$ using sorting are given in Figure 8.12.

```
sort the tuples of R and S on the basis of same unique sort attributes.
i:=1;
j·=1;
while(i<=nR) and (j<=nS) do begin
    if(R(i) < S(j)) then begin
        add R(i) to the result.
        i:=i+1;
    end
    elseif (R(i) > S(j)) then begin
        add S(j) to the result.
        j:=j+1;
    end
    else begin
        add R(i) to the result.
        i:=i+1;
        j:=j+1;     //R(i)=S(j), add only one tuple
    end
end
while(i<=nR) do begin
    add R(i) to the result.     //add remaining tuples
                                     //of R, if any
    i:=i+1;
end
while(j<=nS) do begin
    add S(j) to the result.     //add remaining tuples
                                     //of S, if any
    j:=j+1;
end
```

(a) Implementing UNION Operation

```
sort the tuples of R and S on the basis of same unique sort attributes.
i:=1;
j:=1;
while(i<=nR) and (j<=nS) do begin
    if(R(i) < S(j)) then
        i:=i+1;
    elseif(R(i) > S(j)) then
        j:=j+1;
    else begin
        //R(i)=S(j), add one of the tuples to the result
        add R(i) to thc result.
        i:=i+1;
        j:=j+1;
    end
end
```

(b) Implementing INTERSECTION Operation

Figure 8.12 Implementing Set Operations (Contd...)

```
sort the tuples of R and S on the basis of same unique sort
attributes.
i:=1;
j:=1;
while(i<=nR) and (j<=nS) do begin
    if(R(i) < S(j)) then begin
        add R(i) to the result.
        //R(i) has no matching S(j)
        //so add R(i) to the result
        i:=i+1;
    end
    if(R(i) > S(j)) then
        j:=j+1;
    else begin
        //R(i)=S(j) so skip both the tuples
        i:=i+1;
        j:=j+1;
    end
end
while(i<=nR) do begin
    add R(i) to the result
        //add remaining tuples of R, if any
    i:=i+1;
end
```

(c) Implementing SET DIFFERENCE Operation

Figure 8.12 Implementing Set Operations

15. Discuss the two ways of evaluating a query. Which one is better and why? Does the available buffer space affect the query evaluation speed? If yes, how?

Ans: There are two ways of evaluating a query, namely, materialized evaluation and pipelined evaluation.

- **Materialized evaluation:** In this approach, each operation in the expression is evaluated one by one in an appropriate order and the result of each operation is **materialized** (created) in a temporary relation, which becomes input for the subsequent operations. For example, consider this relation-algebra expression:

$$\pi_{\text{Pname, Email\_id}}(\sigma_{\text{Category="Novel"}}(\text{BOOK}) \bowtie \text{PUBLISHER})$$

This expression consists of three relational operations, join, select and project. The query tree of this expression is given in Figure 8.13.

In materialized evaluation, the lowest-level operations (operations at the bottom of operator tree) are evaluated first. The inputs to the lowest-level operations are the relations in the database. For example, in Figure 8.13, the operation $\sigma_{\text{Category="Novel"}}(\text{BOOK})$ is evaluated first and the result is stored in a temporary relation. The temporary relation and the relation PUBLISHER are then given as inputs to the next-level operation, that is, the join operation. The join operation then performs a join on these two relations and stores the result in another temporary relation, which is given as input to the project operation, which is at the root of the tree.

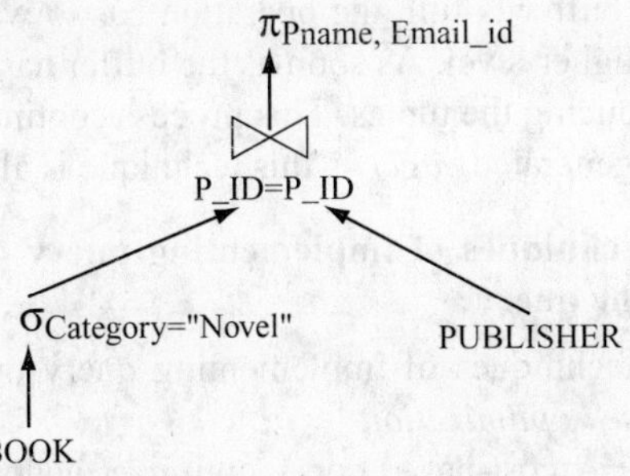

Figure 8.13 Operator Tree for the Expression

- **Pipelined evaluation:** In this type of evaluation, the operations form a queue and results are passed from one operation to another as they are calculated; rather than storing them in temporary relations. For example, the operations given in Figure 8.13 can be placed in a pipeline. As soon as a tuple is generated from the select operation, it is immediately passed to the join operation for processing. Similarly, a tuple generated from the join operation is passed immediately to the project operation for processing. Thus, the evaluation of these three operations in a pipelined manner directly generates the final result without creating temporary relations.

It is clear from our discussion that pipelined evaluation is better as it increases the query-evaluation efficiency by reducing the number of temporary relations. The system maintains one buffer for each pair of adjacent operations to hold the tuples being passed from one operation to the next. Moreover, since the results of the operations are not stored for a long time, lesser amount of memory is required in the pipelining approach. However, the queries that involve aggregate or grouping functions cannot be evaluated using pipelined evaluation because the inputs are not available to the operations for processing all at once in the pipelining.

The available buffer space definitely affects the query evaluation speed. If a single buffer is used to hold the intermediate result, it forces the CPU to wait for an I/O operation to complete. This is because while the filled buffer is being written back to the disk, the CPU has nothing to do. On the other hand, in case of **double buffering**, two buffers are used—one of them continues with the execution of the algorithm while the other being written to the disk. This allows CPU activity to perform in parallel with I/O activity, which in turn results in faster query evaluation.

16. Illustrate the difference between demand-driven and producer-driven pipelining.

Ans: There are two ways of executing pipelines, namely, *demand-driven pipeline* and *producer-driven pipeline*.

- **Demand-driven pipeline:** In this approach, the parent operation requests the next tuple from its child operations as required, in order to output its next tuple. Whenever an operation receives a request for the next set of tuples, it computes those tuples and then returns them. Since, the tuples are generated *lazily*, on demand; this technique is also known as **lazy evaluation**.
- **Producer-driven pipeline:** In this approach, each operation at the bottom of the pipeline produces tuples without waiting for the request from the next higher-level operations. Each operation then puts the output tuples in the output buffer associated with it. This output buffer is used as input buffer by the operation at next higher level. The operation at any other level consumes the tuples from its input buffer to produce the output tuples, and puts them in its output buffer.

In any case, if the output buffer is full, the operation has to wait until tuples are consumed by the operation at the next higher level. As soon as the buffer has some space for more tuples, the operation again starts producing the tuples. This process continues until all the tuples are generated. Since the tuples are generated *eagerly*, this technique is also known as **eager pipelining**.

17. What are the two techniques of implementing query optimization? How would you estimate the cost of the query?

Ans: There are two main techniques of implementing query optimization, namely, *cost-based optimization* and *heuristics-based optimization.*

- **Cost-based optimization:** A cost-based query optimizer generates a number of query-evaluation plans from a given query using a number of equivalence rules, and then chooses the one with the minimum cost. The cost of executing a query include:
  - cost of accessing secondary storage—cost of searching, reading and writing disk blocks.
  - storage cost—cost of storing intermediate results.
  - computation cost—cost of performing in-memory operations.
  - memory usage cost—cost related to the number of occupied memory buffers.
  - communication cost—cost of communicating the query result from one site to another.
- **Heuristic query optimization:** In cost-based optimization, generating a large number of query-evaluation plans for a given query, and finding the cost of each plan can be very time consuming and expensive. Thus, finding the optimal plan from such a large number of plans requires a lot of computational effort. To reduce this cost and computational effort, optimizers apply some heuristics (rules) to find the optimized query-evaluation plan. These rules are known as **heuristics** as they usually (but not always) help in reducing the cost of execution of a query. The heuristic query optimizers simply apply these rules without finding out whether the cost is reduced by this transformation.

The cost of each query can be estimated by collecting the statistical information about the relations such as relation sizes and available primary and secondary indexes from the DBMS catalog. Some of the statistics about database relations is stored in DBMS catalog include:

- the number of tuples in relation R, denoted by n_R.
- the number of blocks containing the tuples of relation R, denoted by b_R.
- the blocking factor of relation R, denoted by f_R is the number of tuples that fit in one block.
- the size of each tuple of relation R in bytes, denoted by s_R.
- the number of distinct values appearing in relation R for the attribute A, denoted by V(A,R). This value is the same as the size of π_A(R). If A is a key attribute, then V(A,R) = n_R.
- height of index i, that is, number of levels in i, denoted by H_i.

Assuming that the tuples of relation R are stored together physically in a file, then

$$b_R = \lceil n_R / f_R \rceil$$

In addition to the relation sizes and indexes height, real-world query optimizers also maintain some other statistical information to increase the accuracy of cost estimates. For example, most databases maintain **histograms** representing the distribution of values for each attribute. The values for the attribute are divided into a number of ranges, and the number of tuples whose attribute value falls in a particular range is associated with that range in the histogram. For example, the histograms for the attributes Price and Page_count of the BOOK relation are shown in Figure 8.14.

A histogram takes very little space so histograms on various attributes can be maintained in the system catalog. A histogram can be of two types, namely equi-width histogram and equi-depth

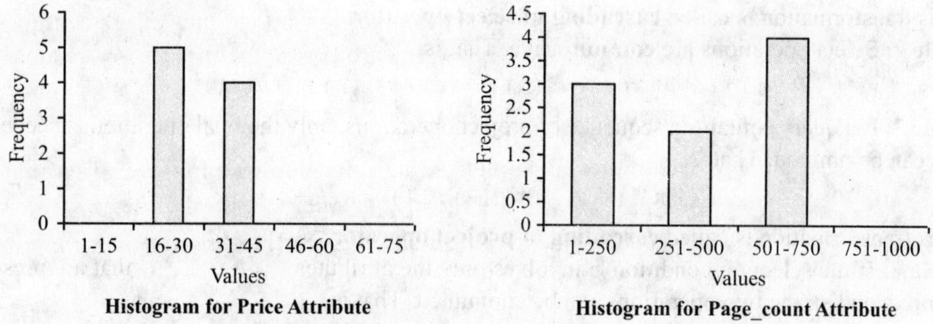

Figure 8.14 Histograms on `Price` and `Page_count`

histogram. In **equi-width histograms**, the range of values is divided into equal-sized sub-ranges. On the other hand, in **equi-depth histograms**, the sub-ranges are chosen in such a way that the number of tuples within each sub-range is equal.

18. When are two relational-algebra expressions said to be equivalent? Explain with the help of an example.

Ans: An expression is said to be **equivalent** to a given relational-algebra expression if, on every legal database instance, it generates the same set of tuples as that of original expression irrespective of the ordering of the tuples. For example, consider a relational-algebra expression for the query "Retrieve the publisher name and category of the book *C++*".

$$\pi_{\texttt{Pname,Category}}(\sigma_{\texttt{Book\_title="C++"}}(\texttt{BOOK} \bowtie \texttt{PUBLISHER}))$$

In this expression, first the join operation between the `BOOK` and `PUBLISHER` relation is performed, and then the tuples with book title *C++* are retrieved from the resultant relation, and finally, the project operation is applied to retrieve the attributes `Pname` and `Category`. When this sequence of operations is followed, it produces a large intermediate relation, which results from the join operation. However, the user is only interested in those tuples having `Book_title="C++"`. Thus, another way to execute this query is to first select only those tuples from the `BOOK` relation satisfying the condition `Book_title="C++"`, and then join it with the `PUBLISHER` relation. This reduces the size of the intermediate relation. The query can now be represented by the following expression:

$$\pi_{\texttt{Pname,Category}}(\sigma_{\texttt{Book\_title="C++"}}(\texttt{BOOK}) \bowtie \texttt{PUBLISHER})$$

This expression is equivalent to the original expression, however, with less number of tuples in the intermediate relation and thus, it is more efficient.

19. What is an equivalence rule? Discuss all equivalence rules.

Ans: An equivalence rule states that expressions of two forms are equivalent if an expression of one form can be replaced by expression of the other form, and vice versa. While discussing the equivalence rules, it is assumed that $c, c_1, c_2, \ldots, c_n$ are the predicates, $A, A_1, A_2, \ldots, A_n$ are the set of attributes and $R, R_1, R_2, \ldots, R_n$ are the relation names.

Rule 1: The selection condition involving the conjunction of two or more predicates can be deconstructed into a sequence of individual select operations. That is,

$$\sigma_{c1 \wedge c2}(R) = \sigma_{c1}(\sigma_{c2}(R))$$

This transformation is called **cascading of select operator**.

Rule 2: Select operations are **commutative**. That is,

$$\sigma_{c1}(\sigma_{c2}(R)) = \sigma_{c2}(\sigma_{c1}(R))$$

Rule 3: If a query contains a sequence of project operations, only the final operation is needed, the others can be omitted. That is,

$$\pi_{A1}(\pi_{A2}(\ldots(\pi_{An}(R))\ldots)) = \pi_{A1}(R)$$

This transformation is called **cascading of project operator**.

Rule 4: If the selection condition c involves only the attributes $A_1, A_2, \ldots, A_n$ that are present in the projection list, the two operations can be commuted. That is,

$$\pi_{A1,A2,\ldots,An}(\sigma_c(R)) = \sigma_c(\pi_{A1,A2,\ldots,An}(R))$$

Rule 5: Selections can be combined with Cartesian products and joins. That is,

a. $\sigma_c(R_1 \times R_2) = R_1 \bowtie_c R_2$

b. $\sigma_{c1}(R_1 \bowtie_{c2} R_2) = R_1 \bowtie_{c1 \wedge c2} R_2$

Rule 6: Cartesian product and join operations are **commutative.** That is,

a. $R_1 \times R_2 = R_2 \times R_1$

b. $R_1 \bowtie_c R_2 = R_2 \bowtie_c R_1$

Rule 7: Cartesian product and join operations are **associative**. That is,

a. $(R_1 \times R_2) \times R_3 = R_1 \times (R_2 \times R_3)$

b. $(R_1 \bowtie R_2) \bowtie R_3 = R_1 \bowtie (R_2 \bowtie R_3)$

Rule 8: The select operation distributes over the join operation in these two conditions:

a. If all the attributes in the selection condition c_1 involve only the attributes of one of the relations (say, R_1), then the select operation distributes. That is,

$$\sigma_{c1}(R_1 \bowtie_c R_2) = (\sigma_{c1}(R_1)) \bowtie_c R_2$$

b. If the selection condition c_1 involves only the attributes of R_1 and c_2 involves the attributes of R_2, then the select operation distributes. That is,

$$\sigma_{c1 \wedge c2}(R_1 \bowtie_c R_2) = (\sigma_{c1}(R_1)) \bowtie_c (\sigma_{c2}(R_2))$$

Rule 9: The project operation distributes over the join operation in these two conditions:

a. If the join condition c involves only the attributes in $A_1 \cup A_2$, where A_1 and A_2 are the attributes of R_1 and R_2 respectively, the project operation distributes. That is,

$$\pi_{A1 \cup A2}(R_1 \bowtie_c R_2) = (\pi_{A1}(R_1)) \bowtie_c (\pi_{A2}(R_2))$$

b. If the attributes A_3 and A_4 of R_1 and R_2, respectively, are involved in the join condition c, but not in $A_1 \cup A_2$, then,

$$\pi_{A1 \cup A2}(R_1 \bowtie_c R_2) = \pi_{A1 \cup A2}((\pi_{A1 \cup A3}(R_1)) \bowtie_c (\pi_{A2 \cup A4}(R_2)))$$

Rule 10: The set operations union and intersection are commutative and associative. That is,

a. Commutative

$$R_1 \cup R_2 = R_2 \cup R_1$$

$$R_1 \cap R_2 = R_2 \cap R_1$$

b. Associative

$$(R_1 \cup R_2) \cup R_3 = R_1 \cup (R_2 \cup R_3)$$

$$(R_1 \cap R_2) \cap R_3 = R_1 \cap (R_2 \cap R_3)$$

Rule 11: The select operation distributes over the union, intersection and set difference operations. That is,

$$\sigma_c (R_1 \cup R_2) = \sigma_c (R_1) \cup \sigma_c (R_2)$$
$$\sigma_c (R_1 \cap R_2) = \sigma_c (R_1) \cap \sigma_c (R_2)$$
$$\sigma_c (R_1 - R_2) = \sigma_c (R_1) - \sigma_c (R_2)$$

Rule 12: The project operation distributes over the union operation. That is,

$$\pi_A (R_1 \cup R_2) = \pi_A (R_1) \cup \pi_A (R_2)$$

20. Explain with the help of an example the importance of optimal join ordering in query optimization.

Ans: An optimal join ordering of join operations results in reducing the size of intermediate results. It is the responsibility of the query optimizer to choose an optimal join order with the minimal cost. Consider the query "Retrieve the publisher name, rating and the name of the authors who have rated the C++ book." The corresponding relational-algebra expression for this query is

$$\pi_{\text{Pname, Rating, Aname}} ((\sigma_{\text{Book\_title="C++"}} (\text{BOOK})) \bowtie \text{PUBLISHER} \bowtie \text{REVIEW} \bowtie \text{AUTHOR}))$$

In this query, first the selection is performed on the BOOK relation. This will generate a set of tuples with book title *C++*. If the operation PUBLISHER⋈REVIEW is performed first, it results in the Cartesian product of these two relations as no common attributes exist between PUBLISHER and REVIEW, which results in a large intermediate relation. As a result, this strategy is rejected. Similarly, the operation PUBLISHER⋈AUTHOR is also rejected for the same reason. If the operation REVIEW⋈AUTHOR is performed, it also results in a large intermediate relation but the user is only interested in the authors who have reviewed the *C++* book. Thus, this order of evaluating join operation is also rejected.

However, if the result obtained after the select operation on BOOK relation is joined with the PUBLISHER, which in turn joined with REVIEW relation, and finally with the AUTHOR relation, the number of tuples is reduced. Thus, the equivalent final expression is

$$\pi_{\text{Pname, Rating, Aname}} ((((\sigma_{\text{Book\_title="C++"}} (\text{BOOK}) \bowtie \text{PUBLISHER}) \bowtie \text{REVIEW}) \bowtie \text{AUTHOR}))$$

21. Discuss the steps followed by heuristic query optimizer to transform an initial query tree into an optimal query tree. Give a suitable example in support of your answer.

Ans: The heuristic query optimizer follows these steps to transform initial query tree into an optimal query tree.

- Conjunctive selection operations are transformed into cascading selection operations (equivalence rule 1—refer Question 23).
- Since the select operation is commutative with other operations according to the equivalence rules 2, 4, 8, 11, it is moved as far down the query tree as permitted by the attributes involved in the selection condition. That is, select operation is performed as early as possible to reduce the number of tuples returned.
- The select and join operations that are more restrictive (result in relations with the fewest tuples) are executed first. That is, the select and join operation are rearranged so that they are accomplished with the least amount of system overhead. This is done by reordering the leaf nodes of the tree among themselves by applying rule 6, 7 and 10 (commutativity and associativity of binary operations).
- Any Cartesian product operation followed by a select operation is combined into a single join operation according to the equivalence rule 5(a).
- The cascaded project operation is broken down and the attributes in the projection list are moved down the query tree as far as possible. New project operation can also be created as required. The

attributes that are required in the query result and in the subsequent operations should only be kept after each project operation. This will eliminate the return of unnecessary attributes (rules 3, 4, 9 and 12).

- The subtrees that represent groups of operations that can be executed by a single algorithm are identified.

For example, consider the following relational-algebra expression:

$$\pi_{\text{Pname, Address}}(\sigma_{\text{Category="Novel"}}(\text{BOOK} \bowtie \text{PUBLISHER}))$$

The initial query tree of this expression is given in Figure 8.15(a). After applying the select operation on the BOOK relation early, the number of tuples can be reduced. Similarly, after applying the project operation to extract the desired attributes P_ID, Pname and Address from the PUBLISHER relation, and P_ID from the result of σ on BOOK relation (P_ID is the join attribute), the size of the intermediate result can be reduced further. The final expression now becomes

$$\pi_{\text{Pname, Address}}((\pi_{\text{P\_ID}}(\sigma_{\text{Category="Novel"}}(\text{BOOK}))) \bowtie (\pi_{\text{P\_ID, Pname, Address}}(\text{PUBLISHER})))$$

The transformed query tree of the final expression after applying the select and project operations earlier is given in Figure 8.15(b).

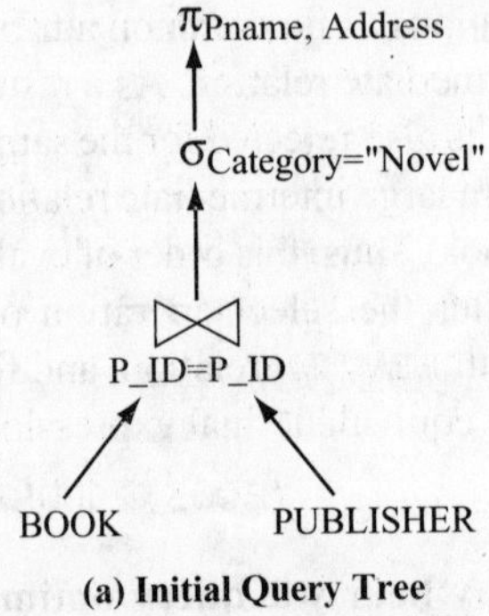

(a) Initial Query Tree

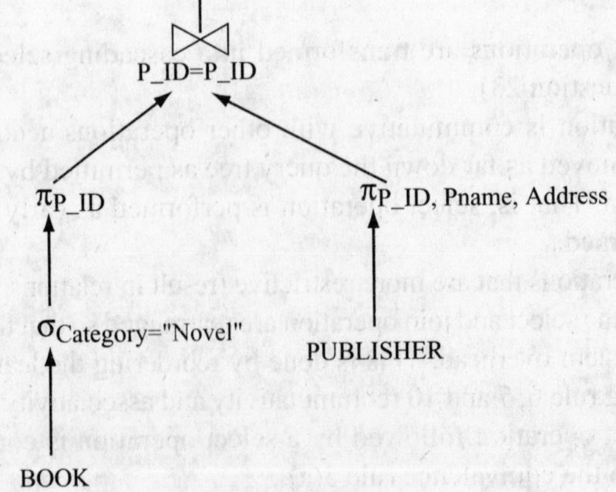

(b) Final Query Tree

Figure 8.15 Transformation from Initial Query Tree to Final Query Tree

22. Consider a file with 10,000 pages and three available buffer pages. Assume that the external sort-merge algorithm is used to sort the file. Calculate the initial number of runs produced in the first pass. How many passes will it take to sort the file completely? How many buffer pages are required to sort the file completely in two passes?

Ans: In the first pass (Pass 0), the number of initial runs (n_i) can be computed as $\lceil b_R/M \rceil$, that is, $\lceil 10000/3 \rceil = 3334$ initial sorted runs each containing 3 pages except the last that will have only one page.

The number of passes required to sort the file completely, including the initial sorting pass, can be calculated as $\lceil \log_{d_M}(n_i) \rceil + 1$. Here, d_M is 2 and n_i is 3334. Therefore, $\lceil \log_2(3334) \rceil + 1 = 12+1=13$ passes are required.

In Pass 0, $\lceil b_R/M \rceil$ runs are produced. In Pass 1, we must be able to merge these runs, that is, $M-1 \geq \lceil b_R/M \rceil$. This implies that M must at least be large enough to satisfy $M*(M-1) \geq b_R$. Thus, with $b_R = 10000$, $M = 101$. Thus, we need 101 buffer pages.

23. Consider three relations R(<u>A</u>, B, C), S(<u>C</u>, D, E) and T(<u>E</u>, F). If R has 500 tuples, S has 1000 tuples, and T has 900 tuples. Compute the size of R⋈S⋈T, and give an efficient way for computing the join.

Ans: Since the join operation is commutative and associative in nature, the relations R, S and T can be joined in any order. Therefore, we will first perform the join operation on R and S based on the common attribute C. Further, the join operation will be performed on the relation T and the result obtained from the previous join operation based on the common attribute E. Thus, we will compute the size based on the strategy of ((R⋈S)⋈T).

The join operation on R and S will yield a relation of at most 500 tuples, because the number of tuples returned by the operation R⋈S is exactly the same as the number of tuples in R, if the common attribute (on the basis of which join is performed) is the primary key in S and foreign key in R.

Similarly, the join operation on T and the result of R⋈S will yield a relation of at most 500 tuples, because the common attribute E is the primary key in T and foreign key in the result obtained from R⋈S. Thus, the operation (R⋈S⋈T) results in 500 tuples.

The efficient way of computing (R⋈S⋈T) is to create an index on the attributes C and E of relations R and S respectively. The index on attribute C can be used to directly retrieve the matching tuples in R that satisfy the join condition. Similarly, the index on attribute E can be used to directly retrieve the matching tuples in the result obtained after R⋈S that satisfy the join condition.

24. How many different join orders are there for a query that joins 5 relations?

Ans: In general, for n relations, there are (2(n-1))!/(n-1)! different join orderings. Therefore, for n=5, the join orderings are 1680.

25. Consider the following relational-algebra queries on the *Online Book* database. Draw the initial query trees for each of these queries.

(a) $\pi_{\text{P\_ID, Address, Phone}}(\sigma_{\text{State="Georgia"}}(\text{PUBLISHER}))$

Ans:

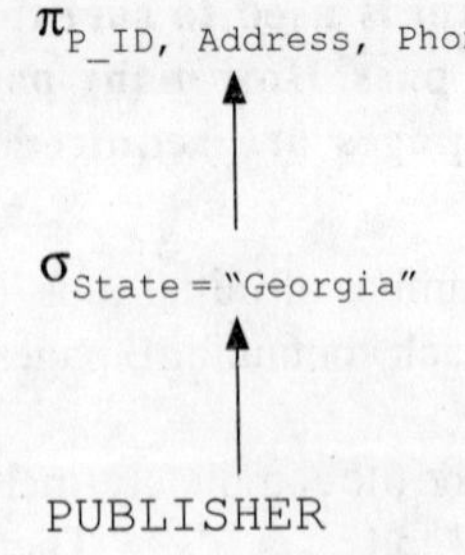

(b) $\sigma_{\text{Category="Textbook"} \wedge \text{State="Georgia"}}(\text{BOOK} \bowtie_{\text{BOOK.P\_ID = PUBLISHER.P\_ID}} \text{PUBLISHER})$

Ans:

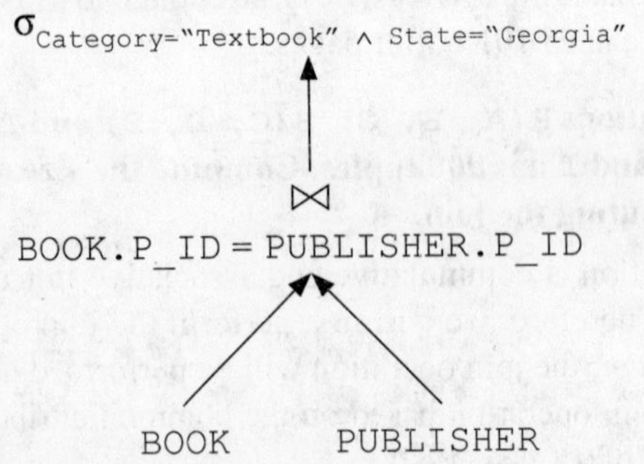

(c) $\pi_{\text{Book\_title, Category, Price}}(\sigma_{\text{Aname="Charles Smith"}}((\text{BOOK} \bowtie_{\text{BOOK.ISBN=AUTHOR\_BOOK.ISBN}} \text{AUTHOR\_BOOK}) \bowtie_{\text{AUTHOR\_BOOK.A\_ID=AUTHOR.A\_ID}} \text{AUTHOR}))$

Ans:

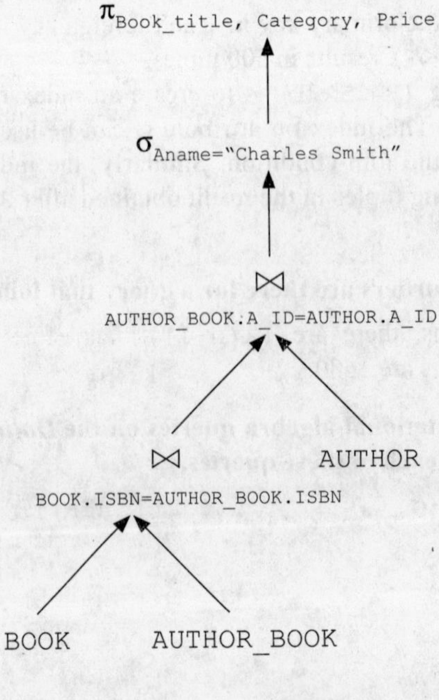

26. Consider the following SQL queries. Which of these queries is faster to execute and why? Draw the query tree also.

(a)
```
SELECT Category, COUNT (*) FROM BOOK
WHERE Category! = 'Novel'
GROUP BY Category;
```

Ans: Query tree for this SQL query is given below:

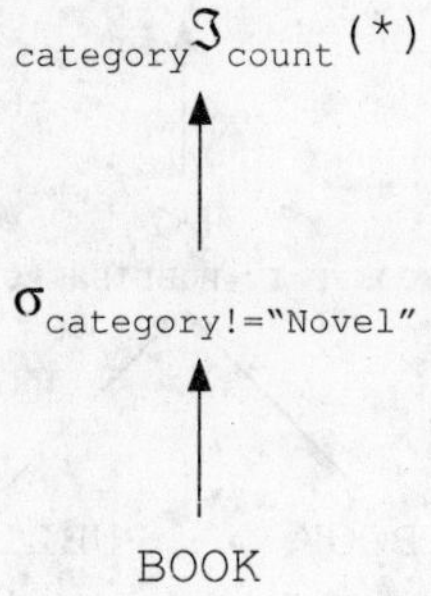

(b)
```
SELECT Category, COUNT (*) FROM BOOK
GROUP BY Category
HAVING Category! = 'Novel';
```

Ans: Query tree for this SQL query is given below:

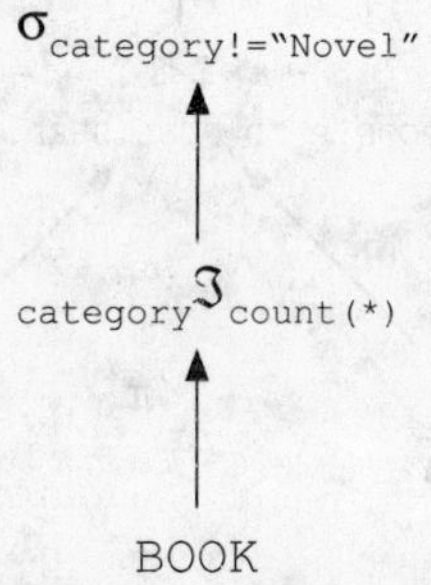

Query (a) is faster to execute than query (b) because `HAVING` clause in query (b) filters the selected tuples only after all the tuples have been fetched. Therefore, it will take more time to execute.

27. Consider the following SQL queries on Online Book database and transform these SQL queries into relational algebra expressions. Draw the initial query trees for each of these expressions, and then derive their optimized query trees after applying heuristics on them.

(a)
```
SELECT P.P_ID, Pname, Address, Phone
FROM BOOK B, PUBLISHER P
WHERE P.P_ID = B.P_ID AND Category = 'Language Book';
```

Ans: $\pi_{\text{P.P\_ID, Pname, Address, Phone}}(\sigma_{\text{Category = "Language Book"}}(\text{BOOK}_{\text{BOOK.P\_ID=PUBLISHER.P\_ID}}\ \text{PUBLISHER}))$

Initial query tree of this expression is given below:

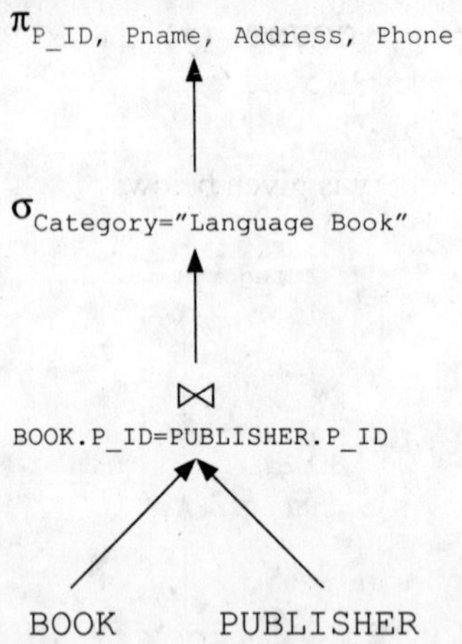

The optimized query tree is given below:

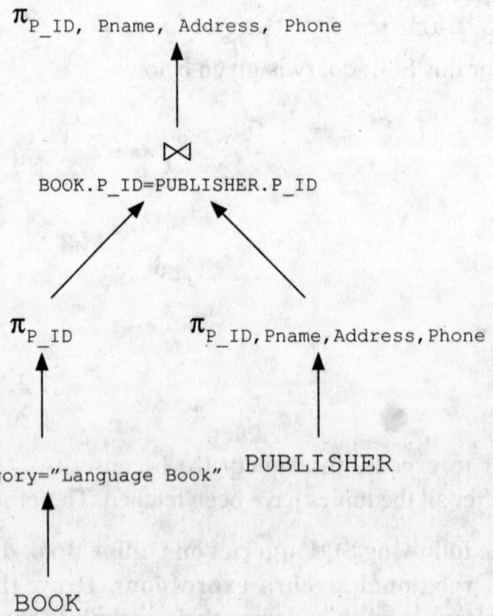

(b) **SELECT** ISBN, Book_title, Category, Price
FROM BOOK B, PUBLISHER P
WHERE P.P_ID = B.P_ID **AND** Pname='Bright Publications'
AND Price>30;

Ans: $\pi_{\text{ISBN, Book\_title, Category, Price}}$ ($\sigma_{\text{Pname="Bright Publications"} \wedge \text{Price>30}}$
(BOOK $\bowtie_{\text{B.P\_ID=P.P\_ID}}$ PUBLISHER))

The initial query tree of this expression is given below:

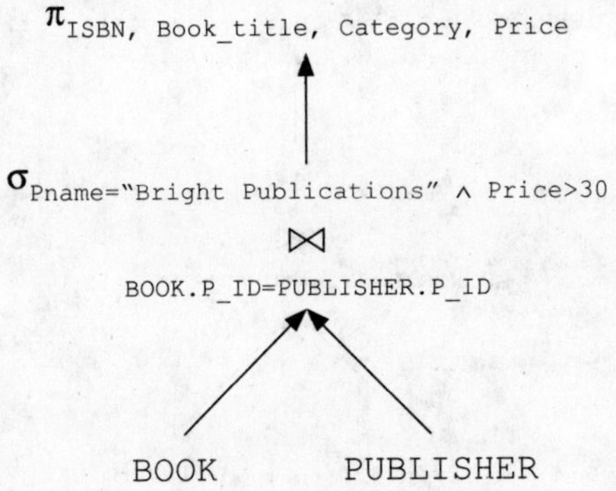

The optimized query tree is given below:

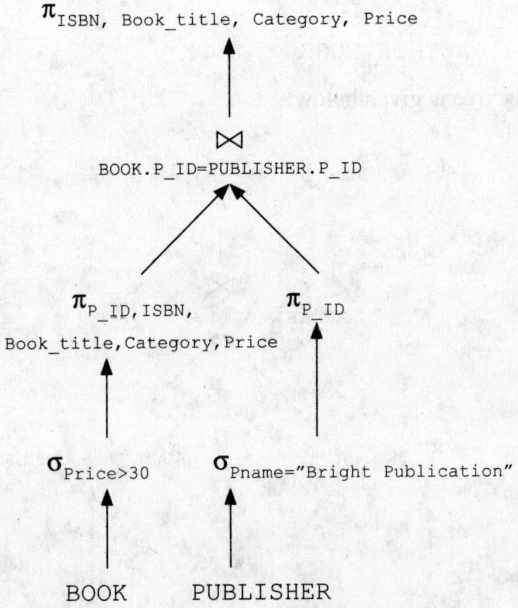

(c) **SELECT** ISBN, Book_title, Year, Page_count, Price
FROM BOOK B, AUTHOR A, AUTHOR_BOOK AB
WHERE B.ISBN = AB.ISBN **AND** AB.A_ID = A.A_ID
AND Aname = 'Charles Smith';

Ans: $\pi_{\text{ISBN, Book\_title, Year, Page\_count, Price}}\ (\sigma_{\text{Aname="Charles Smith"}}$
$((\text{BOOK} \bowtie_{\text{B.ISBN=AB.ISBN}} \text{AUTHOR\_BOOK})$
$\bowtie_{\text{AB.A\_ID=A.A\_ID}} \text{AUTHOR}))$

The initial query tree of this expression is given below:

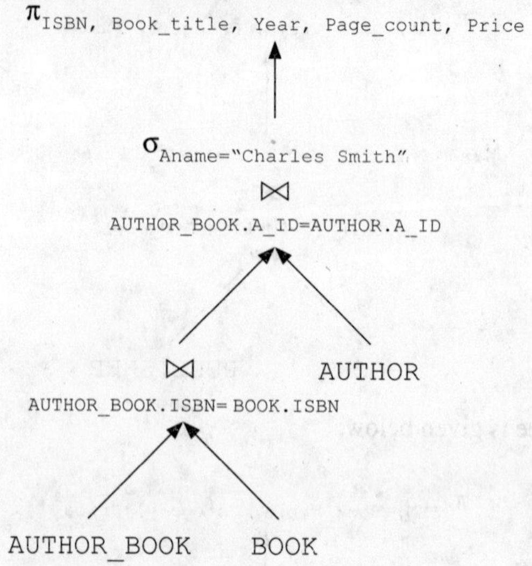

The optimized query tree is given below:

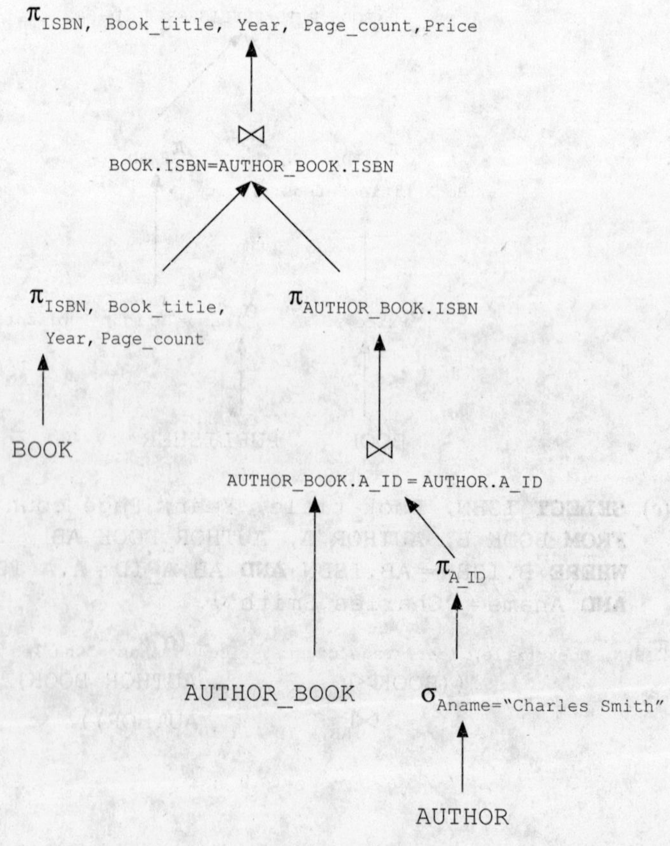

(d)
```
SELECT Book_title, Pname, Aname
FROM BOOK B, PUBLISHER P, AUTHOR A, AUTHOR_BOOK AB
WHERE P.P_ID = B.P_ID AND AB.A_ID=A.A_ID
AND B.ISBN=AB.ISBN AND Category= 'Language book';
```

Ans: $\pi_{\text{Book\_title, Pname, Aname}} (\sigma_{\text{Category="Language Book"}} ((\text{BOOK} \bowtie_{\text{B.P\_ID=P.P\_ID}} \text{PUBLISHER}) \bowtie_{\text{B.ISBN=AB.ISBN}} \text{AUTHOR\_BOOK}) \bowtie_{\text{AB.A\_ID=A.A\_ID}} \text{AUTHOR})$

The initial query tree of this expression is given below:

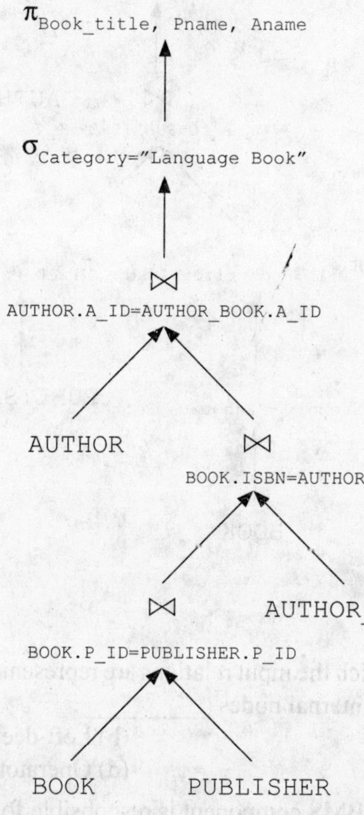

The optimized query tree is given below:

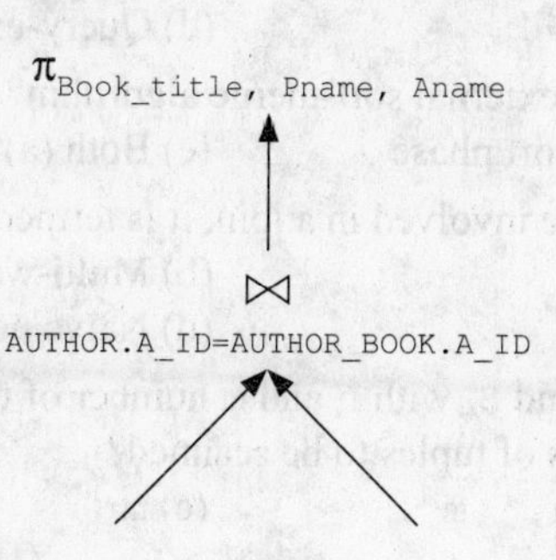

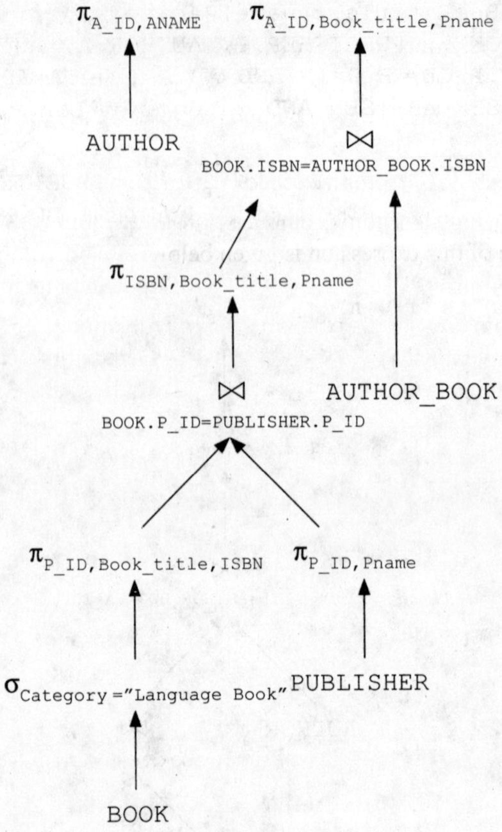

Multiple-choice Questions

1. A tree data structure in which the input relations are represented as the leaf nodes and the relational algebra operations as the internal nodes ___________.
   (a) Query tree (b) Left-deep join tree
   (c) Right deep join tree (d) Operator tree
2. Which of the following DBMS component is responsible for generating a least costly plan?
   (a) Parser (b) Translator
   (c) Query optimizer (d) Query-evaluation engine
3. Which of these is a phase in external sort-merge algorithm?
   (a) Merge phase (b) Sort phase (c) Both (a) and (b) (d) None of these
4. If more than two relations are involved in a join, it is termed as ___________.
   (a) Two-way join (b) Multi-way join
   (c) Nested-loop join (d) Naïve nested-loop join
5. If there are two relations R and S, with n and m number of tuples, respectively, then nested-loop join requires how many pairs of tuples to be scanned?
   (a) n + m (b) n * m (c) m (d) n

6. If there are two relations R and S containing 700 and 900 tuples respectively, then which relation should be taken as outer relation in block nested-loop join algorithm?
(a) S (b) R (c) Any of these (d) None of these
7. An index created by the query optimizer and destroyed when the query is completed is known as ________.
(a) Secondary index (b) Optimized index (c) Temporary index (d) Permanent index
8. Which of the following algorithms combines sort-merge join with indexes?
(a) Hybrid merge-join (b) Nested merge-join
(c) External merge-join (d) Indexed merge-join
9. Which of these evaluations is also known as lazy evaluation?
(a) Materialized evaluation (b) Demand-driven pipeline
(c) Producer-driven pipeline (d) Both (a) and (b)
10. Which of the following operations is not commutative?
(a) Select (b) Union (c) Intersection (d) Set difference
11. Which of these equivalence rules is known as cascading of project operator?
(a) $\pi(\sigma_c(R)) = \sigma_c(\pi_{A1,A2,\ldots,An}(R))$ (b) $\sigma_{c1}(\sigma_{c2}(R)) = \sigma_{c2}(\sigma_{c1}(R))$
(c) $\pi_{A1}(\pi_{A2}(\ldots(\pi_{An}(R))\ldots)) = \pi_{A1}(R)$ (d) $\sigma_{c1 \wedge c2}(R) = \sigma_{c1}(\sigma_{c2}(R))$
12. Given four relations P, Q, R and S. In how many ways these relations can be joined?
(a) 240 (b) 4 (c) 120 (d) 16

Answers

1. (a) 2. (c) 3. (c) 4. (b) 5. (b) 6. (b) 7. (c)
8. (a) 9. (b) 10. (d) 11. (c) 12. (c)

9

Introduction to Transaction Processing

1. Define transaction. What are the properties of a transaction? Explain with the help of an example.

Ans: A collection of operations that form a single logical unit of work is called a **transaction**. The operations that make up a transaction typically consist of requests to access existing data, modify existing data, add new data or any combination of these requests. The statements of a transaction are enclosed within the **begin transaction** and **end transaction** statements.

To ensure the integrity of the data, the database system must maintain some desirable properties of the transaction. These properties are known as **ACID properties**, the acronym derived from the first letter of the terms **a**tomicity, **c**onsistency, **i**solation and **d**urability.

- **Atomicity** implies that either all of the operations that make up a transaction should execute or none of them should occur.
- **Consistency** implies that if all the operations of a transaction are executed completely, the database is transformed from one consistent state to another.
- **Isolation** implies that each transaction appears to run in isolation with other concurrently running transactions.
- **Durability** (also known as **permanence**) implies that once a transaction is completed successfully, the changes made by the transaction persist in the database, even if the system fails.

For example, consider a transaction T_1 that transfers \$100 from account A to account B. Let the initial values of account A be \$2000 and account B be \$1500. The sum of the values of account A and B is \$3500 before the execution of transaction T_1. Since T_1 is a fund-transferring transaction, the sum of the values of account A and B should be \$3500 even after its execution. The transaction T_1 can be written as follows:

T_1:

```
read(A);
A:=A-100;
```

```
write(A);
read(B);
B:= B+100;
write(B);
```

If transaction T_1 is executed, either \$100 should be transferred from account *A* to *B* or neither of the accounts should be affected. If T_1 fails after debiting \$100 from account *A*, but before crediting \$100 to account *B*, the effects of this failed transaction on account *A* must be undone. This is the atomicity property of transaction T_1. The execution of transaction T_1 should also preserve the consistency of the database, that is, the sum of the values of account *A* and *B* should be \$3500 even after the execution of T_1.

Now, let us consider the isolation property of T_1. Suppose that during the execution of transaction T_1 when \$100 is debited from account *A* and not yet credited to account *B*, another concurrently running transaction, say T_2, reads the values of account *A* and *B*. Since T_1 has not yet completed, T_2 will read inconsistent values. The isolation property ensures that the effects of the transaction T_1 are not visible to other transaction T_2 until T_1 is completed. If the transaction T_1 is successfully completed and the user who initiated the transaction T_1 has been notified about successful transfer of funds, then the data regarding the transfer of funds should not be lost even if the system fails. This is the durability property of T_1. The durability can be guaranteed by ensuring that either

- all the changes made by the transaction are written to the disk before the transaction is completed or
- the information about all the changes made by the transaction is written to the disk and is sufficient to enable the database system to reconstruct the changes when the database system is restarted after the failure.

2. Explain state transition diagram. Explain, when a transaction is said to be failed.

Ans: State transition diagram is a diagram that describes how a transaction passes through various states during its execution. Whenever a transaction is submitted to a DBMS for execution, either it executes successfully or fails due to some reasons. During its execution, a transaction passes through various states that are *active*, *partially committed*, *committed*, *failed* and *aborted* as shown in Figure 9.1.

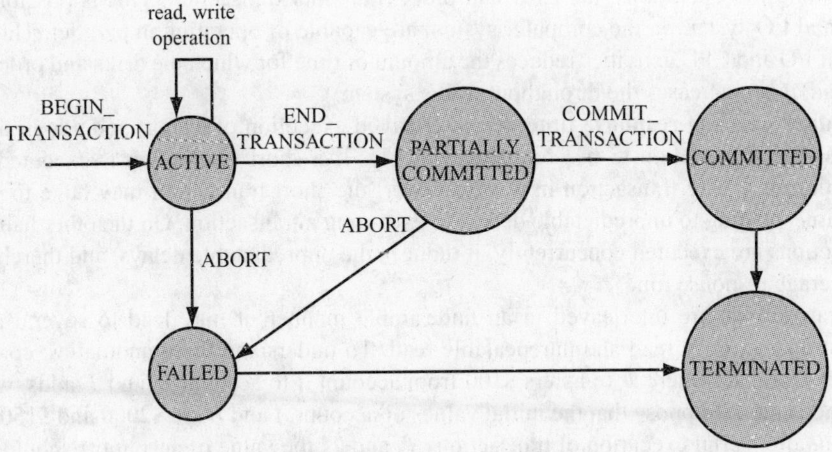

Figure 9.1 State Transition Diagram Showing Various States of a Transaction

A transaction enters into the **active** state with its commencement. At this point, the system marks `BEGIN_TRANSACTION` operation to specify the beginning of the transaction execution. During its execution, the transaction stays in the active state and executes several `READ` and `WRITE` operations on the database. The `READ` operation transfers a data item from the database to a local buffer of the transaction that has executed the read operation. The `WRITE` operation transfers the data item from the local buffer of the transaction back to the database.

Once the transaction executes its final operation, the system marks `END_TRANSACTION` operation to specify the end of the transaction execution. At this point, the transaction enters into the **partially committed** state. The actual output at this point may still be residing in the main memory and, thus, any kind of hardware failure might prevent its successful completion. In such a case, the transaction may have to be aborted.

Before actually updating the database on the disk, the system first writes the details of updates performed by the transaction in the log file. The log file is then written to the disk so that, even in case of failure, the system can re-construct the updates performed by the transaction when the system restarts after the failure. When this information is successfully written out in the log file, the system marks `COMMIT_TRANSACTION` operation to indicate the successful end of the transaction. Now, the transaction is said to be **committed** and all its changes must be reflected permanently in the database.

If the transaction is aborted during its active state or the system fails to write the changes in the log file, the transaction enters the **failed** state. The failed transaction must be rolled back to undo its effects on the database to maintain the consistency of the database. When the transaction leaves the system, it enters into the **terminated** state. At this point, the transaction information maintained in the log file during its execution is removed.

3. Why is it desirable to have concurrent execution of multiple transactions? What are the various anomalies that can occur due to undesirable interleaving of transactions? Explain by giving suitable examples.

Ans: The database system allows concurrent execution of transactions due to two reasons as given below:

- **To increase system throughput:** A transaction performing read or write operation using I/O devices may not be using the CPU at a particular point of time. Thus, while one transaction is performing I/O operations, the CPU can process another transaction. This is possible because CPU and I/O system in the computer system are capable of operating in parallel. This overlapping of I/O and CPU activities reduces the amount of time for which the disks and processors are idle and, thus, increases the throughput of the system.
- **To reduce average response time:** An interleaved execution of a short and a long transaction allows short transaction to be completed quickly. If a short transaction is executed after the execution of a long transaction in a serial order, the short transaction may have to wait for a long time, leading to unpredictable delays in executing a transaction. On the other hand, if these transactions are executed concurrently, it reduces the unpredictable delays, and thereby reduces the average response time.

If the transactions are interleaved in an undesirable manner, it may lead to several anomalies such as lost update, dirty read and unrepeatable read. To understand these anomalies, consider two transactions T_1 and T_2, where T_1 transfers \$100 from account A to account B, and T_2 adds two percent interest to account A. Suppose that the initial values of account A and B are \$2000 and \$1500, respectively. Then, after serial execution of transactions T_1 and T_2, the value of account A should be \$1938 and that of account B should be \$1600.

Suppose that the operations of T_1 and T_2 are interleaved in such a way that T_2 reads the value of account A before T_1 updates its value in the database. Now, when T_2 updates the value of account A in the database, the value of account A updated by the transaction T_1 is overwritten and hence is lost. This is known as **lost update problem**. The value of account A at the end of both the transactions is \$2040 instead of \$1938, which leads to data inconsistency. The interleaved execution of transactions T_1 and T_2 that leads to lost update problem is shown in Figure 9.2(a).

The second problem occurs when a transaction fails after updating a data item, and before this data item is changed back to its original value, another transaction reads this updated value. For example, assume that T_1 fails after debiting \$100 from account A, but before crediting this amount to account B. This will leave the database in an inconsistent state. The value of account A is now \$1900, which must be changed back to the original one, that is, \$2000. However, before the transaction T_1 is rolled back, let another transaction T_2 reads the incorrect value of account A. This incorrect value of account A that is read by transaction T_2 is called **dirty data**, and the problem is called **dirty read** problem. The interleaved execution of transactions T_1 and T_2 that leads to dirty read problem is shown in Figure 9.2(b).

The third problem occurs when a transaction tries to read the value of data item twice, and another transaction updates the same data item in between the two read operations of the first transaction. As a result, the first transaction reads varied values of same data item during its execution. This is known as **unrepeatable read**. For example, consider a transaction T_3 that reads the value of account A. At this point, let another transaction T_4 updates the value of account A. Now if T_3 again tries to read the value of account A, it will get a different value. As a result, the transaction T_3 receives different values for two reads of account A. The interleaved schedule of transactions T_3 and T_4 that leads to a problem of unrepeatable read is shown in Figure 9.2(c).

T_1	T_2
read(A)	
A:= A - 100	
	read(A)
	X:=A * 0.02
	A:=A + X
write(A)	
read(B)	
	write(A)
B:= B+ 100	
write(B)	

(a) Lost Update Problem

T_1	T_2
read(A)	
A:= A - 100	
write(A)	

Figure 9.2 Anomalies Due to Interleaved Execution (Contd...)

(Contd...)

	read(A)
	X:=A * 0.02
	A:=A + X
	write(A)
read(B)	
T_1 fails	

(b) Dirty Read Problem

T_3	T_4
read(A)	
	read(A)
	A:=A + 100
	write(A)
read(A)	
sum:=sum + A	
write(sum)	

(c) Unrepeatable Read

Figure 9.2 Anomalies Due to Interleaved Execution

4. Define the following terms in context of a transaction:

(a) Schedule

Ans: A list of operations (such as reading, writing, aborting or committing) from a set of transactions is known as a **schedule** (or **history**). A schedule should comprise all the instructions of the participating transactions and also preserve the order in which the instructions appear in each individual transaction.

(b) Non-serial schedule

Ans: In a multi-user database system, several transactions are executed concurrently for efficient use of system resources. When two transactions are executed concurrently, the operating system may execute one transaction for some time, then perform a context switch and execute the second transaction for some time, and then switch back to the first transaction, and so on. Thus, when multiple transactions are executed concurrently, the CPU time is shared among all the transactions. The schedule resulted from this type of interleaving of operations from various transactions is known as **non-serial schedule**.

(c) Cascading rollback

Ans: Cascading rollback is a situation in which failure of single transaction leads to a series of transaction rollbacks.

(d) Blind writes

Ans: Blind writes are those write operations which are performed without performing the read operation.

(e) Topological sorting

Ans: The process of ordering the nodes of an acyclic preceding graph is known as **topological sorting**. The topological ordering produces equivalent serial schedule.

(f) Observable external writes

Ans: There are some situations when a transaction needs to perform write operations on a terminal or a printer. These writes are known as **observable external writes**. Since the content once written on the printer or the terminal cannot be erased, the database system allows such writes to take place only after the transaction has entered the committed state.

(g) Compensating transaction

Ans: Compensating transaction is a transaction which reverses the effect of a committed transaction.

5. Define serial schedule. Why is it always considered to be correct?

Ans: **Serial schedule** is a schedule consisting of a sequence of instructions from various transactions, where the operations of one single transaction appear together in that schedule. Each transaction in a serial schedule is executed independently without any interference from the operations of other transactions. As long as every transaction is executed from beginning to end without any interference from other transactions, it gives a correct end result on the database. Therefore, every serial schedule is considered to be correct. Hence, for a set of n transactions, n! different valid serial schedules are possible. The serial schedule of transactions T_1 and T_5 in the order T_5 followed by T_1 is shown in Figure 9.3.

T_1	T_5
	read(B)
	B:= B - 50
	write(B)
	read(C)
	C:= C + 50
	write(C)
read(A)	
A:= A - 100	
write(A)	
read(B)	
B:=B + 100	
write(B)	

Figure 9.3 Serial Schedule in the Order T_5 Followed by T_1

6. Explain serializable schedule by giving an example.

Ans: The consistency of the database under concurrent execution can be ensured by interleaving the operations of transactions in such a way that the final output is the same as that of some serial schedule of those transactions. Such a schedule is referred to as **serializable schedule**. Thus, a schedule S of n transactions $T_1, T_2, T_3, \ldots, T_n$ is serializable if it is equivalent to some serial schedule of the same n transactions.

Figure 9.4 shows a non-serial schedule of transactions T_1 and T_5, which is equivalent to serial schedule shown in Figure 9.3. After the execution of this schedule, the final values of accounts A, B and C are \$*1900*, \$*1550* and \$*550*. Thus, the sum $A + B + C$ is preserved and, hence, it is a serializable schedule.

T_1	T_5
read(A)	
A:=A - 100	
write(A)	
	read(B)
	B:= B - 50
	write(B)
read(B)	
B:=B + 100	
write(B)	
	read(C)
	C:=C + 50
	write(C)

Figure 9.4 Serializable Schedule

7. What are result equivalent schedules? Explain with example.

Ans: Two different schedules may produce the same final state of the database. Such schedules are known as **result equivalent**, since they have the same effect on the database. However, in some cases, two different schedules may accidentally produce the same final state of database. For example, consider two schedules S_i and S_j that are updating the data item `Q`, as shown in Figure 9.5. Suppose that the value of data item `Q` is $*100* then the final state of database produced by schedules S_i and S_j is the same, that is, they produce the same value of `Q` ($*200*).

S_i	S_j
read(Q)	read(Q)
Q:= Q + 100	Q:= Q * 2
write(Q)	write(Q)

Figure 9.5 Result Equivalent Schedules

8. Discuss the two different forms of schedule equivalence.

Ans: Two different forms of schedule equivalence are *conflict equivalence* and *view equivalence* that lead to the notions of *conflict serializability* and *view serializability*.

Conflict equivalence and conflict serializability: Two operations in a schedule are said to **conflict** if they belong to different transactions, access the same data item, and at least one of them is the write operation. On the other hand, two operations belonging to different transactions in a schedule do not conflict if both of them are read operations or both of them are accessing different data items. To understand the concept of conflicting operations in a schedule, consider two transactions T_6 and T_7 that are updating the data items `Q` and `R` in the database. A non-serial schedule of these transactions is shown in Figure 9.6.

T_6	T_7
read(Q)	
write(Q)	
	read(Q)
	write(Q)
read(R)	
write(R)	
	read(R)
	write(R)

Figure 9.6 Non-serial Schedule Showing Conflicting Operations

In Figure 9.6, the `write(Q)` operation of T_6 conflicts with the `read(Q)` operation of T_7 because both the operations are accessing the same data item Q, and one of these operation is the write operation. On the other hand, the `write(Q)` operation of T_7 is not conflicting with the `read(R)` operation of T_6, because both are accessing different data items Q and R.

If a schedule *S* can be transformed into a schedule *S*' by performing a series of swaps of non-conflicting operations, then *S* and *S′* are **conflict equivalents.** Note that while swapping the order of execution of two conflicting operations cannot be changed because if they are applied in different order, they can have different effect on the database or on the other transactions in the schedule. Thus, two schedules are said to be conflict equivalent if the order of any two conflicting operations is same in both the schedules. A schedule, which is conflict equivalent to some serial schedule, is known as **conflict serializable**.

View equivalence and view serializability: Two schedules *S* and *S′* are said to be **view equivalent** if the schedules satisfy these conditions.

- The same set of transactions participates in S and S′, and S and S′ include the same set of operations of those transactions.
- If the transaction T_i reads the initial value of a data item say Q in schedule *S*, then T_i must read the initial value of same data item Q in schedule *S′* also.
- For each data item Q, if T_i executes `read(Q)` operation after the `write(Q)` operation of transaction T_j in schedule *S*, then T_i must execute the `read(Q)` operation after the `write(Q)` operation of T_j in schedule *S′* also.
- If the transaction T_i performs the final write operation on any data item say Q in schedule *S*, then it must perform final write operation on the same data item Q in schedule *S′* also.

A schedule *S* is said to be **view serializable** if it is view equivalent to some serial schedule.

9. What is a precedence graph? How can it be used to test the conflict serializability of a schedule?

Ans: A **precedence graph** is a directed graph `G=(N,E)` where N=$\{T_1, T_2, \ldots, T_n\}$is a set of nodes and E=$\{e_1, e_2, \ldots, e_n\}$is a set of directed edges. For each transaction T_i in a schedule, there exists a node in the graph. An edge e_i in the graph is shown as ($T_i \rightarrow T_j$), where T_i is the **starting node** and T_j is the **ending node** of the edge e_i. The edge e_i is created if one of the operations in T_i appears in the schedule before some conflicting operation in T_j.

The algorithm to test the conflict serializability of a schedule S is given as follows:

1. For each transaction T_i participating in the schedule S, create a node labelled T_i.
2. If T_j executes a read operation after T_i executes a write operation on any data item say Q, create an edge $(T_i \rightarrow T_j)$ in the precedence graph.
3. If T_j executes a write operation after T_i executes a read operation on any data item say Q, create an edge $(T_i \rightarrow T_j)$ in the precedence graph.
4. If T_j executes a write operation after T_i executes a write operation on any data item say Q, create an edge $(T_i \rightarrow T_j)$ in the precedence graph.
5. If the resultant precedence graph is acyclic, that is, it does not contain any cycle, then the schedule S is considered to be conflict serializable. If a precedence graph contains a cycle, the schedule S is not conflict serializable.

An edge from T_i to T_j in the precedence graph implies that the transaction T_i must appear before T_j in any serial schedule S' that is equivalent to S. Thus, if there are no cycles in the precedence graph, a serial schedule S' equivalent to S can be created by ordering the transactions in such a way that whenever an edge $(T_i \rightarrow T_j)$ exists in the precedence graph, T_i must appear before T_j in the equivalent serial schedule S'.

For example, consider the schedule shown in Figure 9.5. The precedence graph of this schedule is shown in Figure 9.7(a). It contains two nodes, one for each transaction—T_6 and T_7. An edge from T_6 to T_7 is created, which is labelled with the data items Q and R that led to the creation of this edge. Since there are no cycles in the precedence graph, this schedule is a conflict serializable schedule. The serial schedule equivalent to *Schedule 5* is shown in Figure 9.6(b).

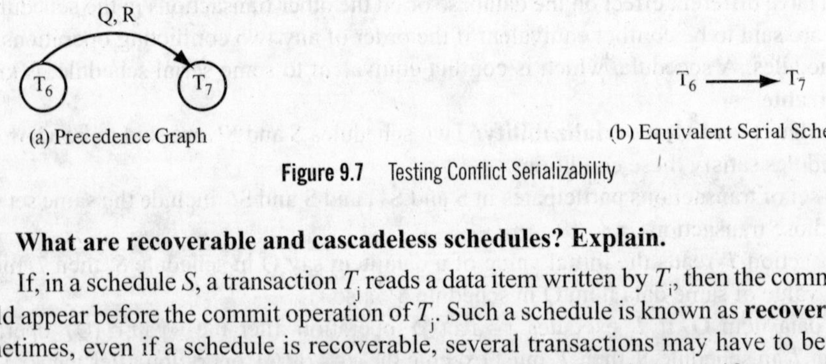

(a) Precedence Graph (b) Equivalent Serial Schedule

Figure 9.7 Testing Conflict Serializability

10. What are recoverable and cascadeless schedules? Explain.

Ans: If, in a schedule S, a transaction T_j reads a data item written by T_i, then the commit operation of T_i should appear before the commit operation of T_j. Such a schedule is known as **recoverable schedule**.

Sometimes, even if a schedule is recoverable, several transactions may have to be rolled back in order to recover completely from the failure of a transaction T_i. It happens if transactions have read the value of a data item written by T_i. For example, consider the schedule shown in Figure 9.8. In this schedule, the transaction T_8 reads the value of data item Q written by transaction T_9, and transaction T_{10} reads the value of data item Q written by transaction T_8.

Now suppose that the transaction T_8 fails due to any reason, it has to be rolled back. Since transaction T_9 has read the data written by T_8, it also needs to be rolled back. The transaction T_{10} also needs to be rolled back because it has in turn read the data written by T_9. Such a situation, in which failure of single transaction leads to a series of transaction rollbacks, is called **cascading rollback**.

Cascading rollback requires undoing of significant amount of work and, thus, is undesirable. Therefore, schedules should be restricted to avoid cascading rollbacks. The schedules that avoid cascading rollbacks are known as **cascadeless schedule**. In cascadeless schedules, transactions T_i and T_j are interleaved in such a way that T_j reads a data item previously written by T_i, however, `commit` operation of T_i appears before the read operation of T_j.

T_8	T_9	T_{10}
read(Q)		
write(Q)		
	read(Q)	
	write(Q)	
		read(Q)

Figure 9.8 Schedule Resulting Cascading Rollback

11. Discuss the four levels of isolation in SQL. What are the possible violations for these levels?

Ans: SQL:92 supports four levels of transaction isolation. The **isolation levels** reduce the isolation between concurrently executing transactions. The level providing the greatest isolation from other transactions is `SERIALIZABLE`. It is the default level of isolation. At this level, a transaction is fully isolated from the changes made by other transactions. The other isolation levels are `READ UNCOMMITTED`, `READ COMMITTED` and `REPEATABLE READ`. `READ UNCOMMITTED` is the lowest level of isolation. At this level, a transaction can read subsequent changes made by other transactions, either committed or uncommitted. With read uncommitted isolation level, one or more of the three problems, namely, *dirty read*, *unrepeatable read* and *phantom read* may occur.

In `READ COMMITTED` isolation level, dirty reads are not possible since a transaction is not allowed to read the updates made by uncommitted transactions. However, unrepeatable reads and phantoms are possible. Phantom read problem occurs when a transaction T_i reads a set of rows from a table based on some condition specified in `WHERE` clause, meanwhile another transaction T_j inserts a new row into that table that also satisfies the condition and commits. Now, if T_i is again executed, then it will see a tuple (or phantom tuple) that previously did not exist.

In `REPEATABLE READ` isolation level, dirty reads and unrepeatable reads are not possible but phantoms are possible. In `SERIALIZABLE` isolation level, dirty reads, unrepeatable reads, and phantoms are not possible. The possible violations for different transaction isolation levels are summarized in Table 9.1.

Table 9.1 Possible violations for different isolation levels

	Dirty Reads	Unrepeatable Reads	Phantoms
Read Uncommitted	Possible	Possible	Possible
Read Committed	Not possible	Possible	Possible
Repeatable Read	Not possible	Not possible	Possible
Serializable	Not possible	Not possible	Not possible

12. Discuss the commit and rollback statements in SQL.

Ans: The `COMMIT` statement terminates the current transaction and makes all the changes made by the transaction permanent in the database. That is, it *commits* the changes to the database. The `COMMIT` statement has the following general format:

```
COMMIT [WORK]
```

where `WORK` is an optional keyword that does not change the semantics of `COMMIT`.

The `ROLLBACK` statement, on the other hand, terminates the current transaction and undoes all the changes made by the transaction. That is, it *rolls back* the changes to the database. The `ROLLBACK` statement has the following general format:

```
ROLLBACK [WORK]
```

In this case also, `WORK` is an optional keyword that does not change the semantics of `ROLLBACK`.

13. Consider two transactions T_1 and T_2 given below:

T_1	T_2
`read(X);`	`read(X);`
`X:=X-10;`	`X:= X*1.02;`
`write(X);`	`Y:= Y*1.02;`
`read(Y);`	`write(X);`
`Y:=Y+10;`	`write(Y);`
`write(Y);`	

Give a serial schedule for these transactions and an equivalent non-serial schedule for these transactions.

Ans: Serial schedule

T_1	T_2
`read(X);`	
`X:=X-10;`	
`write(X);`	
`read(Y);`	
`Y:=Y+10;`	
`write(Y);`	
	`read(X);`
	`X:=X*1.02;`
	`Y:=Y*1.02;`
	`write(X);`
	`write(Y);`

Non-serial schedule

T_1	T_2
`read(X);`	
`X:=X-10;`	
`write(X);`	
	`read(X);`
	`X:=X*1.02;`
`read(Y);`	
`Y:=Y+10;`	
`write(Y);`	
	`Y: =Y*1.02;`
	`write(X);`
	`write(Y);`

14. Consider the following precedence graph. Is the corresponding schedule conflict serializable? Give reasons also.

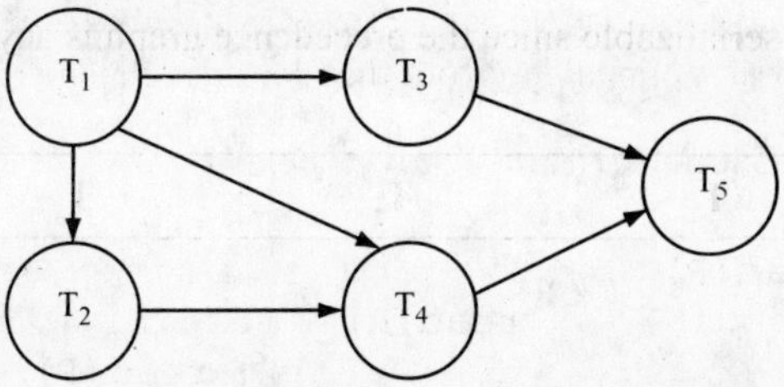

Ans: The corresponding schedule will be conflict serializable as the precedence graph is acyclic.

15. Consider three transactions T_1, T_2 and T_3 and two schedules S_1 and S_2 given below. Draw the precedence graph for schedules S_1 and S_2 and test whether they are conflict serializable or not.

T_1: $r_1(P)$; $r_1(R)$; $w_1(P)$;
T_2: $r_2(R)$; $r_2(Q)$; $w_2(R)$; $w_2(Q)$;
T_3: $r_3(P)$; $r_3(Q)$; $w_3(Q)$;
S_1: $r_1(P)$; $r_2(R)$; $r_1(R)$; $r_3(P)$; $r_3(Q)$; $w_1(P)$; $w_3(Q)$; $r_2(Q)$; $w_2(R)$; $w_2(Q)$;
S_2: $r_1(P)$; $r_2(R)$; $r_3(P)$; $r_1(R)$; $r_2(Q)$; $r_3(Q)$; $w_1(P)$; $w_2(R)$; $w_3(Q)$; $w_2(Q)$;

Ans: Schedule S_1

T_1	T_2	T_3
read(P)		
	read(R)	
read(R)		
		read(P)
		read(Q)
write(P)		
		write(Q)
	read(Q)	
	write(R)	
	write(Q)	

The precedence graph for this schdeule is shown below:

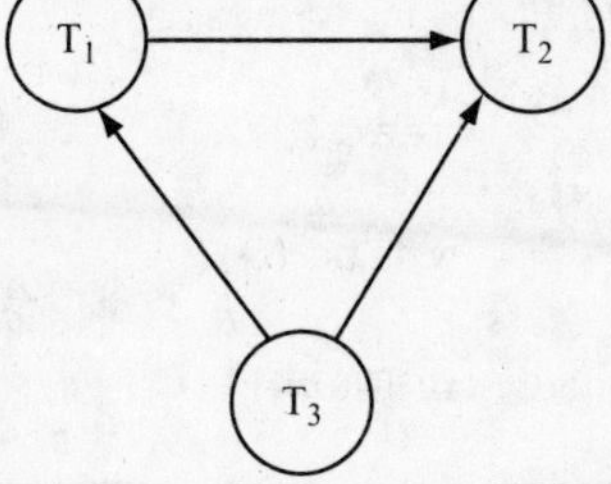

This schedule is conflict serializable since the precedence graph is acyclic.

Schedule S_2

T_1	T_2	T_3
read(P)		
	read(R)	
		read(P)
read(R)		
	read(Q)	
		read(Q)
write(P)		
	write(R)	
		write(Q)
	write(Q)	

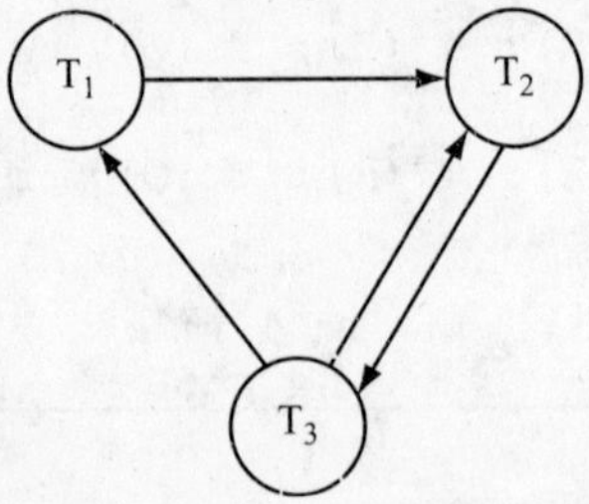

This schedule is not conflict serializable since the precedence graph is cyclic.

16. Consider schedule S_3 given below. Determine whether it is cascadeless, recoverable or non-recoverable.

S_3: $r_1(P)$; $r_2(R)$; $r_1(R)$; $r_3(P)$; $r_3(Q)$; $w_1(P)$; $w_3(Q)$; $r_2(Q)$; $w_3(R)$; $w_2(Q)$; c_1; c_2; c_3

Ans:

T_1	T_2	T_3
read(P)		
	read(R)	
read(R)		
		read(P)
		read(Q)
write(P)		
		write(Q)
	read(Q)	
		write(R)
	write(Q)	
commit		
	commit	
		commit

Here, transaction T_2 reads the data item Q written by T_3. If transaction T_3 fails after T_2 commits, its effects need to be undone. Since T_2 has read the values of Q written by transaction T_3, it also has to be rolled back. However, T_2 has already been committed, thus cannot be rolled back. Therefore, this schedule is a **non-recoverable schedule**.

17. Give an example of SQL transaction.

Ans: An example of an SQL transaction consisting of multiple SQL statements is given in Figure 9.9. In this transaction, two SQL statements are given that update the BOOK and PUBLISHER relations of *Online Book* database. The first statement updates the price of all the books published by publisher *P001*. The next statement updates the email-id of the publisher with P_ID="P002". If an error occurs on any SQL statement, the entire transaction is rolled back. That is, any updated value would be restored to its original value.

```
EXEC        SQL WHENEVER SQLERROR GOTO mylabel;
EXEC        SQL SET TRANSACTION
            READ WRITE,
            ISOLATION LEVEL SERIALIZABLE,
            DIAGNOSTIC SIZE 10;
EXEC        SQL UPDATE BOOK
            SET Price=Price*1.2
            WHERE P_ID="P001";
EXEC        SQL UPDATE PUBLISHER
            SET Email_id="sunsh@sunshinepub.com"
            WHERE P_ID="P002";
EXEC        SQL COMMIT;
GOTO        LAST;
mylabel:    EXEC SQL ROLLBACK;
LAST:...;
```

Figure 9.9 An Example of SQL Transaction

Multiple-choice Questions

1. What does C stand for in transaction ACID properties?
   (a) Correctness (b) Consistency (c) Committed (d) Completeness
2. Once the transaction executes its final operation, it enters into __________ state.
   (a) Committed (b) Terminated
   (c) Partially committed (d) Failed
3. The only way to undo the effects of a committed transaction is to execute a __________.
   (a) Undo transaction (b) Compensating transaction
   (c) Redo transaction (d) None of these
4. Which of these anomalies is also known as WW (write–write) conflict?
   (a) Lost update (b) Dirty read (c) Unrepeatable read (d) None of these
5. Which of these operations is considered for the purpose of recovery and concurrency control?
   (a) `Write` (b) `Commit` (c) `Abort` (d) All of these

6. How many valid serial schedules are possible for four transactions?
(a) 24 (b) 16 (c) 4 (d) 8
7. Two schedules are known as __________ if they produce the same final state of the database.
(a) Serializable (b) Conflict equivalent (c) Result equivalent (d) View equivalent
8. The schedules that avoid cascading rollbacks are known as __________
(a) Cascadeless schedules (b) Recoverable schedules
(c) Serial schedules (d) Non-recoverable schedules
9. How many levels of transaction isolation does an SQL: 92 support?
(a) Two (b) Three (c) Four (d) Five
10. When the two operations in a schedule are said to conflict?
(a) If they belong to different transactions
(b) Access the same data item
(c) Atleast one of the operation is the write operation
(d) All of these
11. Which of the following statements is false?
(a) Cascading rollback is desirable.
(b) The schedules that avoid cascading rollbacks are known as cascadeless schedule.
(c) Every cascadeless schedule is recoverable.
(d) None of these.
12. Which of the following is false with reference to concurrent transaction?
(a) It allows only one operation of any transaction to occur at any given time.
(b) It decreases the throughput of the system.
(c) It reduces the average response time.
(d) None of these.
13. Which of the following operations forms a schedule?
(a) Read (b) Write (c) Commit (d) All of these
14. Which of the following is a form of schedule equivalence?
(a) Result equivalent (b) Conflict equivalence
(c) View equivalence (d) All of these
15. The process of ordering the nodes of an acyclic preceding graph is known as __________.
(a) Bubble sorting (b) Topological sorting
(c) Acyclic sorting (d) None of these
16. Which of the following operations is considered in a schedule to construct a precedence graph?
(a) Read (b) Write (c) Both (a) and (b) (d) None of these
17. Which of the following statements results in making all the changes made by the transaction permanent in the database?
(a) COMMIT (b) ABORT (c) ROLLBACK (d) None of these

Answers

1. (b)	2. (c)	3. (b)	4. (a)	5. (d)	6. (a)	7. (c)
8. (a)	9. (c)	10. (d)	11. (a)	12. (b)	13. (d)	14. (d)
15. (b)	16. (c)	17. (a)				

10

Concurrency Control Techniques

1. What is concurrency control? How is it implemented?

Ans: When several transactions execute concurrently, they may result in interleaved operations, and the isolation property of transaction may no longer be preserved. Thus, it may leave the database in an inconsistent state. To understand, consider a situation in which two transactions concurrently access the same data item. One transaction modifies a tuple, and the other makes a decision on the basis of that modification. Now, suppose that the first transaction rolls back. At this point, the decision of the second transaction becomes invalid. Thus, there is a need to control the interaction among concurrent transactions, which is referred to as concurrency control.

The concurrency control is implemented with the help of concurrency control techniques, which ensure that the concurrent transactions maintain the integrity of a database by avoiding the interference among them and further ensure serializability order in the schedule of transactions. The various concurrency control techniques are locking, timestamp-based, optimistic and the multiversion technique.

2. Define lock. What are the two modes of locking?

Ans: A **lock** is a variable associated with each data item that indicates whether a read or write operation can be applied to the data item. In addition, it synchronizes the concurrent access of the data item. Acquiring the lock by modifying its value is called **locking**. It controls the concurrent access and manipulation of the locked data item by other transactions and, hence, maintains the consistency and integrity of the database. Database systems mainly use two modes of locking, namely, *exclusive locks* and *shared locks*.

Exclusive lock (denoted by X) is the commonly used locking strategy that provides a transaction an exclusive control on the data item. A transaction that wants to read as well as write a data item must acquire an exclusive lock on the data item. Hence, an exclusive lock is also known as the **update** lock or **write** lock. If a transaction (say, T_i) has acquired an exclusive lock on a data item (say, Q), no other transaction is allowed to access Q until T_i releases its lock on Q.

Shared lock (denoted by S) can be acquired on a data item when a transaction wants to only read a data item and not modify it. Hence, it is also known as **read** lock. If a transaction T_i has acquired a shared lock on data item Q, T_i can read but cannot write on Q. In addition, any number of transactions can acquire shared locks on Q simultaneously. However, no transaction can acquire an exclusive lock on Q.

3. What do you understand by lock compatibility? Discuss in detail with examples.

Ans: Whenever a transaction needs to perform some operation on a data item, it should request a lock in appropriate mode on that data item. If the requested data item is not locked by any other transaction, the lock manager grants the request immediately. Otherwise, the lock request may or may not be granted depending on the compatibility of locks. **Lock compatibility** determines whether locks can be acquired on a data item by multiple transactions at the same time.Suppose a transaction T_i requests a lock of mode m_1 on a data item Q on which another transaction T_j currently holds a lock of mode m_2. If mode m_2 is compatible with mode m_1, the request is immediately granted, otherwise rejected. The lock compatibility can be represented by a matrix called the **compatibility matrix** (see Figure 10.1). The term "YES" indicates that the request can be granted and "NO" indicates that the request cannot be granted.

Requested Mode	Shared	Exclusive
Shared	YES	NO
Exclusive	NO	NO

Figure 10.1 Compatibility Matrix

If the mode m_1 is shared, the lock request of transaction T_i is granted immediately, if and only if m_2 is also shared. Otherwise the lock request is not granted and the transaction T_i has to wait. On the other hand, if mode m_1 is exclusive, the lock request (either shared or exclusive) by transaction T_i is not granted and T_i has to wait.

4. How is locking implemented? What is the role of the lock table in implementation? How are requests to lock and unlock a data item handled?

Ans: The locking or unlocking of data items is implemented by a subsystem of the database system known as the **lock manager**. It receives the lock requests from transactions and replies them with a lock grant message or rollback message (in case of deadlock). In response to an unlock request, the lock manager only replies with an acknowledgement. In addition, it may result in lock grant messages to other waiting transactions.

The lock manager maintains a linked list of records for each locked data item in the order in which the requests arrive. Each record of the linked list is used to keep the transaction identifier that made the request and the mode in which the lock is requested. It also records whether the request has been granted. Lock manager uses a hash table known as **lock table**, indexed on the data item identifier, to find the linked list for a data item. Figure 10.2 shows a lock table, which contains locks for three different data items, namely, Q_1, Q_2 and Q_3. In addition, two transactions, namely, T_i and T_j, are shown which have been granted locks or are waiting for locks.

Observe that T_i has been granted locks on the Q_1 and Q_3 in shared mode. Similarly, T_j has been granted lock on Q_2 and Q_3 in shared mode, and is waiting to acquire a lock on Q_1 in exclusive mode, which has already been locked by T_i.

The lock manager handles the requests by the transaction to lock and unlock a data item in the way given here.

- **Lock request:** When a first request to lock a data item arrives, the lock manager creates a new linked list to record the lock request for the data item. In addition, it immediately grants the lock

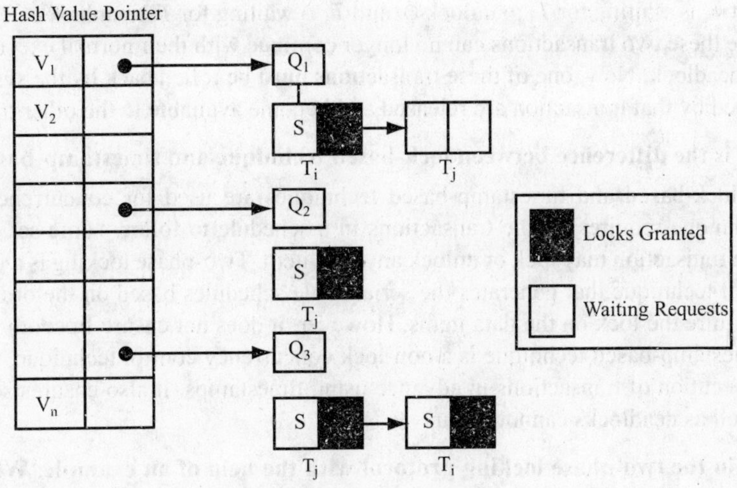

Figure 10.2 Lock Table

request of the transaction. However, if the linked list for the data item already exists, it includes the request at the end of the linked list. The lock request will be granted only if the lock request is compatible with all the existing locks and no other transaction is waiting for acquiring lock on this data item. Otherwise, the transaction has to wait.

- **Unlock request:** When an unlock request for the data items arrives, the lock manager deletes the record corresponding to that transaction from the linked list for the data item. It then checks whether other waiting requests on that data item can be granted. If the request can be granted, it is granted by the lock manager, and the next record, if any, is processed.

If a transaction aborts, the lock manager deletes all waiting lock requests by the transaction. In addition, the lock manager releases all locks acquired by the transaction and updates the records in the lock table.

5. Write a short note on deadlock.

Ans: Deadlock is a situation that occurs when all the transactions in a set of two or more transactions are in a simultaneous wait state and each of them is awaiting for the release of a data item held by one of the other waiting transaction in the set. None of the transactions can proceed until at least one of the waiting transactions releases lock on the data item. For example, consider the partial schedule of transactions T_1 and T_2 shown in Figure 10.3.

T_1	T_2
lock-X(R) -...	
	lock-S(Q)
	...
	lock-S(R)
lock-X(Q)	

Figure 10.3 Partial Schedule

Observe that T_1 is waiting for T_2 to unlock Q, and T_2 is waiting for T_1 to unlock R. Thus, a situation is arrived where these two transactions can no longer continue with their normal execution. This situation is called deadlock. Now, one of these transactions must be rolled back by the system so that the data items locked by that trnsaction are released and become available to the other transaction.

6. What is the difference between lock-based technique and timestamp-based technique?

Ans: Both lock-based and timestamp-based techniques are used for concurrency control. The lock-based technique requires all the transactions in a schedule to follow some set of rules, which indicate when a transaction may lock or unlock any data item. Two-phase locking is a lock-based concurrency control technique that generates the serializable schedules based on the order in which the transactions acquire the lock on the data items. However, it does not ensure freedom from deadlock. In contrast, timestamp-based technique is a non-lock concurrency control technique, which involves ordering the execution of transactions in advance using timestamps. It also ensures serializability of schedules as well as deadlocks cannot occur.

7. Explain the two-phase locking protocol with the help of an example. What are its disadvantages? How can these disadvantages be overcome? What is the benefit of rigorous two-phase locking?

Ans: **Two-phase locking (2PL)** is a lock-based concurrency control technique that requires each transaction to be divided into two phases. During the first phase, the transaction acquires all the locks; during the second phase, it releases all the locks. The phase during which locks are acquired is **growing (or expanding) phase**. In this phase, the number of locks held by a transaction increases from zero to maximum. On the other hand, a phase during which locks are released is **shrinking** (or **contacting**) **phase**. In this phase, the number of locks held by a transaction decreases from maximum to zero. Whenever, a transaction releases a lock on a data item, it enters into the shrinking phase, and from this point, it is not allowed to acquire any lock further. Therefore, until all the required locks on the data items are acquired, the release of the locks must be delayed. The point in the schedule at which the transaction successfully acquires its last lock is called the **lock point** of the transaction.

To understand 2PL technique, consider two transactions T_1 and T_2 along with their lock requests given in Figure 10.4.

T_1	T_2
`lock-X(R)`	`lock-X(sum)`
`read(R)`	`sum := 0`
`R := R - 200`	`lock-S(Q)`
`write(R)`	`read(Q)`
`unlock(R)`	`sum := sum + Q`
`lock-X(Q)`	`unlock(Q)`
`read(Q)`	`lock-S(R)`
`Q := Q + 200`	`read(R)`
`write(Q)`	`sum := sum + R`
`unlock(R)`	`write(sum)`
	`unlock(R)`
	`unlock(sum)`

Figure 10.4 Transactions T_1 and T_2 with their Lock Requests

Figure 10.5 shows the transactions T_1 and T_2 written under two-phase locking.

T_1	T_2
lock-X(R)	lock-X(sum)
read(R)	sum := 0
R := R - 200	lock-S(Q)
write(R)	read(Q)
lock-X(Q)	sum := sum + Q
read(Q)	lock-S(R)
Q := Q + 200	read(R)
write(Q)	sum := sum + R
unlock(R)	write(sum)
unlock(Q)	unlock(Q)
	unlock(R)
	unlock(sum)

Figure 10.5 Transactions T_1 and T_2 in Two-phase Locking

In Figure 10.5, the statements used for releasing the lock are written at the end of the transaction. However, such statements do not always need to appear at the end of the transaction to retain two-phase locking property. For example, the `unlock(R)` statement of T_1 may appear just after the `lock-X (Q)` statement and still maintains the two-phase locking property.

Some disadvantages of the two-phase locking technique are as follows:

- The two-phase locking leads to a lower degree of concurrency among transactions.
- Cascading rollback occurs in two-phase locking.
- There may be a chance of deadlock in 2PL.

To avoid cascading rollback in 2PL, a modification of two-phase locking called **strict two-phase locking** can be used. In the strict two-phase locking, a transaction does not release any of its exclusive-mode locks until it commits or aborts. Strict schedules ensure that no other transaction can read or write the data item exclusively locked by a transaction *T* until it commits. It makes strict schedules recoverable.

Rigorous two-phase locking is another more restrictive version of two-phase locking. The benefit of rigorous two-phase locking is that a transaction does not release any of its locks (both exclusive and shared) until it commits or aborts in it.

8. Define lock conversion. What do you understand by lock upgrade and lock downgrade?

Ans: A transaction can change the mode of locks from one mode to another on a data item on which it already holds a lock. This process of changing the mode of lock is referred to as **lock conversion**. Lock conversion helps in achieving more concurrency.

The changing of lock mode from shared (less restrictive) to exclusive (more restrictive) is known as **lock upgrade**. Similarly, changing the lock mode from exclusive to shared is known as **lock downgrade**. The lock on a data item can be upgraded only in the growing phase. On the other hand, the lock on a data item can be downgraded only in the shrinking phase.

9. Discuss the graph-based locking technique.

Ans: Two-phase locking ensures serializability even when the information about the order in which the data items are accessed is unknown. However, if the order in which the data items are accessed are known in advance, it is possible to develop other techniques to ensure conflict serializability. One such technique is **graph-based locking**.

In this technique, a directed acyclic graph called a **database graph** is formed, which consists of a set S = {A, B, ..., L} of all data items as its nodes, and a set of directed edges. A directed edge from A to B (A → B) in the database graph denotes that any transaction T_i must access A before B when it needs to access both A and B. A simple kind of graph-based locking is **tree-locking** in which all database graphs are tree-structured, and any transaction T_i can acquire only exclusive locks on data items. A tree-structured database graph for the set S is shown in Figure 10.6.

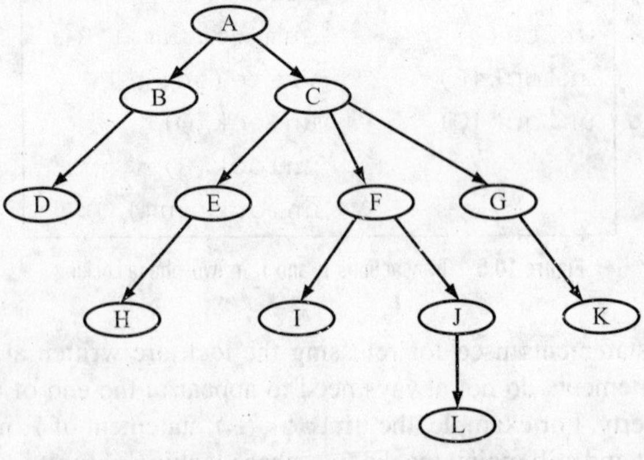

Figure 10.6 Tree-structured Database Graph

A transaction T_i can acquire its first lock on any data item. Suppose T_i requests a lock on data item F, it is granted. After that, T_i can lock a data item only if it has already locked the parent of that data item. For example, if transaction T_i needs to access L, it has to lock J before requesting lock on L. Note that locking the parent of any data item does not automatically lock that data item. Tree locking allows a transaction to unlock a data item at any time. However, once a transaction releases lock on a data item, it cannot relock that data item.

Some advantages of the tree-locking are as follows:

- It ensures conflict serializability as well as freedom from deadlock.
- Unlike two-phase locking, transactions can unlock data items earlier.
- It ensures shorter waiting times and greater amount of concurrency.

The disadvantage of the tree-locking is that in order to access a data item, a transaction has to lock other data items even if it does not need to access them. For example, in order to lock data items A and L in Figure 10.6, a transaction must lock not only A and L, but also data items C, F, and J. Thus, the number of locks and associated locking overhead including possibility of additional waiting time is increased.

10. What is phantom problem for concurrency control and how does index locking resolve this problem?

Ans: Due to the dynamic nature of database, the **phantom problem** may arise. Consider the BOOK relation of *Online Book* database that stores information about books including their price. Now, suppose that the PUBLISHER relation is modified to store information about average price of books that are published by corresponding publishers in the attribute Avg_price. Consider a transaction T_1 that verifies whether the average price of books in PUBLISHER relation for the publisher *P001* is consistent with the information about the individual books recorded in BOOK relation that are published by *P001*. T_1 first locks all the tuples of books that are published by *P001* in BOOK relation and thereafter locks the tuple in PUBLISHER relation referring to *P001*. Meanwhile, another transaction T_2 inserts a new tuple for a book published by *P001* into BOOK relation, and then, before T_1 locks the tuple in PUBLISHER relation referring to *P001*, T_2 locks this tuple and updates it with the new value. In this case, average information of T_1 will be inconsistent even though both transactions follow two-phase locking, since new book tuple is not taken into account. The new book tuple inserted into BOOK relation by T_2 is called a **phantom tuple**. This is because T_1 assumes that the relation it has locked includes all information of books published by *P001*, and this assumption is violated when T_2 inserted the new book tuple into BOOK relation.

Here, the problem is that T_1 did not lock what it logically required to lock. Instead of locking existing tuples of publisher *P001*, it also needed to restrict the insertion of new tuples having P_ID='P001'. This can be done by using the **index locking** technique. In this technique, any transaction that tries to insert a tuple with predicate P_ID = 'P001' must insert a data entry pointing to the new tuple into the index and is blocked until T_i releases the lock. These indexes must be locked in order to eliminate the phantom problem. In order to access a relation, one or more indexes are used. In our example, assume that we have an index on BOOK relation for P_ID. Then, the entry in P_ID will be locked for *P001*. In this way, the creation of phantoms will be prevented since the creation requires the index to be updated and it also requires an exclusive lock to be acquired on that index.

11. Discuss two techniques for concurrency control in tree-structured indexes like B⁺-trees.

Ans: Two techniques for concurrency control in tree-structured indexes like B⁺-trees are as follows:

- **Crabbing:** This technique proceeds in the similar manner as a crab walks, that is, releasing lock on a parent node and acquiring lock on a child node and so on alternately. To understand this technique, consider a transaction T_i that wants to insert a tuple in a relation on which a B⁺-tree index exists. Clearly, T_i also needs to insert a key-value (or corresponding entry) in the appropriate node. For this, the transaction T_i proceeds as follows:
  - T_i first locks the root node of tree in shared mode. Then, it acquires a shared lock on the child node, which is to be traversed next, and releases the lock on the parent node. This process is repeated till we traverse down to the appropriate leaf node.
  - T_i then upgrades its shared lock on leaf node to exclusive lock, and inserts the key-value there, assuming that the leaf node has space for the new entry. Otherwise, the node needs to be split.
  - In case of split, T_i acquires exclusive-mode lock on its parent, performs the splitting operation, and releases its lock on the parent node.
- **B-link tree:** This technique is a variant of the B⁺-tree. In a B-link tree, every node of the tree (not just leaf nodes) maintains a pointer that points to its right sibling. This technique differs from crabbing as it allows the transactions to release locks on nodes even before acquiring locks on the child nodes. Thus, this allows more transactions to operate concurrently.

12. Explain locking granularity, coarse granularity and fine granularity.

Ans: **Locking granularity** is the size of the data item that the lock protects. It is important for the performance of a database system. **Coarse granularity** refers to large data item sizes such as an entire relation or a database, whereas **fine granularity** refers to a small data item sizes such as either a tuple or an attribute.

13. What is multiple-granularity locking? Under what situations is it used?

Ans: Generally, different transactions have dissimilar requests and require different levels of lock granularity on the basis of the operation being performed. For example, an attempt to modify a particular tuple requires only that tuple to be locked while an attempt to modify or delete multiple tuples requires an entire relation to be locked. Thus, it is desirable that the database system provides a range of locking granules called **multiple-granularity locking**. The efficiency of the locking mechanism can be improved by considering the lock granularity to be applied.

Multiple-granularity locking permits each transaction to use levels of locking that are most suitable for its operations. This implies that long transactions use coarse granularity and short transactions use fine granularity. In this way, long transactions can save time by using few locks on a large data item and short transactions do not block the large data item, when its requirement can be satisfied by the small data item.

The size of the data items to be locked influences the level of concurrency. While choosing locking granularity, trade-off between concurrency and overheads should be considered. In other words, the choice is between the loss of concurrency due to coarse granularity and increased overheads of maintaining fine granularity. This choice depends upon the type of the applications being executed and how those applications utilize the database. Since the choice depends upon the type of the applications, it is appropriate for the database system to support or use multiple-granularity locking.

As shown in Figure 10.7, the hierarchy of data items of various sizes can be represented in the form of a tree in which small data items are nested within larger data items. The hierarchy in this figure consists of database DB with three files, namely, F_1, F_2 and F_3. Each file consists of several records as its child nodes. Here, notice the difference between the multiple-granularity tree and tree locking. In the multiple-granularity tree, each non-leaf node represents data associated with its descendents, whereas each node in tree locking is an independent data item.

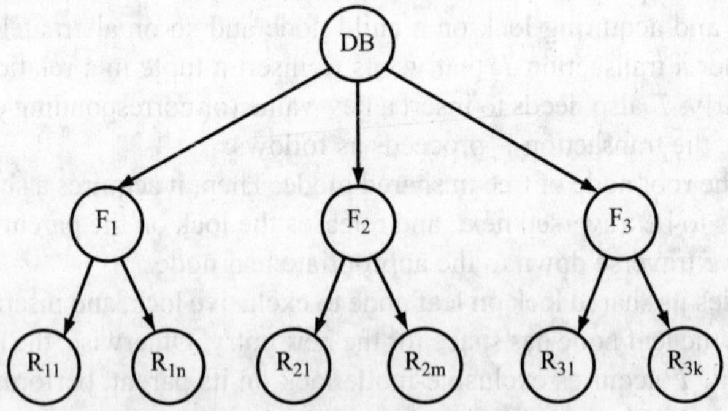

Figure 10.7 Multiple-granularity Tree

Whenever a transaction acquires shared-mode or exclusive-mode lock on a node in multiple-granularity tree, the descendants of that node are implicitly locked in the same mode. Consider the scenario given here to clear this point: Suppose T_i acquires an exclusive lock on file F_1 in Figure 10.7. In that case, it has an exclusive lock on all the records, that is, R_{11}, . . . , R_{1n} of that file. Observe that, in this way, T_i has to acquire only a single lock on F_1 instead of acquiring locks on individual records of F_1. Now, assume that T_j requests a shared lock on R_{11} of F_1. Now, T_j must traverse from the root of the tree to record R_{11} to determine whether this request can be granted. If any node in that path is locked in an incompatible mode, the lock request for R_{11} is denied and T_j must wait.

14. What are intention locks? How does it provide a higher degree of concurrency?

Ans: Intention lock is a type of lock mode used in multiple-granularity locking in which a transaction intends to explicitly lock a lower level of the tree. While traversing from the root node to the desired node, all the nodes along the path are locked in intention mode. In simpler terms, no transaction is allowed to acquire a lock on a node before acquiring an intention-mode lock on all its ancestor nodes. For example, to lock a node R_{11} in Figure 10.7, a transaction needs to lock all the nodes along the path from root node to node R_{11} in an intention mode before acquiring lock on node R_{11}.

To provide a higher degree of concurrency, the intention mode is associated with shared mode and exclusive mode. When intention mode is associated with shared mode, it is called **intention-shared (IS) mode**, and when it is associated with exclusive mode, it is called **intention-exclusive (IX) mode**. To lock a node in shared mode, all its ancestor nodes must be locked in intention-shared (IS) mode. Similarly, to lock a node in exclusive mode, all its ancestor nodes must be locked in intention-exclusive (IS) mode.

It is clear from the discussion that the lower level of the tree has to be explicitly locked in the mode requested by the transaction. However, it is undesirable if a transaction needs to access only a small portion of the tree. Thus, another type of lock mode, called **shared and intention-exclusive (SIX) mode** is introduced. The shared and intention-exclusive mode explicitly locks the subtree rooted by a node in the shared mode, and the lower level of that subtree is explicitly locked in exclusive-mode. This mode provides the higher degree of concurrency than exclusive mode because it allows other transactions to access the part of the subtree that is not locked in the exclusive mode.

15. What are the locking rules for multiple-granularity locking?

Ans: In multiple-granularity locking, each transaction T_i can acquire a lock on node N in any locking mode by following certain rules, which ensure serializability. These rules are given as follows:

- T_i must adhere to the compatibility matrix given in Figure 10.8.
- T_i must acquire any lock on the root of the tree before acquiring any lock on N.
- T_i can acquire S or IS lock on N only if it has successfully acquired either IX or IS lock on the parent of N.
- T_i can acquire X, SIX, or IX lock on N only if it has successfully acquired either IX or SIX lock on the parent of N.
- T_i can acquire additional locks if it has not released any lock. Observe that this is requirement of two-phase locking.
- T_i must release the locks in bottom-up order (that is, leaf-to-root). Therefore, T_i can release its lock on N only if it has released all its locks on the lower level of the subtree rooted by N.

	Current lock on the node				
Requested Mode	**X**	**SIX**	**IX**	**S**	**IS**
X	NO	NO	NO	NO	NO
SIX	NO	NO	NO	NO	YES
IX	NO	NO	YES	NO	YES
S	NO	NO	NO	YES	YES
IS	NO	YES	YES	YES	YES

Figure 10.8 Compatibility Matrix for Different Modes in Multiple-granularity Locking

16. What are the two factors that govern the performance of locking? Discuss how blocking of transactions can degrade the performance.

Ans: The two factors that govern the performance of locking are *resource contention* and *data contention.*

Resource contention refers to the contention over memory space, computing time and other resources. It determines the rate at which a transaction executes between its lock requests. On the other hand, **data contention** refers to the contention over data. It determines the number of currently executing transactions. Assume that the concurrency control is turned off; in that case the transactions suffer from resource contention. For high loads, the system may thrash, that is, the throughput of the system first increases and then decreases. Initially, the throughput increases since only few transactions request the resources. Later, with the increase in the number of transactions, the throughput decreases. If the system has enough resources (memory space, computing power, etc.) that make the contention over resources negligible, the transactions only suffer from data contention.

For high loads, the system may thrash due to **blocking**. Blocking of transactions can degrade the performance as it prevents other transactions to access the data item, which is held by blocked transaction. An instance of blocking is deadlock in which two more transactions are in a simultaneous wait state, and are waiting for some data item, which is locked by one of the other transactions. Hence, the transactions are blocked till the time one of the deadlocked transactions is aborted. Practically, it is seen that there are less than 1% of transactions, which are involved in a deadlock and there are comparatively lesser aborts. Thus, the system thrashes mainly due to blocking.

17. What is timestamp? How does a system generate timestamps?

Ans: Timestamp is a unique identifier assigned to transactions in the order they begin. If transaction T_i begins before transaction T_j, T_i is assigned a lower timestamp. The priority of a transaction will be higher if it is assigned lower timestamp. More precisely, the older transaction has the higher priority since it is assigned a lower timestamp. The timestamp of a transaction T_i is denoted by $\mathtt{TS}(\mathtt{T_i})$. Timestamp can be considered as the *starting time* of the transaction and it is assigned to each transaction T_i in the order in which the transactions are entered in the database system. Suppose a new transaction T_j enters in the system after T_i. In that case, the timestamp of T_i is less than that of T_j, which can be denoted as $\mathtt{TS}(\mathtt{T_i}) < \mathtt{TS}(\mathtt{T_j})$.

The timestamp of each transaction can be generated in two simple ways:

- The value of **system clock** can be used as the timestamp. When a transaction enters the system, it must be assigned a timestamp that is equal to the value (that is, current date/time) of the system clock. It must be ensured that no two transactions are assigned the timestamp values at the same tick of the system clock.
- A **logical counter** can be used which is incremented each time a transaction is assigned a timestamp. When a transaction enters the system, it must be assigned a value that is equal to the value of the counter. The value of the counter may be numbered as 1, 2, 3, … . A counter has finite number of values, so the value of the counter must be reset periodically to zero when no transaction is currently executing for some short period of time.

18. What is timestamp ordering? What are the values associated with timestamps?

Ans: When two concurrently executing transactions, namely, T_i and T_j are assigned the timestamp values $\mathtt{TS}(\mathtt{T_i})$ and $\mathtt{TS}(\mathtt{T_j})$, respectively, such that $\mathtt{TS}(\mathtt{T_i}) < \mathtt{TS}(\mathtt{T_j})$, the system generates a schedule equivalent to a serial schedule in which the older transaction T_i appears before the younger transaction T_j. This is termed as **timestamp ordering (TO)**. Timestamp ordering can be implemented by a number of techniques including basic timestamp ordering, strict timestamp ordering and Thomas' Write Rule.

When the timestamp ordering is enforced, the order in which the data item is accessed by conflicting operations in the schedule does not violate the serializability order. In order to determine this, the following two timestamps values must be associated with each data item `Q`:

- **`read_TS(Q)`:** The **read timestamp** of `Q`; this is the largest timestamp among all the timestamps of transactions that have successfully executed `read(Q)`.
- **`write_TS(Q)`:** The **write timestamp** of `Q`; this is the largest timestamp among all the timestamps of transactions that have successfully executed `write(Q)`.

Whenever new `read(Q)` or `write(Q)` operations are executed, `read_TS(Q)` and `write_TS(Q)` are updated.

19. Discuss basic timestamp ordering. How it is different from strict timestamp ordering protocol?

Ans: The **basic timestamp ordering** ensures that the transaction T_i is executed in the timestamp order whenever T_i requests read or write operation on `Q`. This is done by comparing the timestamp of T_i with `read_TS(Q)` and `write_TS(Q)`. If the timestamp order is violated, the system rolls back the transaction T_i and restarts it with a new timestamp. In this situation, a transaction T_j, which may have used a value of the data item written by T_i, must be rolled back. Similarly, any other transaction T_k, which may have used a value of the data item written by T_j, must also be rolled back, and so on. This situation is known as **cascading rollback**, which is one of the problems with basic timestamp ordering.

Basic timestamp ordering operates as follows:

(1) Transaction T_i requests a read operation on `Q`:

(a) If $TS(T_i) < write\_TS(Q)$, the read operation is rejected and T_i is rolled back. This is because another transaction with higher timestamp (that is, younger transaction) has already written the value of `Q`, which T_i needs to read. The transaction T_i is too late in performing the required read operation and any other values it has acquired are expected to be inconsistent with the modified value of `Q`. Thus, it is better to roll back T_i and restart it with a new timestamp.

(b) If $TS(T_i) \geq write\_TS(Q)$, the read operation is executed, and `read_TS(Q)` is set to the maximum of `read_TS(Q)` and $TS(T_i)$. This is because T_i is younger than the transaction that has written the value of `Q`, which T_i needs to read. If the timestamp of T_i is more than the current value of read timestamp (that is, `read_TS(Q)`), the timestamp of T_i becomes the new value of `read_TS(Q)`.

(2) Transaction T_i requests a write operation on `Q`:

(a) If $TS(T_i) < read\_TS(Q)$, the write operation is rejected and T_i is rolled back. This is because another transaction with higher timestamp (that is, younger transaction) has already read the value of `Q`, which T_i needs to write. Therefore, writing the value of `Q` by T_i violates the timestamp ordering. Thus, it is better to roll back T_i and restart it with a new timestamp.

(b) If $TS(T_i) < write\_TS(Q)$, the write operation is rejected and T_i is rolled back. This is because another transaction with higher timestamp (that is, younger transaction) has already written the value of `Q`, which T_i needs to write. Therefore, the value that T_i is attempting to write becomes obsolete. Thus, it is better to roll back T_i and restart it with a new timestamp.

If TS(T_i) ≥ read_TS(Q) and TS(T_i) ≥ write_TS(Q), the write operation is executed, and the value of TS(T_i) becomes the new value of write_TS(Q). This is because T_i is younger than both the transactions that have last written the value of Q and read the value of Q. Basic timestamp ordering executes the conflict operations in timestamp order; hence, it ensures conflict serializability. In addition, it is deadlock-free since no transaction ever waits.

The **strict timestamp ordering** is a variation of basic timestamp ordering. In addition to the basic timestamp ordering constraints, it follows another constraint when the transaction T_i requests read or write operations on some data item. This constraint ensures a strict schedule, which guarantees recoverability in addition to serializability. Suppose a transaction T_i requests a read or write operation on Q and TS(T_i) > write_TS(Q), T_i is delayed until the transaction, say T_j, that wrote the value of Q has committed or aborted. The strict timestamp ordering is implemented by locking Q that has been written by transaction T_j. Furthermore, the strict timestamp ordering ensures freedom from deadlock, since T_i waits for T_j only if TS(T_i) >TS(T_j).

20. Explain Thomas' Write Rule?

Ans: Thomas' Write Rule is the modification to the basic timestamp ordering, in which the rules for write operations are slightly different from those of basic timestamp ordering. The rules for a transaction T_i that request a write operation on data item Q are as follows:

(1) If TS(T_i) < read_TS(Q), the write operation is rejected and T_i is rolled back. This is because another transaction with higher timestamp (that is, younger transaction) has already read the value of Q, which T_i needs to write. Therefore, the value of Q that T_i is producing was previously needed, and it had been assumed that the value would never be produced.

(2) If TS(T_i) < write_TS(Q), the write operation can be ignored. This is because another transaction with a higher timestamp (that is, younger transaction) has immediately overwritten the value of Q, which T_i wrote. Therefore, no transaction can read the value written by T_i and hence, T_i is trying to write an obsolete value of Q.

(3) If both the conditions given in points (1) and (2) do not occur, the write operation of T_i is executed and write_TS(Q) is set to TS(T_i).

Thomas' Write Rule does not enforce conflict serializability; however, it makes use of view serializability. It is possible to generate serializable schedules using Thomas' Write Rule that are not possible under other techniques like two-phase locking, tree-locking, etc. To illustrate this, consider the schedule shown in Figure 10.9. In this figure, the write operation of T_2 succeeds the read operation and precedes the write operation of T_1. Hence, the schedule is not conflict serializable.

T_1	T_2
read(Q)	
	write(Q)
	commit
write(Q)	
Commit	

Figure 10.9 A Non-conflict Serializable Schedule

Under Thomas' Write Rule, the write(Q) operation of T_1 is ignored. Therefore, the schedule shown in Figure 10.10 is view equivalent to the serial schedule of T_1 followed by T_2.

T_1	T_2
read(Q)	
	write(Q)
	commit
commit	

Figure 10.10 A Schedule Under Thomas' Write Rule

21. How are optimistic concurrency control techniques different from other concurrency control techniques? Why are they named so? Discuss the typical phases of an optimistic technique.

Ans: All the concurrency control techniques including locking and timestamp ordering result either in transaction delay or transaction rollback, thereby named as **pessimistic techniques**. These techniques require performing a check before executing any read or write operation. These checks can be expensive and represent overhead during transaction execution as they slow down the transactions. In addition, these checks are unnecessary overhead when a majority of transactions are read-only transactions. This is because the rate of conflicts among these transactions may be low. Therefore, these transactions can be executed without applying checks and still maintaining the consistency of the system by using an alternative technique, known as **optimistic** (or **validation) technique**. The optimistic technique is named so because the transactions execute optimistically and thereby assumes that few conflicts will occur among the transactions.

In optimistic concurrency control techniques, it is assumed that the transactions do not directly update the data items in the database until they finish their execution. Instead, each transaction maintains local copies of the data items it requires and updates them during execution. All the data items in the database are updated at the end of the transaction execution. In this technique, each transaction T_i proceeds through three phases, namely, *read phase*, *validation phase*, and *write phase*, depending on whether it is a read-only or an update transaction. The three phases of an optimistic technique are as follows:

- **Read phase:** At the start of this phase, transaction T_i is associated with a timestamp `Start(T_i)`. T_i reads the values of data items from the database and these values are then stored in the temporary local copies of the data items kept in the workspace of T_i. All modifications are performed on these temporary local copies of the data items without updating the actual data items of the database.
- **Validation phase:** At the start of this phase, transaction T_i is associated with a timestamp `Validation(T_i)`. The system performs a validation test when T_i decides to commit. This validation test is performed to determine whether the modifications made to the temporary local copies can be copied to the database. In addition, it determines whether there is a possibility of T_i to conflict with any other concurrently executing transaction. In case any conflict exists, T_i is rolled back, its workspace is cleared and T_i is restarted.
- **Write phase:** In this phase, the system copies the modifications made by T_i in its workspace to the database only if it succeeds in the validation phase. At the end of this phase, T_i is associated with a timestamp `Finish(T_i)`.

22. How is a transaction validated in an optimistic concurrency control technique?

Ans: Each transaction in an optimistic concurrency control technique goes through three phases, namely, *read*, *validation* and *write* phase. Accordingly, three different timestamps are assigned to each transaction: `Start(T_i)`, `validation(T_i)` and `Finish(T_i)`.

The validation test for a transaction T_j requires that, for each transaction T_i with `TS(T_i)<TS(T_j)`, one of the following validation conditions must hold:

1. `Finish(T_i)<Start(T_j)`: This condition ensures that the older transaction T_i must complete its all three phases before transaction T_j begins its start phase. Thus, this condition maintains serializability order.
2. `Finish(T_i)<Validation(T_j)`: This condition ensures that T_i completes its write phase before T_j starts its validation phase. It also ensures that the `write_set` of T_i does not overlap with the `read_set` of T_j. In addition, the older transaction T_i must complete its write phase before younger transaction T_j finishes its read phase and starts its validation phase. This is due to the reason that writes of T_j are not overwritten by writes of T_i. Hence, it maintains the serializability order.
3. `Validation(T_i)<Validation(T_j)`: This condition ensures that T_i completes its read phase before T_j completes its read phase. More precisely, this condition ensures that the `write_set` of T_i does not intersect with the `read_set` or `write_set` of T_j. Since T_i completes its read phase before T_j completes its read phase, T_i cannot affect the read or write phase of T_j, which also maintains serializability.

To validate T_j, the first condition is checked for each committed transaction T_i such that TS(T_i)<TS(T_j). Only if the first condition does not hold, the second condition is checked. Further, if the second condition is false, the third condition is checked. If any one of the mentioned validation conditions holds, there is no conflict and T_j is validated successfully. If none of these conditions holds, there is conflict and the validation of T_j fails and it is rolled back and restarted.

23. Discuss the multiversion technique, for what purpose is it used? Discuss multiversion timestamp ordering and multiversion two-phase locking. Compare multiversion two-phase locking with basic two-phase locking.

Ans: **Multiversion technique** is a concurrency control technique, which keeps the old version (or value) of each data item in the system when the data item is updated. In this technique, several versions (or values) of a data item are maintained. When a transaction issues a write operation on the data item `Q`, it creates a new version of `Q`, the old version of `Q` is retained. When a transaction issues a read operation on the data item `Q`, an appropriate version of `Q` is chosen by concurrency control techniques in such a way that the serializability of the currently executing transactions be maintained.

Multiversion timestamp ordering

For each version of a data item, say `Q_i`, the system maintains the value of version and associates the following two timestamps.

- **`read_TS(Q_i)`**: The **read timestamp** of `Q_i`; this is the largest timestamp among all the timestamps of transactions that have successfully read `Q_i`.
- **`write_TS(Q_i)`**: The **write timestamp** of `Q_i`; this is the timestamp of the transaction that has written the value of `Q_i`.

Consider a data item `Q` with the most recent version `Q_i`, that is `write_TS(Q_i)` is the largest among all the versions. Further, assume a transaction T_i with `write_TS(Q_i) <= TS(T_i)`. Now when T_i issues `read(Q)` request, the system returns the value of `Q_i` and updates the value of `read_TS(Q_i)` with `TS(T_i)` if `read_TS(Q_i)<TS(T_i)`. On the other hand, when T_i issues a `write(Q)` request, the following situations may occur:

- `read_TS(Q_i)>TS(T_i)`, which means any younger transaction has already read the value of `Q_i`. In this situation, T_i is rolled back.

- `TS(Ti)=write_TS(Qi)`. In this situation, the contents of Q_i are overwritten.
- If none of the above situation holds, a new version, say Q_j, of Q is created with `read_TS(Qi)=write_TS(Qi)=TS(Ti)`.

The main advantage of the multiversion timestamp ordering technique is that read requests by the transaction are never blocked. Hence, it is important for typical database systems in which read requests are more frequent than write requests. On the other hand, there are two main disadvantages of this technique, which are given here:

- Whenever a transaction reads a data item, `read_TS(Qi)` is updated. It results in accessing the disk twice, that is, one for data item and another for updating `read_TS(Qi)`.
- Whenever two transactions conflict, one of them is rolled back (rather than wait) in order to resolve the conflict, which could result in cascading and hence, can be expensive.

Multiversion two-phase locking

In addition to read and write lock modes, **multiversion two-phase locking** provides another lock mode, that is, **certify**. In order to determine whether these lock modes are compatible with each other or not, consider Figure 10.11.

Requested Mode	Shared	Exclusive	Certify
Shared	YES	YES	NO
Exclusive	YES	NO	NO
Certify	NO	NO	NO

Figure 10.11 Compatibility Matrix for Multiversion Two-phase Locking

The term "YES" indicates that, if a transaction T_i holds the lock on data item Q with the mode specified in column header and another transaction T_j requests to acquire the lock on Q with the mode specified in row header, then the lock can be granted. This is because the requested mode is compatible with the mode of lock held. On the other hand, the term "NO" indicates that the requested mode is not compatible with the mode of lock held, so, the transaction that has requested the lock must wait until the lock is released.

Unlike the locking technique, in multiversion two-phase locking, other transactions are allowed to read a data item while a transaction still holds an exclusive lock on the data item. This is done by maintaining two versions for each data item. One version, known as **certified version**, must be written by any committed transaction and second version, known as **uncertified version**, is created when an active transaction acquires an exclusive lock on a data item. Suppose a transaction, T_j, requests a shared lock on a data item Q, on which another transaction T_i holds an exclusive lock. In this situation, T_j is allowed to read the certified version of Q while T_i is writing the value of uncertified version of Q. However, once T_i is ready to commit, it must acquire a certify lock on Q. Since certify lock is not compatible with other locks (see Figure 10.11), T_i must delay its commit until there is no transaction accessing certified version of the data item in order to obtain the certify lock. Once T_i acquires the certify lock on Q, the value of uncertified version becomes the certified version of Q and the uncertified version is deleted.

The multiversion two-phase locking technique has an advantage over basic two-phase locking that many read operations can execute concurrently with a single write operation on a data item, which is not possible under two-phase locking. This technique, however, has an overhead that the transaction may have to delay its commit until the certify locks are acquired on all the data items it has updated. This technique avoids cascading rollbacks because transactions read certified version instead of uncertified version. Whereas, deadlock may occur if a read lock is allowed to upgrade to a write lock, and they must be handled using the some deadlock handling technique.

24. Explain how to prevent the deadlock.

Ans: Deadlock prevention ensures that deadlock never happens. Generally, this technique is used when the chances of occurring deadlock are high. The approaches to prevent the deadlocks are as follows:

- **Conservative 2PL:** In this approach, each transaction locks in advance all the data items that it needs during its life- time.
- **Assigning an order to all the data items:** In this approach, an ordering is imposed on all the data items in the database. Each transaction acquires locks on the data items in a sequence consistent with that order.
- **Using timestamps along with locking:** In this approach, each transaction is assigned a priority using a unique timestamp, which determines whether a transaction is allowed to wait or is rolled back. A lower timestamp denotes higher priority and vice versa.

The first two approaches can be easily implemented if all the data items that are to be accessed by the transaction are known at the beginning. However, it is not a practical assumption because it is often difficult to predict what data items are needed by a transaction before it begins execution. In addition, both approaches limit concurrency since a transaction locks many data items that remain unused for a long duration. Thus, the third approach is mainly used for deadlock prevention.

25. Discuss "wait-die" and "wound-wait" techniques of deadlock prevention.

Ans: Both wait-die and wound-wait are deadlock prevention techniques using timestamps. To understand, consider a situation in which data item Q is locked by a transaction T_i and another transaction T_j issues an incompatible lock request on Q. In this situation, the wait-die and wound-wait will be described as follows:

- **Wait-die:** If T_i has a lower timestamp (that is, higher priority), T_i is allowed to wait. Otherwise, T_i is rolled back (*dies*).
- **Wound-wait:** If T_i has a lower timestamp (that is, higher priority), T_j is rolled back (T_j is *wounded* by T_i); otherwise, T_i waits.

Both the wait-die and wound-wait techniques have some similarities, which are as follows:

- Starvation is avoided by both the wait-die and wound-wait techniques. In both the techniques, a transaction with the smallest timestamp is not rolled back. In addition, the new transactions are given a higher timestamp than the older transactions. Thus, a transaction that is rolled back repeatedly will eventually become the oldest transaction and has the highest priority. Observe that the oldest transaction has the smallest timestamp. Therefore, it will not be rolled back again and will be granted all the locks that it had requested.
- The request to acquire a lock on a data item held by another transaction does not necessarily involve a deadlock. Therefore, unnecessary rollbacks may occur in both wait-die and wound-wait techniques.

In spite of these similarities, there are certain important differences between the wait-die and wound-wait techniques which are given in Table 10.1.

Table 10.1 Wait-die and Wound-wait Technique

Wait-die Technique	Wound-wait Technique
• In this technique, the waiting that may be required by a transaction with higher priority (that is, older transaction) could be significantly higher.	• In this technique, an older transaction gets the greater probability of acquiring a lock on the data item. It never waits for a younger transaction to release the lock on its data item.
• In this technique, a transaction may be rolled back many times before acquiring the lock on the requested data item. For example, when a younger transaction T_i requests a data item Q held by an older transaction T_j then it is rolled back. When it is restarted, it again requests a lock on Q. Now, if Q is still locked by T_j, T_i will be rolled back again. In this way, T_i may be rolled back several times till it acquires lock on Q.	• Rollbacks in wound-wait technique are less as compared to wait-die technique. For example, when an older transaction T_i requests a data item Q held by a younger transaction T_j then T_j is rolled back. When it is restarted, it requests Q, which is now locked by T_i. In this situation, T_j waits.

26. How is deadlock detected by wait-for graph? What are the measures for recovery from deadlock, explain.

Ans: To detect the deadlock, the system maintains a wait-for graph, which consists of nodes and directed arcs. The nodes of this graph represent the currently executing transactions, and there exists a directed arc from one node to another, if the transaction is waiting for another transaction to release a lock. If there exists a cycle in the wait-for graph, it indicates the deadlock in the system. If there exists a cycle in the wait-for graph, it indicates the deadlock in the system. To understand the creation of a wait-for graph, consider four transactions T_1, T_2, T_3, T_4, whose partial schedule is given in Figure 10.12.

In this schedule, the transaction T_1 waits for transactions T_2 to release the lock on the data item Q_2. Similarly, T_2 waits for T_4, and T_3 waits for T_2. For this situation, the wait-for graph is represented in Figure 10.13.

Observe that there exists no cycle in this graph; thus, there is no deadlock. Now assume that the transaction T_4 requests a lock on the data item Q_4 held by T_3, a directed arc is added in the wait-for graph from T_4 to T_3 (see Figure 10.14). The creation of this directed arc results in a cycle in the wait-for graph, thus, a deadlock occurs in the system in which the transactions T_2, T_3, and T_4 are involved.

T_1	T_2	T_3	T_4
lock-S(Q)			
	lock-X(Q_1)		
	lock-S(Q_2)		
		lock-S(Q_4)	
			lock-X(Q_3)
		lock-X(Q_1)	
	lock-X(Q_3)		
lock-X(Q_2)			

Figure 10.12 A Partial Schedule for T_1, T_2, T_3 and T_4

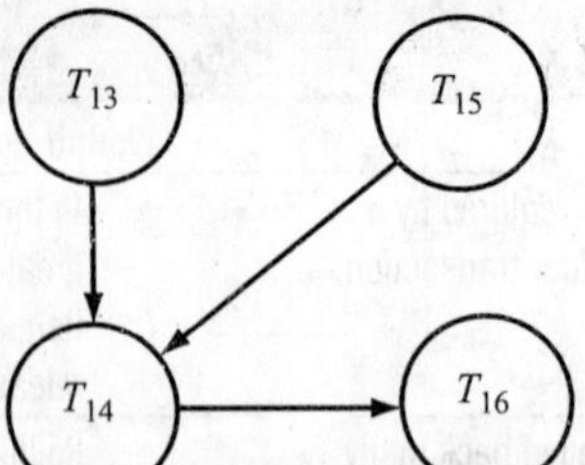

Figure 10.13 Wait-for Graph

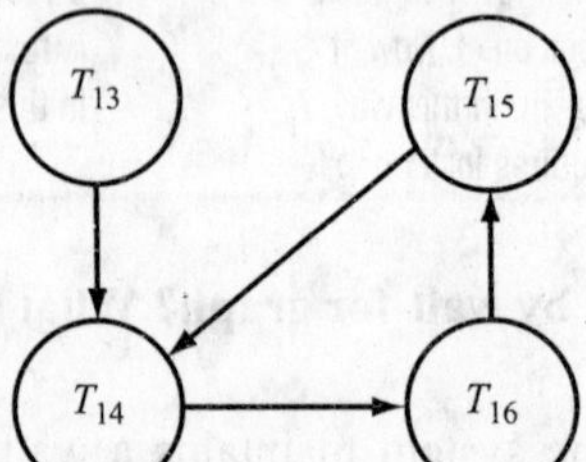

Figure 10.14 Wait-for Graph with Cycle

The wait-for graph is periodically examined by the system to check the existence of deadlock. Once the deadlock is detected, there is a need to recover from the deadlock. The simplest solution is to abort some of the transactions involved in the deadlock, in order to allow other transactions to proceed. The transactions chosen to be aborted are called **victim transactions**. Some criteria should be followed to choose victim transaction, like the transaction with fewest locks, the transaction that has done the minimum work, and so on.

27. Draw a wait-for graph for the following requests and find whether the transactions are deadlocked or not.

T_1	T_2	T_3
S_lock A	–	–
–	X_lock B	–
–	S_lock C	–
–	–	X_lock C
–	S_lock A	–
S_lock B	–	–
S_lock A	–	–
–	–	S_lock A
All the locking requests start from here		

Ans: In the given schedule, transactions T_1 and T_3 are waiting for the transaction T_2 to release lock on the data item B and C respectively. The wait-for graph corresponding to the given schedule of transactions is shown below:

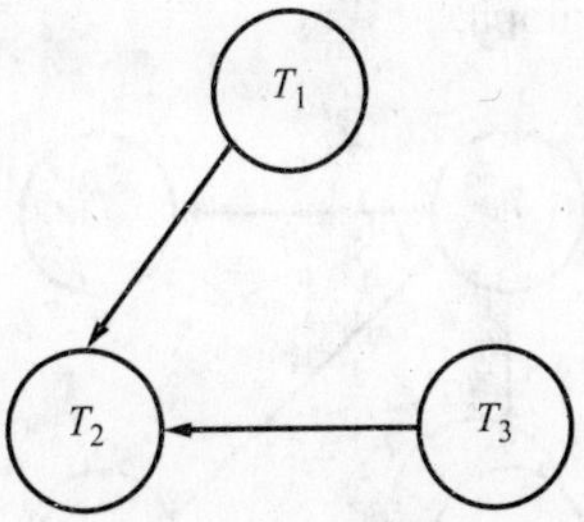

Since there is no cycle in the wait-for graph, the transactions are not deadlocked.

Multiple-choice Questions

1. Strict two-phase locking does not ensure ________.
   (a) Cascadelessness
   (b) Freedom from deadlock
   (c) Serializability
   (d) None of these
2. If a transaction T_i holds a lock on some data item Q in shared and intention-exclusive (SIX) mode, then which of the following is true for another transaction T_j?
   (a) T_j can lock Q in exclusive (X) mode
   (b) T_j can lock Q in intention-exclusive (IX) mode
   (c) T_j can lock Q in intention-shared (IS) mode
   (d) T_j can lock Q in shared (S) mode
3. Strict timestamp-ordering technique ensures________.
   (a) Serializability
   (b) Freedom from deadlock
   (c) Recoverability
   (d) All of these
4. Which of the following is not true in case of tree locking?
   (a) It does not ensure freedom from deadlock
   (b) Unlike two-phase locking, transaction can unlock data items earlier
   (c) It ensures shorter waiting times and greater amount of concurrency
   (d) All of these
5. The number of modes in which a transaction may request a lock in multiple-granularity locking is ________.
   (a) Two (b) Three (c) Five (d) Six
6. Which of the following is true for timestamp ordering?
   (a) Basic timestamp ordering does not ensure conflict serializability
   (b) Strict timestamp ordering ensures freedom from deadlock
   (c) Thomas' Write Rule enforces conflict serializability
   (d) None of these
7. Which phase is not a part of the optimistic technique?
   (a) Execution phase (b) Read phase (c) Write phase (d) Validation phase
8. The techniques used to handle the phantom problem are________.
   (a) Predicate locking (b) Index locking (c) Time stamping (d) Both (a) and (b)

9. Consider the following wait-for graph.

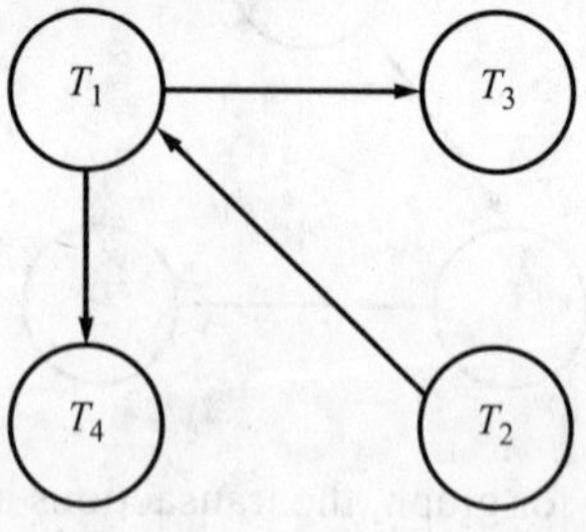

Which of the following statement does not hold true for this wait-for graph?
(a) Transaction T_1 is waiting for the data item locked by transaction T_4
(b) Transaction T_2 is waiting for the data item locked by transaction T_1
(c) If transaction T_2 requests for the data item locked by transaction T_3, deadlock occurs
(d) If transaction T_4 requests for the data item locked by transaction T_2, deadlock occurs

10. Which of the following timestamps is not associated with a transaction T in optimistic technique?
(a) `Start(T)`
(b) `Read(T)`
(c) `Validation(T)`
(d) `Finish(T)`

Answers

1. (b)	2. (c)	3. (d)	4. (a)	5. (c)	6. (d)	7. (a)
8. (d)	9. (c)	10. (b)				

11

Database Recovery System

1. Define recovery manager. What are the properties of transactions that it preserves?

Ans: The component of DBMS that is responsible for performing the recovery operations is called **recovery manager**. The main aim of recovery is to restore the database to the most recent consistent state.

The recovery manager ensures that the two important properties of transactions namely, *atomicity* and *durability* are preserved. It preserves atomicity by undoing actions of uncommitted transactions and durability by ensuring that all the actions of committed transactions survive any type of failure.

2. What information is maintained by recovery manager during normal execution of transactions?

Ans: The recovery manager maintains some information during normal execution of transactions to enable it to perform its task in the event of failure. When a DBMS is restarted after a crash, the control is given to the recovery manager, which is responsible to bring the database to a consistent state. It maintains a system log of all the modifications to the database and stores it on the stable storage, which is guaranteed to survive failures. The stable storage is implemented by storing the database on a number of separate non-volatile storage devices such as disks or tapes (perhaps in different locations). Information residing in stable storage is assumed to be *never* lost.

The amount of work involved during recovery depends on the changes made by the committed transactions that have not been written to the disk at the time of crash. To reduce the time to recover from a crash, the DBMS periodically force-write all the modified buffer pages during normal execution .A process called **checkpointing** also helps in reducing the time taken to recover from a crash.

3. What are the various types of failures that can occur in a system? What is the difference between a system crash and disk crash?

Ans: Various types of failures that can occur in a system are as follows:

- **Logical error:** Transactions may fail due to logical error in the transaction such as incorrect input, integer overflow, division by zero, etc. Certain exception conditions that are not programmed correctly may also result in cancellation of the transaction.
- **System error:** Any undesirable state of the system such as deadlock, incorrect synchronization etc., may also stop the normal execution of the transactions.

- **Computer failure (system crash):** Any type of hardware malfunctioning such as RAM failure, error in application software, bug in operating system, and network problem can also bring the transaction processing to a halt. Such a failure results in the loss of data in volatile storage and does not affect the contents of the non-volatile storage media such as disks.
- **Disk failure:** Disk failure also known as the **media failure**, refers to the loss of data in some disk blocks because of disk read/write head crash, power disruption or error in data transfer operation. These errors also cause the abnormal termination of transaction if occurred during a read/write operation of the transaction.
- **Physical problems and environment disasters:** The physical problems include theft, fire, sabotage, accidental overwriting of secondary storage media, etc. The environment disasters include floods, earthquakes, tsunami, etc.

In case of a system crash, the information residing in the volatile storage such as main memory and cache memory is lost. Therefore, system crash is a non-catastrophic failure as it does not result in the loss of non-volatile storage. On the other hand, disk failure is a catastrophic failure as it results in the loss of non-volatile storage.

4. Define cache directory.

Ans: A directory maintained by the cache manager to keep track of all the data items present in the buffers is called **cache directory**. When an operation needs to be performed on a data item, the cache directory is first searched to determine whether the disk page containing the data item resides in the cache. If it is not present in the cache, the data item is searched on the disk and the appropriate disk page is copied in the cache.

5. Differentiate between in-place updating and shadow paging.

Ans: In **in-place updating** strategy, single copy of the data items are maintained on the disk. The updated buffer is written back to the same original disk location and thus, the old value of any updated data item on the disk is overwritten by the new value. However, in **shadow paging**, multiple copies of the data items can be maintained on the disk. The updated buffer is written at a different location on the disk and thus, the old value of the data item is not overwritten by the new value.

6. What are the differences between steal/no-steal and force/no-force approaches?

Ans: Steal: In this approach, an updated cache page may be written to the disk before the transaction commits. It gives more freedom in selecting buffer pages to be replaced by the cache manager.

No-steal: In this approach, an updated cache page cannot be written to the disk before the transaction commits. The pin bit is set until the updating transaction commits.

Force: In this approach, all the updated cache pages are immediately written to the disk when the transaction commits.

No-force: In this approach, the updated cache pages are not necessarily written to the disk immediately when the transaction commits.

7. Define system log. What types of log records are maintained in it? Explain with the help of an example.

Ans: During the normal transaction processing, the system stores relevant information in a log to make sure that enough information is available to recover from failures. A **system log** is a sequence of log records that contains essential data for each transaction which has updated the database. The various types of log records that are maintained in a log are as follows:

- **Start record:** The log record `[Ti, start]` is used to indicate that the transaction T_i has started.
- **Update log record**: The log record `[Ti, X, Vo, Vn]` is used to indicate that the transaction T_i has performed an update operation on the data item X, having the old value V_o and new value V_n.
- **Read record:** The log record `[Ti, X]` is used to indicate that the transaction T_i has read the data item X from the database.
- **Commit record:** The log record `[Ti, commit]` is used to indicate that the transaction T_i has committed.
- **Abort record:** The log record `[Ti, abort]` is used to indicate that the transaction T_i has aborted, and needs to be rolled back.

To understand how log records are maintained, consider a transaction T_1 that transfers *$100* from account *A* to account *B*. Suppose accounts *A* and *B* have initial values *$2000* and *$1500*, respectively. The transaction T_1 is given here.

```
T1: read(A);
    A:= A - 100;
    write(A);
    read(B);
    B:= B + 100;
    write(B);
```

The log records for the transaction T_1 are shown in Figure 11.1.

```
[T1, start]
[T1, A]
[T1, A, 2000, 1900]
[T1, B]
[T1, B, 1500, 1600]
[T1, commit]
```

Figure 11.1 Log Records for Transaction T_1

8. What are the two types of log-entry information that are maintained during an update operation of a transaction?

Ans: Whenever a transaction needs to update a data item, two types of log-entry information, namely, UNDO-type log entry and REDO-type log entry are maintained. The **UNDO-type log entry** includes the **before-image (BFIM)** of the data item, which is used to undo the effect of an operation on the database. A **REDO-type log entry**, on the other hand, includes the **after-image (AFIM)** of the data item, which is used to redo the effect of an operation on the database, in case the system fails before reflecting the new value of the data item to the database.

9. What is write-ahead logging protocol? Why is it required only for in-place updating strategy?

Ans: Write-ahead logging protocol (WAL) is a protocol that states before making any changes to the database, it is necessary to force-write all log records to the stable storage. In general, write ahead logging protocol states that

- A transaction is not allowed to update a data item in the database on the disk until all its UNDO-type log records have been force-written to the disk.

- The transaction is not allowed to commit until all its REDO-type and UNDO-type log records have been force-written to the disk.

WAL is required only for in-place updating because in shadowing, both BFIM and AFIM of the data item to be modified are kept on the disk; hence, it is not necessary to maintain a log for recovery.

10. Explain log record buffering.

Ans: Each time a log record for a transaction is created, it is immediately written to the stable storage. However, writing each log record individually imposes an extra overhead on the system. To reduce this overhead, multiple log records are first collected in the log buffer in the main memory and then copied to the stable storage in a single write operation. This is called **log record buffering**.

11. Explain checkpoints. How does it help in reducing the amount of time required during recovery? Also discuss the concept of fuzzy checkpointing.

Ans: When the system restarts after a failure, the entire log needs to be scanned to determine the transactions that need to be redone and undone. The main disadvantage of this approach is that scanning of entire log is time consuming. Moreover, the committed transactions that have already written their updates on the database also need to be redone as there is no way to find out the extent to which the changes of committed transactions have been propagated to the database. This causes recovery to take longer time.

To reduce the time for recovery by avoiding redo of the unnecessary work, checkpoints are used. The checkpoint approach is an additional component of the logging scheme. A **checkpoint** is a record periodically written into the log. It is typically written at a point when the system writes out all the modified buffers to the database on the disk. As a result, the transactions that have committed prior to the checkpoint will have their [T_i, commit] record before the [checkpoint] record. The write operations of these transactions need not to be redone in case of a failure as all updates are already recorded in the database on the disk. When a checkpoint is taken, following actions are performed:

1. The execution of the currently running transaction is suspended.
2. All the log records currently residing in the main memory are written to the stable storage.
3. All the modified buffer blocks are force-written to the disk.
4. A [checkpoint] record is written to the log on the stable storage.
5. The execution of suspended transaction is resumed.

Since the transactions committed before the checkpoint time need not be considered during recovery process, it reduces the amount of work required to be done during recovery.

Fuzzy checkpointing: If the number of blocks in the buffer is large, force-writing of all these pages may take long time to finish. The time taken to force-write all modified buffers can result in undesirable delay in the processing of current transactions. For reducing this delay, a technique called **fuzzy checkpointing** is used. In fuzzy checkpointing, a [checkpoint] record (known as **fuzzy checkpoint**) is written in the log before writing the modified buffer blocks to the disk. The system is then allowed to resume the execution of other transactions without having to wait for the completion of step 3. However, a system failure may occur while modified buffer blocks are being written to the disk. In that case, the fuzzy checkpoint would no longer be valid. Thus, the system is required to keep track of the previous checkpoint for which all the actions (1 to 5) have been successfully performed. For this, the system maintains a pointer to that checkpoint and it is updated to point to new checkpoint only when all the modified buffer blocks have been written to the disk.

For example, consider log records of two transactions T_1 and T_2 such as

```
[T1, start]
[T1, P, 20, 25]
[T1, Q, 15, 35]
[T1, commit]
[T2, start]
[T2, R, 50, 70]
[T2, P, 25, 16]
[T2, Q, 35, 18]
[T2, commit]
[checkpoint]
```

If failure occurs after the checkpoint record is written to the log on the stable storage and the system maintains a pointer to checkpoint, the write operations of transaction T_1 and T_2 need not be redone in case of failure as all updates are already recorded in the database on the disk.

12. What are undo and redo operations? Why do these operations need to be idempotent?

Ans: To recover from a failure, basically two operations, namely, *undo* and *redo* are applied with the help of the log on the last consistent state of the database. The undo operation reverses (rolls back) the changes made to the database by an uncommitted transaction and restores the database to the consistent state that existed before the start of transaction. The redo operation reapplies the changes of a committed transaction and restores the database to the consistent state it would be at the end of the transaction. The redo operation is required when the changes of a committed transaction are not or partially reflected to the database on disk. The redo modifies the database on disk to the new values for the committed transaction.

Sometimes the undo and redo operations may also fail due to any reason and this type of failure can occur any number of times before the recovery is completely successful. Therefore, the undo and redo operations for a given transaction are required to be **idempotent**, which implies that executing any of these operations several times must be equivalent to executing it once. That is,

undo(operation)=undo(undo(...undo(operation)...))
redo(operation)=redo(redo(...redo(operation)...))

13. What are log-based recovery techniques? Explain the deferred and immediate- modification versions of the log-based recovery technique with the help of an example.

Ans: The **log-based recovery** techniques maintain transaction logs to keep track of all update operations of the transactions. The log-based recovery techniques are classified into two types, namely, techniques based on deferred update and techniques based on immediate update.

Recovery techniques based on deferred update

The deferred update technique records all update operations of the transactions in the log, but postpones the execution of all the update operations until the transactions enter into the partially committed state. That is, the transaction is not allowed to update the database on disk until the transaction enters into the partially committed state. Once the log records are written to the stable storage under WAL protocol, the database on the disk is updated.

If the transaction fails before reaching its commit point no undo is required as the transaction has not affected the database on the disk. In this case, the information in the log is simply ignored and the failed transaction must be restarted either automatically by the recovery process or manually by the user. However, the redo operation is required in case the system fails after the transaction commits but before all the updates are reflected in the database on the disk. In such a situation, the log is used to redo all the transactions affected by this failure. Thus, this is known as **NO-UNDO/REDO** recovery algorithm. The update log records, in this case, only contain the AFIM of the data item to be modified. The BFIM of the data item is omitted, as no undo operation is required in case of a failure. This technique uses **no-steal/no-force** approach for writing the modified buffers to the database on disk.

For example, consider the transactions T_1 and T_2 given in Figure 11.2(a). The transaction T_1 transfers $*100* from account *A* to account *B* and transaction T_2 deposits *$200* to account *C*. Assume that the initial values of account *A*, *B*, and *C* are *$2000*, *$1500*, and *$500*, respectively. Suppose that these two transactions are executed serially in the order T_1 followed by T_2. The corresponding log records (only for write operations) are shown in Figure 11.2(b).

T₁	**T₂**
`read(A)`	
`A:= A - 100`	
`write(A)`	
`read(B)`	
`B:= B + 100`	
`write(B)`	
	`read(C)`
	`C:= C + 200`
	`write(C)`

(a) Serial Execution of Transactions T_1 and T_2

```
[T1, start]
[T1, A, 1900]
[T1, B, 1600]
[T1, commit]
[T2, start]
[T2, C, 700]
[T2, commit]
```

(b) Log Records for Transactions T_1 and T_2 without BFIMs

Figure 11.2 Transactions and their Log Records

If the system fails before writing the log record `[T1, commit]`, no redo is required as no `commit` record is found in the log. The values of account *A* and *B* remain *$2000* and *$1500*, respectively. If the system fails after writing the log record `[T1, commit]`, but before writing the `commit` record for the transaction T_2, only `redo(T1)` operation is performed. If the system fails after writing the log record `[T2, commit]`, both T_1 and T_2 need to be redone. In general, for each commit record `[Ti, commit]` found in the log, the operation `redo(Ti)` is performed by the system.

Recovery techniques based on immediate update

In the **immediate update** technique, as soon as a data item is modified in cache, the disk copy is immediately updated. That is, the transaction is allowed to update the database in its active state. Like the deferred update technique, the immediate update technique also records the update operations in the log (on the stable storage) first so that the database can be recovered after a failure.

If the system fails before the transaction enters into partially committed state, all the changes made to the database by this transaction must be undone. However, if the immediate update ensures that all the updates made by a transaction are recorded in the database on the disk before the transaction commits, no redo operation is required. Therefore, this recovery algorithm is known as the **UNDO/NO-REDO recovery algorithm**. This technique uses the **steal/force** approach for writing the modified buffers to the database on the disk.

The log records in this case contain only before-image of the data item. The after-image can be omitted, since no redo is required. The undo operation is performed by replacing the current value of a data item in the database by its BFIM stored in the log. For example, consider the transaction T_1 and T_2 given in Figure 11.2(a). The corresponding log records (only for write operations) for these transactions are shown in Figure 11.3.

If the system fails before writing the log record `[T1, commit]`, the operation `undo(T1)` is performed. If the system fails after writing the log record `[T1, commit]` but before writing the `commit` record for the transaction T_2, the operation `undo(T2)` is performed. The operation `redo(T1)` is not required as it is assumed that all updates of transaction T_1 are already reflected to the database on the disk. If the system fails after writing the log record `[T2, commit]`, neither undo nor redo operation is required.

There is a possibility that the immediate update allows a transaction to commit before all its changes are written to the database. In this case, both undo and redo operations may be required. Therefore, this algorithm is known as the **UNDO/REDO recovery algorithm**. This technique uses the **steal/no-force** approach for writing the modified buffers to the database on the disk. The UNDO/REDO algorithm is the most commonly used algorithm. The log records in this case contain both the BFIM and AFIM of the data item to be modified.

For example, consider the transaction T_1 and T_2 given in Figure 11.2(a). The corresponding log records (only for write operations) containing both BFIM and AFIM of the data items to be modified are shown in Figure 11.4.

```
[T1, start]
[T1, A, 2000]
[T1, B, 1500]
[T1, commit]
[T2, start]
[T2, C, 500]
[T2, commit]
```

Figure 11.3 Log Records for Transaction T_1 and T_2 without AFIMs

```
[T1, start]
[T1, A, 2000, 1900]
[T1, B, 1500, 1600]
[T1, commit]
[T2, start]
[T2, C, 500, 700]
[T2, commit]
```

Figure 11.4 Log Records for Transactions T_1 and T_2 with both BFIMs and AFIMs

If the system fails before writing the log record [T$_1$, commit], the operation undo(T$_1$) is performed. If the system fails after writing the log record [T$_1$, commit] but before writing the commit record for the transaction T_2, the operations redo(T$_1$) and undo(T$_2$) are performed. Here, the transaction T_1 should be redone as all updates of T_1 may not be reflected to the database on the disk. If the system fails after writing the log record [T$_2$, commit], the operations redo(T$_1$) and redo(T$_2$) need to be performed.

14. What is shadow paging? How is it different from log-based recovery techniques? What are its disadvantages?

Ans: Shadow paging is a technique in which multiple copies (knows as **shadow copies**) of the data item to be modified are maintained on the disk. Shadow paging considers the database to be made up of fixed-size logical units of storage called **pages**. These pages are mapped into physical blocks of storage with the help of **page table** (or **directory**).The physical blocks are of the same size as that of the logical blocks. A page table with *n* entries is constructed in which the ith entry in the page table points to the ith database page on the disk as shown in Figure 11.5.

The main idea behind this technique is to maintain two page tables, namely, *current page table* and *shadow page table.* The entries in the **current page table** (or **current directory**) points to the most recent database pages on the disk. When a transaction starts, the current page table is copied into a **shadow page table** (or **shadow directory**). The shadow page table is then saved on the disk and the current page table is used by the transaction. The shadow page table is never modified during the execution of the transaction.

Initially, both the tables are identical. Whenever a write operation is to be performed on any database page, a copy of this page is created onto an unused page on the disk. The current page table is then made to point to this copy, and the update is performed on this copy. The shadow page table

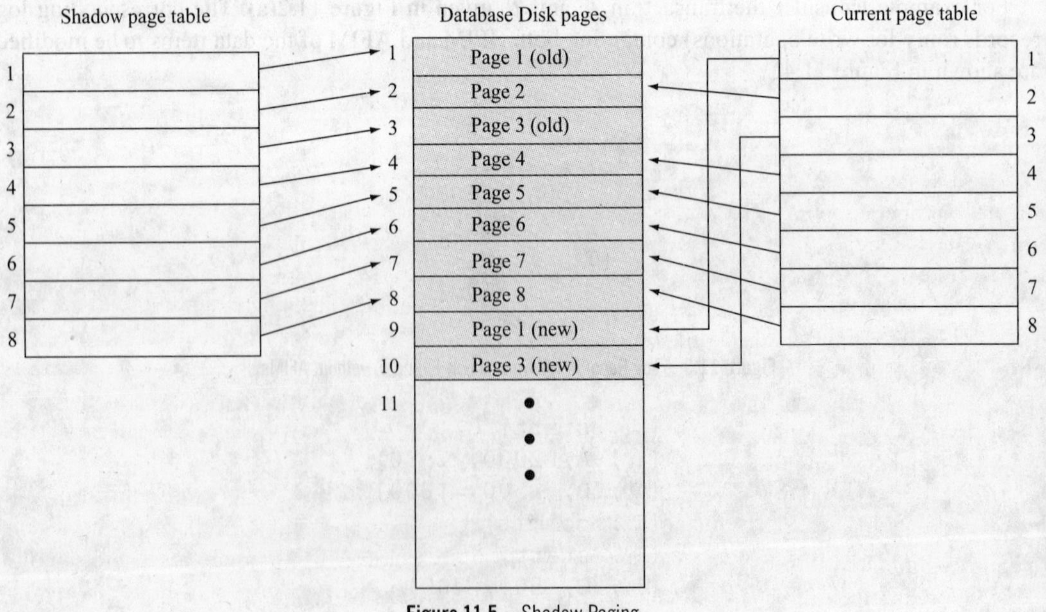

Figure 11.5 Shadow Paging

continues to point to the old unchanged page. The old copy of the page is never overwritten. This implies that for the pages updated by the transactions, two versions are kept. The shadow page table points to the old version and the current page table points to the new version of the page. Figure 11.5 illustrates the concept of shadow and current page table. In this figure, pages 1 and 3 have two versions. The shadow page table references the old versions and current page table references the new versions of pages 1 and 3.

The shadow paging technique is different from the log-based recovery techniques in a way that it does not require the use of log in an environment where only one transaction is active at a time. However, in an environment where multiple transactions are executing concurrently, the log is maintained for the concurrency control method. This technique assumes that only one transaction is active at a time and thus, can be used as an alternative to log-based recovery technique in case the transactions are executed serially. This recovery technique is simple to implement but not as efficient as log-based recovery techniques.

The shadow paging technique has several disadvantages, which are as follows:

- **Data fragmentation:** Shadow paging technique causes the updated database pages to change locations on the disk. This makes it difficult to keep the related database pages together on the disk.
- **Garbage collection:** Whenever a transaction commits, the database pages containing the old version of data are considered as garbage as they do not contain any usable information. Thus, it is necessary to find all of the garbage pages periodically and add them to the list of free pages. This process of finding garbage pages periodically is known as **garbage collection**.
- **Harder to extend:** It is difficult to extend the algorithm to allow transactions to run concurrently.

15. Discuss the recovery techniques in a multi-user environment.

Ans: The log-based recovery algorithms can also be extended to handle multiple transactions running concurrently. Regardless of the number of transactions, the system maintains a single log for all the transactions. Consider a system in which strict two-phase locking protocol is used for concurrency control, and checkpoints are also maintained at regular intervals to minimize the work of a recovery manager. Two lists, namely active list and commit list are maintained by the recovery system. All the active transactions T_A are entered in the **active list** and all the committed transactions T_C since the last checkpoint are entered in the **commit list**.

First, consider the case when **UNDO/REDO** recovery algorithm is used. During recovery process, the write operations of all the transactions in the commit list are redone in the order in which they were written to the log. The write operations of all the transactions in the active list are undone in the reverse of the order in which they were written to the log.

For example, consider five transactions T_1, T_2, T_3, T_4, and T_5 executing concurrently as shown in Figure 11.6. Suppose a checkpoint is made at time t_c and the system crash occurs at time t_f. During the recovery process, transactions T_2 and T_3 (present in commit list) need to be redone, as they are committed after the last checkpoint. Since thc transaction T_1 is committed before the last checkpoint, its operations need not be redone. The transactions T_4 and T_5 (present in the active list) were not committed at the time of system crash and hence, need to be undone.

If the **NO-UNDO/REDO** algorithm is followed, the transactions in the active list are simply ignored, as these transactions have not affected the database on the disk and, hence, need not be undone. Similarly, if the **UNDO/NO-REDO** technique is followed, the transactions in the commit list are ignored as their effects are already reflected in the database on the disk.

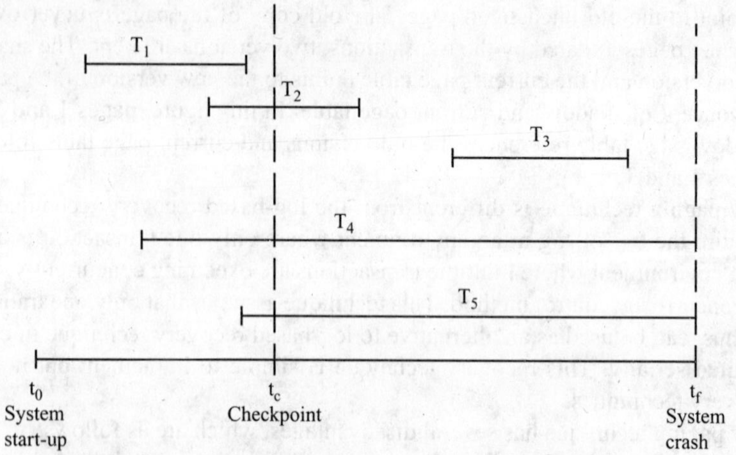

Figure 11.6 Recovery with Concurrent Transactions

16. What is ARIES? What are the principles on which it is based?

Ans: Algorithm for Recovery and Isolation Exploiting Semantics (ARIES) is an example of the recovery algorithm, which is widely used in the database systems. It uses the steal/no force approach for writing the modified buffers back to the database on the disk. This implies that ARIES follows the UNDO/REDO technique. The ARIES recovery algorithm is based on the disk. This implies that ARIES follows the UNDO/REDO technique. The ARIES recovery algorithm is based on three main principles which are as follows:

- **Write-ahead logging:** This principle states that before making any changes to the database, it is necessary to force-write the log records to the stable storage.
- **Repeating history during redo:** When the system restarts after a crash, ARIES retraces all the actions of database system prior to the crash to bring the database to the state which existed at the time of the crash. It then undoes the actions of all the transactions that were not committed at the time of the crash.
- **Logging changes during undo:** A separate log is maintained while undoing a transaction to make sure that the undo operation once completed is not repeated in case the failure occurs during the recovery itself, which causes restart of the recovery process.

17. How does the ARIES recovery algorithm maintain a log file and checkpoints?

Ans: In ARIES, each log record is assigned a unique id called the **log sequence number (LSN)** in monotonically increasing order. This id indicates the address of the log record on the disk. The ARIES algorithm splits a log into a number of sequential log files, each of which is assigned a file number. When a particular log file grows beyond a certain limit, a new log file is created and new records are added to that file. The new file is assigned a number higher by 1 than the previous log file. In this case, the LSN consists of a file number and an offset within the file. Every data page has a **pageLSN** field that is set to the LSN of the log record corresponding to the last update on the page. During the redo operation, the log records with LSN less than or equal to pageLSN of the page should not be executed as their actions are already reflected in the database.

The set of all log records for a particular transaction is stored in the form of a linked list. Every log record includes some common fields such as prevLSN (previous LSN), transaction ID and type of the log record. The **prevLSN** contains the address of the previous log record of the transaction. It is required to traverse the linked list in backward direction. The **transaction ID** field contains the id of the transaction for which the log record is maintained. The **type** field contains the type of the log record. The update log record also contains some additional fields such as **pageID** containing the data item, **length** of the updated item, its **offset** from the beginning of the page, and the **BFIM** and **AFIM** of the data item being modified.

The most recent portion of the log, which is kept in main memory, is called the **log tail**. The log tail is periodically forced-written to the stable storage. A log record is written for each of these actions:

- updating a page (write operation)
- committing a transaction
- aborting a transaction
- undoing an update
- ending a transaction

The log records for update operation and committing and aborting a transaction have already been discussed in previous questions. For undoing an update operation, a **compensation log record** (CLR) is maintained that records the actions taken during the rollback of a particular update operation. It is appended to the log tail as any other log record. The CLR contains an additional field, called the **UndoNextLSN**, which contains the LSN of the log record that needs to be undone next, when the transaction is being rolled back. Unlike update log records, the CLRs describe the actions that have already been undone and hence, will not be undone again because we never need to undo an action that has already been undone. The number of CLRs written during undo is the same as of the number of update log records for transactions that were not committed at the time of the crash.

When a transaction is committed or aborted, some additional actions (like removing its entry from the transaction table, etc.) are taken after writing the commit or abort log record. When these actions are completed, the **end** (or **completion**) **log record** containing the transaction id is appended in the log. Thus, this record notes that a particular transaction has been committed or aborted.

A checkpoint is also maintained by writing a `begin_checkpoint` and `end_checkpoint` record in the log. The LSN of the `begin_checkpoint` record is written to a special file which is accessed during recovery to find the last checkpoint information. When an `end_checkpoint` record is written, the contents of both the transaction table and the dirty page table are appended to the end of the log. To reduce the cost of checkpointing, fuzzy checkpointing is used so that DBMS can continue to execute transactions during checkpointing.

18. What is the purpose of the transaction table and dirty page table in ARIES?

Ans: In addition to the log, two tables, namely, transaction table and dirty page table are also maintained in ARIES for efficient recovery. The **transaction table** contains a record for each active transaction. The record contains the information such as transaction ID, transaction status (active, committed or aborted), and the LSN of the most recent log record (called **lastLSN**) for the transaction. The **dirty page table** contains a record for each dirty page in the buffer. Each record consists of a pageID and recLSN. The **recLSN** is the LSN of the first log record that has updated the page. This LSN gives the earliest log record that might have to be redone for this page when the system restarts after a crash. During normal operation, the transaction table and the dirty page table are maintained by the transaction manager and buffer manager, respectively.

19. Discuss the three phases of the ARIES recovery algorithm.

Ans: When a system restarts after a crash, the ARIES recovers from the crash in three phases:

- **Analysis phase:** This phase starts from the `begin_checkpoint` record and proceeds till the end of the log. When the `end_checkpoint` record in the log is encountered, the transaction table and the dirty page table are accessed, which were written in the log during checkpointing. During analysis, these two tables are reconstructed as follows:

- If an end log record for a transaction T_i is encountered in the transaction table, its entry is deleted from that table.
- If any other type of log record for a transaction T_j is encountered, its entry is inserted into the transaction table (if not present) and the last LSN is modified accordingly.
- If the log record specifying a change in page P is encountered, an entry is made for that page (if not already present) in the dirty page table and associated recLSN field is modified.

At the end of analysis phase, the necessary information for redo and undo phase has been compiled in transaction table and dirty page table.

- **Redo phase:** The redo phase actually reapplies the updates from the log to the database. In ARIES, the redo operation is not applied to only the committed transactions, rather, a starting point from which the redo phase should start is determined first, and from this point the redo phase begins. The smallest LSN, which indicates the log position from where the redo phase needs to be started, is determined from the dirty page table. Before this point, the changes to dirty pages have already been reflected to the database on disk.
- **Undo phase:** This phase rolls back all transactions that were not committed at the time of failure. A backward scan of the log is performed and all the transactions in the undo-list are rolled back. A compensating log record for each undo action is written in the log. After the undo phase, the recovery process is finished and normal processing can be started again.

20. Discuss the technique used to handle disk failures and natural disasters. How is the database recovered from these failures? Explain.

Ans: The main technique used to handle disk failures and natural disasters is **database backup** (also known as **dump**). In this technique, the entire contents of the database and the log are copied periodically onto a cheap storage medium such as magnetic tapes.

When a database backup is taken, the following actions are performed:

1. The execution of the currently running transactions is suspended.
2. All the log records currently residing in the main memory are written to the stable storage.
3. All the modified buffer blocks are force-written to the disk.
4. The contents of the database are copied to the stable storage.
5. A `[dump]` record is written to the log on the stable storage.
6. The execution of suspended transactions is resumed.

In case of disk failure the most recent dump of the database is loaded from the magnetic tapes to the disk. The system log is then used to bring the database to the most recent consistent state by reapplying all the operations since the last backup. In case of natural disasters when the primary site fails, the remote site takes over the processing. However, before that the recovery is performed at the remote site using the most recent backup of the data (may be outdated) and the log records received from the primary site. Once the recovery has been performed, the remote site can start the processing of the transactions. Each time the updates are performed at the primary site; the updates must be propagated to the remote site so that the remote site remains synchronized with the primary site. This can be achieved by sending all the log records from the primary site to the remote site where the backup is taken.

21. Consider the following log records for the transactions T_1, T_2, T_3, T_4 and T_5. Describe the recovery process from a system crash if immediate update technique is followed. Also

assume that the system maintains the checkpoints. Determine the list of transactions that need to be undone and that need to be redone.

```
[T1, start]
[T1, P, 20, 25]
[T1, Q, 15, 35]
[T1, commit]
[T2, start]
[T2, R, 50, 70]
[T2, P, 25, 16]
[T2, Q, 35,18]
[T2, commit]
[checkpoint]
[T3, start]
[T3, R, 70, 45]
[T4, start]
[T4, P, 16, 22]
[T4, Q, 18, 25]
[T5, start]
[T5, Q, 25, 32]
[T5, R, 45, 25]
[T5, commit]
[T3, P, 22, 24]
```

System Crash

Ans: Since the log records shown here contain both the BFIM and AFIM of the data item to be modified, the UNDO/REDO recovery algorithm is followed. According to this algorithm, the transactions T_3 and T_4 need to be undone as these transactions are not committed at the time of system crash; hence, they may have left the database in inconsistent state. On the other hand, the transaction T_5 needs to be redone as it has been committed at the time of system crash, but there is no checkpoint record at this point of time, which implies that this transaction may not have updated the database completely. Finally, the transactions T_1 and T_2 need not be undone or redone as these transactions have been committed and a checkpoint record also exists after the commit records of these transactions.

22. **Consider the following log records containing only AFIMs of the data item being modified. Describe the recovery process from a system crash if deferred update technique is followed.**

```
[T1, start]
[T1, P, 25]
[T1, Q, 35]
[T1, commit]
[T2, start]
[T2, R, 70]
[T2, P, 16]
[T2, Q, 18]
[T2, commit]
```

```
[checkpoint]
[T3, start]
[T3, R, 45]
[T4, start]
[T4, P, 22]
[T4, Q, 25]
[T5, start]
[T5, Q, 32]
[T5, R, 25]
[T5, commit]
[T3, P, 24]
```

System Crash

Ans: Since the log records shown here contain only the AFIM of the data item to be modified, the NO-UNDO/REDO recovery algorithm is followed. According to this algorithm, the transactions T_3 and T_4 need not be undone or redone as there is no commit record for these transactions. However, the transaction T_5 has to be redone as the system fails after its commit record, and no checkpoint exists as this point of time. The transactions T_1 and T_2 need not be redone as a checkpoint record exists after their commitment and before system crash, which implies that the database is already updated.

Multiple-choice Questions

1. Which of the following is a type of environmental disaster?
   (a) Earthquake (b) Integer overflow (c) Logical error (d) None of these
2. Which of these strategies can be used for copying modified data in cache to the disk?
   (a) In-place updating (b) Shadow paging (c) Page caching (d) Both (a) and (b)
3. Which of these terms is not included in DBMS recovery terminology?
   (a) Steal (b) No-force (c) Force (d) None of these
4. Which of these is a type of log record maintained in a log?
   (a) Start record (b) Update log record (c) Abort record (d) All of these
5. In which of the following technique, as soon as a data item is modified in cache, the disk copy is immediately updated?
   (a) Immediate update technique (b) Deferred update technique
   (c) Both (a) and (b) (d) None of these
6. Which of the following is false?
   (a) The undo operation reverses (rolls back) the changes made to the database.
   (b) Undo and redo operations for a given transaction are required to be idempotent.
   (c) The deferred update technique does not record update operations of the transactions in the log.
   (d) None of these.
7. The UNDO/REDO recovery algorithm uses __________ approach for writing the modified buffers to the database on the disk.
   (a) Steal/force (b) No-steal/force (c) No-steal/no-force (d) Steal/no-force
8. Which of these terms is associated with shadow paging?
   (a) Shadow copies (b) Page directory (c) Current directory (d) All of these

9. Which of the following is the disadvantage of shadow paging?
   (a) Data fragmentation (b) Garbage collection (c) Harder to extend (d) All of these
10. The UNDO-type log entry includes the __________ of the data item which is used to undo the effect of an operation on the database.
    (a) BFIM (b) AFIM (c) AFMI (d) BFMI
11. Which of the following techniques maintain transaction logs to keep track of all update operations of the transactions?
    (a) Log-based recovery (b) Shadow paging
    (c) Both (a) and (b) (d) None of these
12. The log record in UNDO/REDO recovery algorithm contains __________.
    (a) AFIM (b) BFIM (c) Both (a) and (b) (d) None of these
13. The ARIES algorithm is based on the principle of __________.
    (a) Write-ahead logging (b) Logging changes during undo
    (c) Repeating history during redo (d) All of these
14. In ARIES, each log record is assigned a unique id called the __________ in monotonically increasing order.
    (a) Transaction ID (b) Page ID
    (c) Log sequence number (d) None of these
15. The most recent portion of the log, which is kept in main memory is called __________.
    (a) Log top (b) Log head (c) Log tail (d) None of these
16. For which of the following actions a log record is written?
    (a) Committing a transaction (b) Aborting a transaction
    (c) Undoing an update (d) All of these
17. Which of the following is not a phase of ARIES algorithm?
    (a) Analysis phase (b) Logging phase (c) Redo phase (d) Undo phase
18. Which of the following phase of ARIES algorithm actually reapplies the updates from the log to the database?
    (a) Analysis phase (b) Redo phase (c) Undo phase (d) None of these
19. Which of these actions is not performed while taking database backup?
    (a) All the modified buffer blocks are force-written to the disk.
    (b) The contents of the database are copied to the stable storage.
    (c) Continue with the execution of currently running transactions.
    (d) A [dump] record is written to the log on the stable storage.
20. The remote site at which the database backup is taken is known as __________.
    (a) Primary site (b) Secondary site (c) Tertiary site (d) None of these

Answers

1. (a)	2. (d)	3. (d)	4. (d)	5. (a)	6. (c)	7. (d)
8. (d)	9. (d)	10. (a)	11. (a)	12. (c)	13. (d)	14. (c)
15. (c)	16. (d)	17. (b)	18. (b)	19. (c)	20. (b)	

12

Database Security

1. What is database security? Why is it important? Also discuss the various security issues.

Ans: Database security refers to protecting the database against unauthorized access or manipulation. The database system manages large bodies of information which needs to be protected from unauthorized persons. Thus, security plays an important role in database systems.

Database security covers the following issues.

- **Privacy:** Only authorized persons should be allowed to access the database. In addition, only the part of the database that is required for the functions they perform should be available to them. In other words, users are allowed to access only the information that is pertinent to their jobs.
- **Database integrity:** Database should be protected from improper modifications, either intentional or accidental, to maintain database integrity. Only the type of operations that need to be performed by the user should be allowed to them. For example, an employee who does not belong to accounts department should not be allowed to modify the balance sheet of the organization. The employees of accounts department only should be allowed to do so.
- **Database availability:** Security should not restrict the authorized users to perform their actions on the part of the database available to them. For example, an accounts department employee should not be restricted to update the balance sheet.

2. What are the various types of threats?

Ans: There are various types of threats that adversely affect the database system. Threats are classified into two categories, namely, *accidental* and *malicious* (or *intentional*) *threats*.

Accidental threats

- Due to any system error, a user can get access to the portion of the database that should not be accessible to him/her.
- Improper authorization can be accidentally assigned to a user by the authorizer, which could lead to security violations.
- Failure of the memory protection hardware could result in diversified response from the database.
- Concurrent usage of the database could lead to database inconsistency, if a proper synchronization mechanism is not implemented.

Malicious or intentional threats

- Hackers can get into the system parts that they are not authorized to access. They could then intentionally update or even delete the secret and precious information from the database.
- Authorized user of an organization could give valuable information to the competitors for personal gain.
- Programmers and/or developers of database development team could easily access database files, although not authorized to do so, and can update the data.

3. Who is responsible for the overall security of the database system? What are his/her responsibilities?

Ans: The database administrator (DBA) is responsible for the overall security of the database system. The two main responsibilities of DBA are managing user accounts and performing database audit.

Managing user accounts

It includes creation and deletion of accounts as well as granting and revoking privileges to/from the accounts. For this, the DBA has a **system** or **superuser account** in the DBMS, which provides powerful capabilities to control access to the database. He/She must restrict the user's access to the data so that the user can perform only the necessary action on the portion of the database to which they are authorized. DBA deals with the following:

- Creation of user account
- Granting and revoking of privileges
- Classification of user accounts

It is the responsibility of DBMS to keep the user accounts and passwords secure and confidential. For this, it maintains an encrypted table with two fields, namely, `Account_Number` and `Password`. At the time of creation of a new account, a new entry is inserted into the table and at the time of deletion of an account, the corresponding entry must be deleted from the table.

Database audit

Whenever a user logs in, the DBMS records his/her account number and the terminal ID from where the user has logged in. Once the user has logged in, it is the responsibility of DBMS to keep track of all the changes (insert/delete/update) applied to the database. For this, a system log that includes an entry for each update operation can be used. The entry in the system log can be further modified to include the user's account number and terminal ID from where the changes have been applied. In case of database tampering, a review of log is carried out to examine all the operations applied to the database during a certain period of time. This review of log is called **database audit.** It helps the DBA to find out which illegal or unauthorized operation has been performed. It also helps in determining the account number and terminal ID from where this illegal operation has been performed. A database log that is mainly used for database security is generally called an **audit trail.**

4. What is authorization? What is the role of access matrix? Discuss with the help of an example.

Ans: Authorization is the granting of privileges to users, which enable them to access certain portion of the database. Since database users perform different roles, they are permitted to access only the part of database that is pertinent to their job. In addition, each user is allowed to perform only the necessary operation on the database that is required to perform their function. Such type of permission is given to database users by granting different privileges to them. The person who is responsible for granting privileges to database users is called **authorizer**.

The system maintains the authorization information in a table called **access matrix**, which the database system consults each time an access request is issued in the system. The columns of access matrix represent **objects** and rows represent **subjects**. Object is any part of the database that needs to be protected from unauthorized access. Subject is an active user or account who operates on various objects in the database. For example, a file or a relation and its attribute can be considered as an object. An application program can also be considered as a subject. Each subject is given some access rights on some or all objects. The type of access that a subject has with respect to an object is represented by an entry in the access matrix at the intersection of the corresponding row and column as shown in Figure 12.1

SUBJECTS	OBJECTS		
	OBJECT 1	OBJECT 2	OBJECT 3
USER 1	Select Update	Select Insert	Select
USER 2	Insert Delete	Select Modify	Select Insert
USER 3	Select Drop Alter	Select Delete	Select Update Propagate
USER 4	Select Insert	Select Delete	Select Reference

Figure 12.1 Access Matrix

5. Discuss various access privileges that a user can have on a relation.

Ans: The various access privileges that a user can have on a relation are:

- **SELECT:** A user having select privilege on relation R is allowed to select or retrieve tuples from R.
- **MODIFY:** A user having modify privilege on relation R is allowed to modify the tuples of R. This privilege is further divided into three types, namely, INSERT, UPDATE and DELETE. User having any of the privilege is allowed to apply the corresponding command to R.
- **REFERENCES:** The references privilege on R allows the user to reference the attributes of R while specifying integrity constraints. This privilege can also be restricted to some specific attributes of R.
- **DROP:** A drop privilege allows the user to delete existing relation of the database.
- **ALTER:** A user having alter privilege on relation R is allowed to add new attributes to the relation R. The user is also allowed to drop or delete the existing attributes of R.
- **PROPAGATE ACCESS CONTROL:** A user having propagate right on relation R is allowed to pass all or part of his or her privileges on R to other users.

6. Describe authorization tree.

Ans: Propagate access control privilege allows the users to pass either entire or part of their rights to other users, who may also be allowed to pass their rights as well. Such a series of authorization from one user to another user leads to a tree termed as **authorization tree.** Database users become the nodes in the tree with authorizer as the root node. Edge from one node to another node exists if rights are passed from one user to another user represented by these two nodes. For example, consider an authorization tree shown in Figure 12.2.

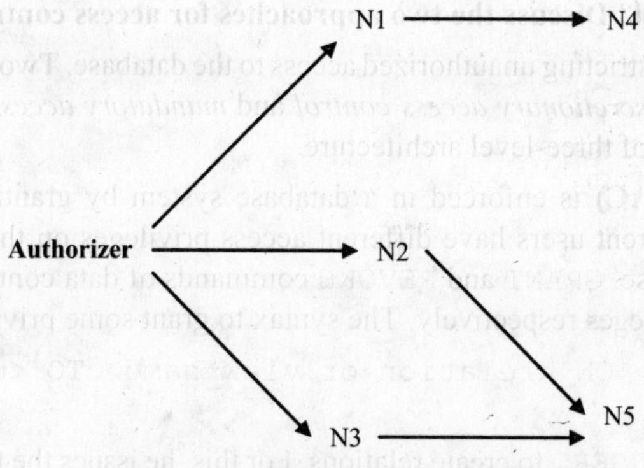

Figure 12.2 Authorization Tree

Here, authorizer assigns some access rights to the users represented by the nodes N1, N2 and N3. N1 assigns access rights to N4, which in turn assigns access rights to N6. Further, N2 and N3 together assign access rights to N5. A user has some access rights, if there is any path from the root node (that is, authorizer) to the node representing that user. In case all the access rights need to be removed from a user, all the incoming edges to that user in authorization tree should be removed. In addition, all the privileges propagated by this user to the other users should automatically be removed by the system.

For example, suppose that the authorizer revokes the access rights from N3. In this situation, N5 loses its access rights that are granted by N3; however it retains all those rights that are granted by N2. Further, if the authorizer revokes the access rights from N2 also, then N5 loses all of its access rights. However, if authorizer revokes access rights from N1 then both N4 and N6 lose their authorization, since both N4 and N6 has their access rights from N1.

7. What is authentication? What are the various techniques that can be used to authenticate a user?

Ans: The process of verifying the identity of a user is termed as **authentication**. Some of the various techniques that can be used to authenticate a user are a secret password, some physical characteristics of the user, a smart card, or a key given to the user.

- **Password authentication:** In this scheme, the user is asked to enter the user name and password to log in into the database. The DBMS then verifies the combination of user name and password to authenticate the user, and allows him/her access to the database if he/she is the legitimate user, otherwise access is denied.
- **Physical characteristics of user:** In this method, the physical characteristics of the users such as fingerprints, voiceprint, length of fingers of hand, face structure and so on are used for the identification purpose. These characteristics of users are known to be unique, and have a very low probability of duplication.
- **Smart card:** In this method, a database user is provided with a smart card that is used for identification. The smart card has a key stored on an embedded chip, and the operating system of smart card ensures that the key can never be read. Instead, it allows data to be sent to the card for encryption or decryption using a private key. The smart card is programmed in such a way that it is extremely difficult to extract values from smart card, thus, it is considered as a secure device.

8. What is an access control? Discuss the two approaches for access control in DBMS.

Ans: Access control refers to restricting unauthorized access to the database. Two main approaches in DBMS for access control are *discretionary access control* and *mandatory access control*. Access control works at the external level of three-level architecture.

Discretionary access control (DAC) is enforced in a database system by granting and revoking privileges to/from the users. Different users have different access privileges on the object (either a base table or a view) of the database. GRANT and REVOKE commands of data control language corresponds to grant and revoke privileges respectively. The syntax to grant some privileges to a user is

```
GRANT <privilege_list> ON <relation or view_name> TO <user_list>
[WITH GRANT OPTION];
```

Suppose DBA decides to allow USER1 to create relations. For this, he issues the following GRANT statement.

```
GRANT createtab TO USER1;
```

Now, suppose USER1 creates a relation R1 and decides to give some privileges to two other users USER2 and USER3. For this, he issues the following statements.

```
GRANT SELECT, INSERT, UPDATE ON R1 TO USER2;
GRANT SELECT, DELETE, UPDATE ON R1 TO USER3 WITH GRANT OPTION;
```

The first statement allows USER2 to retrieve, insert and update tuples in relation R1. However, USER2 is not allowed to propagate SELECT, INSERT and UPDATE privileges on R1 to other users. On the other hand, the second statement allows USER3 to retrieve, delete and update tuples in R1. Moreover, the WITH GRANT OPTION in this statement enables USER3 to further propagate its privileges on R1 to other users.

It is also possible to restrict a user to access only few attributes or tuples of a relation. Following statement allows USER4 to UPDATE only A1 and A2 attribute of relation R1.

```
GRANT UPDATE (A1, A2) ON R1 TO USER4;
```

Note that only INSERT or UPDATE privilege can be given on a set of attributes of a relation. SELECT and DELETE privilege on a set of attributes can easily be specified by creating views containing that set from the base relation and granting privilege on that view. In order to create a view, the user must have SELECT privilege on all the base relations involved in creating the view. In case, the owner of a view loses SELECT privilege on the underlying base relations then the view may be dropped.

To cancel or revoke the previously assigned privileges from a user, the REVOKE command is used. The syntax to revoke some privilege from the user is

```
REVOKE <privilege_list> ON <relation or view_name> FROM <user list>;
```

For example, the following statement revokes the privileges of USER2 on relation R1:

```
REVOKE SELECT, INSERT, UPDATE ON R1 FROM USER2;
```

Mandatory access control (MAC) enforces multilevel security by classifying **subjects** (for example, database users, programs, etc.) and **objects** (for example, relations, views, etc.) of database system in different security classes. The **Bell-LaPadula** model is commonly used to implement multilevel security. In this model, each object is assigned a **security class** (for example, top secret, secret, confidential and unclassified) and each subject has some **clearance** (generally the same as security classes). The class assigned to a subject or an object, say Z, is denoted as class(Z).

The security classes are assumed to form a hierarchy as top secret (TS) > secret (S) > confidential (C) > unclassified (U). It means the class TS is the highest level and U is the lowest level. In other words, the data of class TS are much more sensitive than class S data and so on. This model imposes two rules on subjects to access objects.

- Subject `S` is allowed to read object `O` if and only if the clearance level of `S` is greater than or equal to the classification level of `O`, that is `class(S) >= class(O)`. This property is known as **simple security property**.
- Subject `S` is allowed to write object `O` if and only if the clearance level of `S` is less than or equal to the classification level of `O`, that is `class(S) <= class(O)`. This property is known as **star property** (*-property).

These two rules, in combination with discretionary access control, enforce additional security for database. Thus, in order to retrieve or write an object, the subject should have necessary access privileges on the object and in addition, the security classes of subject and object must satisfy the above stated rules. The first rule or simple security property is very obvious, which states that a subject can read an object whose security classification is lower than or equal to the security clearance of subject itself. For example, a subject with clearance level TS can read object of all classes (including TS) but the subject should have required access privileges (through `GRANT` command) on that object. The second rule or star property restricts a subject from writing an object whose security classification is lower than the security clearance of the subject. For example, a subject with clearance S can write objects of class TS and class S, since object with TS or S classification is at higher or equal classification than that of subject clearance. However, subject with clearance S cannot write objects of class C and class U.

9. What are multilevel relations? Explain these terms in context of multilevel relations: *apparent key, filtering, covert channel and polyinstantiation.*

Ans: To implement mandatory access control in relational DBMS, attribute values and tuples are considered as objects and therefore, assigned a security class. Each attribute in a relation is associated with a **classification attribute**, say `Y`, and each attribute value is associated with a corresponding security classification. In addition, a **tuple classification** attribute, say `TY`, is added to the relation to classify each tuple as a whole. This situation leads to a **multilevel relation**. A multilevel relation schema `R` with *m* attributes would be represented as

$R(A_1, Y_1, A_2, Y_2, \ldots\ldots, A_m, Y_m, TY)$

where Y_i represents the classification attribute associated with attribute A_i, and `TY` is tuple classification attribute. The value of tuple classification attribute for each tuple is the highest level of all classification attribute value associated with the attributes within that tuple.

The set of attributes that would have served as the primary key in the regular relation is termed as an **apparent key** in a multilevel relation. For example, consider the modified `PUBLISHER` relation from *Online Book* database shown in Figure 12.3 (for simplicity, only selected attributes and tuples are shown). The apparent key of the `PUBLISHER` relation is `P_ID`, and the classification attribute value of each attribute is written next to the attribute value.

P_ID	Pname	State	TY
P001 U	Hills Publication U	Georgia C	C
P002 C	Sunshine Publishers Ltd S	New Jersey C	S
P003 S	Bright Publications S	Hawaii S	S

Figure 12.3 Instance of `Publisher` Relation

A multilevel relation has a surprising property that the users of different security classes view a different collection of rows within the same relation. For example, in response to the query SELECT * FROM PUBLISHER, the users with clearance S and TS get all the rows, since all the tuple classifications are less than or equal to S and TS. However, the users with clearance C are not allowed to see the third row. Moreover, they are not allowed to see the value of attribute Pname in the second row, since it has a higher classification in the second row. The value for the attribute Pname in the second row would appear to be NULL [see Figure 12.4(a)]. Similarly, the users with clearance U get only the first row, and in that the value of attribute State appears to be NULL [see Figure 12.4(b)]. This process, where a single tuple is stored at a higher classification level, however, can be produced at lower-level classification levels, is known as **filtering**.

Further, assume that a user with clearance U is trying to insert a new row <P002, Wesley Publications, Nevada, U>. In such situations, a problem arises in choosing between the following two alternatives:

- If the user is allowed to insert that row, the relation will contain two distinct tuples with P_ID = "*P002*", which violates the primary key constraint.
- On the other hand, if the user is denied to insert the new row because of violation of primary key constraint, the user with clearance U deduce that there exist a publisher with P_ID = "*P002*" whose classification is higher than U. Doing so violates the principle that users should not be able to deduce any information about objects of the higher classification level. This flow of information from a higher classification level to a lower classification level, through indirect means, is called **covert channel**.

This problem can be solved by treating the combination of P_ID and TY as primary key for the relation, instead of just P_ID, and allowing the user to insert the new tuple. The relation instance after insertion is shown in Figure 12.5.

P_ID	Pname	State	TY
P001 U	Hills Publication U	Georgia C	C
P002 C	NULL C	New Jersey C	C

(a)

P_ID	Pname	State	TY
P001 U	Hills Publication U	NULL U	U

(b)

Figure 12.4 (a) Appearance for Clearance Level C and (b) Appearance for Clearance Level U

P_ID	Pname	State	TY
P001 U	Hills Publication U	Georgia C	C
P002 U	Wesley Publication U	Nevada U	U
P002 C	Sunshine Publishers Ltd. S	New Jersey C	S
P003 S	Bright Publications S	Hawaii S	S

Figure 12.5 Relation Publisher After Insertion

It is clear from Figure 12.5 that the PUBLISHER relation has two different tuples for the same value of P_ID = "*P002*" for the users of different clearance level. This concept, where several tuples can have the same apparent key value but have different attribute values at different classification levels, is called **polyinstantiation**.

10. Discuss the advantages and disadvantages of DAC and MAC.

Ans: Discretionary access control (DAC) policies are generally very effective and flexible. Due to their high degree of flexibility, they are well suited for large variety of applications. However, DAC suffers with certain weaknesses. Their vulnerability to malicious attacks, such as Trojan horse, is the major limitation of DAC. Using Trojan horse scheme, an unauthorized user can change application program of DBMS to infer sensitive data from authorized user. This is because the discretionary models do not impose any control on flow of information, once it has been accessed by authorized users.

In contrast, mandatory access control (MAC) policies overcome such problems of DAC. MAC controls any illegal flow of information using the two rules discussed in Question 9. Thus, MAC ensures a high degree of protection, which makes them suitable for highly secure applications, such as military applications. However due to their rigid nature, mandatory policies are applicable to a very few applications.

11. What is Role-based Access Control (RBAC)? Which SQL commands are used for creating and destroying roles? What are role hierarchies in RBAC? Why is RBAC considered superior to DAC and MAC?

Ans: Role-based access control (RBAC) is an alternative approach to traditional DAC and MAC. This approach restricts the system access to authorized users only. It appears to be promising approach for controlling what information computer users can utilize, the programs that they can run and the modifications that they can make. In this approach, permissions to perform certain operations are associated with arbitrary roles and these roles are assigned to database users based on their responsibilities in the organization. Only the operations that need to be performed by the members of a role are granted to the role.

Roles can be created and destroyed using CREATE ROLE and DESTROY ROLE commands, respectively. The GRANT and REVOKE commands can then be used to assign and revoke privileges from roles. Since, users are not assigned to the permissions directly; they acquire a set of permissions through their assigned roles. It reduces the amount of administrative effort required to add or delete accounts of database users. In addition, roles can be updated without updating the privileges for every user on an individual basis.

Under RBAC, roles can have overlapping responsibilities and permissions, that is, users belonging to different roles may need to perform common operations. In this situation, it would be inefficient and administrative cumbersome to repeatedly specify those operations for each role. Alternatively, **role hierarchies** can be established to provide the natural structure of an organization. In the role hierarchy, a role may contain other roles that means, one role implicitly includes the operations that are associated with another role. Usually, roles in the hierarchy include the operations that are associated to the lower level roles.

RBAC is considered superior to DAC and MAC because in addition to traditional DAC and MAC policies, it also supports user-defined or organization-specific policies. Moreover, RBAC models have several other desirable features such as flexibility, better management and administrative support make them suitable for implementing security plan for Web-based applications. In contract, DAC and MAC models lack capabilities to support the security requirements of Web-based applications.

12. What do you understand by encryption and decryption of data? Discuss the features of a good encryption algorithm. What are the two types of encryption? Explain them briefly.

Ans: Encryption is a means of maintaining security of data in an insecure environment, such as while transmitting data over an insecure communication link. It involves applying an **encryption algorithm** to the data or **plain text** using a pre-defined **encryption key**. The algorithm produces encrypted version of the plain text as the output. For example, assume that the encryption algorithm substitutes each character of plain text with the next third character in the alphabetical sequence. In this algorithm, three is the key for circularly shifted alphabets. Thus, we have the following substitution format.

Plain text: a b c d e f g h i j k l m n o p q r s t u v w x y z
Cipher text: d e f g h i j k l m n o p q r s t u v w x y z a b c

By this substitution, the text *principle* becomes *sulqflsoh*. It is difficult for an unauthorized user or intruder to understand the meaning of *sulqflsoh*. This encrypted data need to be decrypted using a **decryption algorithm** to recover the original data. The decryption algorithm requires **decryption key** to decrypt the encrypted data.

Features of a good encryption algorithm are as follows:

- Security should not only depend on the secrecy of the algorithm, rather it should also depend on the encryption key.
- It should be simple for the authorized user to encrypt and decrypt the data.
- It should be extremely difficult for an unauthorized user to guess the encryption key.

Most encryption algorithms belong to one of the two categories, *symmetric key encryption* or *public key encryption*.

- **Symmetric key encryption:** The type of encryption in which the same key is used for both encryption and decryption of data is called **symmetric key encryption**. Data Encryption Standard (DES) is an example of symmetric key encryption. The DES algorithm is parameterized by a 56-bit encryption key. The DES algorithm has a total of 19 distinct stages and encrypts the plain text in blocks of 64 bits, producing 64 bits of cipher text. The first stage is independent of the key and performs transposition on the 64-bit plain text. The last stage is the exact inverse of first stage transposition. The preceding stage of the last one exchanges the first 32 bits with the next 32 bits. The remaining 16 stages perform encryption by using parameterized encryption key. Since the algorithm is symmetric key encryption, it allows decryption to be done with the same key as encryption. All the steps of algorithm are executed in the reverse order to recover the original data.

  With the increasing speed of computer, it is estimated that a special-purpose chip can crack DES in under a day by searching 2^{56} possible keys. Thus, after questioning the adequacy of DES, the National Institute of Standards and Technology (NIST) adopted the **Rijndael Algorithm** (by V. Rijmen and J. Daemen) in 2000 as a new symmetric encryption standard called the **Advanced Encryption Standard (AES)**. It supports key lengths of 128, 192 and 256 bits and specifies the block size of 128 bits. Since the key length is 128 bits, there are 2^{128} possible keys. It is estimated that a fast computer that can crack DES in 1 second could take trillions of years to crack the 128-bit AES key. The main problem with a symmetric algorithm is that the key must be shared among all the authorized users. This increases the chance of the key becoming known to an intruder. The main problem with the symmetric algorithm is that the key must be shared among all the authorized users. This increases the chance of the key becoming known to an intruder.

- **Public key encryption:** It is based on mathematical functions rather than operations on bit patterns. It uses two different keys for encryption and decryption. The key used for encryption is referred to as **public key** and the key used for decryption is termed as **private key**. Each authorized user has a pair of public key and private key. The public key of each user is known to everyone, whereas the private key is known to its owner only, thus, avoiding the weakness of DES. For example, suppose user `A` wants to transfer some information to user `B` securely. The user `A` encrypts the data by using the public key of `B` and sends the encrypted message to `B`. On receiving the encrypted message, `B` decrypts it by using his or her private key. Since the decryption process requires private key of user `B`, which is only known to `B`, the information is transferred securely.

13. Explain the RSA Algorithm.

Ans: In 1978, a group at M. I. T discovered a strong method for public key encryption. It is known as **RSA**, the name derived from the initials of the three discoverers Ron **R**ivest, Adi **S**hamir, and Len **A**dleman. The algorithm requires keys of at least 1024 bits for good security. The algorithm consists of the following steps to determine the encryption key and decryption key:

1. Take two large distinct prime numbers, say m and n (about 1024 bits).
2. Calculate $p = m * n$ and $q = (m - 1)*(n - 1)$.
3. Find a number that is relatively prime to q, say D (that is, $gcd\ (q, D) = 1$). That number is the decryption key.
4. Find encryption key E such that $E * D = 1\ mod\ q$ or $E = D^{-1}\ mod\ q$.

Using these calculated keys, a block `B` of plain text is encrypted as $T_e = B^E \bmod p$. To recover the original data, compute $B = (T_e)^D \bmod p$. E and p are needed to perform encryption, whereas, D and p are needed to perform decryption. Thus, the public key consists of (E, p), and the private key consists of (D, p). An important property of RSA algorithm is that the roles of E and D can be interchanged.

14. Write a short note on digital signatures.

Ans: Digital signature is a very useful application of public key encryption technique. Similar to a physical handwritten signature, **digital signatures** are used to verify the authenticity of electronic document. The private key of the user is used to digitally sign an electronic document, and the signed document can be made public. Any user can easily verify the authenticity of the document by using the public key that means it can be easily verified that the data is originated by the person who claims for it. However, no one can sign the document without having the private key.

Digital signatures also ensure **non-repudiation** that means no party or person can later deny that they never created such a document, which is digitally signed by them.

15. What is statistical database? Explain with example. Also discuss the various security problems raised in these databases. How can we prevent them?

Ans: A statistical database contains confidential information about individuals or events. These databases are mainly used to generate statistical information about the stored information. Such databases accept only **statistical queries**, which involve statistical functions such as `SUM`, `AVG`, `COUNT`, `MIN`, `MAX` and so on. However, users are not allowed to retrieve information about a particular individual.

Consider a relation `BankEmp` with the attributes `ECode`, `EName`, `Sex`, `State`, `Salary`, `Branch` and `Designation`. Using statistical queries, one can retrieve the number of clerks, maximum salary, average salary of clerks and so on. However, users are not allowed to retrieve the salary of a particular employee.

Implementing security in such a database raises new problems because it is possible to infer the information about specific individuals from a sequence of statistical queries. For example, suppose that the user is interested in retrieving the salary of *John Macmillan* living in *New York*, who is a clerk in *Los Angeles* branch. User issues a statistical query to count the number of clerks in *Los Angeles* branch who are living in *New York*. The query can be defined as

```
SELECT COUNT (*) FROM BankEmp WHERE (State = 'New York' AND Sex
= 'M' AND Designation = 'Clerk' AND Branch = 'Los Angeles');
```

If the result of this query is 1, the next statistical query can be issued with the same condition to find the `Salary` of John Macmillan. The query can be defined as

```
SELECT SUM (Salary) FROM BankEmp WHERE (State = 'New York' AND
Sex = 'M' AND Designation = 'Clerk' AND Branch = 'Los Angeles');
```

Even if the result of the first query is not 1 but a small value, say 4 or 5, the approximate salary of John Macmillan could be inferred by applying `MAX`, `MIN`, and `AVG` functions in statistical queries.

One possible approach to prevent the chances of inferring information about individual is to reject certain statistical queries. For example, if the number of tuples specified by selection condition falls below a particular number, say `N`, the statistical query can be rejected. Alternatively, by rejecting the sequence of statistical queries from the same user that refers to the same set of tuples, it is possible to prevent retrieval of individual information. Another approach is database partitioning, in which records are classified and stored in small size groups. In this case, any statistical query can refer to complete group or set of groups, but the query referring to subset of any group is rejected.

16. Consider the relation `BankEmp` and assume yourself to be a database administrator. Write the SQL statements to grant privileges for the following:
Note: Create views wherever required.
(a) Allow USER1 to retrieve `ECode`, `EName` and `Salary` only and also allow USER1 to update the `Salary` of any employee.
(b) Allow USER2 to act as an authorizer for all privileges on `BankEmp`.
(c) Allow USER3 to retrieve or modify the relation but he or she should not be able to propagate privileges to other users.

Ans: (a) `GRANT SELECT(ECode, Ename, Salary),UPDATE(Salary)ON BankEmp to USER1;`

(b) `GRANT SELECT, INSERT, UPDATE, DELETE ON BankEmp TO USER2 WITH GRANT OPTION;`

(c) `GRANT SELECT, INSERT, UPDATE, DELETE ON BankEmp TO USER3;`

17. Suppose using any substitution system the plain text *Strong Security* becomes *Fgebat Frphevgl*. Using the same substitution system, compute the cipher text for the plain text *It is really hard* and also list the complete substitution format.

Ans: Plain text: It is really hard.
Cipher text: vg vf ernyyl uneq

List of complete substitution format is:

Plain text: a b c d e f g h i j k l m n o p q r s t u v w x y z
Cipher text: n o p q r s t u v w x y z a b c d e f g h i j k l m

18. Suppose you are given two small prime numbers 11 and 3. Using the RSA Algorithm, compute the public key and the private key.

Ans: Here, $m = 11$ and $n = 3$

According to RSA algorithm

$p = m * n = 11 * 3 = 33$

Thus, $p = 33$

Now, $q = (m-1) * (n-1) = (11-1) * (3-1) = 10 * 2 = 20$

Thus, $q = 20$

$D = 3$ (number relatively prime to 20, that is, $gcd(20, 3) = 1$))

Now, $E * D = 1 \bmod q$

That is, $E * 3 = 1 \bmod 20$

Therefore, $E = 7$

As we know, the public key consists of (E, p), and the private key consists of (D, p).

Therefore,

Public key is (7, 33)

Private key is (3, 33)

Multiple-choice Questions

1. Which of the following issues are covered by database security?
   (a) Privacy (b) Database availability
   (c) Database Integrity (d) All of these
2. The person who is responsible for the overall security of the database system is ________.
   (a) Programmer (b) Database users
   (c) Database administrator (d) All of these
3. Which of the following is an example of malicious attack?
   (a) System error that leads to accessibility to the portion of database.
   (b) Improper authorization can be accidentally assigned to user by authorization.
   (c) Hackers, who can get into system parts that they are not authorized to access.
   (d) None of these
4. Managing user account includes ________.
   (a) Creation of user accounts (b) Granting of privileges
   (c) Classification of user accounts (d) All of these
5. To keep track of database users and their passwords, the DBMS maintains an encrypted table having ________ fields.
   (a) One (b) Two (c) Three (d) Four
6. When a user logs in successfully, the DBMS records its ________.
   (a) Account number (b) Terminal ID (c) Both (a) and (b) (d) None of these
7. Which of the following statements is false?
   (a) DBA can assign privileges to different users.
   (b) A user can assign privileges to any user on its own relations only.
   (c) A user can assign privileges to any user on any relation.
   (d) All of these

8. A part of database that needs to be protected from unauthorized access is ________.
   (a) Object (b) Subject (c) Both (a) and (b) (d) None of these
9. Which of the following access privileges a user can have on a relation?
   (a) SELECT (b) Propagate access control
   (c) REFERENCES (d) All of these
10. Which of the following statements is false?
    (a) Passwords itself need to be secured from unauthorized access.
    (b) The key stored on embedded chip in the smart card cannot be read.
    (c) Relatively high security of database can be achieved by using physical characteristics of user for identification.
    (d) None of these
11. Which of these privileges can be given on a set of attributes of a relation?
    (a) `SELECT` (b) `INSERT` (c) `UPDATE` (d) Both (b) and (c)
12. Which of the following privileges the user must have on all the base relations in order to create a view?
    (a) `SELECT` (b) `UPDATE` (c) `CREATE` (d) None of these
13. The command used for destroying roles in RBAC is ________.
    (a) `CREATE ROLE` (b) `DESTROY ROLE` (c) `DROP ROLE` (d) None of these
14. The type of encryption in which the same key is used for both encryption and decryption is called ________.
    (a) Symmetric key encryption (b) Public key encryption
    (c) Digital signature (d) None of these
15. Which of the following is an example of symmetric key encryption?
    (a) AES (b) DES (c) Both (a) and (b) (d) None of these

Answers

1. (d) 2. (c) 3. (c) 4. (d) 5. (b) 6. (c) 7. (c)
8. (a) 9. (d) 10. (d) 11. (d) 12. (a) 13. (b) 14. (a)
15. (c)

13

Database System Architecture

1. What do you understand by parallel processing? Explain main architectures for building parallel database systems.

Ans: The simultaneous use of computer resources such as central processing units (CPUs) and disks to perform a specific task is known as **parallel processing**. In parallel processing, many tasks are performed simultaneously on different CPU's. Parallel DBMS seeks to improve performance by carrying out many operations in parallel, such as loading data, processing queries and so on. The three main architectures for building parallel database systems are as follows:

- **Shared memory:** In shared-memory architecture, all the processors have access to a common memory and to storage disks via an interconnection network (bus or switch).
- **Shared disk:** In shared-disk architecture, each processor has a private memory and shares only storage disks via the interconnection network.
- **Shared-nothing:** In shared-nothing architecture, each processor has private memory and one or more private disk storage. No two processors can access the same storage. The processors communicate through an interconnection network.

All these three architectures are shown in Figure 13.1.

2. What is a distributed database system? What are its advantages?

Ans: In a distributed database system, data are physically stored across several computers. The computers are geographically dispersed and are connected with one another through various communication media such as high-speed networks or telephone lines. The computers in a distributed system are referred to as **sites** and each site is managed by a DBMS that is capable of running independent of other sites. The overall distributed system can be regarded as a kind of partnership among the individual local DBMSs at the individual local sites. The necessary partnership functionality is provided by a new software system at each site. This new software is logically an extension of local DBMS. The combination of this new software together with the existing DBMSs is called **distributed database management system (DDBMS)**.

The distributed database system has various advantages, some of which are as follows:

- **Sharing data:** The primary advantage of DDBMS is the ability to share and access data in an efficient manner. DDBMS provides an environment where users at a given site are able to access

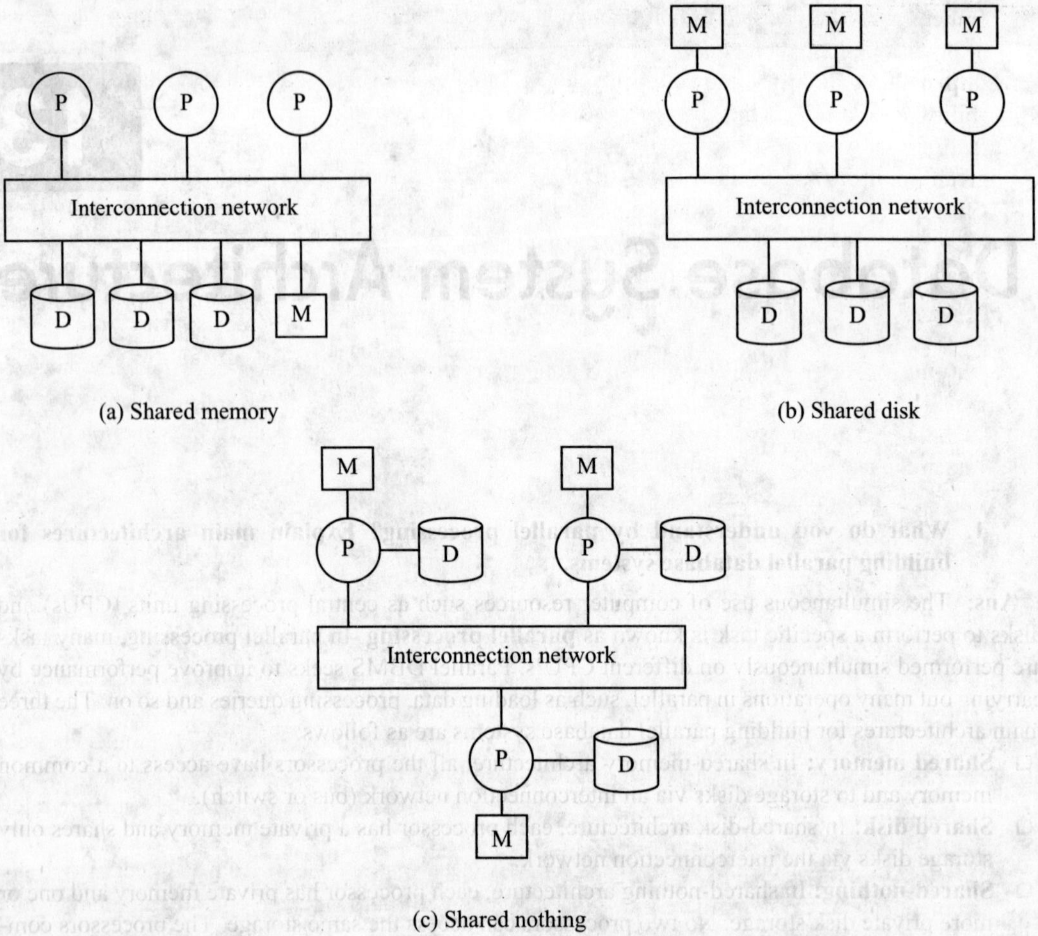

Figure 13.1 Parallel Database Architecture

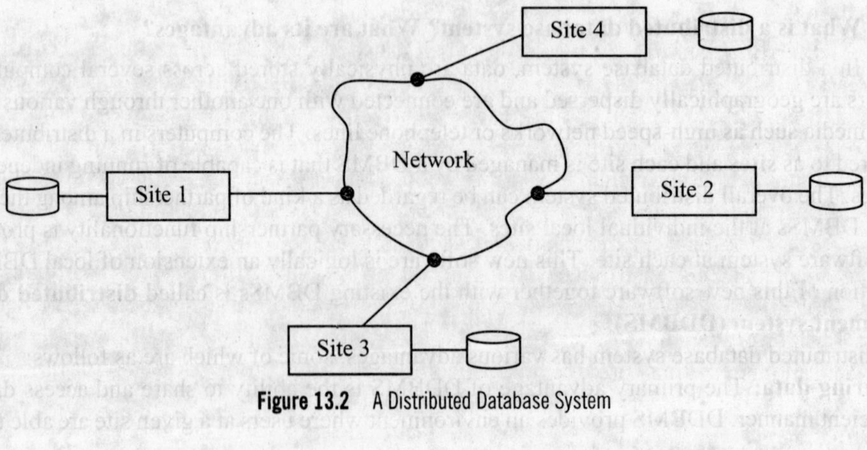

Figure 13.2 A Distributed Database System

data stored at other sites. For example, consider an organization having many branches. Each branch stores data related to that branch; however, a manager of a particular branch can access information of any branch.

- **Improved availability and reliability:** Distributed systems provide greater availability and reliability. Availability is the probability that the system is running continuously throughout a specified period, whereas reliability is the probability that the system is running (not down) at any given point of time. In distributed database systems, since, data are distributed across several sites, failure of a single site does not halt the entire system. The other sites can continue to operate in case of failure of one site. Only the data that exist at the failed site cannot be accessed. This means, some of the data may be inaccessible but other parts of database may still be accessible to the users. Furthermore, if the data are replicated at one or more sites, further improvement can be achieved.
- **Autonomy:** The possibility of local autonomy is the major advantage of distributed database system. Local autonomy implies that all operations at a given site are controlled by that site. It should not depend on any other site. Further, the security, integrity and representation of local data are under the control of the local site.
- **Easier expansion:** Distributed systems are more modular, hence, they can be expanded easily as compared to centralized systems, where upgrading a system with changes in hardware and software affects the entire database. In a distributed system, the size of the database can be increased, and more processors or sites can be added as needed with little effort.

3. Compare shared-nothing parallel database system with distributed database system.

Ans: Though the shared-nothing parallel database system resembles distributed database system, there are certain differences between the two:

- The shared-nothing parallel database system is implemented on a tightly coupled multiprocessor and comprises a single database system. While in the distributed database system, databases are geographically separated across the sites that share no physical components and are separately administered.
- In shared-nothing architecture, there is symmetry and homogeneity of sites. However, in a distributed database system, there may be heterogeneity of hardware and operating system at each site.

4. Differentiate between homogenous distributed database system and heterogeneous database system.

Ans: The distributed database system in which all sites share a common global schema and run the identical DBMS software is known as the **homogeneous distributed database system**. In such a system, DBMS software on different sites are aware of one another, and agree to work together in processing a user request at any site exactly as if data were stored at the user's own site. In addition, the software must agree in exchanging information about transactions so that a transaction can be processed across multiple sites. Local sites relinquish a certain degree of control in terms of their right to change schemas or database management system software to some other site.

On the other hand, the distributed database system in which different sites may have different schemas and run different DBMS software, essentially autonomously, is known as the **heterogeneous distributed database system** or **multidatabase system**. In such a system, the sites may not be aware of one another and may provide limited facilities for cooperation in transaction processing. The differences in schemas also cause a problem in query processing. In addition, differences in software obstruct the processing of transactions that access multiple sites.

5. Describe the methods of storing data in a distributed database system.

Ans: In distributed DBMS, the relations are stored across several sites using two methods, namely, *fragmentation* and *replication*.

- **Fragmentation:** A relation is divided into several fragments (or smaller relations), and each fragment can be stored at sites where they are more often accessed.
- **Replication:** Several identical copies or replicas of each relation are maintained and each replica is stored at many distinct sites.

6. Explain different techniques of database fragmentation with suitable illustrations.

Ans: Fragmentation of a relation R consists of breaking it into a number of fragments $R_1, R_2, \ldots R_n$ such that it is always possible to reconstruct the original relation R from the fragments $R_1, R_2, \ldots R_n$. The fragmentation can be *horizontal, vertical* (see Figure 13.3) or *mixed*.

- **Horizontal fragmentation:** Horizontal fragmentation breaks a relation R by assigning each tuple of R to one or more fragments. In horizontal fragmentation, each fragment is a subset of the tuples in the original relation. Since each tuple of a relation R belongs to at least one of the fragments, original relation can be reconstructed. Generally, a horizontal fragment is defined as a selection on the relation R. For instance, fragment R_i can be constructed as shown here.

$$R_i = \sigma_{\text{condition(i)}} (R)$$

The relation R can be reconstructed by applying union on all fragments, that is,

$$R = R_1 \cup R_2 \cup \ldots \cup R_n$$

TID	ISBN	Book_title	Category	Price	Copyright_date	Year	Page_count	P_ID
T1	003-456-433-6	Introduction to German Language	Language Book	22	2003	2004	200	P004
T2	003-456-533-8	Learning French Language	Language Book	32	2005	2006	500	P004
T3	001-354-921-1	Ransack	Novel	22	2005	2006	200	P001
T4	002-678-880-2	Call Away	Novel	22	2001	2002	200	P002
T5	001-987-760-9	C++	Textbook	40	2004	2005	800	P001
T6	002-678-980-4	DBMS	Textbook	40	2004	2006	800	P002
T7	004-765-409-5	UNIX	Textbook	26	2006	2007	550	P003
T8	004-765-359-3	Coordinate Geometry	Textbook	35	2006	2006	650	P003
T9	001-987-650-5	Differential Calculus	Textbook	30	2003	2003	450	P001

Vertical Fragment

Horizontal Fragment

Figure 13.3 Horizontal and Vertical Fragmentation

For example, the relation book can be divided into several fragments on the basis of attribute `Category` as shown here:

$$BOOK1 = \sigma_{Category = \text{"Novel"}}(BOOK)$$
$$BOOK2 = \sigma_{Category = \text{"Textbook"}}(BOOK)$$
$$BOOK3 = \sigma_{Category = \text{"LanguageBook"}}(BOOK)$$

Here, each fragment consists of tuples of `Book` relation that belongs to a particular category. Further, the fragments are disjoint. However, by changing the selection condition, a particular tuple of R can appear in more than one fragment.

- **Vertical fragmentation:** Vertical fragmentation breaks a relation by decomposing schema of relation R. In vertical fragmentation, each fragment is a subset of the attributes of the original relation. A vertical fragment is defined as a projection on the relation R as

$$R_i = \pi_{Ri}(R)$$

The relation should be fragmented in such a way that the original relation can be reconstructed by applying natural join on the fragments. That is,

$$R = R_1 \bowtie R_2 \bowtie \ldots \bowtie R_n$$

To ensure the reconstruction of a relation from the fragments, one of the following options can be used:

  - Include key attributes of R in each fragment R_i.
  - Add a unique tuple id to each tuple in the original relation—this id is attached to each vertical fragment.

- **Mixed fragmentation:** It is the combination of horizontal and vertical fragmentation. The fragments obtained by horizontally fragmenting a relation can be further partitioned vertically or vice versa. The original relation is obtained by the combination of join and union operations.

7. What do you understand by data replication? What are its advantages and disadvantages?

Ans: Replication means storing a copy (or replica) of a relation or relation fragments in two or more sites. Distribution of an entire relation at all sites is known as **full replication**. When only some fragments of a relation are replicated, it is called **partial replication**. In partial replication, the number of copies of each fragment can range from one to the total number of sites in the system.

Replication provides the following advantages:

- **Increased availability of data:** If a site containing the relation R fails, then the same relation can be found as long as at least one replica is available at some other site. Thus, the system can continue to process queries involving R, despite the failure of one site. Further, if the local copies of remote relations are available, we are less vulnerable to failure of remote site.
- **Better performance:** The system can process queries faster by operating on local copy of relation instead of communicating with remote sites. In case there are more replicas of a relation, the probability of the needed data at the site where the transaction is initiated is more. Thus, data replication minimizes the overhead due to the movement of data between sites.

The disadvantages of replication are as follows:

- In case of full replication, update operations incur greater overhead. The system must ensure that all the replicas of a relation are consistent to avoid erroneous result. This requirement slows down the update operations and makes the distributed database system more complex.
- Concurrency control and recovery procedures are quite expensive as compared to if there were no replication.

8. Discuss the types of transparencies supported in a distributed system.

Ans: In a distributed system, the users are not required to know where the data are physically stored and how the data can be accessed at the specific local site. Hiding all such details from the users is referred to as **data transparency**. DDBMS provides the following types of transparencies:

- **Location transparency** (also known as **location independence**): Users should not know the physical location of the data. Users should be able to access the data as if all the data were stored at their own local site.
- **Fragmentation transparency** (also known as **fragmentation independence**): User should not be aware of the data fragmentation.
- **Replication transparency** (also known as **replication independence**): User should not be aware of the data replication. Data may be replicated either for better availability or performance. Users should be able to work as if data is not replicated at all.
- **Naming transparency:** Data items such as relations, fragments and replicas must have unique names. This property can be ensured easily in a centralized system. However, in a distributed database, care must be taken to ensure that no two sites have same name for distinct data items so that once a name is assigned to a data item, that named data item can be accessed unambiguously.

9. Discuss different strategies for executing simple equijoin of two relations located at different sites. What factors affect the cost of data transfer?

Ans: The join operation is one of the most expensive operations to perform. Consider the following relational algebra expression:

$$\pi_{\text{ISBN, Price, P\_ID, Pname}} \text{ (BOOK} \bowtie_{\text{BOOK.P\_ID=PUBLISHER.P\_ID}} \text{PUBLISHER)}$$

Suppose relations BOOK and PUBLISHER are stored at sites S_1 and S_2, respectively, and the result is to be produced at site S_3. Further, suppose that there are 500 tuples in BOOK where each tuple is 100 bytes long and 100 tuples in PUBLISHER where each tuple is 150 bytes long. Thus, the size of BOOK relation is 500 * 100 = 50,000 bytes and the size of PUBLISHER relation is 100 * 150 = 15,000 bytes. The result of this query has 500 tuples where each tuple is 75 bytes long (assuming that the attributes ISBN, Price, P_ID, Pname are 15, 6, 4 and 50 bytes long).

The different possible strategies that can be employed for processing this query are as follows:

- Transfer replicas of both the relations to site S_3 and process the query at this site to obtain the result. In this strategy, a total of 50,000 + 15,000 = 65,000 bytes must be transferred.
- Transfer replica of relation PUBLISHER to site S_1 for processing the entire query locally at site S_1 and then ship result to site S_3. In this strategy, the bytes equivalent to the size of the query result and the size of relation PUBLISHER must be transferred. That is, 37,500 + 15,000 = 52,500 bytes must be transferred.
- Transfer replica of relation BOOK to site S_2 for processing the entire query locally at site S_2 and then ship result to site S_3. In this case, 50,000 + 37,500 = 87,500 bytes must be transferred.

If minimizing the amount of data transfer is the criteria for optimization, strategy 2 must be chosen. However, in addition to the amount of data transfer, the optimal choice also depends on the communication cost between a pair of sites and the relative speed of processing at each site.

10. Discuss the semijoin strategy for executing an equijoin of two relations located at different sites. What are its advantages over simple join processing?

Ans: In **semijoin** strategy, instead of sending entire relation, the joining attribute of one relation is sent to the site where another relation is present. This attribute is then joined with the relation and then the join attributes along with the required attributes are projected and transferred back to the original site. For example, consider the following relational algebra expression:

$$\pi_{\texttt{ISBN, Price, P\_ID, Pname}}(\texttt{BOOK} \bowtie_{\texttt{BOOK.P\_ID = PUBLISHER.P\_ID}} \texttt{PUBLISHER})$$

where, BOOK and PUBLISHER are stored at different sites S_1 and S_2, respectively. Further, suppose that system needs to produce the result at site S_2. This relational algebra expression can be evaluated using the strategy as follows:

- Project the join attribute (P_ID) of PUBLISHER at site S_2 and transfer it to S_1. A total of 100*4 = 400 bytes will be transferred.
- Join this transferred attribute with the BOOK relation and transfer the required attributes from the resultant relation to site S_2. A total of 500 * 25 (size of attribute ISBN + size of attribute Price + size of attribute P_ID), that is, 12,500 bytes are required to be transferred.
- Evaluate the expression by joining the transferred attributes with PUBLISHER relation at site S_2.

Here, 12,900 (12,500 + 400) bytes are required to be transferred. This strategy is more advantageous if small fraction of tuples of BOOK relation participates in join.

Semijoin strategy reduces the size of a relation that is to be transmitted to other site and hence, the communication cost while performing the join operations.

11. Differentiate between local transaction and global transaction.

Ans: The transaction that accesses and updates data only at the site where it is initiated is known as **local transaction**. The transaction that accesses and updates data from several sites or the site other than the site at which the transaction is initiated is known as **global transaction**.

12. Differentiate between coordinator site and participating site.

Ans: A transaction that requires data from remote sites is broken into one or more subtransactions. These subtransactions are then distributed to the appropriate sites where they are executed independently. The site at which the transaction is initiated is referred to as **coordinator site** and the sites where subtransactions are executed are called **participating sites**.

13. Discuss various locking techniques that can be applied in distributed systems along with their advantages and disadvantages.

Ans: There are various locking techniques that can be applied in distributed systems. These techniques include *single lock manager*, *distributed lock manager*, *primary copy* and *majority locking*.

Single lock manager

In this technique, the system maintains a single lock manager that resides in any single chosen site and all the requests to lock and unlock the data items are sent to that site. When a transaction needs to acquire lock on a specific data item, it sends request to the site where the lock manager resides. The lock manager checks whether the lock can be granted immediately. If the lock can be granted, the lock manager sends a message to the site from which the request for lock was initiated. Otherwise, the request is delayed until it can be granted. In case of a read lock request, the data item at any one of the sites (at which replica of data item is present) is locked in the shared mode and then read. In case of a write lock request, all the replicas of the data item are locked in the exclusive mode and then modified.

The advantages of this technique are as follows:

- It is relatively easy to implement as it is merely a simple extension of the centralized approach.
- Since all requests to lock and unlock data items are made at one site, deadlock can be detected by applying directed graph directly.

The disadvantages of this technique are as follows:

- Sending all locking requests to a single site can overload that site which can cause bottleneck.
- The failure of the site containing lock manager disrupts the entire system as all the locking information is kept at that site.

Distributed lock manager

In this technique, each site maintains a local lock manager, which is responsible for handling the lock and unlock request for those data items that are stored in that site. When a transaction needs to acquire lock on a data item (assume that the data item is not replicated) that resides at site say S, a message is sent to the lock manager at site S requesting appropriate lock. If the lock request is incompatible with the current state of locking of the requested data item, the request is delayed. Once it has ascertained that the lock can be granted, the lock manager sends a corresponding message to the site at which the request was initiated.

The advantages of this technique are as follows:

- This approach is also simple to implement.
- It reduces the degree to which the coordinator is a bottleneck.

The disadvantages of this technique are as follows:

- Deadlock detection is more complex. Since lock requests are directed to a number of different sites, there may be intersite deadlocks even when there is no deadlock within a single site. Thus, the deadlock-handling algorithm needs to be modified to detect **global deadlocks** (deadlock involving two or more sites).

Primary copy

This technique deals with the replicated data by designating one copy of each data item (say, Q) as a **primary copy**. The site at which the primary copy of Q resides is called **primary site** of Q. All requests to lock or unlock Q are handled by the lock manager at the primary site, regardless of the number of copies existing for Q. If the lock can be granted, the lock manager sends a message to the site from which the request for lock was initiated. Otherwise, the request is delayed until it can be granted.

The advantages of this technique are as follows:

- Concurrency control for replicated data can be handled the same way as for unreplicated data. This similarity permits for a simpler implementation.
- The load of processing lock requests is distributed among various sites by having primary copies of different data items stored at different sites.

The disadvantages of this technique are as follows:

- If the primary site of a specific data item fails, the data item no longer remains accessible even though some other site containing a replica of that data item is accessible.

Majority locking

In this technique, majority of the copies must be locked in case of both read and write lock request for a data item. Lock request is sent to more than one-half of the sites that contain a copy of the required data item. The local manager at each site determines whether the lock can be granted or not and acts similarly as discussed in earlier techniques. In this technique, a transaction cannot operate on a data item until the lock has been granted on a majority of the replica of the data item. Further, any number of transactions can simultaneously acquire a read lock on a majority of the replicas of a data item, since a read lock is shareable. However, only one transaction can acquire a write lock on a majority of these replicas. No transaction can majority lock a data item in the shared mode if it is already locked in the exclusive mode.

The advantages of this technique are as follows:

- This technique is considered as a truly distributed concurrency control method, since most of the sites are involved in decision in the locking process.

The disadvantages of this technique are as follows:

- This technique is more complicated to implement than earlier discussed techniques. It is because, it has higher message traffic among sites.
- In addition to the problem of global deadlocks due to the use of a distributed lock manager, deadlock can occur even if only one data item is being locked. To illustrate this, consider a system with four sites S_1, S_2, S_3, and S_4 having data replicated at all sites. Suppose that transactions T_1 and T_2 need to lock a data item Q in exclusive mode. Further, suppose that transaction T_1 succeeds in locking Q at sites S_1 and S_4, while transactions T_2 succeeds in locking Q at sites S_2 and S_3. Now, to acquire the third lock, each of the transactions must wait. Hence, a deadlock has occurred.

14. How are timestamps generated in a distributed system?

Ans: In timestamping approach, each transaction in the system is assigned a unique timestamp to determine its serialization order. For generating global unique timestamps in distributed systems, there are two primary methods, namely, *centralized* and *distributed.*

- **Centralized scheme:** In this scheme, a single site is responsible for generating the timestamps. The site can use either a logical counter or value of its own clock for this purpose.
- **Distributed scheme:** In this scheme, each site generates a unique local timestamp by using either a logical counter or local clock. This unique local timestamp is concatenated with the site identifier (which must also be unique) to get a unique global timestamp (see Figure 13.4). The order of concatenation is important. The site identifier must be at the least significant position so that the global timestamps generated in one site is not always greater than those generated in another site. That is, the transactions are always ordered on the basis of the time of their occurrence not on the basis of the site from which they are initiated.

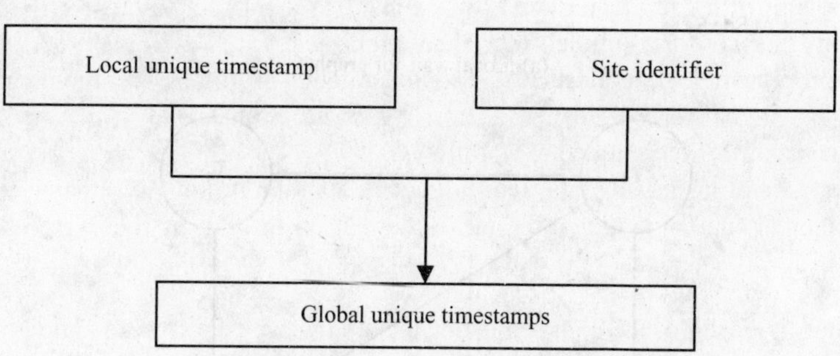

Figure 13.4 Generation of Global Unique Timestamps

15. How are deadlocks handled in a distributed database system?

Ans: In distributed systems, even when there is no deadlock within a single site, there may be intersite deadlocks. In other words, a deadlock involving two or more sites can occur. The two commonly used techniques for deadlock handling are as follows:

Wait-for graph

This technique requires each site to maintain its own **local wait-for graph** where the nodes represent all the local as well as non local transactions that are currently holding or requesting any of the items local to that site. To illustrate, consider a system having two sites S_1 and S_2 with the following situation:

- At site S_1, transaction T_1 is waiting to acquire lock on the data item held by transaction T_2. Transaction T_2 is waiting to acquire lock on the data item held by transaction T_4. Transaction T_3 is waiting to acquire lock on the data item locked by transaction T_1 and T_2.
- At site S_2, transaction T_4 is waiting to acquire lock on the data item locked by transaction T_3

Figure 13.5(a) shows the local-wait graphs maintained at site S_1 and S_2. Transactions T_3 and T_4 are present in both the graphs indicating that transactions have requested data items at both sites.

The local wait-for graphs on sites S_1 and S_2 are acyclic, indicating that there is no deadlock on these sites. However, absence of cycle in the local wait-for graph does not imply that there is no deadlock. This means, global deadlock cannot be detected solely on the basis of local wait-for graph. For this, **global wait-for graph** [see Figure.13.5(b)] is constructed simply by the union of the local wait-for graphs and maintained at a single chosen site for deadlock detection. Since this site is responsible for handling global deadlocks, it is known as **deadlock detection coordinator**.

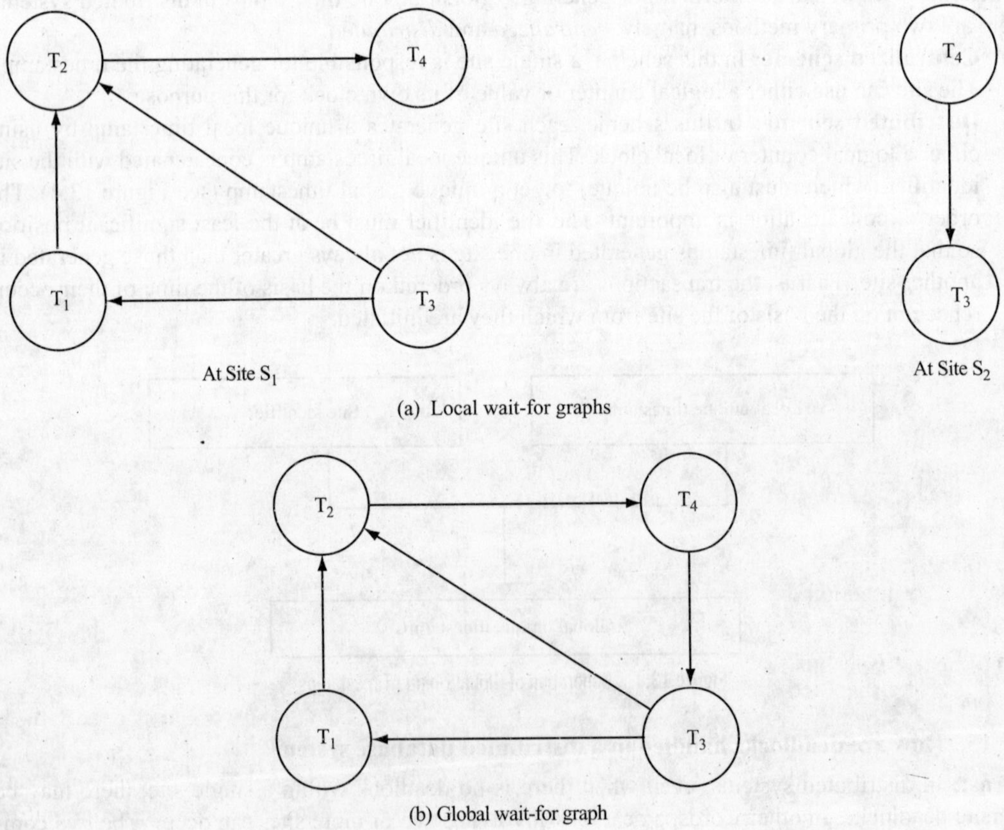

Figure 13.5 Distributed Deadlock

The disadvantage of this technique is that it incurs communication overhead, as it requires sending all local wait-for graphs to the coordinator site. The other disadvantage is that delays in propagating local wait for graphs may cause deadlock detection algorithms to identify deadlocks that do not really exist. Such deadlocks are known as **phantom deadlocks**. These types of deadlocks may lead to unnecessary rollbacks.

Time-out based technique

In this technique, a transaction is allowed to wait for a fixed interval of time for required data item. If a transaction waits longer than specified time interval, it is aborted. Though this algorithm may cause unnecessary restarts, the overhead of deadlock detection is low. Moreover, if the participating sites do not cooperate to the extent of sharing their waits-for graphs, it may be the only option.

16. What is the role of commit protocol in a distributed database? Describe two phase commit (2PC) protocol.

Ans: The recovery system must ensure atomicity property, that is, either all the sub transactions of a given transaction must commit or abort at all sites. This property must be guaranteed despite any kind of failure. This guarantee is achieved using the commit protocol. The two commonly used protocols are *two-phase commit protocol* (*2PC*) and *three-phase commit protocol* (*3PC*).

Two-phase commit (2PC)

In a distributed system, since a transaction is being executed at more than one site, the commit protocol may be divided into two phases, namely, *voting phase* and *decision phase*. Consider a transaction *T* initiated at site S_i where the transaction coordinator is C_i. When *T* completes its execution, that is, all the sites at which *T* has executed inform C_i that *T* has completed, C_i initiates the 2PC protocol. The two phases of this protocol are as follows.

- **Voting phase:** In this phase, the participating sites vote on whether they are ready to commit *T* or not. During this phase, the following actions are taken:
  1. C_i inserts a prepare record `[T, prepare]` in the log and force-writes the log onto stable storage. After this, C_i sends the `prepare T` message to all the participating sites.
  2. When the transaction manager at a participating site receives the `prepare T` message, it determines whether the site is ready to commit *T* or not. If the site is ready to commit *T*, it inserts a `[T, ready]` record in the log; otherwise it inserts `[T, not-ready]` record. It then force-writes the log onto stable storage and sends the `ready T` or `abort T` message to C_i accordingly.
- **Decision phase:** In this phase, the coordinator site decides whether the transaction *T* can be committed or it has to be aborted. The decision is based on the responses to `prepare T` message that C_i receives from all the participating sites. The following responses may be received at the coordinator site.
  1. A `ready T` message from all the participating sites. In this case, C_i decides to commit the transaction and inserts `[T, commit]` record to the log. It then force-writes the log onto stable storage and sends `commit T` message to all the participating sites.
  2. At least one `not-ready T` message or no response from any participating site within the specified time-out interval. In this case, C_i decides to abort the transaction and inserts `[T, abort]` record to the log. It then force-writes the log onto stable storage and sends `abort T` message to all the participating sites.

Once the participating sites receive either the `commit T` or `abort T` message from C_i, they insert the corresponding record to the log, and force-write the log onto stable storage. After that, each participating site sends an `acknowledge T` message to C_i. Upon receiving this message from all the sites, C_i force-writes the `[T, complete]` record to the log.

17. What types of failures can occur during the execution of the 2PC protocol? How are these failures handled?

Ans: While the 2PC protocol is being executed, either one of the participating sites or the coordinator may fail.

If any participating site fails, there are two possibilities. First, the site fails before sending `ready T` message. In this case, the coordinator does not receive any reply within the specified time interval. Thus, the transaction is aborted. Second, if the site fails after sending `ready T` message, the coordinator simply ignores the failure of participating site and proceeds in the normal way.

When the participating site restarts after failure, the recovery process is invoked. During recovery, the site examines its log to find all those transactions that were executing at the time of the failure. To decide the fate of those transactions, the recovery process proceeds as follows:

- If the log contains the `[T, commit]` or `[T, abort]` record, the site simply executes `redo(T)` or `undo(T)`, respectively, and sends the `acknowledgement T` message to the coordinator.
- If the log contains the `[T, ready]` record, the site contacts the coordinator to determine whether to commit or abort *T*.
- If no such record exists in the log, the site decides unilaterally to abort the transaction and execute `undo(T)`, since the site could not have voted before its failure.

In case the coordinator fails, all the participating sites communicate with each other to determine the status of *T*. If any participating site contains the `[T, commit]` or `[T, abort]` record in its log, the transaction has to be committed or aborted respectively. On the other hand, if any participating site does not contain `[T, ready]` record in its log, it means that site has not voted for *T* and without that vote, the coordinator could not have decided to commit *T*. Thus, in this case, it is preferable to abort *T*. However, if none of the discussed cases holds, the participating sites have to wait until the coordinator recovers, and all the locks acquired by *T* are held. This leads to **blocking problem** at the participating sites, since the transactions that require locks on data items locked by *T* have to wait.

When the coordinator restarts after failure, the recovery process is invoked at the coordinator site. The coordinator examines its log to determine the status of *T*.

- If the log contains `[T, commit]` or `[T, abort]` record, it executes `redo(T)` or `undo(T)`, respectively, and periodically resends the `commit T` or `abort T` message to the participating sites, until it receives `acknowledgement T` message from each participating site.
- If the log contains `[T, prepare]` record, the coordinator unilaterally decides to abort *T* and conveys it to all the participating sites.

18. How does three-phase commit (3PC) protocol avoid the problem of blocking?

Ans: The **three-phase commit protocol (3PC)** is an extension of the two-phase commit protocol that avoids blocking even if the coordinator site fails during recovery. To avoid the blocking problem, this protocol requires some conditions, which are as follows.

- There is no network partitioning.
- At least there is one available site.
- At most `K` sites fail, where `K` is some predetermined number.

If these conditions hold, 3PC protocol avoids blocking by introducing third phase between voting phase and the decision phase. In this phase, multiple sites are involved in the decision to commit. The basic idea of 3PC protocol is that when the coordinator sends `prepare T` message and receives yes votes from all the participant sites; it sends all participants pre-commit message instead of commit message. After ensuring that at least K other participating sites know about the decision to commit, the coordinator force-writes a commit log record and sends a commit message to all participants. The coordinator effectively postpones the decision to commit until it is sure that enough sites know about the decision to commit. If the coordinator site fails, the other sites choose a new coordinator. This new coordinator communicates with the remaining other sites to check whether the old coordinator had decided to commit.

19. Discuss the three layers of three-tier client/server architecture used in developing distributed system.

Ans: Three-tier client/server architecture has been used in developing distributed systems, particularly in web applications. The three layers of this architecture are *presentation layer*, *application layer* and *database server*.

- **Presentation layer (client):** This layer provides an interface to handle user input and display the needed information. At this layer, Web interfaces or forms are provided through which the user can issue request, provide input, and the formatted output generated by application layer is displayed. For this purpose, Web browsers are used. HTML is the basic data presentation language that is used to communicate data from the presentation layer to the application layer. The other languages which can be used are Java, JavaScript, etc. This layer communicates with the application layer via HTTP protocol.
- **Application layer:** This layer executes the business logic of the application. It controls what data needs to input before an action can be executed, and what action are taken under what conditions. The languages that can be used to program business logic are Java servlets, JSP, etc. This layer can communicate with one or more databases using standards such as ODBC, JDBC, etc. Apart from the business logic, it also handles functionality like security checks, identity verification and so on.
- **Database server:** This layer processes the query requested by the application layer and send the results to it. Thus, it is the layer that accesses data from the database system. Generally, SQL is used to access the database if it is relational or object-relational. Stored procedures can also be

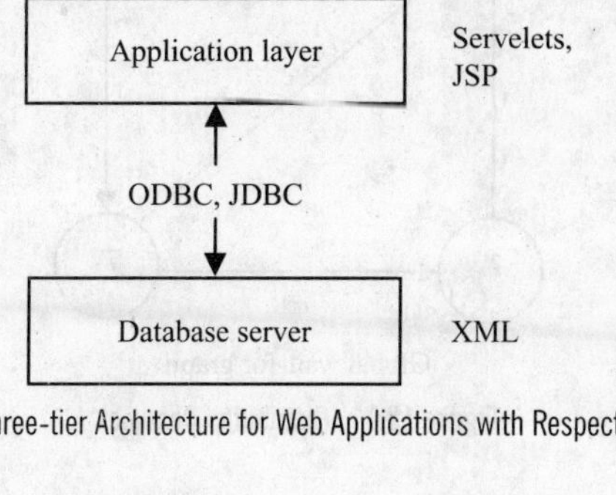

Figure 13.6 Three-tier Architecture for Web Applications with Respective Technologies

used for the same purpose. At this level, XML may be used to exchange information regarding the query between the application server and the database server.

20. Given four relations R, S, T and U stored at sites S_1, S_2, S_3 and S_4, respectively. None of these relations are either fragmented or replicated. Suggest a strategy to compute the join of these four relations in parallel and obtain the result at site S_1.

Ans: The query can be evaluated in parallel by using the strategy given here.

Relation R is transferred to site S_2 where R ⋈ S can be evaluated. At the same time, relation T is transferred to site S_4 where T ⋈ U can be evaluated. Site S_2 can ship tuples of R ⋈ S to S_1 as they are generated, instead of waiting for the entire join to be computed. Similarly, Site S_4 can ship tuples of T ⋈ U to S_1. Once tuples of R ⋈ S and T ⋈ U reach at S_1, the computation of R ⋈ S ⋈ T ⋈ U can start. Hence, the computation of the final join result at S_1 can be done in parallel with the computation of R ⋈ S at S_2 and T ⋈ U at S_4.

21. Give an example of a distributed DBMS with three sites such that no two local waits-for graphs reveal a deadlock, yet there is a global deadlock.

Ans:

In Figure 13.7, each local wait-for graph is acyclic, indicating that there is no deadlock within the sites. Global wait-for graph is constructed by the union of the local wait-for graphs and maintained at a single chosen site, which indicates the presence of a global deadlock.

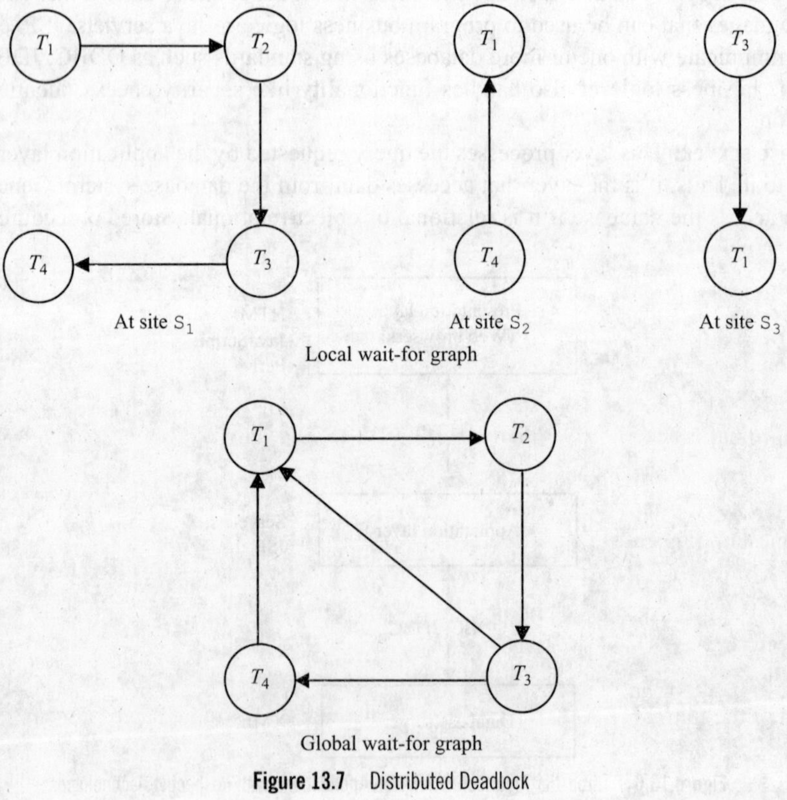

Figure 13.7 Distributed Deadlock

22. Consider a database of a company where a relation `Employee (name, address, salary, branch)` is fragmented horizontally by branch. Assume that each fragment has two replicas: one stored at site A and one stored locally at the branch site. Describe a good strategy for the following queries entered at site B:

(i) Find the name and address of all employees at site C.
(ii) Find the average salary of all employees.
(iii) Find the lowest-paid employee in the company.

Ans: **(i)** Send the query $\pi_{\texttt{name, address}}$ `(Employee)` to site C and send back the result to site B.

(ii) Send the query $£_{\texttt{AVG(price)}}$ `(Employee)` to the site A as it contains a copy of all the replicas, compute the average salary at site A and send back the result to site B.

(iii) Send the query to find the lowest-paid employee to site A, compute the query at site A and send back the result to site B.

Multiple-choice Questions

1. The important metric(s) for measuring the efficiency of a parallel database system is __________.
(a) Speedup (b) Scaleup (c) Both (a) and (b) (d) None of these
2. In which fragmentation is each fragment a subset of the tuples in the original relation?
(a) Horizontal (b) Vertical (c) Both (a) and (b) (d) None of these
3. In which of these transparencies are users allowed to access the data as if the data are stored at their own local site?
(a) Fragmentation transparency (b) Replication transparency
(c) Naming transparency (d) Location transparency
4. Which of the following is not an advantage of replication?
(a) Better performance (b) Reliability
(c) Increased availability (d) All of these
5. The strategy that is used to reduce the communication cost in performing a join operation is __________.
(a) Equijoin (b) Semijoin (c) Parallelism (d) Transparency
6. Which of the following transactions accesses and updates data only at the site where it is initiated?
(a) Global (b) Local (c) Horizontal (d) Vertical
7. The site at which the transaction is initiated is referred to as __________.
(a) Coordinator site (b) Primary site (c) Participating site (d) None of these
8. Which of the following techniques is considered as a truly distributed concurrency control method?
(a) Timestamping (b) Majority locking
(c) Primary copy (d) Distributed lock manager
9. Which of the following technologies is not used in presentation layer of three-tier client/server architecture?
(a) JSP (b) Browsers (c) Javascript (d) HTML
10. Which of the following layers can communicate with one or more databases using standards such as ODBC, JDBC, etc.?
(a) Database server (b) Application layer (c) Presentation layer (d) None of these

11. Which of these layer issues SQL queries to the database server formats the query result and sends to the client for presentation?
(a) Application layer (b) Presentation layer (c) Database server (d) None of these

Answers

1. (c)	2. (a)	3. (d)	4. (b)	5. (b)	6. (b)	7. (a)
8. (b)	9. (a)	10. (b)	11. (a)			

14

Data Warehousing, OLAP, and Data Mining

1. What are decision-support systems? What are the various tools and techniques that support decision-making activities?

Ans: Decision-support systems (DSS) are systems that aim to extract high-level information stored in traditional databases (such as network, hierarchical, relational and object-oriented), and use that information in making a variety of decisions that are important for the organization. The various tools and techniques that support decision-making activities are data warehousing, online analytical processing (OLAP) and data mining. Data warehouses contain consolidated data from many sources, augmented with summary information, and covering a long time period. OLAP refers to the analysis of complex data from the data warehouse, and data mining refers to the mining or discovery of new information in terms of patterns or rules from a vast amount of data.

2. What is a data warehouse? How does it differ from an OLTP system?

Ans: A **data warehouse (DW)** is a repository of suitable operational data (data that document the everyday operations of an organization) gathered from multiple sources, stored under a unified schema, at a single site. It can successfully answer any ad hoc, complex, statistical or analytical queries. The data once gathered can be stored for a longer period, allowing access to historical data. The data warehouse is more than just data—it is also the process involved in getting that data from various sources to tables and in getting the data from tables to analysts. Data warehouses are different from traditional transaction-processing systems that record information about the day-to-day operations of an organisation. The key differences between a data warehouse and an OLTP system are listed in Table 14.1.

Table 14.1 Differences between data warehouse and OLTP system

Data Warehouse	OLTP System
A data warehouse is mainly designed to handle ad hoc queries.	OLTP systems support only predefined operations like insertion, deletion, updates and retrieval of data.

(Contd...)

Table 14.1 (Contd...)

Data Warehouse	OLTP System
A data warehouse is updated on a regular basis (nightly or weekly) using bulk data modification techniques. This modification is done by extraction, transformation and load (ETL) tools. The end users are not allowed to directly update the data warehouse.	The database of an OLTP system is always up to date, and reflects the current state of each business transaction. The end users are allowed to directly update the database.
A data warehouse generally uses de-normalized or partially de-normalized schemas to optimize query performance.	OLTP systems use fully normalized schemas to optimize insert, delete and update performance.
A typical data warehouse query accesses thousands or millions of records.	A typical query in an OLTP system accesses only a few records at a time.
A data warehouse usually stores data of many months or years to support historical analysis.	OLTP systems usually store data of only a few weeks or months.

3. What is a data mart?

Ans: A **data mart** is a subset of data warehouse that is designed for a particular department of an organization such as sales, marketing or finance.

4. Discuss the basic characteristics of a data warehouse.

Ans: The four basic characteristics of a data warehouse are:

- **Subject oriented**: A data warehouse is organized around a major subject such as customer, products and sales. That is, data are organized according to a subject instead of application. For example, an insurance company using a data warehouse would organize its data by customer, premium and claim instead of by different policies.
- **Nonvolatile:** A data warehouse is always a physically separated store of data. Due to this separation, data warehouse does not require transaction processing, recovery, concurrency control and so on. The data are not overwritten or deleted once they enter the data warehouse, but are only loaded, refreshed and accessed for queries.
- **Time varying:** Data are stored in a data warehouse to provide a historical perspective. Thus, the data in the data warehouse are time-variant or historical in nature.
- **Integrated:** A data warehouse is usually constructed by integrating multiple, heterogeneous sources such as relational databases and flat files. The database contains data from most or all of an organization's operational applications, and these data are made consistent.

5. What are the advantages of using a data warehouse?

Ans: The main advantage of using a data warehouse is that a data analyst can perform complex queries and analyses of the information stored in a data warehouse without affecting the OLTP systems. It has some more advantages, which are as follows:

- It provides historical information that can be used in different forms to perform comparative and competitive analyses.
- It increases the quality of the data and tries to make it complete.
- With the help of other backup resources, it can also help in recovery from disasters.
- It can be used in determining many trends and patterns through the use of data mining.
- The users of a data warehouse can generate high-level information from it by analyzing the data stored in it.

6. Give a schematic representation of the architecture of a data warehouse. Give a brief description of each component of a data warehouse.

Ans: A data warehouse basically consists of three components, namely, the data sources, the ETL process and the metadata repository. The architecture of a typical data warehouse is shown in Figure 14.1.

- **Data sources:** Large companies have various data sources, which include operational databases (databases of the organizations at various sites) and external sources such as Web, purchased data, etc. These data sources may have been constructed independently by different groups and likely to have different schemas. If the companies want to use such diverse data for making business decisions, they need to gather these data under a unified schema for efficient execution of queries.
- **ETL process:** After the schema is designed, the warehouse must acquire data so that it can fulfill the required objectives. Acquisition of data for the warehouse involves the following steps:
  1. The data are **extracted** from multiple, heterogeneous data sources.
  2. The data sources may contain some minor errors or inconsistencies. For example, the names are often misspelled, and street, area or city names in the addresses are misspelled, or zip codes are entered incorrectly. These incorrect data, thus, must be **cleaned** to minimize the errors and fill in the missing information when possible. The task of correcting and preprocessing the data is called **data cleansing**. These errors can be corrected to some reasonable level by looking up a database containing street names and zip codes in each city. The approximate matching of data required for this task is referred to as **fuzzy lookup**. In some cases, the data managers in the organization want to upgrade their data with the cleaned data. This process is known as **backflushing**. These data are then **transformed** to accommodate semantic mismatches.
  3. The cleaned and transformed data is finally **loaded** into the warehouse. Data are partitioned, and indexes or other access paths are built for fast and efficient retrieval of data. Loading is a slow process due to the large volume of data. For instance, loading a terabyte of data sequentially can take weeks and a gigabyte can take hours. Thus, parallelism is important for loading warehouses. The raw data generated by transaction-processing system may be too large to store in a data warehouse; therefore, some data can be stored in the summarized form. Thus, additional preprocessing such as sorting and generation of summarized data is performed at this stage.

This entire process of getting data into the data warehouse is called **extract, transform and load (ETL)** process. Once the data are loaded into a warehouse, it must be periodically **refreshed** to reflect the updates on the relations at the data sources and periodically **purge** old data.

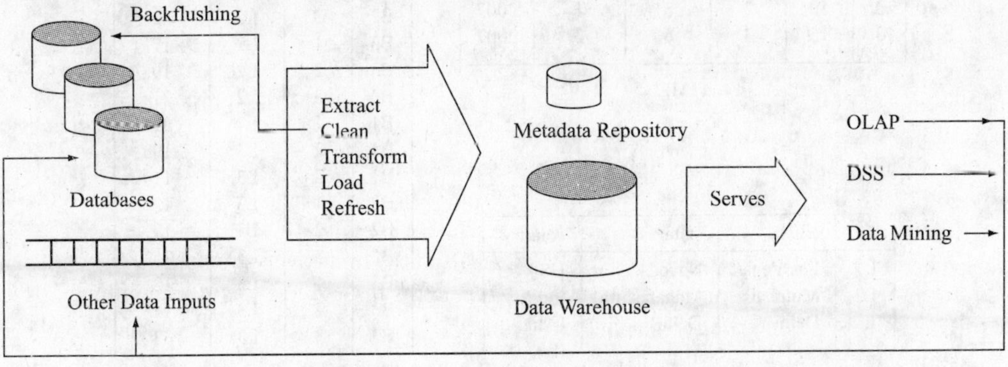

Figure 14.1 Typical Data Warehouse Architecture

- **Metadata repository:** It is the most important component of the data warehouse. It keeps track of currently stored data. It contains the description of the data including its schema definition. The metadata repository includes both technical and business metadata. The **technical metadata** includes the technical details of the warehouse including storage structures, data description, warehouse operations, etc. The **business metadata**, on the other hand, includes the relevant business rules of the organization.

7. Discuss the multidimensional modeling for a data warehouse.

Ans: The data in a warehouse are usually **multidimensional data** having measure attributes and dimension attributes. The attributes that measure some value and can be aggregated upon are called **measure attributes**. On the other hand, the attributes that define the dimensions on which the measure attributes and their summaries are viewed are called **dimension attributes**.

The relations containing such multidimensional data are called **fact tables**. The fact tables contain the primary information in the data warehouse, and thus are very large. Consider a bookshop selling books of different categories such as textbooks, language books and novels, and it maintains an *Online Book* database for its customers so that they can buy books online. The bookshop may have several branches in different locations. The `SALES` relation shown in Figure 14.2 is an example of the fact table that stores the sales information of various books at different locations in different time periods. The attribute `number` is the measure attribute, which describes the number of books sold.

bid	b_title	category	price
B1	C++	Textbook	40
B2	Ransack	Novel	22
B3	Learning French Language	Language book	32

BOOK

tid	date	week	month	quarter	year
1	15	3	12	4	2006
2	10	2	3	1	2007
3	15	3	6	2	2007

TIME

lid	city	state	country
L1	Las Vegas	Naveda	USA
L2	Mumbai	Maharashtra	India
L3	Delhi	Delhi	India

LOCATION

bid	tid	lid	number
B1	1	L1	25
B1	2	L1	18
B1	3	L1	10
B2	1	L1	11
B2	2	L1	12
B2	3	L1	18
B3	1	L1	16
B3	2	L1	10
B3	3	L1	8
B1	1	L2	12
B1	2	L2	10
B1	3	L2	11
B2	1	L2	23
B2	2	L2	9
B2	3	L2	8
B3	1	L2	17
B3	2	L2	19
B3	3	L2	21
B1	1	L3	22
B1	2	L3	19
B1	3	L3	11
B2	1	L3	12
B2	2	L3	17
B2	3	L3	15
B3	1	L3	12
B3	2	L3	14
B3	3	L3	33

SALES

Figure 14.2 Dimension Tables and Fact Tables

Each tuple in the SALES relation gives information about which book is sold, from which location the book was sold, and at what time the book was sold. The dimension attributes bid, tid and lid in the fact tables are the primary keys in other tables called **dimension tables** (or **lookup tables**), which store additional information about the dimensions. For example, the *book* dimension can have the attributes b_title, category and price. Similarly, the *location* dimension can have the attributes city, state, country. The *time* dimension can have the attributes date, week, month, quarter and year. This information about *book*, *location* and *time* is stored in the dimension tables BOOK, LOCATION and TIME, respectively, as shown in Figure 14.2.

8. What are the two ways in which multidimensional data in a data warehouse can be represented?

Ans: The multidimensional data in a data warehouse can be represented either using a *star schema* or a *snowflake schema*. The **star schema** is the simplest data warehouse schema, which consists of a fact table with a single table for each dimension. The centre of the star schema consists of a large fact table and the points of the star are the dimension tables. The star schema for a data warehouse is given in Figure 14.3(a). The **snowflake schema** is a variation of star schema, which may have multiple levels of dimension tables. For example, the attribute Book_title in BOOK relation can be a foreign key in another relation, say, BOOK_DETAILS with an additional attribute Descr that gives details of the book. Similarly, the attribute Quarter in the TIME relation can be a foreign key in another relation, say, QTR_DETAILS with two additional attributes, Beg_date and End_date that give the starting and ending dates of each quarter, respectively. The snowflake schema for our running example is shown in Figure 14.3(b).

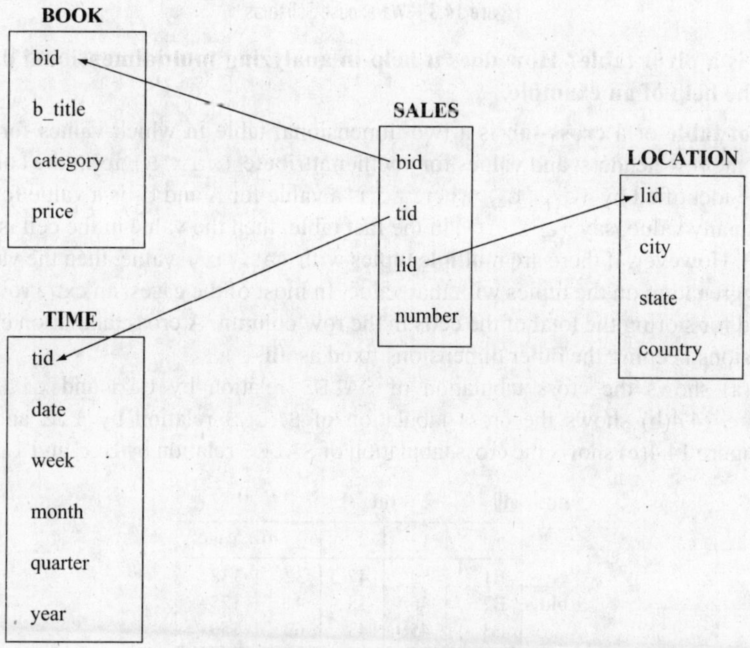

(a) **Star Schema for a Data Warehouse**

Figure 14.3 Warehouse Schemas (Contd...)

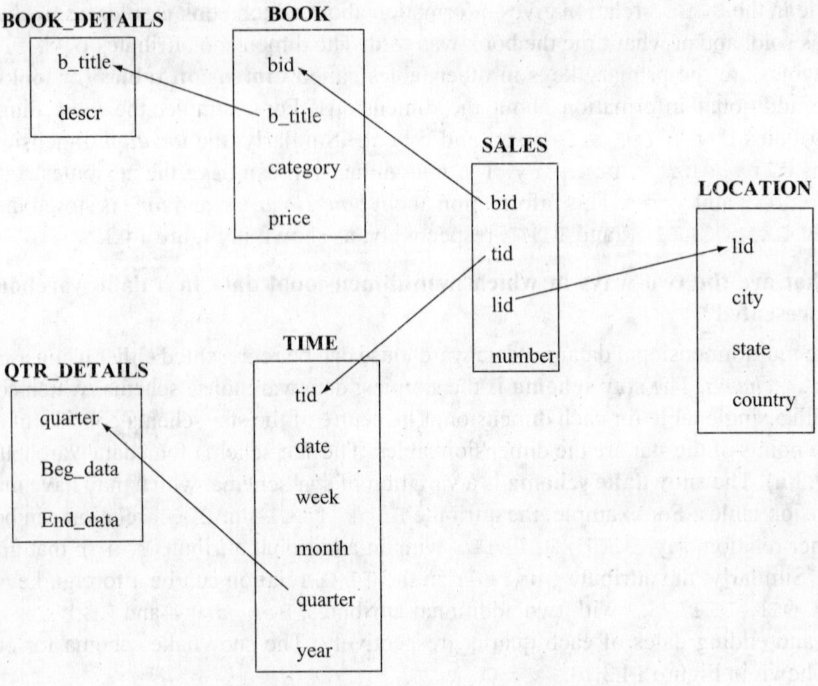

(b) Snowflake Schema for a Data Warehouse

Figure 14.3 Warehouse Schemas

9. What is a pivot table? How does it help in analyzing multidimensional data? Explain with the help of an example.

Ans: A **pivot table** or a **cross-tab** is a two-dimensional table in which values for one attribute `(say A)` form the row headers, and values for another attribute `(say B)` form the column headers. Each cell can be identified by (a_i, b_j) where a_i is a value for A and b_j is a value for B. If there is single tuple with any value, say (a_i, b_j), in the fact table, then the value in the cell is derived from that single tuple. However, if there are multiple tuples with (a_i, b_j) value, then the value in the cell is derived by aggregation on the tuples with that value. In most of the cases, an extra row and an extra column are used for storing the total of the cells in the row/column. A cross tabulation can be done on any two dimensions keeping the other dimensions fixed as **all**.

Figure 14.4(a) shows the cross tabulation of `SALES` relation by `bid` and `tid` for all `lid`. Similarly, Figure 14.4(b) shows the cross tabulation of `SALES` relation by `lid` and `tid` for all `bid`. Finally, Figure 14.4(c) shows the cross tabulation of `SALES` relation by `bid` and `lid` for all `tid`.

lid: all **tid**

		1	2	3	Total
	B1	59	47	32	138
bid	B2	46	38	41	125
	B3	45	43	62	150
	Total	150	128	135	413

(a) Cross Tabulation of `SALES` by `bid` and `tid`

Figure 14.4 Cross Tabulation of `SALES` Relation (Contd...)

bid: all

		tid			
		1	2	3	Total
lid	L1	52	40	36	128
	L2	52	38	40	130
	L3	46	50	59	155
	Total	150	128	135	413

(b) Cross Tabulation of `SALES` by `lid` and `tid`

tid: all

		lid			
		L1	L2	L3	Total
bid	B1	53	33	52	138
	B2	41	40	44	125
	B3	34	57	59	150
	Total	128	130	155	413

(c) Cross Tabulation of `SALES` by `bid` and `lid`

Figure 14.4 Cross Tabulation of `SALES` Relation

10. Write a short note on OLAP. Define data cube in context of the OLAP system. What are the different operations that can be performed on a data cube?

Ans: Online Analytical Processing (OLAP) is a category of software technology that enables analysts, managers and executives to analyze the complex data derived from the data warehouse. The term *online* indicates that the analysts, managers and executives must be able to request new summaries and get the responses online, within a few seconds. OLAP enables data analysts to perform an ad hoc analysis of data in multiple dimensions, thereby providing the insight and understanding they need for better decision making.

In the core of any OLAP system, there is a concept of **data cube** (also called a **multidimensional cube** or **OLAP cube** or **hypercube**), which is the generalization of a 2D cross-tab to `n` dimensions. A three-dimensional data cube on the `SALES` relation is shown in Figure 14.5. In this figure, *book* dimension is shown on the x axis, *time* on the y axis, and *location* on the z axis. The value for a dimension may be **all**, in which case the cell contains a summary over all values of that dimension like a cross tabulation.

Different operations that can be performed on a data cube are given below:

- **Pivoting:** The technique of changing from one-dimensional orientation to another is known as **pivoting** (or **rotation**). The pivoted version of the data cube in Figure 14.5 is shown in Figure 14.6. In this figure, *book* dimension is shown on the x axis, *location* on the y axis and *time* on the z axis.
- **Slice and dice:** The data cube is full of data, and there are many thousands of combinations in which it can be viewed. In case a cross tabulation is done for a specific value other than *all* for the fixed third dimension, it is called **slice** operation or **slicing**. Slicing can be thought of as viewing a slice of the data cube. Slicing is sometimes called **dicing** when two or more dimensions are fixed. Slice and dice operations enable users to see the information that is most meaningful to them and examine it from different viewpoints. For example, an analyst may want to see a cross tab of `SALES` relation on the attributes `bid` and `lid` for `tid=1`, instead of the sum across all time periods. The resultant cross tab is shown in Figure 14.7, which can be thought of as a slice orthogonal to the `tid` axis. In this figure, `tid=1` is displayed on the top of the cross tab instead of **all**.

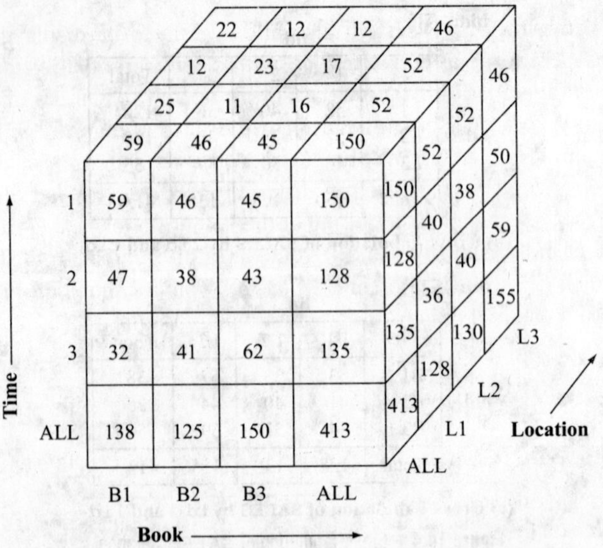

Figure 14.5 Three-dimensional Data Cube for SALES Relation

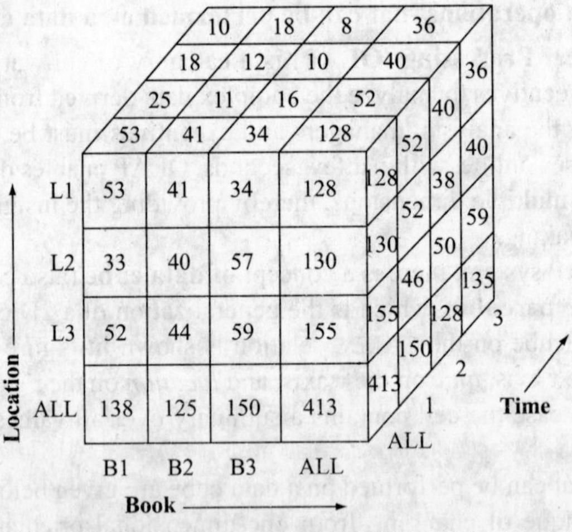

Figure 14.6 Pivoted Version of Data Cube

tid: 1

		lid			
		L1	L2	L3	Total
bid	B1	25	12	22	59
	B2	11	23	12	46
	B3	16	17	12	45
	Total	52	52	46	150

Figure 14.7 Slicing the Cube for `tid=1`

- **Rollup and drill down:** OLAP system also allows data to be displayed at various levels of granularity. The operation that converts data with a finer granularity to the coarser granularity with the help of aggregation is known as **rollup** operation. On the other hand, an operation that converts data with a coarser granularity to the finer granularity is known as **drill down** operation. For example, an analyst may be interested in viewing the sales of books category wise (*textbooks*, *language books* and *novels*) in different countries, instead of looking at individual sales. On the other hand, the analyst looking at the level of books categories may drill down the hierarchy to look at individual sales in different states of each country. The resultant cross tabs after rollup and drill down operations on SALES relation are shown in Figure 14.8. The values are derived from the fact and dimension tables shown in Figure 14.2.

Book Categories	Country: India	USA	Grand Total
Textbook	85	53	138
Language book	84	41	125
Novel	116	34	150
Subtotal	285	128	413

(a) The Rollup Operation

	India: Maharashtra	India: Delhi	USA: Naveda	Grand Total
Textbook	33	52	53	138
Language book	40	44	41	125
Novel	57	59	34	150
Subtotal	130	155	128	413

(b) The Drill Down Operation

Figure 14.8 Applying Rollup and Drill Down Operations on SALES Relation

11. What are the various ways of implementing OLAP?

Ans: There are three ways of implementing the OLAP system. The traditional OLAP systems used multidimensional arrays in memory to store data cubes and, thus, are referred to as **multidimensional OLAP (MOLAP)** systems. The OLAP systems that work directly with relational databases are called **relational OLAP (ROLAP)** systems. In ROLAP systems, the fact tables and dimension tables are stored as relations, and new relations are also created to store the aggregated information. MOLAP systems generally use specialized indexing and storage optimizations and, hence, deliver better performance. MOLAP also needs less storage space compared to ROLAP, because the specialized storage typically includes compression techniques. Moreover, ROLAP relies more on the database to perform calculations; thus, it has more limitations in the specialized functions it can use. However, ROLAP is generally more scalable.

The systems that include the best of ROLAP and MOLAP are known as **hybrid OLAP (HOLAP)**. These systems use the main memory to hold some summaries, and relational tables to hold base data and other summaries. Therefore, it can generally preprocess quickly, scale well, and offer good function support.

12. What is data mining? Why are data in data warehouses more suitable for the data mining process?

Ans: The extraction of hidden and predictive information from large databases is known as **data mining**. Data mining tools predict future trends and behaviours, which allow organizations to make proactive and knowledge-driven decisions.

Some of the reasons for using data of data warehouses for data mining are listed as follows:

- ❑ A data warehouse consists of data from multiple sources. Thus, the data in data warehouse are integrated and subject oriented.
- ❑ In a data warehouse, the data are first extracted, cleaned and transformed before loading, thus, maintaining the consistency of the data.
- ❑ The data in a data warehouse are in a summarized form. Hence, the data mining process can directly use these data without performing any aggregations.
- ❑ A data warehouse also provides the capability of analysing the data by using OLAP operations.

13. Define the term knowledge discovery in databases (KDD). Discuss the different phases of KDD process. What are the types of knowledge discovered during data mining?

Ans: Knowledge discovery in databases (KDD) is the non-trivial extraction of implicit, previously unknown, and potentially useful information from the databases. The process of KDD is divided into six phases that are given as follows:

- ❑ **Data selection or extraction:** The entire raw dataset is examined to identify the target subset of data and the attributes of interest.
- ❑ **Data cleansing or preprocessing:** The data are cleaned to minimize errors and fill in missing information, wherever possible.
- ❑ **Enrichment:** The data are enhanced with additional sources of information.
- ❑ **Data transformation or encoding:** The data are categorized under different groups in terms of categories, ranges, geographical regions and so on. This may be done to reduce the amount of data stored in the database.
- ❑ **Data mining:** The data mining is applied to discover useful patterns and rules.
- ❑ **Interpretation or evaluation:** The patterns are presented to the users in easily understandable and meaningful formats such as listings, graphical outputs, summary tables or visualizations.

The knowledge discovered from the database during data mining includes the following:

- ❑ **Association rules:** Association describes a relationship between a set of items that people tend to buy together. For example, if customers buy two-wheelers, there is a possibility that they also buy some accessories such as seat cover, helmet, gloves, etc. A good salesman, therefore, exploits them to make additional sales. However, our main aim is to automate the process so that the system itself may suggest accessories that tend to be bought along with two-wheelers. The association rules derived during data mining correlate a set of items with another set of items that do not intersect.
- ❑ **Classification:** The goal of classification is to partition the given data into predefined disjoint groups or classes. For example, an insurance company can define the insurance worthiness level of a customer as excellent, good, average or bad depending on the income, age and prior claims experience of the customers.

- **Clustering:** The task of clustering is to group the data into set of similar elements so that similar elements belong to the same class. The principle of clustering is to maximize intra-class similarity and minimize the inter-class similarity.

14. What are association rules in the context of data mining? Describe the terms support and confidence with the help of suitable examples.

Ans: **Association** describes a relationship between a set of items that people tend to buy together. For example, if customers buy two-wheelers, there is a possibility that they also buy some accessories such as seat cover, helmet, gloves, etc. Discovery of association rules is one of the major tasks involved in data mining. The task of mining association rules is to find an interesting relationship among various items in a given dataset. Consider some examples of associations given below:

- A person who buys a mobile is also likely to buy some accessories such as mobile cover, hands free, etc.
- A person who buys bread is also likely to buy butter and jam.
- Someone who buys eggs is also likely to buy bread.
- Someone who bought the book *Data Structure using C* is also likely to buy *Programming in C*.

An association rule has a form X ⇒ Y, where X=$\{x_1, x_2, \ldots, x_n\}$ and Y=$\{y_1, y_2, \ldots, y_n\}$ are the disjoint sets of items, that is, X∩Y=∅. It states that if a person buys an item X, he or she is likely to buy an item Y. The set X ∪ Y is called an **itemset**—a set of items a customer tends to buy together. The item X is called the **antecedent**, while Y is called the **consequent** of the rule. An example of the association rule is

mobile ⇒ mobile cover, hands free

For an association rule to be of interest to an analyst, the rule should satisfy two interest measures, namely, *support* and *confidence*.

- **Support** (also known as **prevalence**): It is the percentage or fraction of the population that satisfies both the antecedent and consequent of the rule. If the support is low, it implies that there is no strong evidence that the items in the itemset X ∪ Y are bought together. For example, suppose only 0.002% of the customers buy mobile and chocolates; thus, the support for the rule *mobile ⇒ chocolates* is low.
- **Confidence** (also known as **strength**): It is the probability that a customer will buy the items in the set Y if he or she purchases the items in the set X. It is computed as

support(X ∪ Y)/support(X)

For example, the association rule *mobile ⇒ mobile cover* has the confidence of 80% if 80% of the purchases that include mobile also include mobile cover.

15. What do you mean by large itemsets? Discuss the apriori algorithm for generating large itemsets. Apply this algorithm for generating a large itemset on the following dataset:

Transaction ID	Items Purchased
T1	1, 3, 4
T4	2, 3, 5
T10	1, 2, 3, 5
T20	2, 5

Also discuss the algorithm for generating association rules with the help of an example.

Ans: The itemsets that have support above the minimum prespecified support are known as **large** (or **frequent**) **itemsets.**

Apriori algorithm uses the downward closure property, which states that each subset of a large itemset must also be large. It takes a database `D` of `t` transactions and minimum support, `minSup`, represented as a fraction of `t`, as input. Apriori algorithm generates all possible large itemsets L_1, L_2, ..., L_k as output. The algorithm is shown in Figure14.9. The algorithm proceeds iteratively. In the first pass, only the sets with single items are considered for generating large itemsets. This itemset is referred to as large 1-itemsets (itemset with one item). In each subsequent pass, large itemsets identified in the previous pass are extended with another item to generate larger itemsets. Therefore, the second pass considers only sets with two items, and so on. Thus, by considering only the itemsets obtained by extending the large itemsets, we reduce the number of candidate large itemsets. The algorithm terminates after *k* passes, if no large *k*-itemsets is found.

```
Step 1: k = 1;
Step 2: Find large itemset Lk from Ck;      //Ck is the set of all
                                            //candidate itemsets
Step 3: Form Ck+1 from Lk;
Step 4: k = k+1;
Step 5: Repeat steps 2, 3, and 4 until Ck is empty;
```

Figure 14.9 Apriori Algorithm

Step 2 is called the large itemset generation step and Step 3 is called the candidate itemset generation step. The details about Steps 2 and 3 are explained in Figure 14.10.

Step 2: Large itemset generation

```
Step 2a: Scan the database D and count each itemset in Ck;
Step 2b: If the count is greater than minSup then
              add that itemset to Lk;
```

Step 3: Candidate itemset generation

```
Step 3a: For k = 1, C1 = all itemsets of length 1;
         For k > 1, generate Ck from Lk-1 as follows:
       The join step:
            Ck = k-2 way join of Lk-1 with itself;
            If both {I1,..,Ik-2, Ik-1} and {I1,.., Ik-2, Ik} are in
            Lk-1 then
                  add {I1,..,Ik-2, Ik-1, Ik} to Ck;
       //assuming that the items I1,...,Ik are always sorted
       The prune step:
            Remove {I1, …,Ik-2, Ik-1, Ik}, if it does not contain
            a large (k-1) subset;
```

Figure 14.10 Details of Steps 2 and 3 of Apriori Algorithm

Consider the given dataset. Let the value of `minSup` be 50%, that is, the item in the candidate set should be included in at least two transactions. In the first pass, the database `D` is scanned to find the candidate itemset C_1 from which large 1-itemset L_1 is produced. Since the support for itemset {4} is less than the `minSup`, it is not included in L_1. In the second pass, candidate itemset C_2 is generated from L_1, which consists of {1,2}, {1,3}, {1,5}, {2,3}, {2,5} and {3,5}. Then the database D is scanned to find the support for these itemsets and produce large 2-itemsets L_2. Since the support for itemsets {1, 2} and {1, 5} is less than the `minSup`, they are not included in L_2. In the third pass, candidate itemset C_3 is generated from L_2, which includes {2,3,5}. The database D is again scanned to find the support for this itemset and produce large 3-itemsets L_3, which is the desired large itemset.

Database D

Transaction_ID	Items
T1	1 3 4
T4	2 3 5
T10	1 2 3 5
T20	2 5

Scan D → C_1

Itemset	Support
{1}	2
{2}	3
{3}	3
{4}	1
{5}	3

({4}: less than minSup) → L_1

Itemset	Support
{1}	2
{2}	3
{3}	3
{5}	3

C_2

Itemset	Support
{1,2}	1
{1,3}	2
{1,5}	1
{2,3}	2
{2,5}	3
{3,5}	2

({1,2}: less than minSup; {1,5}: less than minSup) → L_2

Itemset	Support
{1,3}	2
{2,3}	2
{2,5}	3
{3,5}	2

C_3

Itemset	Support
{2,3,5}	2

L_3

Itemset	Support
{2,3,5}	2

desired large itemset

Figure 14.11 Generating Large ItemSets on the Given DataSet

Once the large itemsets are identified, the next step is to generate all possible association rules. Association rules can be found from every large itemset L with the help of another algorithm shown in Figure 14.12.

For example, consider the large itemset L ={2, 3, 5} generated earlier with support 50%. Proper non-empty subsets of L are: {2, 3}, {2, 5}, {3, 5}, {2}, {3}, {5} with supports = 50%, 75%, 50%, 75%, 75% and 75%, respectively. The association rules from these subsets are given in Table 14.2.

```
For every non-empty subset S of L
Find B = L - A.
A ⇒ B is an association rule if
    confidence(A ⇒ B)>=minConf
                //confidence(A ⇒ B)=support(A∪B)/
support(A)
```

Figure 14.12 An Algorithm for Finding Association Rules

Table 14.2 Set of association rules

Association Rule A ⇒ B	Confidence Support(A ∪ B)/Support(A)
{2, 3} ⇒ {5}	50% / 50% = 100%
{2, 5} ⇒ {3}	50% / 75% = 66.67%
{3, 5} ⇒ {2}	50% / 50% = 100%
{2} ⇒ {3, 5}	50% / 75% = 66.67%
{3} ⇒ {2, 5}	50% / 75% = 66.67%
{5} ⇒ {2, 3}	50% / 75% = 66.67%

16. What is classification in context of data mining? Why is it called supervised learning? Explain decision tree classification with the help of an example.

Ans: Classification refers to partitioning the given data into predefined disjoint groups or classes. The task of classification is to predict the class of a new item; given that items belong to one of the classes, and given past instances (known as **training instances**) of items along with the classes to which they belong. For example, consider an insurance company that wants to decide whether or not to provide insurance facility to a new customer. The company maintains records of its existing customers, which may include name, address, gender, income, age, types of policies purchased and prior claims experience. Some of this information may be used by the insurance company to define the insurance worthiness level of the new customers. For instance, the company may assign the insurance worthiness level of excellent, good, average or bad to its customers depending on the prior claims experience. New customers cannot be classified on the basis of prior claims experience as this information is unavailable for new customers. Therefore, the company attempts to find some rules that classify its current customers on the basis of the attributes other than the prior claim experience. Consider four such rules that are based on two attributes, age and income.

Rule 1: ∀*customer C, C.age<30 and C.income<=30,000* ⇒ *C.insurance=bad*

Rule 2: ∀*customer C, C.age≥30 and C.age<50 and C.income>75,000* ⇒ *C.insurance=excellent*

Rule 3: ∀*customer C, (C.age≥50 and C.age≤60) and (C.income≥30,000 and C.income≤75,000)* ⇒ C.insurance=good

Rule 4: ∀*customer C, C.age>60 and C.income>30,000* ⇒ *C.insurance=average*

This type of activity is known as **supervised learning** since the partitions are done on the basis of the training instances that are already partitioned into predefined classes. The actual data, or the population, may consist of all new and the existing customers of the company.

A **decision tree** (also known as **classification tree**) is a graphical representation of the classification rules. Each internal node of the decision tree is labelled with an attribute A_i. Each arc is labelled with the predicate (or condition) which can be applied to the attribute at the parent node. Each leaf node is labelled with one of the predefined classes. Therefore, each internal node is associated with a predicate and each leaf node is associated with a class. An example of a decision tree is shown in Figure 14.13.

In this figure, the attribute *age* is chosen as a partitioning attribute, and four child nodes—one for each partitioning predicate 0-30, 30-50, 50–60 and over 60—are created. For all these child nodes, the attribute *income* is chosen to further partition the training instances belonging to each child node. Depending on the value of the income, a class is associated with customer. For example, if the age of the customer is between 50 and 60, and his income is greater than 75,000, then the class associated with him is "excellent".

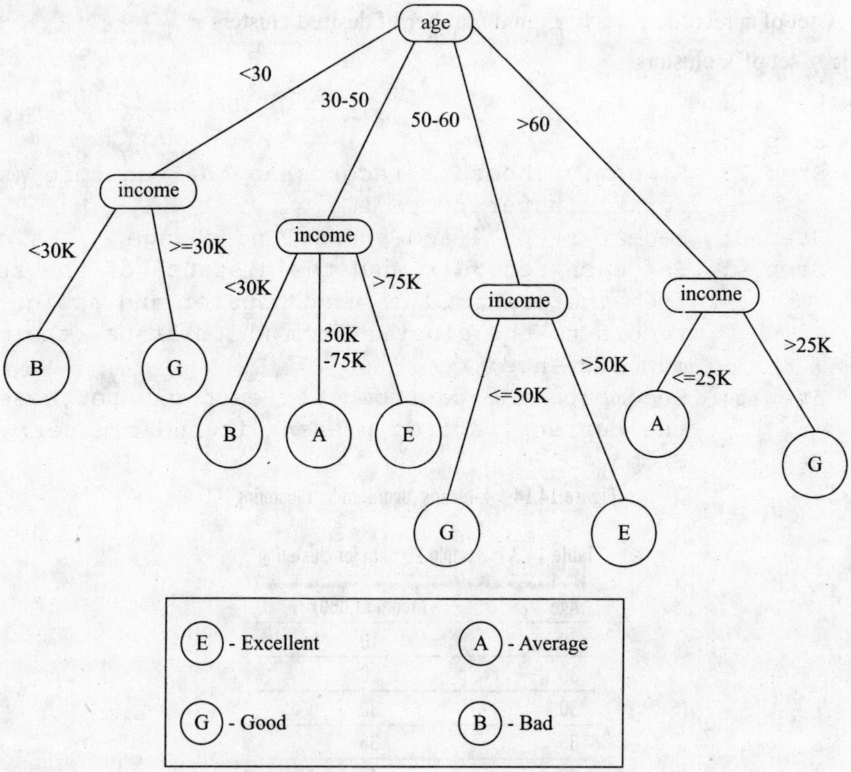

Figure 14.13 An example of a Decision Tree

17. What is clustering? How is it different from classification? Discuss the *k*-means algorithm for clustering with the help of an example.

Ans: The process of grouping the records together so that the degree of association is strong between the records of the same group and weak between the records of different groups is known as **clustering**. Unlike classification, clustering is **unsupervised learning** as no training sample is available to guide partitioning. The groups created in this case are also disjoint. Grouping of customers on the basis of similar buying patterns, grouping of students in a class on the basis of grades (A, B, C, D, E or F), etc., are some of the common examples of clustering.

The most commonly used algorithm for clustering is *k*-means algorithm, where *k* is the number of desired clusters, is shown in Figure 14.14.

Consider a sample of 2D records shown in Table 14.3. Assume that the number of desired clusters *k*=2. The centroid (mean) of a cluster C_i containing *m* *n*-dimensional records can be calculated as follows:

$$\overline{C_i} = \left(\frac{1}{m} \sum_{\forall r_j \in C_i} r_{ji}, \ldots, \frac{1}{m} \sum_{\forall r_j \in C_i} r_{jn} \right)$$

Input: A set of m records $r_1, \ldots, r_m$ and number of desired clusters k

Output: A set of k clusters

Process:

```
Step 1:  Start
Step 2:  Randomly choose k records as the centroid (mean)
         for k clusters;
Step 3:  Repeat steps 4 and 5 until no change
Step 4:  For each record ri find the distance of the record
         from the centroid of each cluster and assign that
         record to the cluster from which it has the mini-
         mum distance;
Step 5:  Recompute the centroid for each cluster based on
         the current records present in the cluster;
Step 6:  Stop
```

Figure 14.14 k-means Algorithm for Clustering

Table 14.3 Sample 2D data for clustering

Age	Income (,000)
20	10
30	20
30	30
35	35
40	40
50	45

Step 1: Let the algorithm randomly choose record 2 for cluster C_1 and record 5 for cluster C_2. Thus, the centroid for C_1 is (30, 20) and C_2 is (40, 40).

Step 2: Calculate the distance of the remaining records from the centroid of both C_1 and C_2, and assign the record to the cluster from which it has the minimum distance as shown in Table 14.4. The distance between two n-dimensional records (records with n attributes) r_i and r_j can be computed as follows:

$$D(r_i, r_j) = \sqrt{\left|r_{i1} - r_{j1}\right|^2 + \left|r_{i2} - r_{j2}\right|^2 + \ldots + \left|r_{in} - r_{jn}\right|^2}$$

Table 14.4 Distance of records from centroids of C_1 and C_2

Record	Distance from C_1	Distance from C_2	Cluster Selected
1	14.14	36.05	C_1
3	18.02	14.14	C_2
4	14.81	7.07	C_2
6	32.01	11.18	C_2

Now, records 1 and 2 are assigned to cluster C_1 and records 3, 4, 5 and 6 are assigned to cluster C_2.

Step 3: Recompute the centroid of both the clusters. The new centroid for C_1 is (25, 15) and for C_2 is (38.75, 37.5). Again calculate the distance of all six records from the new centroid and assign the records to the appropriate cluster as shown in Table 14.5.

Table 14.5 Distance of all six records from new centroids of C_1 and C_2

Record	Distance from C_1	Distance from C_2	Cluster Selected
1	7.07	33.28	C_1
2	7.07	19.56	C_1
3	14.81	11.52	C_2
4	22.36	4.51	C_2
5	29.15	2.80	C_2
6	39.05	13.52	C_2

After Step 3, records 1 and 2 are assigned to cluster C_1 and records 3, 4, 5 and 6 are assigned to cluster C_2. Since after Step 3, the records remain in the same cluster as they were in Step 2, the algorithm terminates after this step.

18. What are the various applications of data mining?

Ans: The various applications of data mining technology are as follows:

- **Market-basket analysis:** Companies can analyze the customer behaviour based on their buying patterns, and may launch products according to the customer needs. The companies can also decide their marketing strategies such as advertising, store location, etc. They can also segment their customers, stores or products based on the data discovered after data mining.
- **Investment analysis:** Customers can also look at the areas such as stocks, bonds and mutual funds where they can invest their money to get good returns.
- **Fraud detection:** By finding the association between frauds, new frauds can be detected using data mining.
- **Manufacturing:** Companies can optimize their resources like machines, manpower and materials by applying data mining technologies.
- **Credit risk analysis:** Given a set of customers and an assessment of their credit worthiness, descriptions for various classes can be developed. These descriptions can be used to classify a new customer into one of the classes.

Multiple-choice Questions

1. Which of the following is not a basic characteristic of a data warehouse?
   (a) Subject oriented (b) Volatile (c) Time varying (d) Integrated
2. Which of the following statements is incorrect for a data warehouse?
   (a) A data warehouse is mainly designed to handle ad hoc queries
   (b) Data warehouses generally use denormalized or partially denormalized schemas to optimized query performance
   (c) A data warehouse is always up to date, and reflects the current state of each business transaction.
   (d) None of these

3. The OLTP systems use __________ schemas to optimize query performance.
   (a) Denormalized (b) Fully normalized
   (c) Partially normalized (d) None of these
4. Which of the following is a basic component of a data warehouse?
   (a) Data sources (b) ETL process
   (c) Metadata repository (d) All of these
5. Which of the following tables contain the primary information in the data warehouse?
   (a) Primary table (b) Dimension table (c) Fact table (d) Lookup table
6. The technique of changing from one-dimensional orientation to another is known as __________.
   (a) Pivoting (b) Slicing (c) Dicing (d) Drill down
7. Which of the following OLAP systems work directly with relational databases?
   (a) HOLAP (b) ROLAP (c) MOLAP (d) None of these
8. Which of the following is not a part of the KDD process?
   (a) Data selection (b) Data cleansing (c) Enrichment (d) Data warehousing
9. The percentage or fraction of the population that satisfies both the antecedent and consequent of the rule is known as __________.
   (a) Support (b) Population (c) Confidence (d) Instance
10. Which of the following techniques is used for classification during data mining?
    (a) Apriori algorithm (b) *k*-means algorithm (c) Decision tree (d) Any of these
11. Which of the following is an application area of data mining?
    (a) Market-basket analysis (b) Fraud detection
    (c) Investment analysis (d) All of these
12. The old data that has already been classified by using the domain of the experts' knowledge is known as __________.
    (a) Training instances (b) Training set (c) Data mining (d) Partitioning attribute

Answers

1. (b)	2. (c)	3. (b)	4. (d)	5. (c)	6. (a)	7. (b)
8. (d)	9. (a)	10. (c)	11. (d)	12. (b)		

15

Information Retrieval

1. What is information retrieval (IR)? Differentiate between database system and IR system.

Ans: The process of extracting information from unstructured textual data is referred to as **information retrieval** (IR). The process of information retrieval consists of locating relevant documents based on user inputs. The users of IR systems request to retrieve a particular set of documents by providing a set of words (keywords).

Table 15.1 Differences between database system and IR system

Database System	IR System
Data in database system are rigidly structured and support searching based on a very general class of queries.	IR system deals with unstructured data and supports approximate searching based on the keywords.
It supports the notion of transaction and its associated requirements, such as concurrency control and durability.	Notion of transaction is less significant in IR systems and it is mainly designed to handle read-mostly workload.
Database systems do not order the search result in terms of its relevance to the query.	Ranking of search documents in terms of their relevance to the keyword is the main feature of the IR system.

2. Explain how documents are represented by using the vector space model with the help of suitable example. What are the limitations of this model?

Ans: One of the most widely used model for document representation is the *vector space model*. In this model, each document is transformed from full text version to a document vector, which describes the contents of the document. Each word that appears in the collection of documents corresponds to a dimension in the vector, and each document is represented as a vector with one entry per word.

For instance, if a given word *t* appears *n* times in a document *d*, the vector for document *d* contains value *n* in position *t*. The document vector for any document *d* contains a non-zero value for the word that appears in *d*.

Consider a set of text documents shown in Figure 15.1. Each document in the set can be represented as a document vector, which is shown in Figure 15.2. In this representation, each row corresponds to a document and each dimension corresponds to a term in the collection of documents. Such a vector representation of the documents is called a **vector space model**.

ID	Document Contents
A	computer keyboard mouse memory mobile
B	keyboard language memory device driver
C	mouse CPU keyboard mobile mouse

Figure 15.1 Text Documents with Some Records

ID	computer	CPU	device	driver	keyboard	language	memory	mobile	mouse
A	1	0	0	0	1	0	1	1	1
B	0	0	1	1	1	1	1	0	0
C	0	1	0	0	1	0	0	1	2

Figure 15.2 An Example of Document Vector

Limitations of the vector space model

- Representation of long documents is poor because of their poor similarity values.
- Similar context documents having different term vocabulary cannot be associated.
- The order of term appearance in the document is lost in this representation.

3. Discuss TF/IDF-based ranking.

Ans: In the document vector, the value for a term is the number of occurrences of that word in the document or simply the **term frequency (TF)**. It gives the impression that higher the TF, more relevant the document is. However, just counting the number of occurrences is not a good idea. It is because some words appear more frequently in the document than other words. Secondly, the number of occurrences also depends on the length of the document.

However, TF can be used to measure the relevance R of a document *d* to a given term *t* using the following formula:

$$R(d, t) = \log(1 + a(d, t)/a(d))$$

where $a(d, t)$ represents TF (the number of times term *t* appears in the document *d*) and $a(d)$ represents the total number of terms in the documents. The relevance of document $R(d, t)$ increases with TF. However, it is not directly proportional to TF because the formula takes the document length into account.

Some common words that appear in almost all the documents are not very useful in searches. For instance, all textual documents in English contain words such as '*a*', '*an*', '*the*', '*and*' and so on. A set of these most common words, called **stop words**, are defined by IR systems, and documents are pre-processed to ignore these words while searching.

Even after ignoring stop words, all the terms used as keywords are not equally significant. This is because some terms appear more frequently than others in the set of documents. Suppose a query contains two terms "MBA" and "course". It is likely to have much more frequency of occurrence of term "course" than "MBA". To get better results, we should give more importance to the term "MBA" than the term "course".

This can be achieved by assigning weights to terms in the document vector by using the **inverse document frequency (IDF)**. The IDF of a term *t* is defined as $1/a(t)$, where $a(t)$ represents the total number of documents that contains term *t*. The relevance of a document *d* to a query *Q* is defined as

$$R(d, Q) = \sum_{t \in Q} a(d, t) * \text{IDF}(t)$$

This approach of using term frequency and inverse document frequency as a measure of the relevance of a document is called TF/IDF approach.

4. Discuss similarity-based retrieval.

Ans: **Similarity-based retrieval** allows users to retrieve documents that are similar to a given document d. Similarity between two documents may be defined on the basis of common terms. A set of n terms in the document d with highest values of a(d, t)* IDF(t) are used as a query to find other relevant documents. The document that is most similar to the query is ranked highest.

Consider *n* terms $t_1, t_2, \ldots, t_n$ that appear in the collection of documents. The document vector for the document collection can be visualized as an *n*-dimensional space, in which each dimension corresponds to a term. Any document *d* is represented by a point in this space, with the value of jth coordinate of the point being $R(d, t_j)$. For a two-dimensional space, Figure 15.3 shows document vector for two documents d_1 and d_2, along with a query *Q*.

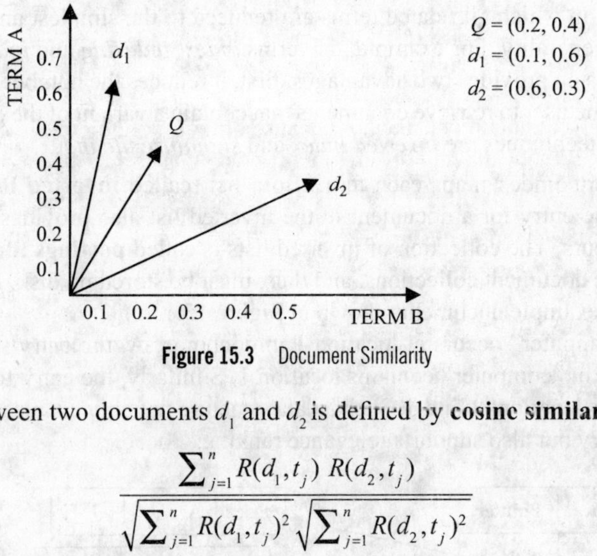

Figure 15.3 Document Similarity

The similarity between two documents d_1 and d_2 is defined by **cosine similarity** metric as

$$\frac{\sum_{j=1}^{n} R(d_1,t_j)\, R(d_2,t_j)}{\sqrt{\sum_{j=1}^{n} R(d_1,t_j)^2}\sqrt{\sum_{j=1}^{n} R(d_2,t_j)^2}}$$

where $R(d, t) = A(d, t) * \mathrm{IDF}(t)$. Note that the metric derives its name "cosine similarity" from the fact that it computes the cosine of the angle between two vectors, each of which represents a document.

5. Define the term relevance feedback.

Ans: If the system finds a large set of documents that are similar to the query document *d*, it may present only a few highest ranked documents, and allow the user to select the most relevant few. After this, the system starts searching documents that are similar to *d and* to the selected documents. The set of documents returned by the system is likely to be what the user is looking for. This scheme of searching is called **relevance feedback**. This scheme can also be used to find relevant documents from a large set of documents that match the given query keywords.

6. How will you measure the performance of IR systems?

Ans: The performance of anIR system is evaluated in order to determine the accuracy or quality of the retrieved result. The two widely used measures for evaluating the performance of IR systems are *recall* and *precision*. **Precision** is defined as the percentage of retrieved documents that are relevant to the query. **Recall** is defined as the percentage of relevant documents in the database, which are retrieved in response to the query.

In information retrieval, a perfect recall of 100% means that every relevant document is retrieved but it does not guarantee that irrelevant documents are not retrieved. On the other hand, a perfect precision of 100% means that every retrieved document is relevant but it does not guarantee that all relevant documents are retrieved.

Often, there is an inverse relationship between recall and precision. It means that it is possible to increase one at the cost of other. Generally, it is relatively easy for an IR system to achieve either high recall or high precision; however, it is challenging to achieve both.

7. What is the importance of indexing? Explain various indexing techniques.

Ans: Efficient index structure plays an important role in efficient processing of queries in an IR system. The size of the index depends on the number of terms in the document collection. Thus, documents are pre-processed to eliminate irrelevant terms such as stop words. In addition, IR system may also apply **stemming**, in which all related terms are reduced to the simplest and the most significant form without loss of generality. For example, the terms *index*, *indexing* and *indexed* stem to the simplest term *index*. This step provides two advantages, first, it reduces the number of terms for indexing, and second, it allows the user to retrieve documents that contain a variant of the exact query term. Two widely used indexing techniques are *inverted index* and *signature file index*.

Inverted index: Invertedindex maps each term *t* to a list (called **inverted list**) of documents that contain the term *t*. The entry for a document in the inverted list also provides a location within the document where *t* occurs. The collection of inverted lists is called **postings file**. An inverted list can be very large for large document collections, and thus, must be stored on disk. Figure 15.4 shows the inverted index of our example documents shown in Figure 15.1.

Since the term "computer" occurs at location 1 in document A, the entry for document A in the inverted list for the term "computer" contains location 1. Similarly, the entry for document C for the term "mouse" contains locations 1 and 4. Such a data structure not only enables fast retrieval of documents for a given query but also supports relevance ranking.

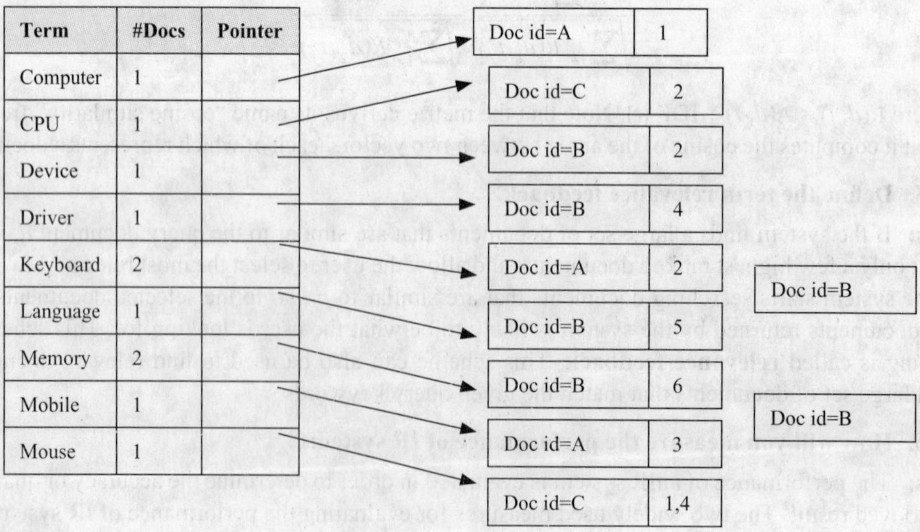

Figure 15.4 An Example of Inverted Index

To quickly find the inverted list for a given query keyword, a second index structure such as B^+ tree or hash index is created for all the possible keywords. This index, called the **lexicon**, not only contains the address of inverted lists on disks, but it may also contain some additional information such as the number of documents in which the term occurs, etc. Lexicon is much smaller than the postings file, and is kept in the memory. Thus, it enables quick retrieval of the inverted list for a given query term.

Signature files: In this technique, each document is associated with an index record called **signature** of the document. Each signature is represented by a fixed size of bits called **signature width**. To calculate the signature of a document, first the hash value of each word in the document is calculated by applying a hash function. A hash function may group different words to same buckets. For instance, suppose a hash function is applied on each word in the set of documents as shown in Figure 15.1, and the hash values we get for each word is shown in Figure 15.5.

Word	Hash Value
computer device	0001
CPU driver	0010
keyboard language mobile	0100
mouse memory	1000

Figure 15.5 Words with Hash Value

For each word in the document, we set the bits in the signature that are set in the hash value of the word. Signature file for the set of documents is shown in Figure 15.6.

ID	Document Contents	Signature
A	computer keyboard mouse memory mobile	1101
B	keyboard language memory device driver	1111
C	mouse CPU keyboard mobile mouse	1110

Figure 15.6 An Example of Signature File

Since the signature does not uniquely identify the words contained in a document, all the retrieved documents must be checked to determine whether they actually contain the required words.

8. Explain the working of a Web search engine.

Ans: Web search engines are designed to locate information on the World Wide Web. Web search engines **crawl** the Web to locate and gather information found in the documents to a combined index. Crawling consists of several processes that run on multiple machines. Crawling starts at a collection of pages with many hyperlinks. These hyperlinks are followed to find new pages. All the hyperlinks that are to be visited are stored in a database. The new hyperlinks found during a crawl are inserted into the database, and may be assigned to another crawler program, or may be visited later. All the pages found during a crawl are given to an **indexing system**, which creates inverted lists for the terms that occur in the document. The process is iterated, keeping track of the hyperlinks that have been visited to avoid re-visiting them in a single crawl. Since, the process retrieves enormous amount of pages, creating an index of them is an expensive task. This task is parallelizable, so indexing systems run on multiple machines in parallel.

To keep the index up to date, the pages are re-fetched periodically to obtain the updated information. Pages of new launched sites are added in the index, and the sites that no longer exist are discarded. Generally, two copies of index are maintained—one is used to handle queries and another is updated by adding new pages. The two copies are switched over periodically; with the old one being updated and the new one being used to handle queries.

9. What is a Web page? Discuss its two types.

Ans: A Web page is a collection of hyperlinked documents. Web pages are classified into two types, *hubs* and *authorities*. The **hub** is a page that itself may not contain the actual information on a topic, but stores links to many related pages that contain actual information. On the other hand, **authority** is a page that contains actual information on a topic; however, it may not contain links to other related pages.

10. Briefly discuss link-based search algorithm, the HITS algorithm.

Ans: The **HITS algorithm**, a link-based algorithm retrieves highly relevant pages in response to a given query. The algorithm represents the Web as a directed graph with each node corresponding to a Web page. If there is a hyperlink from page *X* to page *Y*, there exists an edge in the graph between the two corresponding nodes. This algorithm proceeds in two steps, namely, *sampling step* and *iteration step*. In the **sampling step**, the algorithm collects the pages that are most relevant to the given query using some traditional method. For instance, all the Web pages that contain the occurrence of query terms are collected. The resulting set of pages is called the **root set**. Since some relevant authoritative pages may not contain the query words, the root set may not contain all the relevant pages. However, it may be the case that some pages in the root set contain hyperlinks to those relevant authoritative pages or that some of those authoritative pages have hyperlinks to pages in the root set. Such a page is called a **link page**, if it is linked to some pages in the root set. All link pages are added in the root set to collect all the potentially relevant pages. The resultant set of pages is called the **base set**, which includes all the root pages and all the link pages. A Web page in the base set is referred to as **base page**.

Since, the base set can be quite large, each base page is associated with a hub-prestige value and an authority-prestige value. Hub-prestige value indicates the quality of the page as a hub, and the authority-prestige value indicates the quality of the page as an authority. A hub is considered a good hub and assigned higher hub-prestige value if it stores hyperlinks to many pages with high authority-prestige value. On the other hand, an authority is considered a good authority and is assigned higher authority-prestige value if many good hubs have link to it. The pages with good authority-prestige value and hub-prestige value among the base pages are located in the **iteration step.**

Initially we do not know which pages are good hubs and authorities, so all the values are assigned to one. Later, authority-prestige and hub-prestige values are updated iteratively. Rather taking into account the words that occur in the base page, the iteration step is concerned with the hyperlinks that the base pages store.

For instance, consider a page *b* in the base set with authority-prestige value V_a and hub-prestige value V_h. In each iteration, the value V_a is updated to the sum of V_h of all the pages that have a link to *b*. On the other hand, the value V_h is updated to the sum of V_a of all the pages that are pointed to by *b*.

Multiple-choice Questions

1. The user of IR systems requests to retrieve a particular set of documents by providing ________.
   (a) Keywords (b) Index (c) Vector (d) None of these
2. Which of the following is incorrect?
   (a) Database system deals with unstructured data.
   (b) Database system supports the notion of transaction.
   (c) Database system orders the search result according to its relevance to query.
   (d) Both (a) and (c)
3. A query containing keywords without any of the logical connectives is assumed to have ________ implicitly.
   (a) Or (b) And (c) Not (d) Both (a) and (c)
4. The vector space model is widely used for ________.
   (a) Information retrievall (b) Indexing
   (c) Relevance ranking (d) All of these
5. In TF/IDF approach, which of the following term is used as a measure of relevance of document?
   (a) Term frequency (b) Inverse document frequency
   (c) Both (a) and (b) (d) None of these
6. Which of the following should be ignored while searching documents?
   (a) Keywords (b) Term (c) Stop words (d) Term frequency
7. Which of these statements is correct with reference to the information retrieval system?
   (a) Two widely used indexing techniques in the IR system are the inverted index and the signature file index.
   (b) The collection of inverted lists is called postings file.
   (c) Two copies of index are maintained—one is used to handle queries and the other is updated by adding new pages.
   (d) All of these
8. The HITS algorithm involves ________.
   (a) Sampling step (b) Iteration step (c) Both (a) and (b) (d) None of these
9. The pages with good authority-prestige value and hub-prestige value among the base pages are located in the ________.
   (a) Sampling step (b) Iteration step (c) Root set (d) None of these
10. A Web page in the base set is referred to as the ________.
   (a) Base page (b) Root page (c) Link page (d) None of these

Answers

1. (a) 2. (d) 3. (b) 4. (d) 5. (c) 6. (c) 7. (d)
8. (c) 9. (b) 10. (a)

16

Miscellaneous Questions

1. Write a short note on PostgreSQL. Discuss its various features.

Ans: PostgreSQL is the most advanced and widely used open source object-relational database system. It comes with a BSD license that allows everyone to use, modify and distribute its code and documentation for any purpose without any charge. The current version of PostgreSQL is fully ACID compliant and has full support for foreign keys, joins, triggers, views, stored procedures, multiversion concurrency control and write ahead logging. It includes most of the SQL92 and SQL99 data types and allows users to define new data types also. In addition, it has interfaces for many programming languages like C, C++, Java, Perl, and Python and it runs on almost all the major operating systems including Linux, UNIX, Solaris, Apple Macintosh OS X and Windows.

PostgreSQL is highly scalable in terms of the number of concurrent users it can handle and the amount of data it can manage. It supports database of virtually any size, and a table in PostgreSQL can contain any number of rows. However, there is an upper limit on the size of a table (32 TB), row (1.6TB) and field (1GB). PostgreSQL employs a client/server architecture in which clients send their requests to the server, which processes the requests and returns the result back to the client.

Features of PostgreSQL

PostgreSQL is rich in features that an organization looks for in a database system. The data types in PostgreSQL include integer, numeric, Boolean, date, varchar, etc., and it also allows defining new types as per the needs of specific applications. To maintain data integrity, PostgreSQL allows applying SQL constraints such as unique, primary key, foreign key with restricting and cascading updates/deletes, check and not null. It also supports triggers, which are executed automatically as a result of SQL DML statements. Some additional features of PostgreSQL are as follows:

- **Extensibility**: Since the source code of PostgreSQL is available (without any cost) under the BSD license, staff of any organization can extend the features of PostgreSQL as well as add new features to it to meet their needs.
- **Cross-platform**: PostgreSQL is available for almost all the major operating systems. Though earlier versions were made Windows compatible via the Cygwin framework, version 8.0 and higher have native Windows support.

- **GUI support**: PostgreSQL supports graphical user interface along with the command-line interface. Several commercial as well as open-source GUI tools are available for database design and administration.

2. Briefly describe query-rewrite system supported by PostgreSQL.

Ans: PostgreSQL supports a rule system (also called **query-rewrite system**), which allows users to define how SQL queries on a given table or view should be modified into alternate queries. The modified queries are then submitted for the execution. Using rules is advantageous in many situations. For example, suppose a new edition of an existing book in the `BOOK` relation of *Online Book* database is published. In this case, it is required to have information about the new edition in the `BOOK` relation instead of having information about the old edition. Further, it is required to keep the information of old edition in some other relation. To perform all this, we can declare a new relation, say `oldEditions`, having the same attributes as that of the `BOOK` relation and define the following rule:

```
CREATE RULE editions AS ON INSERT TO BOOK
WHERE new.Book_title = old.Book_title
DO INSERT INTO oldEditions VALUES( old.ISBN,
                                   old.Book_title,
                                   old.Category,
                                   old.Price,
                                   old.Copyright_date,
                                   old.Year,
                                   old.Pagecount,
                                   old.P_ID
                                 );
```

Now, a query to insert the information of a new edition of book into the `BOOK` relation automatically transfers the information of old edition of the book into the `oldEditions` relation. Note that rules can also be used by PostgreSQL to implement views and handle update queries on view.

3. Create a rule in PostgreSQL for inserting the ISBN and the old price of book in a new relation whenever the price of a book in the BOOK relation is updated.

Ans:

```
CREATE RULE prices AS ON UPDATE TO BOOK
WHERE new.ISBN = old.ISBN
DO INSERT INTO oldPrices VALUES(old.ISBN, old.Price);
```

4. Write a short note on Oracle. Discuss its various features of Oracle.

Ans: There are several DBMSs available in the market today, out of which Oracle is the most popular one. It was the first commercial relational database management system. The first version of Oracle was written in Assembly language and was never released. The version of Oracle released in 1979 was version 2.0. Today, Oracle technology can be found in almost every industry. The latest release of this database is Oracle 11g. There are several tools available to access a database created in Oracle. The most popular and simplest tool is `SQL*PLUS`, which allows users to interactively query the database using SQL commands as well as executing PL/SQL programs.

Features of Oracle

Oracle supports all the core features of SQL99 in addition to object-relational features. Some object-relational features supported by Oracle are as follows:

- **Defining types**: New types can be defined as objects in Oracle using the following syntax:

```
CREATE TYPE newtype AS OBJECT (
    Declarations of attributes and methods
);
/
```

  The use of slash (/) is mandatory at the end of the type definition. It lets Oracle to process the type definition. Once a type is defined, it can be used like other types of SQL.
- **Dropping types**: The new types defined by the users can be dropped by using the following syntax:

```
DROP TYPE newtype;
```

- **Defining methods**: Oracle allows declaring methods in `CREATE TYPE` statement using `MEMBER FUNCTION` or `MEMBER PROCEDURE`. These methods are then defined separately in a `CREATE TYPE BODY` statement or in a programming language like Java or C.
- **Nested tables**: Oracle supports nested tables, which means in a relation, the value of an attribute in one tuple can be an entire table.
- **XML as a data type**: Oracle has XML as its native data type, which is used to store XML documents.

Some additional features of Oracle are as follows:

- It provides support for embedding SQL in programming languages. For example, to embed SQL in Java, it supports SQLJ.
- It allows referencing external sources (such as flat files) in the `FROM` clause of a query. It is particularly important for ETL process in a data warehouse.
- It allows executing queries that need data from tables residing at different sites. It has in-built capability to optimize such queries, that is, it attempts to minimize the amount of data transfer in order to evaluate the query successfully and efficiently.
- It provides a standby database feature known as **Data Guard**. A **standby database** is a copy of the regular database maintained on a separate system. In case, a catastrophic failure occurs at the site where the regular database is maintained, the standby database is activated, which then takes over the processing. This feature minimizes the effect of failure and thus, provides high availability of the database.

5. What is the use of `INSTEAD OF` trigger in Oracle?

Ans: The `INSTEAD OF` trigger is created on view to specify the actions that need to be taken on the base table as a consequence of DML operation on the view. Whenever the DML operation for which the trigger is defined is performed on the view, Oracle executes the trigger and not the DML operation.

6. Write a short note on Microsoft SQL Server. Discuss its various features.

Ans: SQL Server is a relational model database server developed by Microsoft. It is used to generate databases that can be accessed from desktops or laptops or through handheld devices like PocketPCs and PDAs. The latest release of this software is SQL Server 2008. SQL Server contains SQL Server Management Studio that provides a variety of functionality for managing the server using graphical user interface. SQL Server Management Studio is the tool that allows creating, editing, and deleting database objects like tables, views, procedures, triggers, etc.

Features of Microsoft SQL server

T-SQL is the core language that is used in SQL Server for data access. It is a CLR (Common Language Runtime) compliant language, which means, a .NET language. SQL Server 2008 introduces several new T-SQL programmability features and enhances some existing ones. Some of its key features are as follows:

- It allows initializing variables as a part of the variable declaration statements, whereas in earlier versions, separate `DECLARE` and `SET` statements had to be used.
- New compound assignment operators are introduced, which includes += (plus equals), -= (minus equals), *= (multiplications equals), /= (division equals), and %= (modulo equals). These assignment operators can be used wherever assignment is allowed. These operators help abbreviating the code of assignments.
- Four new date and time data types are introduced, namely, `DATE`, `TIME`, `DATETIME2`, and `DATETIMEOFFSET`. These data types provide improved accuracy and support for larger date and a time zone element. Some new functions that operate on these new types are also introduced and existing ones are enhanced.
- The SQL server's new data compression feature helps reducing the size of tables, indexes or a subset of their partitions. Although space savings that can be achieved depends on the schema and data distribution, one can expect 50% to 70% reduction. SQL backups can also be compressed to significantly save space on disk media.
- Database mirroring feature that Microsoft introduced in SQL Server 2005 is enhanced in SQL Server 2008. This enhanced feature provides database administrators a low-cost disaster recovery solution.

7. Write a short note on IBM DB2 Universal Database. Discuss its various features.

Ans: DB2 Universal Database (UDB) is one of IBM's families of RDBMS software products. It is strong enough to meet the needs of large organizations and flexible enough to serve the medium-sized and small business organizations. Initially, DB2 was available on IBM's mainframes only, but later it spanned to a wide variety of platforms including Windows 2000, Window XP, variants of UNIX like Linux, Solaris, AIX, HP-UX, etc. Today, different editions and versions of DB2 are available that run on devices ranging from handhelds (such as PDAs) to mainframes. In mid-2009, IBM announced version 9.7 of this product on distributed platforms.

Similar to the free version of Oracle and Microsoft SQL Server, a free version of DB2 called **DB2 Express-C** is also available. This free version has no limit on the number of concurrent users and database size, but the database engine (the software component responsible for storing, processing, and retrieving data) uses only two CPU cores and supports a maximum of 2 GB of RAM.

Features of IBM DB2

DB2 is a true client/server architecture, which allows applications running on client machines to interact with the databases residing on the server machine. It comes with an expansion of SQL which supports recursive queries, active database features (such as constraints and triggers), etc. It also includes a collection of object-oriented features that allow manipulating large objects such as text, images, video, etc. Some important features of DB2 are as follows.

- **Scalable**: DB2 runs on laptops or handheld devices to massive parallel systems with several GBs of data and many concurrent users.
- **Business intelligence support**: DB2 supports business intelligence applications such as data warehousing and online analytical processing (OLAP).

- **Open database**: It is an open database and runs on almost all the popular and widely used platforms. It also supports popular development platforms like J2EE and Microsoft .NET and has APIs for .NET CLI, Perl, Python, Java, C, C++, FORTRAN, and many other popular programming languages. This capability enables organizations to reduce cost by utilizing their current investment in hardware, software, and skills.
- **Data compression technology**: The data compression technology of DB2 can help reduce the storage need for data, indexes, temporary tables, and other large database objects significantly. Increased storage efficiency along with automated administration, simple deployment of virtual appliances, and improved performance reduce the cost of data management.
- **Easy to use and manage**: DB2 can be administered by either command-line interface or graphical user interface (GUI). Its GUI contains several wizards that enable novice users to interact with it easily.
- **Support for XML data**: DB2 has native support for XML data and contains several XML functions including `xmlelement`, `xmlagg`, and `xmlattributes`.
- **Support for user-defined types, functions and methods**: DB2 supports user-defined types and allows users to define distinct or structured types. **Distinct types** are based on built-in types of DB2 but user can define additional semantics to the new types. These are defined using `CREATE DISTINCT TYPE` statement, and user can use them as a type for fields of tables. **Structured types** are complex types and can contain more than one attribute. These are defined using `CREATE TYPE` statement and can be used to define **typed tables** (a table whose rows are of user-defined type) or nested attributes inside a column of table.

DB2 also enables users to define their own functions and methods. Users can write functions in programming languages (such as C or Java) or scripts (such as Perl). These functions can generate either single attribute or tables as their result.

8. Discuss the object relation database management systems.

Ans: Object relational database management systems (ORDBMS) are the relational database systems that have been extended to include the features of object-oriented paradigm. SQL:1999 extends the SQL to support the complex data types and object-oriented features such as inheritance. SQL:1999 allows us to create user-defined data types that can be used to represent composite attributes as well as multivalued attributes of E-R diagrams are represented efficiently. For example, a composite attribute `Address` with component attributes `HouseNo`, `Street`, `City`, `State`, and `Zip` can be specified as follows:

```
CREATE TYPE AddressType AS
      (HouseNo     VARCHAR(30),
       Street      VARCHAR(15),
       City        VARCHAR(12),
       State       VARCHAR(6),
       Zip         INTEGER(6));
```

Multivalued attributes can be specified using an array type. For example, an author can have many phone numbers, thus, the attribute `Phone` can be represented using array type in the type `AuthorType` as follows:

```
CREATE TYPE AuthorType AS(
   Aname       VARCHAR(30)       NOT NULL,
   State       VARCHAR(15),
   City        VARCHAR(15),
```

```
Zip          VARCHAR(10),
Phone        VARCHAR(20)    ARRAY[5],
URL          VARCHAR(30));
```

We can also include methods in the type definition as follows:

```
CREATE TYPE PublisherType AS(
P_ID         VARCHAR(20),
Pname        VARCHAR(50),
Paddress     VARCHAR(25))
METHOD ShowName (P_ID VARCHAR(20))
RETURNS VARCHAR(20));
```

9. Discuss the different concepts of object-oriented database management system (OODBMS), which is beneficial for certain applications than the other database management systems.

Ans: Traditional database applications like airline reservation and employee management consist of data-processing tasks with relatively simpler data types such as integers, date/time and strings, which are well suited to the relational model. However, complex database applications such as Computer Aided Design (CAD), Computer Aided Software Engineering (CASE) and Geographical Information System (GIS) demand the use of complex data types to represent multivalued attributes, composite attributes and inheritance. It is very difficult to represent these features in traditional database systems. Moreover, traditional databases seem to be difficult to use with software applications that are developed in object-oriented languages such as C++, Smalltalk or Java. These limitations led to the development of object-oriented database management systems (OODBMS). Object-oriented databases are designed in such a way that they can be directly integrated with the applications that are developed using object-oriented programming language.

An object-oriented database system extends the concept of object-oriented programming language with persistence, concurrency control, data recovery, security and other capabilities as shown in Figure 16.1.

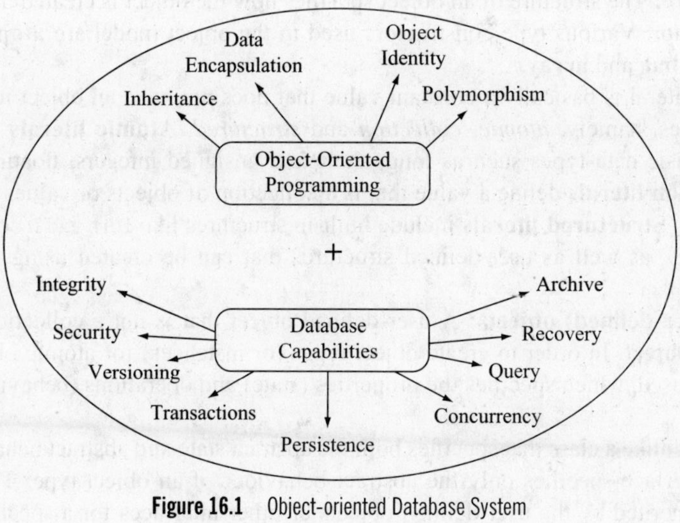

Figure 16.1 Object-oriented Database System

Persistence is one of the most important characteristics of object-oriented database systems. In an object-oriented programming language (OOPL), objects are transient in nature, that is, they exist only during program execution and disappear after the program terminates. In order to convert an OOPL into a persistent programming language (or database programming language), the objects need to be made persistent, that is, objects should persist even after the program termination. OO databases store persistent objects permanently on the secondary storage so that they can be retrieved and shared by multiple programs. Whenever a persistent object is created, the system returns a persistent object identifier. Persistent OID is implemented through a **persistent pointer**, which points to an object in the database and remains valid even after the termination of program.

Another important feature of OODBMS is **versioning**. Versioning allows maintaining multiple versions of an object, and OODBMS provide capabilities for dealing with all the versions of the object. This feature is especially useful for designing and engineering applications in which the older version of the object that contains tested and verified design should be retained until its new version is tested and released.

10. Write a short note on the ODMG object model.

Ans: The object data management group (ODMG), a subgroup of the object management group (OMG), has designed the object model for object-oriented database systems. In 1993, the first release of the ODMG was published which was called **ODMG-93** or **ODMG 1.0** standard. Later, it was revised into ODMG 2.0. Various concepts and terminologies related to object model are discussed here.

- **Objects:** An object is the most basic element of an object model and it consists of two components: **state** and **behaviour**. An object in the object model is described by four characteristics, namely, *identifier*, *name*, *lifetime*, and *structure*.
  - **Identifier:** Each object is assigned a unique system generated identifier (**OID**) that identifies it within the database.
  - **Name:** Some objects are also assigned a unique name within a particular database that can be used to refer to that object in the program.
  - **Lifetime:** The lifetime of an object specifies whether the object is persistent or transient.
  - **Structure:** The structure of an object specifies how the object is created using a certain type constructor. Various type constructors used in the object model are **atom**, **tuple** (or **row**), **set**, **list**, **bag** and **array**.
- **Literal:** A literal is basically a constant value that does not have an object identifier. It can be of three types, namely, *atomic*, *collection* and *structured*. **Atomic literals** correspond to the values of basic data types such as long, short and unsigned integers, floating point numbers, etc. **Collection literals** define a value that is a collection of objects or values such as set, array, list, bag, etc. **Structured literals** include built-in structures like `Date`, `Interval`, `Time` and `Timestamp`, as well as user-defined structures that can be created using the `struct` type constructor.
- **Atomic (user-defined) objects:** A user-defined object that is not a collection object is called an **atomic object**. In order to create object types (or instances) for atomic objects, the `class` keyword is used, which specifies the properties (state) and operations (behaviour) for the object types.
- **Interface:** Unlike a class that specifies both the abstract state and abstract behaviour of an object type, an interface specifies only the abstract behaviour of an object type. The operations that are to be inherited by the user-defined objects or other interfaces for a specific application are

defined in an interface. In addition, an interface cannot be instantiated that means objects cannot be created for an interface. An interface is defined using the keyword `interface`.

- **Inheritance:** The object model employs two types of inheritance relationships. One is **behaviour inheritance** or **interface inheritance** in which the supertype is an interface and the subtype is either a class or an interface. The behaviour inheritance is specified using the colon (:) symbol. Another kind of inheritance relationship is **EXTENDS** relationship, which requires both the supertype and the subtype to be classes. This type of inheritance is specified using the keyword `extends`, and it cannot be used for implementing multiple inheritance.
- **Extents:** In the ODMG object model, an extent can be declared for any object type (defined using class declaration), and it contains all the persistent objects of that class. An extent is given a name and is declared using the keyword `extent`.

11. Discuss the two types of object database languages.

Ans: The two object database languages are object definition language (ODL) and object query language (OQL).

Object definition language

Object definition language, a part of ODMG 2.0 standard, has been designed to represent the structure of an object-oriented database. ODL serves the same purpose as DDL and is used to support various constructs specified in the ODMG object model. The database schema is defined independently of any programming language. The main purpose of ODL is to model object specifications (classes and interfaces) and their characteristics. Any class in the design process has three characteristics that are attributes, relationships and methods. For example, the BOOK object of *Online Book* database can be defined as follows:

```
class BOOK
{
    attribute string ISBN;
    attribute string Book_title;
    attribute enum Book_type
          {Novel,Textbook,Languagebook} Category;
};
```

In the same way, another object CUSTOMER can also be defined as follows:

```
class CUSTOMER
{
     attribute string Cust_id;
     attribute string Name;
     attribute string Cust_address
     relationship set <BOOK> purchases
           inverse BOOK :: purchasedby;
     void find_cust(in string city; out string cust_name)
           raises(city_not_valid);
};
```

In this class definition, for each object of the class CUSTOMER, there is a reference to BOOK object and the set of these references is called `purchases`. This relationship helps us to find the books purchased by a particular customer. In addition to relationships, operations (or methods) can also be specified by including their signatures within the class declaration. For example, a method find_cust() that finds the name of the customer residing in a particular city is included in the CUSTOMER class definition as shown above.

The concept of inheritance can be implemented using the keyword extends as shown below:

```
class JOURNAL extends BOOK
{
    attribute string VOLUME;
    attribute string Emailauthor1;
    attribute string Emailauthor2;
};
```

Similar to the relation instance of a relation schema, ODL defines an extent of a class, which contains the current set of the objects of that class. For example, an extent books of the class BOOK can be defined as shown here.

```
class BOOK (extent books)
{
    . . .   //same as in
    . . .   //BOOK class
};
```

A class with an extent can have one or more keys associated with it that uniquely identify each object in the extent. A key for a class can be declared using the keyword key as shown below:

```
class CUSTOMER (extent FirstCustomer key Cust_id)
{
    . . .   //same as in
    . . .   //CUSTOMER class
};
```

Object query language

OQL is a standard query language designed for the ODMG object model. It resembles SQL but it also supports object-oriented concepts of the object model, such as object identity, inheritance, relationship sets, operations, etc. An OQL can query object databases either interactively (that is by writing ad hoc queries) or OQL queries can be embedded in object-oriented programming languages.

Each query in OQL needs an **entry point** to the database for processing. Generally, the name of an extent of a class is used as an entry point; however, any named persistent object (either an atomic object or a collection object) can also be used as a database entry point. For example, the query to retrieve the titles of all textbooks can be specified as follows:

```
SELECT b.Book_title
FROM books b
WHERE b.Category = 'Textbook';
```

In order to access the related attributes and objects of the object under collection, we can specify a **path expression**. For example, consider a query that displays the titles of all the books purchased by *Allen*, which is shown here.

```
SELECT b.Book_title
FROM books b
WHERE b.purchasedby.Name = 'Allen';
```

Here, the query retrieves a collection of all the books that are purchased by the customer *Allen* using the path expression "`b.purchasedby.Name`".

We can also use the `ORDER BY` clause in the OQL statement as shown below:

```
SELECT DISTINCT b.Book_title
FROM books b
WHERE b.purchasedby.Name = 'Allen'
ORDER BY b.Category ASC, b.Price DESC;
```

In this query, a list of books purchased by *Allen* is displayed in the ascending order by `Category` and in the descending order by `Price`.

In addition, a number of aggregate operators like `SUM`, `AVG`, `COUNT`, `MAX`, and `MIN` can also be used in OQL. For example, the following query returns the average price of books purchased by *Allen*.

```
AVG ( SELECT b.Price
      FROM books b
      WHERE b.purchasedby.Name = 'Allen');
```

12. Discuss briefly the various graphical notations for representing ODL schema constructs with the help of an example.

Ans: In ODL, various schema constructs like class, interface, relationships, and inheritance can be represented graphically. The graphical notations for representing ODL schema constructs are shown in Table 16.1.

Using these notations, a graphical object database schema for *Online Book* database can be represented as shown in Figure 16.2.

Table 16.1 Graphical notations for representing ODL schema constructs

Schema Construct	Graphical Notation
Interface	
Class	
Relationships	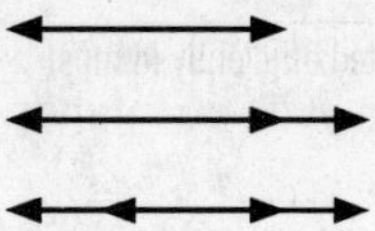 1:1 1:N M:N
Inheritance	 interface inheritance via ":" class inheritance via "extends"

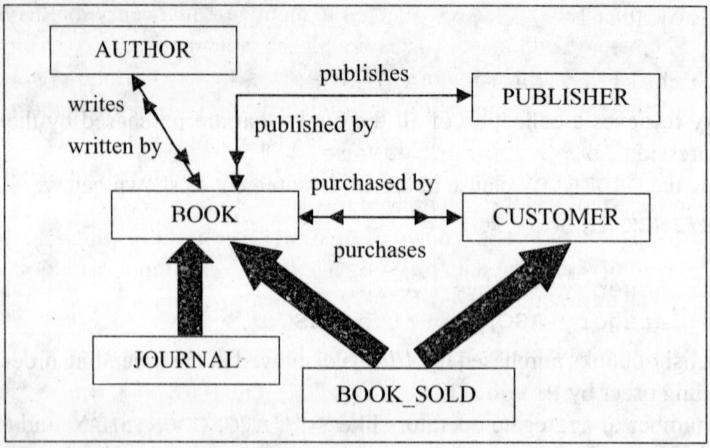

Figure 16.2 Graphical Object Database Schema for Online Book Database

13. Compare and contrast OODBMS and ORDBMS.

Ans: OODBMS and ORDBMS are similar in terms of their functionalities. Both the databases support structured types, object identity and reference types and inheritance. In addition, both support a query language for accessing and manipulating complex data types, and common DBMS functionality such as concurrency control and recovery. In spite of these similarities, there exist certain differences between them, which are discussed in Table 16.2.

Table 16.2 Differences between OODBMS and ORDBMS

OODBMS	ORDBMS
It is created on the basis of persistent programming paradigm.	It is built by creating object-oriented extensions of a relational database system.
It supports ODL and OQL for defining and manipulating complex data types.	It supports an extended form of SQL.
It aims to achieve seamless integration with object-oriented programming languages such as C++, JAVA or SMALLTALK.	Such an integration is not required as SQL:1999 allows us to embed SQL commands in a host language
Query optimization is difficult to achieve in these databases.	The relational model has a very strong foundation for query optimization, which helps in reducing the time taken to execute a query.
The query facilities of OQL are not supported efficiently in most OODBMS.	The query facilities are the main focus of ORDBMS. The querying in these databases is as simple as in relational database system, even for complex data types and multimedia data.
It is based on object oriented programming languages; any error of data type made by programmer may affect many users.	It provides good protection against programming errors.

14. Explain structured, semistructured and unstructured data.

Ans: The data that are represented in a strict format is called **structured data**. A relation in a relational database is an example of structured data because each record in the relation has a format consistent with other records in that relation.

However in some applications, data are collected in an ad hoc manner before having information regarding how it will be stored and managed. Although the collected data may have a certain structure, not all the data have an identical structure. Different entities may have different sets of attributes that means there is no predefined schema. Such type of data is known as **semistructured data**. In such type of data, the schema information is mixed in with the data values because there may be different attributes associated with each data object that are not known in advance. Thus, semistructured data are also sometimes referred to as **self-describing data**.

A third category of data that exists is known as **unstructured data** in which there is very limited indication about the type of data. The data in Web pages represented in a markup language, such as HTML, are considered as unstructured data.

15. When HTML is widely accepted as markup language, then why is XML needed?

Ans: A well-designed document in HTML enables users to easily understand the contents of the document, and navigate through the document. In addition, HTML document includes the information about how to display the contents of this document. However, it does not include the schema information about the type of data. Therefore, it becomes very difficult for a computer program to interpret the source HTML documents automatically. For example, suppose an HTML document is sent from one application to another application. The second application can display this document well, but it cannot distinguish the contents in a tag from the contents in another tag because tags do not specify the semantics of data. This shortcoming of HTML makes it unsuitable for the applications that require exchanging documents and also led to the development of XML. Unlike HTML, which defines a set of valid tags and their meanings, XML allows the set of tags to be chosen for each individual application. This feature makes XML a suitable language for data representation as well as data exchange.

16. Describe the structure of an XML document. Also explain when an XML document is considered a well-formed document.

An: To understand the structure of XML document, consider a sample XMI. document shown in Figure 16.3.

```
<?xml version="1.0" encoding="UTF-8"?>
<PUBLISHERLIST>
<PUBLISHER P_ID="P001">
    <NAME>Hills Publications</NAME>
    <ADDRESS>
        <HNO>12</HNO>
        <STREET>Park street</STREET>
        <CITY>Atlanta</CITY>
    </ADDRESS>
    <STATE>Georgia</STATE>
    <PHONE>7134019</PHONE>
    <EMAIL>h_pub@hills.com</EMAIL>
</PUBLISHER>
<PUBLISHER P_ID="P002">
    <NAME>Sunshine Publishers Ltd.</NAME>
```

```
        <ADDRESS>
            <HNO>45</HNO>
            <STREET>Second street</STREET>
            <CITY>Newark</CITY>
        </ADDRESS>
        <STATE>New Jersey</STATE>
        <PHONE>6548909</PHONE>
    </PUBLISHER>
    <PUBLISHER P_ID="P003">
        <NAME>Bright Publications</NAME>
        <ADDRESS>
            <HNO>123</HNO>
            <STREET>Main street</STREET>
            <CITY>Honolulu</CITY>
        </ADDRESS>
        <STATE>Hawaii</STATE>
        <PHONE>7678985</PHONE>
        <EMAIL>bright@bp.com</EMAIL>
    </PUBLISHER>
    </PUBLISHERLIST>
```

Figure 16.3 Sample XML Document

An XML document uses two main constructs: elements and attributes. An **element** is a pair of a start tag and a matching end tag and all the contents enclosed between them. For example, `<PHONE>...</PHONE>` is an element used in our sample XML document. XML allows nesting of elements. It means an element can appear completely within another element. For example, the `HNO`, `STREET` and `CITY` elements are nested in the `ADDRESS` element, which in turn is nested in the `PUBLISHER` element.

Elements can have attributes associated with them. An **attribute** provides information about the element and takes the form of `attributename=value` pair. This pair appears inside the start tag of an element just after the name of element. For example, `P_ID` of publisher appears as an attribute in the `PUBLISHER` element as shown in the sample document.

The message in XML documents is easy to understand with the presence of user-defined tags, but sometimes we may want to include notes in an XML document. So XML allows inserting **comments** anywhere in the document (except within other tags). Comments do not become a part of the processed or displayed content, but are useful for the one who is reading the source XML document. Every comment in an XML document begins with `<!--` and ends with `-->`.

An XML document is considered **well formed** if it follows a few structural guidelines. First, it must start with an XML declaration, which takes the form as the first line in our sample document. This declaration specifies the version of XML for which the document is written and the character-encoding system to describe the non-ASCII characters in the document. Second, the document must have a single **root** element, which contains all other elements in the document. In our sample document, the `PUBLISHERLIST` element serves the purpose of the root element. Finally, all the elements in the XML document must be properly nested. That is, if an element has its start tag within another element, then it must also have its end tag within the same enclosing element.

17. What is DTD?

Ans: A **DTD** (Document Type Definition) is a set of rules that defines a set of elements and attributes that can appear within a document. In addition, it specifies a structure (or pattern) in which elements can be nested. An XML document is considered a **valid** document if it conforms to the DTD associated with it. To understand the notations used for specifying elements, consider a sample DTD shown in Figure 16.4.

```
<!DOCTYPE PUBLISHERLIST [
<!ELEMENT PUBLISHERLIST (PUBLISHER)*>
    <!ELEMENT PUBLISHER (NAME, ADDRESS, STATE, PHONE?, EMAIL?)>
        <!ELEMENT NAME (#PCDATA)>
        <!ELEMENT ADDRESS (HNO, STREET, CITY)>
            <!ELEMENT HNO (#PCDATA)>
            <!ELEMENT STREET (#PCDATA)>
            <!ELEMENT CITY (#PCDATA)>
        <!ELEMENT STATE (#PCDATA)>
        <!ELEMENT PHONE (#PCDATA)>
        <!ELEMENT EMAIL (#PCDATA)>
]>
```

Figure 16.4 Sample DTD

Every DTD is in the form of `<!DOCTYPE root [declarations]>`, where `root` is the name of the root element in the XML document and `declarations` are the rules of the DTD. Various notations are used in the above DTD while specifying the elements and their subelements. The first declaration is:

```
<!ELEMENT PUBLISHERLIST (PUBLISHER)*>
```

It specifies that the `PUBLISHERLIST` element contains zero or more occurrences of the `PUBLISHER` element; the * indicates zero or more occurrences. If we were to specify that the `PUBLISHERLIST` element must have at least one occurrence of `PUBLISHER` element, then in place of *, we would use + (which indicates one or more occurrences) as follows:

```
<!ELEMENT PUBLISHERLIST (PUBLISHER)+>
```

The next declaration specifies that the `PUBLISHER` element can contain `NAME`, `ADDRESS`, `STATE`, `PHONE`, and `EMAIL` elements as its subelements. Note that the ? with `PHONE` and `EMAIL` elements specifies zero or one occurrence of the element. It means that the `PHONE` and `EMAIL` elements are optional for the `PUBLISHER` element. Note that the elements that appear without +, *, or ? in the DTD must appear exactly once in the document.

In the next declaration, the `NAME` element is declared. This declaration specifies that the `NAME` element does not contain any subelement; instead it contains textual data. It is specified by the special symbol `#PCDATA`, which stands for *parsed character data*. Like `#PCDATA`, the two other special symbols are allowed.

- **EMPTY:** It specifies that the element is empty, that is, the element has no contents. Such elements need not have an end tag. They can simply be specified as `<ELEMENT/>`.
- **ANY:** It specifies that there is no restriction on the subelements of the element, which means an element may contain any elements, even those that are not specified in the DTD, as its subelements.

The declaration of the ADDRESS element specifies that it contains HNO, STREET, and CITY elements as its subelements. Finally, the HNO, STREET, CITY, STATE, PHONE and EMAIL elements are declared to contain textual data.

Although none of the declarations in our sample DTD declares the allowable attributes for the elements, they are also declared in the DTD. The general structure for the declaration of attribute(s) of an element is

```
<!ATTLIST ele_name (att_name att_type default)+>
```

The beginning of an attribute declaration in DTD is indicated by the keyword ATTLIST. Following this keyword, the name of the element appears with which the attribute(s) are associated; here the word ele_name is used for this purpose. After the name of the element comes the declaration of the attribute(s). The strings att_name and att_type are the attribute name and type, respectively. Several allowable types for an attribute defined by XML are as follows:

- **CDATA:** An attribute of type CDATA can contain character data.
- **ID:** An attribute of type ID is used to provide the element with a unique identifier. It means a value that appears in an ID attribute of an element cannot occur in any attribute of any other element in the same document. Further, an element can have at most one attribute of type ID.
- **IDREF** and **IDREFS:** An attribute of type IDREF contains a value that appears in the ID attribute of some element in the same document. It means IDREF attribute is a reference to some element. The type IDREFS is almost similar to type IDREF except that the former allows a list of references.

In an attribute declaration, the attribute name and type are followed by the default specification. The default specification can consist of a default value, or #REQUIRED, or #IMPLIED. If the default value is specified for an attribute of an element, then whenever this element appears without any value for the attribute, the attribute automatically takes the default value. The default specification #REQUIRED states that a value for the attribute must be specified whenever the associated element appears. The default specification #IMPLIED states that no default value has been specified for the attribute and every appearance of associated element in the document is not bound to provide a value for the attribute.

18. What are the limitations of DTD?

Ans: Despite the widespread use of DTD, it has several limitations, which are as follows:

- The allowable types in XML cannot be further typed, which means we cannot constrain an element or attribute to have values in some given range.
- It is difficult to specify the elements as an unordered set.
- DTD mechanism follows its own syntax, which is different from the XML syntax. This creates the need of specialized processors for processing XML schema description and the XML document.

Due to these limitations of DTD, a replacement of DTD, that is, XML schema language is developed.

19. Describe the XPath and Xquery with an example.

Ans: The **XPath** language queries XML documents on the basis of path expressions and returns a set of elements that match the patterns specified in the expression. A **path expression** consists of a sequence of element names (or attribute names) in the XML document with each pair of names separated by a **separator**, either a slash (/) or a double slash (//). A / specifies that the name following the slash must be nested directly within the element before the slash. On the other hand, a // specifies that the name following the double slash can be nested anywhere within the element before the double slash. XPath also allows specifying conditions based on which we want to retrieve data from XML documents. The conditions must be specified in square brackets as illustrated in the following expression:

```
//PUBLISHER[NAME="Bright Publications"]/ADDRESS
```

The expression returns the address of the publisher whose name is *Bright Publications*. This expression can also be written as follows when the full path is known to us.

```
/PUBLISHERLIST/PUBLISHER[NAME="Bright Publications"]/ADDRESS
```

XPath language becomes a basic building block for the World Wide Web Consortium (W3C) standard query language **XQuery**. A typical query in XQuery takes the form of a **FLWOR expression**. The letters of FLWOR (pronounced as flower) denote the five main clauses of XQuery language:

- **FOR:** It binds a variable to each element returned by XPath expression.
- **LET:** It binds a variable to a collection of elements returned by XPath expression.
- **WHERE:** It performs some tests to determine whether an element should appear in the result or not.
- **ORDER BY:** It allows ordering of result in some sorted order.
- **RETURN:** It constructs the result of XQuery in XML.

A query can be constructed using some of the clauses of XQuery language. It means a query is not bound to contain all the clauses always. For example, consider the following query in XQuery to retrie‥e the names of all the publishers in the sample XML document.

```
FOR $res IN
    /PUBLISHERLIST/PUBLISHER/NAME
RETURN <Result> $res </Result>
```

The FOR clause binds the variable res to each element returned by the path expression, that is, the names of all the publishers. To mark that res is a variable name, it is prefixed with a dollar ($) sign. The RETURN clause then constructs the result of the query, which is the following XML document:

```
<Result><NAME>Hills Publications</NAME></Result>
<Result><NAME>Sunshine Publishers Ltd.</NAME></Result>
<Result><NAME>Bright Publications</NAME></Result>
```

Note that each name is enclosed in the Result tag. This is because the variable res gets bound with every individual element and the RETURN clause constructs result using res. However, if the FOR clause in the query is replaced with the LET clause, then the variable res binds to the collection of elements, and the result of the query is the following XML document:

```
<Result>
    <NAME>Hills Publications</NAME>
    <NAME>Sunshine Publishers Ltd.</NAME>
    <NAME>Bright Publications</NAME>
</Result>
```

XPath returns the result set in which elements appear in the same order as they are in the XML document itself. However, XQuery allows sorting of result in some other order using the ORDER BY clause. For example, the following query lists the names of all the publishers in the sorted order:

```
FOR $res IN
    /PUBLISHERLIST/PUBLISHER
ORDER BY $res/NAME
RETURN <Result>$res/NAME</Result>
```

20. What is spatial data? Discuss the spatial databases in detail.

Ans: Certain applications such as Geographical Information Systems (GIS) need to store geographical data about objects like countries, states, rivers, cities, roads, lakes, oceans, etc., in the form of maps. Certain other applications such as computer-aided-design (CAD) and Computer-aided manufacturing (CAM) need to store data related to objects like buildings, aircrafts, cars, or layouts of ICs, or electronic devices. Such type of data is known as **spatial data**. Several attempts had been made to manage such type of data in database systems resulting in spatial database systems. A **spatial database system** is designed to store information related to spatial locations. It also supports efficient querying and indexing on the basis of spatial locations.

All the objects stored in spatial databases have spatial or geometric characteristics that describe them. These characteristics may either be static or dynamic depending upon the type of object. For example, the objects like cities, forests, hospitals, etc., have static characteristics whereas the objects like vehicles have characteristics that may change with time. To represent these geometric characteristics, a spatial data model is required. A **spatial data model** is a hierarchical structure that consists of three parts, namely, *element*, *geometry* and *layer*.

- **Element:** An element is the basic building block of spatial databases. It consists of various geometric constructs such as a point, a linestring (a connected sequence of line segments), or a polygon. These elements are used to represent spatial locations. For example, a building location can be represented using a point, a bridge can be represented using a linestring and a country can be represented using a polygon.
- **Geometry:** A geometry also called a **geometric object** is an ordered collection of elements. Each geometric object in the database is assigned a unique numeric **geometry identifier (GID)** that associates the geometric object with its corresponding attribute set.
- **Layer:** A layer is constructed from a heterogeneous collection of geometric objects having the same attribute set.

In order to retrieve data from spatial databases, special type of queries known as spatial queries, are used. A **spatial query** allows the use of spatial or geometric data types. For example, the queries like "to find the nearest telephone booth" or "to find all the cities within 50 miles of a given city" involve spatial locations and can be answered using spatial queries. Spatial queries can be categorized into three types as discussed here.

- **Range query:** A range query (also known as **region** or **proximity query**) requests for the objects of a particular type that fall within a specified spatial region or within the specified range from the query object. For example, a query to find all the libraries within a city or all the schools within 2 kilometers from a given location is a spatial range query.
- **Nearest neighbor query:** It is a special case of proximity query that requests for an object of a particular type that is closest to the query object. For example, a query to find the nearest post office from a given location is a nearest neighbor query.
- **Spatial join query:** It requests for the join of the objects of two types on the basis of some spatial condition, such as the objects that intersect or overlap spatially or objects having a specified distance from one another. For example, a query to find pairs of countries that are 500 miles apart or a query to find all the motels on Delhi to Mumbai highway is a spatial join query.

In order to facilitate faster searching and better optimization of spatial queries, special indexing techniques are required. Some of the most commonly used techniques are *R-trees* and *quadtrees*.

- **R-tree:** An R-tree (where R stands for a rectangle) is a balanced tree structure used for indexing of objects such as points, lines, rectangles and other polygons. Like B^+-tree, the objects to be indexed (say, polygons) are stored in the leaf nodes; however, each node of an R-tree is associated with a rectangular bounding box called **minimum bounding rectangle** (**MBR**) rather than a range of values. The bounding box of each internal node stores the bounding boxes of its child nodes along with the pointers to child nodes. The bounding box of each leaf node contains the indexed objects and sometimes the bounding boxes of the objects. Note that the bounding box of an object stores the object itself.

An R-tree splits the space into hierarchically nested and overlapping bounding boxes. The criterion for splitting the space is to minimize the rectangular area that results in faster searching by limiting the search space. For example, consider the query "find all the objects in a given area that intersect the query object". To answer this query, the search is limited only to those subtrees whose bounding boxes overlap with the bounding box of the query object.

- **Quadtree:** It is an alternative method of indexing two-dimensional data. The structure of a quadtree is based on successive decomposition of the space into four equal-sized quadrants. Depending on the type of data that quadtrees represent, they are classified into point quadtrees and region quadtrecs. Point quadtrees are useful for indexing point data, whereas the region quadtrees are useful for indexing point as well as region data.

21. Write a short note on multimedia databases.

Ans: With the technological advancements in computing, multimedia data such as images, audio, video, text or document, and other graphic objects are being used in a wide variety of software applications. Examples of such applications are Internet video, video conferencing, art and entertainment, digital libraries, journalism and many more. The databases that allow users to store different types of multimedia objects and also provide support for efficient querying and indexing of multimedia data are known as **multimedia databases**.

Since multimedia data need a huge amount of storage space, it is mandatory to store and transmit multimedia data in compressed form in order to save the storage space. For example, to compress images to a lesser number of bytes, different compression standards like JPEG (Joint Picture Experts Group) or GIF (Graphical Image Format) are used. For compressing video data, a different series of standard MPEG (Moving Picture Experts Group) is used as it exploits the common features and thus, reduces the size to a greater extent. Different standards used for encoding audio data are MP3, Real Audio, Windows Media Audio, etc.

In addition to multimedia objects, multimedia databases require one to store several aspects related to the multimedia objects. The various contents of multimedia data are described here.

- **Media data:** It includes the actual multimedia object such as an image or an audio clip or a video clip stored in the database usually in a compressed form so as to save the storage space.
- **Format data:** It includes information related to format of multimedia data such as encoding scheme used, resolution, sampling rate etc. Format data is used to represent the retrieved information.
- **Keyword data:** It includes keyword description usually related to the creation of multimedia data. For example, date, time, place, creator, etc. of multimedia data. This information is also referred to as **content descriptive data**.
- **Feature data:** It includes information that characterizes multimedia data. For example, shapes, colors, textures used in an image. This information is also referred to as **content dependent data**.

In multimedia databases, user queries not always result in textual form; rather it may require generating a multimedia representation that satisfies the user queries. Some types of multimedia data like audio and video require the retrieval of data from the database at a constant rate, thus, called **isochronous** or **continuous media data**. For example, if audio data are retrieved at a variable rate, then either there will be gaps in the sound or data may be lost due to overflow of system buffers. In addition, synchronization between multiple media streams is one of the most important requirements for some multimedia applications. For example, during retrieval of a movie, there must be synchronization between audio and video data so that lips' movement of the person must match with the voice of the person.

The main type of queries imposed on multimedia databases request for multimedia data containing certain objects or activities. For example, a user might want to search images based on its color or texture or shapes present in the image or any other information that can be derived from the image from a Web-based photo gallery. Such types of queries that retrieve multimedia objects from multimedia databases based on their contents are referred to as **content-based queries** or **content-based retrieval**.

In some cases, the user may also need to find the images in the database that are similar to a given image. These types of queries can be answered by comparing the given image with each image in the database on the basis of visual attributes. Since it is rare to find the exact match, the matching of two images is based on similarity measuring function for visual attributes. To check the similarity between two images, different approaches can be used. In one of the most widely used approach, each visual attribute is assigned a particular weight, and a similarity measuring function calculates the relative distance (known as **score**) between the two images being compared. The score for each visual attribute determines the degree of similarity between the two images and the image with a least score reflects the closest match. This type of retrieval is also referred to as **similarity-based retrieval** and most often used in fingerprints matching systems, retailing stores, medical imaging, etc.

22. Give a brief overview of deductive databases.

Ans: In deductive database systems, some rules are specified using a declarative language such as Prolog and Datalog in which we need to specify only what to achieve rather than how to achieve it. The system has an **inference engine** (or **deduction mechanism**) that interprets these rules to deduce new facts from the database. The field of logic programming and the **Prolog** language form the basis for deductive database systems. Another language called **Datalog**, which is a variation of Prolog, is used to define rules declaratively in conjunction with an existing set of relations, which are themselves treated as literals in the language. Though the language structure of Prolog and Datalog are similar, their operational semantics (how the programs are executed in each of them) are different.

A deductive database system mainly uses two types of specifications, namely, *facts* and *rules*. **Facts** in deductive databases are specified in the similar way as relations are specified in relational databases. The only difference is that it is not mandatory to include attribute names while specifying the facts. In relational database system, a tuple of a relation represents some real-world fact whose meaning can be determined by the attribute names. However, in deductive database system, the meaning of an attribute value can be determined by its position in the tuple.

Rules in deductive databases correspond to views in the relational databases, with the only difference that rules may involve recursion and hence may generate virtual relations that cannot be defined in terms of basic relational views. The deductive databases enable the users to specify recursive rules, and also provide a framework through which new information can be inferred based on the specified rules. The general form of specifying a rule in a Prolog notation is as follows:

```
Head:-body
```

where

`Head` or the left-hand side (LHS) of the rule consists of a single predicate—also known as the **conclusion** of the rule

`Body` or the right-hand side (RHS) of the rule consists of one or more predicates—also known as **premise(s)** of the rule

The symbol :- can be read as "if and only if"

A **predicate** has an implicit meaning which is indicated by the name of the predicate. Each predicate has a fixed number of parameters (or arguments). The arguments in a predicate can be variable symbols such as A, B, C, etc., or can be constant values. A predicate which takes constants as arguments is called **ground** or **instantiated predicate**. A rule specifies that if we assign some specific constant values to the variables in the RHS predicates, which makes all the RHS predicates *true*, then assigning the same constant values to the variables in the LHS predicate also makes it *true*. This process of assigning constant values to the variables in the body of the rule is known as **binding**.

To understand the concept of facts and rules, consider an example where we have three predicate names `superior`, `supervise` and `subordinate`. The predicate `supervise` can be defined as follows:

```
supervise(supervisor, supervisee)
```

The predicate `supervise` accepts two arguments: name of the supervisor and the name of supervisee, which is the direct subordinate of that supervisor. This predicate is defined as a set of facts, which correspond to the actual data stored in the relations in the database. For example, the predicate `supervise(A,B)` states the fact that "A supervises B". After assigning some constant values to the variables A and B, we can define some facts, which are as follows:

```
supervise(John, Joe)                    (i)
supervise(John, Anthony)                (ii)
supervise(Joe, Smith)                   (iii)
supervise(Joe, Adams)                   (iv)
supervise(Anthony, Williams)            (v)
supervise(Anthony, Brooks)              (vi)
```

The other two predicates `superior` and `subordinate` can be defined by rules as given below:

```
superior(A,B):- supervise(A,B)                      (1)
superior(A,C):- supervise(A,B),superior(B,C)        (2)
subordinate(B,A):- superior(A,B)                    (3)
```

Rule (1) states the fact that if "A supervises B", then A will be the superior of B. Similarly, rule (2) states the fact that if "A supervises B" and "B is a superior of C", then A will also be the superior of C (though C will not be the direct subordinate of A). Finally, rule (3) states the fact that if "A is a superior B", then "B is a subordinate of A". Based on the given facts and rules, we can deduce new facts. Some of these new facts are given below:

```
superior(John, Joe)              (by applying fact (i) and rule (1))
superior(John, Anthony)          (by applying fact (ii) and rule (1))
superior(Anthony, Williams)      (by applying fact (v) and rule (1))
superior(John, Williams)         (by applying fact (ii) and rule (2))
subordinate(Anthony, John)       (by applying fact (ii) and rule (3))
subordinate(Williams, Anthony)   (by applying fact (v) and rule (3))
```

Thus, we can conclude from the above discussion that the facts are considered as **ground axioms** that are given to be true, as they always contain constant values as their arguments. The rules, on the other hand, are called **deductive axioms** that contain variables as arguments, and can be used to deduce new facts.

23. Write a short note on mobile databases.

Ans: Development of wireless technologies and widespread use of portable devices such as laptops, palmtops, and notebook have given rise to a new type of computing called **mobile computing**. With mobile computing, it is nowadays common for employees to perform office tasks and other activities like meeting while being away from their offices. Employees are able to access data virtually at anytime and from anywhere. Organizations having their branches geographically dispersed are especially interested in mobile computing. To utilize the power of mobile computing, they provide their employees with portable devices and also setup the wireless network. The portable device (or **mobile unit**) uses the wireless network to access the central database managed by the server(s) and usually has a copy of DBMS software to perform local transactions.

The backbone of mobile computing architecture is the wired network to which numerous computers are connected. These computers, referred to as **base stations** or **mobile support stations**, help mobile units to communicate with the wired network. Every base station covers a small geographical area (referred to as **cell**) and manages only the mobile units within its cell. Since mobile units are allowed to move between cells, the transfer of control of mobile unit from one base station to another is required.

Mobile computing seems similar to a distributed database system in which database is distributed among the base stations or among the base stations and mobile units. Hence, mobile computing has the same problems that distributed DBMS has including transaction management and data management. However, solving these problems is more difficult here mainly because of unreliable connectivity of wireless networks, limited battery life of mobile unit, changing network topology due to movement of mobile units, etc.

Base stations and mobile units communicate through wireless medium that has significantly less bandwidth (around 10 times) than wired medium. Further, mobile units operate upon battery, which provide power supply for limited time. To compensate for both these problems, the mobile units can cache the replicas of frequently accessed data items. This eliminates the need of power-consuming wireless communication for accessing each data item, which not only increases the data availability but conserves the battery power also.

Mobile units may move from one cell to another and their control may transfer from one base station to another. Ideally, this transfer of control over mobile unit must be transparent to it and should not affect its working negatively. However while transferring the control, the connection of mobile unit with the network may break.

Security of data in wireless communication that is widely used in mobile computing is another challenge. Hence, proper authorization of users before critical data access is a necessity. Further, provision for data backup and proper techniques for data recovery is must to recover from data loss.

Mobile computing also presents problems for data management. Locations of mobile units must be known so that messages can be transmitted to them. Further, the data required by a mobile unit must be kept at a position which is closest to it so that wireless network traffic can be minimized or data can be transmitted quickly. However, keeping data at a fixed location is a problem as mobile unit may move away from that location.

Multiple-choice Questions

1. Which of these features are supported by PostgreSQL?
   (a) Extensibility (b) Cross-platform (c) GUI support (d) All of these
2. Which of the following support query-rewrite system?
   (a) Oracle (b) PostgreSQL
   (c) IBM DB2 (d) Microsoft SQL Server
3. Which of the following statements is incorrect?
   (a) Oracle supports only some of features of SQL99.
   (b) New types can be defined as objects in Oracle.
   (c) Oracle supports nested tables.
   (d) Oracle has XML as its native data type which is used to store XML documents.
4. Which of the following is the core language for data access in SQL server?
   (a) SQL99 (b) T-SQL (c) SQL92 (d) None of these
5. In which of the following release of SQL Server is database mirroring introduced?
   (a) SQL Server 2000 (b) SQL Server 2005 (c) SQL Server 2008 (d) None of these
6. To which organization does DB2 belong?
   (a) Microsoft (b) Apple (c) IBM (d) Sun Microsystems
7. Which of these is/are the most important characteristics of OODBMS?
   (a) Persistence (b) Versioning (c) Both (a) and (b) (d) None of these
8. __________ is a standard query language designed for the ODMG object model.
   (a) DDL (b) OQL (c) ODL (d) DML
9. The data in which there is very limited indication about the type of data is known as ______.
   (a) Structured data (b) Unstructured data
   (c) Semistructured data (d) All of these
10. A __________ is a set of rules that defines a set of elements and attributes that can appear within an XML document.
    (a) Document type definition (b) Structured definition
    (c) XML definition (d) HTML definition
11. Which of the following language queries XML documents on the basis of path expressions?
    (a) XPath (b) XQuery (c) Both (a) and (b) (d) None of these
12. The letters of FLWOR denote the five main clauses of XQuery language, in which W stands for __________.
    (a) What (b) Where (c) Who (d) Which
13. Which of the following database systems is designed to store geographical data about countries, states, rivers, cities, roads, lakes, oceans, etc., in the form of maps?
    (a) Geographical information system (b) Spatial database system
    (c) Deductive database system (d) Multimedia databases
14. Which of the following standards is used to compress video data in multimedia databases?
    (a) GIF (b) JPEG (c) MP3 (d) MPEG
15. Which of the following indexing techniques is used for in spatial database systems?
    (a) R-trees (b) Quadtrees (c) K-d trees (d) All of these

16. Which of these statements is correct for deductive databases?
    (a) In deductive database systems, some rules are specified using a declarative language.
    (b) The system has an inference engine (or deduction mechanism) that interprets these rules to deduce new facts from the database.
    (c) A deductive database system mainly uses two types of specifications, namely, facts and rules.
    (d) All of these.

Answers

1. (d)	2. (b)	3. (a)	4. (b)	5. (b)	6. (c)	7. (c)
8. (b)	9. (b)	10. (a)	11. (a)	12. (b)	13. (b)	14. (d)
15. (d)	16. (d)					

Index